T0270920

EXPERIMENTS IN FINANCIAL DEMOCRACY

This book is a detailed historical description of the evolution of corporate governance and stock markets in Brazil in the late nineteenth and twentieth centuries. The analysis details the practices of corporate governance, in particular the rights that shareholders have had to restrict the actions of managers, and how that shaped different approaches to corporate finance over time. The book argues that companies are not necessarily constrained by the institutional framework in which they operate. In the case of Brazil, even if the protections for investors included in national laws were relatively weak before 1940, corporate charters contained a series of provisions that protected minority shareholders against the abuses of large shareholders, managers, or other corporate insiders. These provisions ranged from limits on the number of votes a single shareholder could have to restrictions on the number of family members who could act as directors simultaneously. The investigation uses the Brazilian case to challenge some of the key findings of a recent literature that argues that legal systems (e.g., common vs. civil law) shape the extent of development of stock and bond markets in different nations. The book argues that legal systems alone cannot determine the course of stock and bond markets over time, because corporate governance practices and the size of these markets vary significantly over time, while the basic principles of legal systems are stable.

Aldo Musacchio is an assistant professor in the Business, Government, and International Economy Unit of Harvard Business School and a Research Fellow of the National Bureau of Economic Research, Cambridge, Massachusetts. Before joining Harvard in 2004, Professor Musacchio was a Fellow of the Center for Democracy, Development, and the Rule of Law at Stanford University and a Fellow of the Institute for Humane Studies at George Mason University. His primary fields of expertise are the business and economic history of Latin America, corporate governance, the political economy of development, and new institutional economics. Professor Musacchio's current research explores the role of property rights and the legal environment for long-run economic development, including the ways in which firms adapt to adverse economic conditions. His paper "Can Civil Law Countries Get Good Institutions? Lessons from the History of Creditor Rights and Bond Markets in Brazil" won the Arthur H. Cole Prize for best paper in the *Journal of Economic History*, 2007–2008. Professor Musacchio received his Ph.D. in economic history of Latin America from Stanford University.

STUDIES IN MACROECONOMIC HISTORY

SERIES EDITOR: Michael D. Bordo, *Rutgers University*

EDITORS: Marc Flandreau, *Institut d'Etudes Politiques de Paris*
Chris Meissner, *University of California, Davis*
François Velde, *Federal Reserve Bank of Chicago*
David C. Wheelock, *Federal Reserve Bank of St. Louis*

The titles in this series investigate themes of interest to economists and economic historians in the rapidly developing field of macroeconomic history. The four areas covered include the application of monetary and finance theory, international economics, and quantitative methods to historical problems; the historical application of growth and development theory and theories of business fluctuations; the history of domestic and international monetary, financial, and other macroeconomic institutions; and the history of international monetary and financial systems. The series amalgamates the former Cambridge University Press series *Studies in Monetary and Financial History* and *Studies in Quantitative Economic History*.

Other books in the series:

Howard Bodenhorn, *A History of Banking in Antebellum America*

Michael D. Bordo, *The Gold Standard and Related Regimes*

Michael D. Bordo and Forrest Capie (eds.), *Monetary Regimes in Transition*

Michael D. Bordo and Roberto Cortés-Conde (eds.), *Transferring Wealth and Power from the Old to the New World*

Claudio Borio, Gianni Toniolo, and Piet Clement (eds.), *Past and Future of Central Bank Cooperation*

Richard Burdekin and Pierre Siklos (eds.), *Deflation: Current and Historical Perspectives*

Trevor J. O. Dick and John E. Floyd, *Canada and the Gold Standard*

Barry Eichengreen, *Elusive Stability*

Barry Eichengreen (ed.), *Europe's Postwar Recovery*

Caroline Fohlin, *Finance Capitalism and Germany's Rise to Industrial Power*

Michele Fratianni and Franco Spinelli, *A Monetary History of Italy*

Mark Harrison (ed.), *The Economics of World War II*

Continued after the index

Experiments in Financial Democracy

*Corporate Governance and Financial Development
in Brazil, 1882–1950*

ALDO MUSACCHIO

Harvard Business School

CAMBRIDGE
UNIVERSITY PRESS

CAMBRIDGE UNIVERSITY PRESS
Cambridge, New York, Melbourne, Madrid, Cape Town,
Singapore, São Paulo, Delhi, Mexico City

Cambridge University Press
32 Avenue of the Americas, New York, NY 10013-2473, USA

www.cambridge.org
Information on this title: www.cambridge.org/9780521518895

© Aldo Musacchio 2009

First published 2009
Reprinted 2013

A catalog record for this publication is available from the British Library.

Library of Congress Cataloging in Publication Data

Musacchio, Aldo.
Experiments in financial democracy : corporate governance and financial development in Brazil,
1882–1950 / Aldo Musacchio.
   p. cm. – (Studies in macroeconomic history)
Includes bibliographical references and index.
ISBN 978-0-521-51889-5
1. Stockholders–Brazil–History. 2. Corporate governance–Brazil–History. 3. Finance–Brazil–
History. I. Title. II. Series.
HG5338.M87 2009
338.60981–dc22   2009025734

ISBN 978-0-521-51889-5 Hardback

Para Haydeé y Humberto

… most of the fundamental errors currently committed in economic analysis are due to lack of historical experience more often than to any other shortcoming of the economist's equipment.

— Joseph Schumpeter, *History of Economic Analysis*, p. 13

C'est une immense démocratie financière qu'on ne rencontre nulle part ailleurs et qui est la force et la sauvegarde de notre pays (It's an immense financial democracy that cannot be found elsewhere and is the force and safeguard of our country)…

— Alfred Neymarck, "Les chemineaux de l'épargne," p. 125,
referring to France

Contents

Figures and Tables

FIGURES

TABLES

Preface

When I started to do research for this book, debate about the policies and legal institutions necessary for the development of financial markets around the world was intensifying both in academic circles and in international financial agencies. As academics reached near consensus on the importance of financial development to foster economic growth, the development of financial markets became a goal of international development agencies and governments in most countries. Discussion moved from how important it was to have stock markets versus banks to how countries could develop financial markets in general. To devise policies that could help countries develop financial markets, however, academics and policy makers first had to understand why financial markets are more developed in some countries than in others.

A natural candidate for explaining these differences was variation in legal institutions across countries. But although social scientists agree that institutions are important in explaining economic and financial development, there is no agreement as to which institutions generate, and which are incidental to, financial prosperity. It could be the case, for example, that important changes in institutions and regulations in the already highly developed U.S. financial system were demanded by actors to further improve the functioning of that market. If so, institutions that favor the development of financial markets might be a consequence rather than a cause of financial development.

Researchers therefore sought to explain the variance in financial markets by looking for institutional differences across countries that would not be a consequence of financial market development. The logical way to do this was to go back in history before the emergence of modern financial markets to look for factors that might account for the variation in institutions across countries.

A number of papers that follow this methodological approach argue that contemporary institutional and financial outcomes are a consequence of the persistent effects of the legal traditions countries adopted decades or centuries ago. This literature, termed the "law and finance" literature, advances the idea that a country's legal tradition determines the degree to which the legal system protects investors from the abuses of managers and corporate insiders, and this influences how willing savers are to participate in financial markets and, ultimately, how deep these markets will be. In fact, their statistical work suggests that common law countries (Australia, Canada, England, the United States, and others) have, on average, stronger protections for creditors and shareholders, and larger financial markets, than countries that followed the civil law tradition (Brazil, countries in continental Europe, most of Latin America, and others).

Because most countries adopted or inherited their legal traditions before legislators enacted investor protections, even, in fact, before modern financial markets developed, legal systems are thought to be exogenous to finance. Also implicit in the law and finance literature's statistical results is the notion that there exists a relationship between legal origin and financial market development. If being a civil law country is highly correlated with having smaller financial markets and poor investor protections today, this relationship between legal origin and financial outcomes should be observable at any time in the country's past. Yet, most of the work in this literature has focused on finding relationships between a time-invariant variable such as legal origin and investor protections and financial development, which seem to vary a great deal over time. As I did the research for this book, I found that only a few researchers were looking into the historical trajectories of institutions and financial development over a long time span. I realized that we needed detailed case studies that tracked institutions and markets over time in order to inform our understanding of how, if at all, legal traditions determined the economic development paths countries followed in subsequent years.

As I tried to understand the origins, institutional and otherwise, of the large stock and bond markets that developed in Brazil since the nineteenth century, I realized that the logic employed by the law and finance literature to explain differences in financial market development did not square with my evidence. If the effects of legal traditions persist over time, Brazil should have had weak investor protections in the past as well as today. But my evidence showed that the first period of financial development, roughly between 1882 and 1915, was accompanied by strong investor protections. This suggested a lack of support for the idea of persistent effects of legal traditions. It remained to identify the specific investor protections that aided the development of stock and bond markets after 1882, and to determine how the Brazilian government and Brazilian corporations were able to provide these protections. I found strong creditor rights not only in Brazil, but also in other countries during the nineteenth century, likely due to the influence of Napoleon's commerce code, which led most countries to impose harsh punishments on debtors in default and judges in many countries, especially Brazil, to strongly protect creditors. Because bondholders also benefited from these practices, when corporations were allowed by law to issue bonds, the Brazilian bond market gained momentum. The takeoff in bond markets in Brazil was thus related to legal institutions that protected creditors and court practices that protected bondholders during corporate bankruptcies.

Curiously, I did not find strong protections for shareholders in either the Commerce Code or Brazil's national company laws. Yet Brazil's stock markets enjoyed a bonanza period between 1882 and 1915, and minutes of large corporations' shareholder meetings revealed that in many cases corporate ownership was relatively dispersed and distribution of votes among shareholders relatively egalitarian in many corporations. How was it that these savers, who were not protected directly by national regulations, were willing to invest in Brazilian corporations and showing up in significant numbers at shareholder meetings?

The answer, I found, was that the investor protections absent from national laws were incorporated in the bylaws or provided through the actions of corporations and the information made available to investors before equity was sold in financial markets. I found this also to be the case in other countries in which national protections for investors were weak or absent. For instance, while I was writing this book researchers studying the evolution of stock markets and ownership concentration in Chile, Germany, Italy, Japan, and the United Kingdom showed that in those countries, too, financial markets had grown rapidly at the end of the nineteenth century and beginning of the twentieth century despite the lack of legal protections for shareholders in national laws. Some of these researchers surmised that financial intermediaries such as universal banks and stock exchanges were the source of the trust needed to induce investors to buy the equity and participate in the ownership of publicly traded corporations. The evidence for Chile, England, and Japan was to a large extent similar to that for Brazil: corporations included in their bylaws voting provisions that explicitly protected small investors by limiting, for example, the maximum number of votes per shareholder.

The idea that the kind of investor protections we observe today is a consequence of the legal tradition countries follow stems directly from the way the law and finance literature conceptualizes history. If there are clear and systematic differences in legal protections for investors across countries, and those are strongly correlated with legal origin, then in order to justify the causality from those protections to financial development it must be the case that the systematic differences were determined by legal origin years and years ago. Yet, the evidence presented in this book shows that this is not the case: before 1913 investor protections were very different in Brazil, and perhaps in many countries, from what they are today. History did not occur the way the literature assumes and the only way to know the evolution of investor protections over time is actually to do historical work. Therefore, the first main objective of this book is to defend the use of explicit historical research rather than relying on the merely implicit historical work done by most studies in the law and finance literature. As Joseph Schumpeter argued in his *History of Economic Analysis,* perhaps this is one of those instances in which the use of detailed historical work could aid the development of an economic theory of the relationship between legal institutions and financial development.

The second important contribution of this book is to bring the corporation back into the forefront of the debate about investor protections and access to capital. Most of the literature that studies investor protections and other regulations that promote financial development emphasizes the importance of regulations and government monitoring, relegating companies, shareholders, and mangers to a secondary role. The recipes for developing financial markets promulgated by the law and finance literature are for governments and regulatory agencies (and largely dependent on information disclosure by corporations issuing equity and bonds). According to this literature, which is followed closely by the World Bank and other international organizations, the best way to improve investor protections is through the reform of national company and bankruptcy laws (not to mention influencing judiciary behavior and improving the monitoring capacity of regulatory agencies). Once legal systems (and with them investor protections) are improved, this story goes, masses of new investors will participate in stock and bond markets, which will deepen, causing the cost of capital for corporations to fall.

My historical evidence shows that in the absence of investor protections in national laws, Brazilian companies and their founding shareholders induced smaller investors to buy equity on a massive scale before 1915 through the dissemination of information (e.g., the names and interests of all corporate insiders) and inclusion of friendly provisions in their bylaws. I document, for example, some important provisions in corporate bylaws that limited the power of large shareholders and show how they operated in practice. In fact, corporations with provisions that limited the power of large shareholders exhibited less concentration of ownership and voting power. I found many instances of shareholders who held large portions of equity that afforded them less than proportional voting rights, reflecting, I believe, democratic attitudes on the part of investors and a rooted tradition of "financial democracy" in some of Brazil's largest corporations.

Of course, democratic practices at the company level did not exist in a void of government regulation and oversight. In fact, Brazil had a system of fairly advanced company laws that provided limited liability to shareholders, mandated a two-tier board system, permitted shareholders to sue managers for fraud and mismanagement, and required corporations to make public everything from financial statements and shareholder meeting minutes to executive compensation.

That many of Brazil's largest corporations financed growth through bond issues was a consequence, I maintain, of improvements in creditor rights in 1890 that led to increased investor participation in the bond markets. After that year, the republican government that replaced the Brazilian monarchy started a series of regulatory and constitutional changes. As a consequence of one such reform, bondholders were strongly protected on paper and in practice.

However, the institutional settings that promoted financial development in Brazil were not long lasting. The disruption in trade and capital markets generated by World War I and the subsequent inflation in Brazil and other countries increased the cost of capital for corporations and reduced real returns for investors. The economic shock of World War I and the changes in international markets that followed (especially after the Great Depression) altered the equilibrium that existed until 1914, radically changing corporate governance practices and promoting the rise of bank-based financing for corporations. The book ends with this "great reversal" of conditions and draws some lessons for the future.

Acknowledgments

This book is the product of a long effort that benefited from the support and help of many colleagues around the world. To my advisor and friend, Steve Haber, who contributed to the design of this project from its very early stages, I am particularly grateful. Many of the ideas advanced in these pages had their genesis in conversations we had in his office or at the academic seminars and conferences he organized. I am also grateful to Gavin Wright, Zephyr Frank, and Avner Greif at Stanford University, who essentially taught me economic history and kindly gave of their time to discuss many of the ideas that have ended up in this book.

However much the process of writing a book is an individual experience, it also has been for me a collaborative experience involving a succession of fruitful debates and interactions with colleagues and friends the world over. The encouragement I needed to embark on the project was provided by Gary Libecap and the late Ken Sokoloff, who provided extremely positive feedback after my first presentation at the Economic History Association meetings. With the initial boost from Ken, Gary, and Steve, and the further encouragement of Naomi Lamoreaux and Jean-Laurent Rosenthal at UCLA and Phil Hoffman at Caltech, I decided to press ahead with the project and write a dissertation and a book about the history of corporate governance and financial market development in Brazil. As my work progressed, many colleagues provided valuable feedback on early versions of some of the chapters of this book. I wish to thank especially Rawi Abdelal, Dan Bogart, John Coatsworth, Paul David, Gustavo del Ángel, Rafael DiTella, Alan Dye, Stan Engerman, Jeff Fear, Niall Ferguson, Marc Flandreau, Zephyr Frank, Carola Frydman, Claudia Goldin, Aurora Gómez-Galvarriato, Peter Gourevitch, Avner Greif, Tim Guinnane, Anne Hanley, Pierre-Cyrille Hautcoeur, Eric Hilt, Lakshmi Iyer, Stephen Krasner, Ross Levine, Juliette Levy, David Moss, Doug North, Mary O'Sullivan, Enrico Perotti, Jim Robinson, Armin

Schwienbacher, Jérôme Sgard, Mary Shirley, Andrei Shleifer, Rich Sicotte, Jordan Siegel, Alberto Simpser, Bill Summerhill, Dick Sylla, Gail Triner, Richard Vietor, John Wallis, Barry Weingast, Eric Werker, Jeff Williamson, and Gavin Wright. I am also grateful for feedback I received from participants in seminars and conferences at Stanford, Harvard, UCLA, Yale, Stern-NYU, the Observatoire Francais des Conjonctures Économiques, the University of Antwerp, the École des Hautes Études en Sciences Sociales, and the All-UC Economic History Group. Carol H. Shiu provided useful criticisms of the first draft of the project when it was selected as one of the Gerschenkron dissertation prize finalists by the Economic History Association.

From the comfort of my home in Cambridge, Massachusetts, I was the beneficiary of abundant help via e-mail from colleagues scattered, and even moving, around the globe. Les Hannah, whether in Tokyo or in transit to sundry destinations, answered a thousand questions and kindly shared his data and research with me. Lyndon Moore, in Australia, whom I have yet to meet in person, promptly answered frequent and numerous queries from me and shared his data. Dan Bogart not only provided insightful feedback on some of the chapters, but also initiated intriguing debate about the effects of legal origins on the railway sector. Zephyr Frank also made himself readily available, sharing his unpublished data with me and answering my questions promptly. Ranald Michie was ever helpful, and shared his work as well before it was published. Steve Haber, Eric Hilt, Tom Nicholas, Noel Maurer, and Jean-Laurent Rosenthal also kindly placed themselves on what amounted to almost permanent standby in order to provide timely answers to the near continual stream of questions with which I bombarded them. My friend Ian Read also read the whole manuscript and provided helpful comments. Finally, the exchange of communications with Phil Hoffman and the detailed comments he made to my findings on creditor rights and bond market development shaped much of the discussion of Chapters 7, 9, and 10.

My colleagues in the Business, Government, and the International Economy (BGIE) Unit at Harvard Business School were extremely supportive of this project and provided valuable feedback on many of the book's chapters. The book is better for significant contributions from every one of them, for which I am most grateful. I am particularly grateful to Niall Ferguson, who took the time to help me structure the book and reorganize the argument, and Noel Maurer, who helped me to design the book from the very beginning and provided crucial feedback in the last stages of writing. The main lessons of the book were partly a product of helpful discussions with Rawi Abdelal. Conversations with David Moss shaped and enriched most of the discussion of creditor rights and bankruptcy law. Jeff Fear provided constant support for the project and because of our intense discussions on corporate governance in Europe I was able to write parts of the book with a comparative perspective. Rafael DiTella, who was and continues to be a great mentor, provided useful criticisms to the project. The encouragement and support of Geoff Jones and Tom Nicholas in the Business History group are also gratefully acknowledged. Geoff, during his tenure as director of research, did everything he could to make my research more successful. Tom Nicholas read the first draft of the book over one weekend and gave me detailed criticisms. Conversations with Tarun Khanna, Jordan Siegel, and Mikołaj Jan Piskorski, in the Strategy Unit, greatly improved my understanding of corporate governance and business networks, and helped frame some of the chapters that treat those topics. Tarun pointed out a large literature in accounting that I had missed and pushed me to refine my argument. Jordan read the entire manuscript and gave me detailed comments and helpful criticisms. Mark Roe, from Harvard Law School, was also a great source of inspiration and feedback. He provided meticulous comments on the entire manuscript and encouraged me to make a stronger case against the law and finance literature.

In Brazil, when I was a visiting scholar at Ibmec São Paulo in 2002, I received immensely helpful comments on an early version of Chapter 7 from Flávio Saes, Renato Marcondes, Renato Colistete, and Teresa C. de Novaes Marques. The support of Claudio Haddad and Carlos da Costa at Ibmec were fundamental to my research there. I am grateful as well to the librarians of Ibmec São Paulo, especially Josi Amato, who helped me locate materials from the stock exchange archives housed at Ibmec Rio de Janeiro. Conversations, both formal and informal, with my colleagues at Ibmec contributed greatly to the development of the book. I am especially grateful to Pedro C. de Mello, Eduardo Andrade, Sergio Lazzarini, Carlos Melo, Regina Madalozzo, Antonio Zoratto Sanvicente, Pedro Valls, and Rinaldo Artes. My archival work while in Brazil was greatly facilitated by conversations with Lise Sedrez, Joe Ryan, and Alison Adams. At the Comissão de Valores Mobiliários (CVM) I cannot thank enough the unconditional help of my friend Aline Menezes. While at the São Paulo Stock Exchange (Bovespa) Wang Jiang Horng was always willing to help.

The book is in part dedicated to the economic historians who studied the financial history of Brazil before me. In particular, it would not have been possible if it were not for the careful research left by the late Mária Bárbara Levy and the late Raymond Goldsmith. Levy's history of the Rio de Janeiro Stock Exchange inspired me in the initial stages of research. She also compiled the Rio de Janeiro Stock Exchange Archive, from which I generated most of the data used herein, Raymond Goldsmith was the father of the field of economics that studies financial development and his book on Brazil was extremely influential for my work.

Behind every book there is always an army of librarians and archivists that usually does not get much credit. I would like to acknowledge the help of Sátiro Nunez of the Arquivo Nacional in Rio de Janeiro, who guided me through the Stock Exchange Archive and the court cases used for this book. The personnel at the Arquivo do Estado de São Paulo and the Museu Banespa, which houses documents I needed to examine and copy, were also extremely helpful. Invaluable support was also provided by Sonia Moss, Mary Louise Munhill, and all the personnel of Stanford University's Green and SAL libraries. Laura Linard and Deb Wallace of Baker Library made sure I had all the materials I needed from the Harvard libraries (and others around the world) to finish the book.

In Brazil, I was most fortunate to have met families that helped me immerse myself in the culture, politics, and society of the country. Carolina Mota and Janice Theodoro da Silva opened the door to their country and got me interested in Brazilian history. Suzana, Lucas, and Clara Martins became my adoptive family in Rio de Janeiro, and Alejandra Meraz and Marcos Natali my adoptive Mexican family in São Paulo. Maira Evo Magro helped me greatly during my stay in São Paulo to understand the local culture and improve my Portuguese.

I am also fortunate to have worked with a team of superb research assistants and editors over the past few years. I am grateful, in particular, for the meticulous work of Carlos L. de Góes Góes and Elsa Campos in Brazil, and the outstanding research of Claire Gilbert at Harvard University. Research assistance in different stages of the book was also ably provided by Silvana Jeha, Ricardo Tancredi, Veronica A. Santarosa, Alexandre Rostoworoski, Danilo Caccaos, and Lucía Madrigal. I am grateful to the late Jack McNamara, who edited the early versions of some of the chapters, and to John Simon, who worked on the final versions, for their copyediting and suggestions to improve the manuscript.

Funding for this project was provided by the Social Science History Institute at Stanford University, the Institute of Humane Studies in Washington, D.C., the Center for Democracy, Development and the Rule of Law at Stanford University, and the Division of Research and Faculty Development at Harvard Business School.

I do not have enough words to acknowledge the generosity of Carmen Peralta in providing support during the initial stages of the project. I will always be in her debt for her support and affection.

Finally, this book would not have been possible without the love and support of my family, Haydeé, El Doc, Marusia, Natalia, Humberto, and Duska, my exwife Paola, and my friends Aurora Gómez-Galvarriato, Ian Read, Zephyr Frank, Gustavo del Ángel, Alberto Simpser, Esteban Rossi-Hansberg, Maria José Sordo, and Lucas Martins.

ONE

Introduction

At the end of 2007, the financial press celebrated that the São Paulo Stock Exchange (Bovespa) had successfully promoted the issue of new shares for 27 companies in that year alone. Abetted by low interest rates and improvements in corporate governance, corporations in Brazil had accomplished what seemed to be an all-time record number of initial public offerings (IPOs) in a single year.[1] Yet, Brazil experienced a period of relative stability in interest rates and intense activity in stock markets before 1920 that by some measures represents even more of an historical peak than today's boom. Many of the better years between 1890 and 1913 saw more than 30 new initial public offerings of stock on the Rio de Janeiro and São Paulo stock exchanges combined. Moreover, both the number of traded companies per million people (a common measure of stock market development) and the capitalization of corporate bond issues to gross domestic product (GDP) were nearly twice at the beginning of the twentieth century than they are today. How did Brazil develop such an impressive market for corporate securities – perhaps even more impressive than today's market – before World War I?

This book examines the institutional conditions that prevailed at the turn of the twentieth century when Brazilian companies were selling large amounts of equity and bonds to foreign and domestic investors. The argument of the book is that in a relatively favorable macroeconomic environment, with significant flows of external capital, Brazilian corporations were able to attract large numbers of shareholders and bondholders by providing protections against potential mismanagement and abuse by managers and insiders. These often took the form of corporate bylaws that constrained

---

[1] See, for example, "Brazilian Markets: The View from Cloud Nine," *The Economist,* October 27, 2007, p. 88.

the power of large investors and bankruptcy laws that protected the rights of bondholders in the event of default. An important sidebar to this story is that Brazilian investors circa 1900 had access to more detailed information about the ownership and financial health of, and executive compensation in, corporations than is available even to relatively well-informed investors today. Such information was at that time recorded in official documents and reported in the financial press.

These conditions had a significant effect on the country's industrialization because it was through the issue of corporate securities that companies mobilized the resources needed to finance Brazil's earliest development of domestic railways, manufacturing companies, utilities, and banks as well as businesses in other sectors. This book contributes to the historiography of Brazil two important insights. First, its detailed analysis of the development of stock and bond markets in Brazil reveals that financial markets mattered, especially in an environment in which banks focused on short-term lending and the financing of the coffee export complex. Second, Brazil's early industrialization was financed largely through stock and bond issues because Brazilian investors trusted these securities thanks to a complex set of institutions that protected them. A richly detailed narrative of how this institutional system evolved and worked between 1882 and 1950 reveals investor protections to have been stronger at the turn of the twentieth century than one might imagine given the country's relatively "adverse" institutional heritage.[2]

---

[2] According to recent literature that links current levels of institutional and economic development in excolonies, Brazil at the time of colonization had all the worst possible initial conditions, including an adverse, disease-ridden environment that complicated European settlement, vast expanses of land that encouraged plantation agriculture resulting in a low proportion of European settlers to native and African slaves, and the French civil law system inherited from the Portuguese, which affords only weak protections of investors' rights and enforcement of complex financial contracts. Under these conditions, Brazil should throughout its history have had a weak institutional environment, especially with respect to the enforcement of contracts, and thus low levels of financial and economic development. These initial conditions were related to subsequent levels of institutional and economic development by Daron Acemoglu, Simon Johnson, and James Robinson, "The Colonial Origins of Comparative Development: An Empirical Investigation," *American Economic Review* 91 (2001): 1369–1401. Most of the discussion of the importance of initial endowments was originally developed by Stanley Engerman and Kenneth Sokoloff, "Factor Endowments, Institutions, and Differential Paths of Growth," in Stephen Haber (ed.), *Why Latin America Fell Behind*, Stanford: Stanford University Press, 1997, pp. 260–304. But none of these latter authors attributes a path-dependent effect to these initial conditions, insisting instead that initial conditions would influence but not determine future paths of development (see p. 262).

LAW AND FINANCIAL DEVELOPMENT

There is a general agreement that financial markets matter for economic growth. Among other things, firms and individuals finance their investment and consumption by borrowing from banks, and stock and bond markets connect corporations that need capital to make investments with savers who are interested in high returns and want a diversified portfolio. In fact, economists and economic historians have been able to demonstrate significant causal links between financial development and economic growth. Levels of financial intermediation, stock market liquidity, and banking development, for example, are good predictors of long-run economic growth. There is also evidence that firms that rely more heavily on external sources of finance to expand operations have grown disproportionately faster in countries that have more developed financial markets. What is not so clear is why financial markets are more developed in some countries than in others.[3]

An explanation for differences observed in financial development around the world might logically be sought in variation in institutions across countries. If we think of institutions as a combination of formal (e.g., laws) and informal (e.g., norms, conventions, and cultural beliefs) rules that constrain or enable actions on the part of the economic actors in a society, then the relevant question becomes, Which rules constrain and which enable the development of financial markets?[4]

---

[3] The finance-growth link has been established by, among others, Raymond W. Goldsmith, *Comparative National Balance Sheets: A Study of Twenty Countries, 1688–1978*, Chicago: University of Chicago Press, 1985; Robert G. King and Ross Levine, "Finance and Growth: Schumpeter Might Be Right," *Quarterly Journal of Economics* 108, 3 (1993): 717–737; Ross Levine and Sara Zervos, "Stock Markets, Banks, and Economic Growth," *American Economic Review* 88 (June 1998): 537–558; Raghuram G. Rajan and Luigi Zingales, "Financial Dependence and Growth," *American Economic Review* 88 (June 1998): 559–586 and "Financial Systems, Industrial Structure, and Growth," *Oxford Review of Economic Policy* 17-4 (2001): 467–482; and Peter L. Rousseau and Richard Sylla, "Financial Revolutions and Economic Growth: Introducing this EEH Symposium," *Explorations in Economic History* 43, 1 (2006): 1–12 and "Emerging Financial Markets and Early U.S. Growth," *Explorations in Economic History* 42, 1 (2005): 1–26.

[4] "[I]nstitutions," according to Douglass C. North, "are the humanly devised constraints that structure human interaction. They are made up of formal constraints (rules, laws, constitutions), informal constraints (norms of behavior, conventions, and self imposed codes of conduct), and their enforcement characteristics. Together, they define the incentive structure of societies and specifically economies." See Douglass C. North, "Economic Performance Through Time," Nobel Prize Lecture, Stockholm, December 9, 1993. (Nobel Prize Lecture, December 9, 1993). See also Douglass C. North, *Institutions, Institutional Change, and Economic Performance*, Cambridge: Cambridge University Press, 1990.

Even if social scientists have agreed that institutions are important in explaining economic and financial development, it is not yet clear which institutions generate and which are incidental to financial prosperity. Researchers looking for institutional differences across countries that can explain variation in financial markets, but that are not a consequence of financial market development, have logically gone back in history in search of exogenous factors that might have come into play before the emergence of modern financial markets. This was the approach followed by, among others, Rafael La Porta, Florencio Lopez-de-Silanes, Andrei Shleifer, and Robert Vishny in a series of papers that belong to what has become known as the "law and finance" literature. They relate financial development to the extent of a country's legal protections for investors (shareholders and creditors), arguing that "when investor rights such as the voting rights of the shareholders and the reorganization and liquidation rights of the creditors are extensive and well enforced by regulators or courts, investors are willing to finance firms."[5] They divide the world into two main legal traditions, civil law and common law, and four legal families, common law, French civil law, German civil law, and Scandinavian civil law. They find that "legal rules protecting investors vary systematically among legal traditions or origins, with the laws of common law countries (originating in English law) being more protective of outside investors than the laws of civil law (originating in Roman law) and particularly French civil law countries."[6] They further argue that because "countries typically adopted their legal systems involuntarily (through conquest or colonization)," legal families can "be treated as exogenous to a country's structure of corporate ownership and finance."[7]

Implicit in the methodological approach used by this literature is the idea that the effects of legal institutions persist over time. If being a civil law country is highly correlated with having smaller financial markets and poorer

I prefer to define institutions as not only "constraints" but also enablers of behavior, an idea advanced by Avner Greif, "Cultural Beliefs and the Organization of Society: A Historical and Theoretical Reflection on Collectivist and Individualist Societies," *Journal of Political Economy* 102, 5 (October 1994): 912–950, especially pp. 915 and 943, and *Institutions and the Path to the Modern Economy: Lessons from Medieval Trade*, Cambridge: Cambridge University Press, 2006.

[5] See Rafael La Porta, Florencio Lopez-de-Silanes, Andrei Shleifer, and Robert Vishny, "Investor Protection and Corporate Governance," *Journal of Financial Economics* 58, 1 (2000): 1–25, quote from p. 5.

[6] For a survey of this literature, see Rafael La Porta, Florencio Lopez-de-Silanes, and Andrei Shleifer, "The Economic Consequences of Legal Origins," *Journal of Economic Literature* 46, 2 (June 2008): 285–332, quote from the unpublished version, October 2007, p. 3.

[7] See Rafael La Porta, Florencio Lopez-de-Silanes, Andrei Shleifer, and Robert Vishny, "Law and Finance," *Journal of Political Economy* 106–6 (1998): 1113–1155, esp. p. 1126.

investor protections today, this relationship should thus be observable at any time in the country's past as well. Even if there is now a larger literature looking at the historical trajectories of institutions and financial development over time, economists and policy makers have largely ignored them, especially when it comes to making policy recommendations. This book contributes to the debate, but rather than focusing only on the evolution of national laws protecting investors, it examines how corporate governance practices evolved at the company level.

ARGUMENT OF THE BOOK

This book argues that the legal traditions adopted or inherited in the past neither determine nor constrain the faith of countries. The evidence presented here shows that there is significant variation in levels of investor protections and financial development over time and calls into question the persistent effects of legal traditions in the long run.

The book explores the significant variation in financial development and, especially, in investor protections in Brazil between 1882 and 1950. After documenting, in Chapter 2, the development of large stock and bond markets in the country between roughly 1882 and 1915, I study the institutional conditions that enabled and supported this development. I show that (1) Brazil had strong protections for shareholders and creditors in the past (perhaps even stronger than today), and (2) the protections enjoyed by shareholders were provided and enforced not by the government through national laws but by corporations and their managers largely through the organizations' bylaws.

These findings draw on and strengthen the findings of Raguram Rajan and Luigi Zingales, who showed, among other things, that circa 1913 French civil law countries had, on average, larger stock markets than common law countries.[8] The contribution of this book to the literature that studies the conditions that promoted financial development across countries is that it clearly explains the protections that both shareholders and creditors received before 1915 based on archival research and company-level data. Chapter 9 uses the Brazilian case to test some of the hypotheses of Rajan and Zingales and others who have explained the decline of stock

---

[8] See Raghuram Rajan and Luigi Zingales, "The Great Reversals: The Politics of Financial Development in the 20th Century," *Journal of Financial Economics* 69 (2003): 5–50, esp. Table 3, and *Saving Capitalism from the Capitalists: Unleashing the Power of Financial Markets to Create Wealth and Spread Opportunity*, New York: Crown Business, 2003, p. 212.

markets across countries after World War I. The main finding is that inflation may have played a strong role in the demise of stock and bond markets.
Moreover, inflation and interest rate ceilings explain to a large extent the
switch to a system of corporate finance based on bank credit.

Although the evidence for Brazil casts doubt on the idea that the effects
of legal tradition on investor protections and financial development persist
over time, I do not therefore suggest that the principle advanced in the law
and finance literature that investor protections matter does not hold historically. In fact, evidence that investor protections mattered to and aided the
development of stock markets before World War I is to be found in most of
the chapters of this book.

AGENCY COSTS AND INVESTOR PROTECTIONS ACCORDING
TO THE LAW AND FINANCE LITERATURE

The body of scholarly work known as the "law and finance" literature has
been instrumental in focusing researchers' attention on investor protections
and the legal environment as important determinants of the greater financial development of some countries than others.[9] The main idea advanced
by this literature is that investors cannot be expected to participate in
financial markets without legal protections because "when outside investors finance firms, they face a risk, and sometimes near certainty, that the
returns of their investments will never materialize because the controlling
shareholders or managers expropriate them."[10] This book takes this part of
the argument of the law and finance literature as given and examines how
companies actually provided protections against such risks.

---

[9] Representative works include: Rafael La Porta, Florencio Lopez-de-Silanes, Andrei Shleifer,
    and Robert Vishny, "Legal Determinants of External Finance," *Journal of Finance* 52, 3
    (1997): 1131–1150; La Porta et al., "Law and Finance," 1113–1155; La Porta et al., "Investor
    Protection and Corporate Governance," 1–25; Rafael La Porta, Florencio Lopez-de-Silanes,
    and Andrei Shleifer, "Corporate Ownership around the World," *Journal of Finance* 54, 2
    (1999): 471–517; Simon Johnson, Rafael La Porta, Florencio Lopes-de-Silanes, and Andrei
    Shleifer, "Tunneling," *The American Economic Review Papers and Proceedings* 90 (2000):
    22–27; Thorsten Beck and Ross Levine, "Legal Institutions and Financial Development,"
    in Claude Menard and Mary Shirley (eds.), *The Handbook of New Institutional Economics*,
    Dordrecht, The Netherlands: Springer, 2005, pp. 251–279; Thorsten Beck, Asli Demirgüç-
    Kunt, and Ross Levine, "Law and Finance: Why Does Legal Origin Matter?," *Journal of
    Comparative Economics* 31 (2003a): 653–675; "Law, Endowments, and Finance," *Journal
    of Financial Economics* 70, 2 (2003b): 137–181; and Daniel Berkowitz, Katharina Pistor,
    and Jean-Francois Richard, "Economic Development, Legality, and the Transplant Effect,"
    European Economic Review 47 (2003): 165–195.
[10] La Porta et al., "Investor Protection and Corporate Governance," p. 4.

The idea that the separation of ownership from control in large corporations generates agency costs goes back to the work of Adolf A. Berle and Gardiner C. Means (*The Modern Corporation and Private Property*, 1967[1932]) and the formalization of the theory of the firm by Michael C. Jensen and William H. Meckling, among others.[11] In Jensen and Meckling's view, the agency costs (or conflict between the respective interests of shareholders and "insiders") arise because the decisions of the agent or manager running the company for the shareholders will be based not only on

the benefits he derives from pecuniary returns but also [on] the utility generated by various non-pecuniary aspects of his entrepreneurial activities such as the physical appointments of the office, the attractiveness of the secretarial staff, the level of employee discipline, the kind and amount of charitable contributions ... a larger than optimal computer to play with, purchase of production inputs from friends, etc.[12]

More recently, this view was nuanced to include the fact that controlling shareholders, the "insiders," have incentives to steal profits directly – to, for example, "sell the output, the assets, or the additional securities in the firm they control to another firm they own at below market prices," take advantage of outside investors by giving managerial positions to unqualified family members, obtain inflated salaries for themselves and for other executives, or use the company's private jet for personal jaunts.[13]

Therefore, the theory goes, investors and banks are willing to finance firms as shareholders or creditors in exchange for the power to limit the abuses of directors and insiders. Agency costs, according to the theory, can be reduced by effectively monitoring management (as by requiring disclosure) or devising contracts that align the incentives of managers and outside investors, whether creditors or shareholders (as by awarding stock options to managers who increase the value of the company). Other important

---

[11] See Adolf A. Berle and Gardiner C. Means, *The Modern Corporation and Private Property*, New York: Hartcourt, Brace & World, Inc., rev. ed., 1967 [1932]; Michael C. Jensen and William H. Meckling, "Theory of the Firm: Managerial Behavior, Agency Costs and Ownership Structure," *Journal of Financial Economics* 3, 4 (October 1976): 305–360; Oliver Hart and John Moore, "Property Rights and the Nature of the Firm," *Journal of Political Economy* 98, 6 (December 1990): 1119–1158; and Oliver Hart, *Firms, Contracts, and Financial Structure*, Oxford: Clarendon Press, New York: Oxford University Press, 1995. On the rise of managerial capitalism, see Alfred D. Chandler, *The Visible Hand: The Managerial Revolution in American Business*, Cambridge, Mass.: Belknap Press of Harvard University Press, 1977, esp. Ch. 3 and 12.

[12] Jensen and Meckling, "Theory of the Firm," p. 312.

[13] La Porta et al., "Investor Protection and Corporate Governance," p. 4.

provisions identified in the law and finance literature that can strengthen the position of outside investors relative to managers and insiders include the right to "change directors, to force dividend payments, to stop a project or a scheme that benefits the insiders at the expense of the outside investors, to sue directors and get compensation, or to liquidate the firm and receive the proceeds," and restrictions on voting rights that preclude the disproportionate exercise of power by insiders or managers.[14] In fact, in the United States, the evidence at the firm level suggests that companies with weaker protections for shareholders have lower returns for investors, perhaps because of the larger agency costs.[15]

The law and finance literature maintains that because shareholder and creditor protections provided at the company level are often embodied in financial contracts or company bylaws that, because of their exceeding complexity, impede enforcement by the courts, such provisions instead should be written into national company, bankruptcy, and securities laws, and, indeed, research has found financial markets to be more developed in countries that have legislated more shareholder and creditor protections.[16] The literature classifies countries in terms of how many basic shareholder and creditor protections are incorporated into national laws. It considers these basic rights to include for shareholders the right to vote (one-share, one-vote provisions), to participate in shareholders' meetings, to challenge director or insider decisions, to subscribe new issues of stock to preserve their share of ownership, and to call extraordinary shareholders' meetings, among other provisions aimed at ensuring opportunities to participate in decision making. The literature includes among basic rights for creditors the rights to claim collateral in the event of default, of seniority during bankruptcy, to control company assets during bankruptcy, and to nominate new managers. Investors also require access to accurate financial information and so are concerned about disclosure and accounting rules that provide information they need to exercise other rights.

Incorporation of these investor protections in national laws has been found to be highly correlated with a country's legal tradition.[17] Moreover, countries that follow the common law legal tradition currently provide stronger protections for investors than do countries that follow any of

---

[14] La Porta et al., "Investor Protection and Corporate Governance," p. 5.
[15] See Paul Gompers, Joy Ishii, and Andrew Metrick, "Corporate Governance and Equity Prices," *Quarterly Journal of Economics* 118, 1 (February 2003): 107–155.
[16] La Porta et al., "Legal Determinants of External Finance" and "Law and Finance."
[17] This argument was initially developed in La Porta et al., "Legal Determinants of External Finance," "Law and Finance," and "Investor Protection and Corporate Governance."

the three civil law traditions (French, German, and Scandinavian), and currently French civil law countries have been observed to have the worst protections for investors and smallest financial markets.[18] "[C]ommon law countries give both shareholders and creditors – relatively speaking – the strongest, and French civil law countries the weakest, protections. German civil law and Scandinavian civil law countries generally fall between the other two."[19] Common law countries also have been found to have more developed equity and debt markets than do any of the civil law countries, and French civil law countries have the least developed financial markets, no matter what measure of financial development is used. A description of the basic features of each of the legal families is in Table 1.1.

In countries with national laws that afford only weak protections for investors, ownership of large corporations tends to be more concentrated.[20] Concentrated ownership is an expected outcome in the face of high agency costs and weak investor protections for at least two reasons. First, because smaller outside investors would be disinclined to participate in the owner-ship of a corporation from which managers and insiders have unrestricted power to "extract value" for their private benefit, entrepreneurs likely would have to provide the bulk of financing, which would effectively concentrate ownership. Second, ownership concentration can compensate for weak investor protections inasmuch as shareholders with large blocks of votes will have both the incentive and the power to monitor, dismiss, and name new managers.

This book uses the basic approach of the law and finance literature to explore the relationship between investor protections and financial develop-ment in Brazil. Yet it challenges the idea that investor protections are stron-ger or weaker (on paper and in practice) according to the legal tradition of a country and looks for other explanations for how investor protections arose and became relatively strong in Brazil at the turn of the twentieth century.

Other recent additions to the law and finance literature tie financial development more strongly to the degree to which a country's legal sys-tem relies on case law and facilitates the adaptation of laws to new mar-ket conditions. For instance, according to some of this literature German and Scandinavian civil law rely more heavily than does French civil law on judicial interpretation of statutes and are, thus, more adaptable to chang-ing conditions. According to this logic, common law countries have more

---

[18] See, for instance, La Porta et al., "Law and Finance," Tables 2 and 4.
[19] See, for instance, La Porta et al., "Law and Finance," p. 1116.
[20] La Porta et al., "Corporate Ownership around the World."

Table 1.1. *Main features of the four legal families according to the law and finance literature*

Legal tradition	Main features
French civil law	Legal family in which the application of the law is based on the rules established in codes and statutes that were created by legislatures.[a] This form of civil law emerged after the French Revolution and is based on the codification of Roman law by Justinian (6 A.D.), who "took the view that what was in his compilation would be adequate for the solution of legal problems without the aid of further interpretations or commentary by legal scholars."[b] This legal system was also reaction to the power that French judges had before the French Revolution. According to comparative lawyer John H. Merryman: "Before the French Revolution, judicial offices were regarded as property that one could buy, sell, and leave to one's heir on one's death," and "judges were an aristocratic group who supported the landed aristocracy against the peasants and the urban working and middle classes, and against the centralization of governmental power in Paris."[c] Thus, Napoleon, in an attempt to put the state above the courts, suppressed the lawmaking capacity of judges and limited their discretion to the pure application of what was in the codes and statutes passed by legislatures. As a way to reduce judge discretion and corruption, these reforms also included more procedural formalism that in the long run generated an inefficient legal system.[d] Different codes were passed during the Napoleonic era and the French civil law tradition was diffused to other parts of the world throughout the nineteenth century by colonization and cultural influence, reaching the Near East, some parts of Africa, Indochina, Oceania, the French Caribbean, some Swiss cantons, and Luxembourg. Other areas of influence were Spain, Italy, Belgium, Portugal, and their colonies.
German civil law	This legal family was part of Bismarck's effort to unify the legal system of Germany after 1871. Most of the codes were created in the next two decades, mostly modifying the main procedures of French civil law but allowing jurisprudence a more central role. It was created with the "idea that "lawyers would be needed" and that "they would engage in interpreting and applying the law, and that the code they prepared should be responsive to the needs of those trained in the law."[e] German civil law, then, intended to incorporate the principles of German legal tradition, which gave much weight to interpretation of the law and precedent (very much in the spirit of common law) and the principles of French civil law and the Roman tradition with comprehensive codes to regulate all areas of law. This legal tradition prevails in Germany, Austria, Czechoslovakia, Greece, Hungary, Switzerland, Yugoslavia, Japan, Korea, China, and Taiwan.

Common law	The main feature of common law is that the judges are the main source of law (precedent determines the law). Codes are also used in the common law world, but experts in comparative law argue that "where such codes exist, they make no pretense of completeness. The judge is not compelled to find a basis for deciding a given case within the code."[b] The main advantage of having law emerging from cases or precedent is that judges can, supposedly, adapt the legal system more rapidly to changing conditions. According to the law and finance literature, one difference of common law and French civil law is that after the Glorious Revolution of 1688 (in England) the law was placed above the Crown in order to limit its power to alter property rights. Thus this legal system is focused on the protection of private property rather than on trying to assert the power of the state over the legal system. The countries that follow the common law tradition are the United Kingdom and all of the former British colonies.
Scandinavian civil law	Scandinavian civil law is less derivative of Roman law (codified law) than are the French and German families. Since it evolved independently from the other legal traditions in the seventeenth and eighteenth centuries, it relies less on codified law and more on precedent or jurisprudence.
Exceptions and hybrid systems	The law and finance literature has ignored the fact that in most countries that follow the civil law tradition judge-made law or jurisprudence is indeed important. Also, most commercial, bankruptcy, and corporate law in common law countries is regulated through national codes rather than purely on the basis of precedent. Furthermore, many countries have hybrid legal systems. For instance, Japan followed German law before World War II and then adopted more features of common law; the Netherlands follows a variation of Roman law called Roman-Dutch law with influences from French civil law; South Africa has a mixture of common and Roman-Dutch law; China adopted the German codes in the late nineteenth century (e.g., the Company law in 1904), but kept many features of Chinese legal practice (common law); and in jurisdictions such as Quebec, Louisiana, and Puerto Rico common law and French civil law operate simultaneously.

Notes:

[a] Jurisprudence plays an important role in the evolution of laws in French civil law countries, even if the law and finance literature tends to ignore it.

[b] John Henry Merryman, *The Civil Law Tradition*, Stanford: Stanford University Press, 1985, p. 7. Other legal traditions that influenced the first codes of French civil law were cannon law and commercial law.

[c] John Henry Merryman, *The Civil Law Tradition*, p. 15.

[d] For a summary of the characteristics of each legal family and the origins of French civil law see Thorsten Beck and Ross Levine, "Legal Institutions and Financial Development," in Claude Menard and Mary Shirley (eds.), *The Handbook of New Institutional Economics*, Dordrecht, The Netherlands: Springer, 2005, pp. 251–279, especially p. 254–255. On the issue of excessive formalism and the effects that can have other important markets (e.g., credit markets) see Simeon Djankov, Rafael La Porta, Florencio Lopez de Silanes, and Andrei Shleifer, "Courts: The Lex Mundi Project," *Quarterly Journal of Economics* 118, 2 (May 2003): 453–517.

[e] John Henry Merryman, *The Civil Law Tradition*, p. 31.

[f] John Henry Merryman, *The Civil Law Tradition*, p. 32.

11

flexible and adaptable legal systems because judges are the most important source of changes to laws.[21]

This idea has been taken further to suggest that countries that do not adapt their adopted legal system to local conditions and provide flexibility in the interpretation of the statues will find it more difficult to have a strong rule of law. The research in this stream of the literature has been more historical and has looked at how during the nineteenth century many countries, for example in Latin America, copied European codes of commerce and later adapted them to local conditions.[22]

More recently, the debate within the law and finance literature has shifted away from investor protections in national laws (and the importance of public enforcement) and toward the conditions that facilitate private enforcement of shareholder (and creditor) rights. Work by Rafael La Porta, Florencio Lopez-de-Silanes, and Andrei Shleifer acknowledges, for instance, that "public enforcement plays a modest role at best in the development of stock markets" because what seems to induce investors to buy equity is "extensive disclosure requirements and a relatively low burden of proof on investors seeking to recover damages resulting from omissions of material information from the prospectus [of a new stock issue]," which implies that even in the absence of strong protections in national laws, investors can gauge the trustworthiness of a stock issue as long as its prospectus discloses detailed information about the firm's directors and their ownership shares as well as pertinent financial information. This book agrees with this part of the literature and in fact provides supporting evidence that private

---

[21] See, for instance, Beck et al., "Law and Finance," 653–675; "Law, Endowments, and Finance," 137–181.

[22] According to Berkowitz et al., the determinants of the level of legal order are related to the degree to which a country is an originator (e.g., France, Germany, England) or recipient of a legal system. A recipient or *transplant* is a country that inherited or adopted its legal system from an originator country. *Transplants* can be either *receptive* (i.e., able to adapt the legal system to local conditions and practices) or *unreceptive* (i.e., adopt the law with little adaptation to local customs and traditions). The hypothesis of such studies is that *receptive transplants* and originators tend to have a stronger rule of law than *unreceptive transplants*, legality being defined in terms of indices of perceived contract enforcement by country. Among *receptive* countries, the United States, in playing a special role as an innovator in commercial law, enjoys a higher level of "legality" than an *unreceptive transplant* country such as Brazil. Katherina Pistor, Yoram Keinan, Jan Kleinheisterkamp, and Mark West are more specific, classifying recipient countries according to the degree to which they adapted their legal systems to local conditions (even analyzing in detail the evolution of the codes of the countries they discuss). See Berkowitz et al., "Economic Development, Legality, and the Transplant Effect," 165–195; and Katharina Pistor, Yoram Keinan, Jan Kleinheisterkamp and Mark West, "Innovation in Corporate Law," *Journal of Comparative Economics* 31, 4 (2003): 676–694.

enforcement (as well as public) was crucial for the development of Brazil's capital markets.[23]

What is less clear for the Brazilian case is whether there is a clear correlation between the conditions that facilitate the private enforcement of shareholder and creditor rights and legal origins. For instance, the work of La Porta and coauthors looking at the private enforcement of investor protections argues that their "findings further clarify why legal origin predicts stock market development" because "the benefit of common law ... appear to lie in its emphasis on private contracting and standardized disclosure and in its reliance on private dispute resolution using market-friendly standards of liability."[24] This book shows that the same facility to enforce equity contracts existed in Brazil at the turn of the twentieth century.

CHALLENGES TO THE LAW AND FINANCE LITERATURE

There has been a significant pushback against the law and finance literature from at least two camps. First, historians and economic historians have done more historical work examining the evolution of investor protections, company laws, and corporate governance practices in general. The findings of these works show that corporate governance in both common and civil law countries varies significantly over time. By focusing mostly on the rights of equity holders, the literature has challenged the idea that there is path dependence between legal origins and investor protections.

The findings of this book confirm this line of argumentation and add two new elements. The first one is that we observe variation over time not only in the rights of shareholders, but also in the protections creditors had in Brazil. Second, the book argues that perhaps the main source of variation in shareholder protections over time exists at the corporate level – in the type of protections companies include in their company bylaws – rather than in national laws.[25]

---

[23] Rafael La Porta, Florencio Lopez-de-Silanes, and Andrei Shleifer. "What Works in Securities Laws?" *Journal of Finance* 61, 1 (February 2006): 1–32, quote from p. 20.

[24] La Porta et al., "What Works in Securities Laws?," p. 22.

[25] Some representative works examining the historical trajectories of corporate governance institutions are Naomi Lamoreaux and Jean-Laurent Rosenthal, "Corporate Governance and the Plight of Minority Shareholders in the United States before the Great Depression," in Edward Glaeser and Claudia Goldin (eds.), *Corruption and Reform*, Chicago: University of Chicago Press, 2006, pp. 125–152; Colleen Dunlavy, "Corporate Governance in Late-19th Century Europe and the U.S.: The Case of Shareholder Voting Rights," in Klaus J. Hopt, H. Kanda, Mark J. Roe, E. Wymeersch, and S. Prigge (eds.), *Corporate Governance: The State of the Art of Emerging Research*, Oxford: Clarendon Press, 1998, pp. 5–39; Eric

The second pushback against the law and finance literature comes from a growing number of works in the political economy of finance and the literature on political institutions and financial development. The main idea of this work is that financial development is generated or hindered by policies and regulations that are the products of political interactions. The literature can be divided into two segments: the political economy view and the political institutions and financial development view.

In the political economy view, the interaction of interest groups and the relative power they have determines what kind of financial regulation and investor protections governments put in place and, thus, determines the extent to which a country can develop deep stock and bond markets (as well as large banking systems). For instance, Mark Roe, Raghuram Rajan and Luigi Zingales, Marco Pagano and Paolo Volpin, Enrico Perotti and Ernst-Ludwig von Thadden, and Peter Gourevitch and James Shinn have different political economy models to explain how investor protections in national laws and the configuration of corporate finance are the product of politics (mostly in developed countries). According to these models we need to understand the political process and the shocks that caused a change in the preferences of powerful interest groups in order to comprehend the divergence in investor protections and corporate governance regimes across countries.[26]

The literature on political institutions and financial development argues that the configuration of the political system has a direct impact on the capacity of governments to commit to protect property rights and enforce financial contracts. Beginning with the seminal paper by Douglass C. North and Barry Weingast, there is a large literature linking political systems that

Hilt, "When Did Ownership Separate from Control?: Corporate Governance in the Early Nineteenth Century," *Journal of Economic History* 68, 3 (September 2008): 645–685; Randall Morck (ed.), *A History of Corporate Governance around the World: Family Business Groups to Professional Managers* (National Bureau of Economic Research Conference Report), Chicago: University of Chicago Press, 2004; Julian Franks, Colin Mayer and Hannes F. Wagner, "The Origins of the German Corporation: Finance, Ownership and Control," *Review of Finance* 10, 4 (2006): 537–585. Unpublished detailed historical work includes Gonzalo Islas Rojas, "Does Regulation Matter?: An Analysis of Corporate Charters in a Laissez-faire Environment," unpublished manuscript, University of California Los Angeles, September 2007.

[26] See Rajan and Zingales, "The Great Reversals"; Mark J. Roe, *Political Determinants of Corporate Governance*, New York and Oxford: Oxford University Press, 2003; Marco Pagano and Paolo Volpin, "The Political Economy of Corporate Governance," *American Economic Review* 95, 4 (September 2005): 1005–1030; and Enrico Perotti and Ernst-Ludwig von Thadden, "The Political Economy of Corporate Control and Labor Rents," *Journal of Political Economy* 114, 1 (2006): 145–175.

constrain the executive (through a functioning system of checks and balances) with more developed financial markets. The basic logic behind this literature is that a government strong enough to uphold and enforce property rights is also strong enough to expropriate its citizens. Therefore limited governments can credibly commit to enforce financial contracts and protect the (property) rights investors have to the cashflows and assets of companies that trade stocks and bonds.[27]

‏ This book agrees with the view that both politics and political institutions are crucial to understand the configuration of financial systems at any point in time. Without basic protections for property rights and strong court enforcement of financial contracts Brazilian companies could not have committed credibly to protect investors by adding specific bylaws in their corporate charters. A basic legal and political infrastructure had to be in place for Brazilian companies sucessfully to attract investors to buy their shares and bonds. Yet the argument of this book is that companies can partly overcome some of the shortcomings of a country's legal system and political institutions by protecting investors in their corporate bylaws. Governments do not have to protect investors explicitly in national laws; companies can offer those protections in their bylaws, but courts have to be committed to enforce such contracts if a problem arises. Obviously an unconstrained government that can expropriate a company or its shareholders will make it unattractive for investors to buy shares or bonds, notwithstanding the attractiveness of a company's bylaws. In sum, this book borrows heavily from the political economy view and the political institutions and financial development view when it discusses the general framework under which Brazilian companies offered protections for investors, but goes further by saying that a limited government is not sufficient to develop equity and bond markets. Brazil had a limited government (a constitutional monarchy) from independence in 1824 all the way to 1888 and the country did not develop large markets for private securities until the legal system facilitated the private enforcement of property rights.[28]

[27] See Douglass C. North and Barry Weingast, "Constitutions and Commitment: The Evolution of Institutions Governing Public Choice in Seventeenth Century England," *Journal of Economic History* 49 (1989): 803–832, and the collection of essays in Stephen Haber, Douglass C. North, and Barry Weingast (eds.), *The Politics of Financial Development*, Stanford: Stanford University Press, 2007.
[28] The argument that Brazil had a limited government throughout most of the nineteenth century and did not develop a large stock market is defended with detailed quantitative evidence by William R. Summerhill III in "Sovereign Credibility with Financial Underdevelopment: The Case of Nineteenth-Century Brazil," unpublished manuscript, University of California, Los Angeles, May 2007.

This book thus borrows heavily from the historical and the political economy approaches and synthesizes the evolution of investor protections and the financial development of Brazil over time. The main objective is to provide new insights that should inform not only policy makers, but also corporate managers interested in improving corporate governance standards in their firms.

THE BRAZILIAN CASE: TIME PRESENT AND TIME PAST

Using Brazil as a case study through which to explore the link between legal origin and investor protections makes sense because it is currently a French civil law country with somewhat poor shareholder protections, a terrible profile of creditor rights, and weak contract enforcement. If we believe that the effects of legal traditions persist over time, we would not expect Brazil to have had better institutions in the past.

Yet, there is clear evidence that Brazil was more financially developed in the past than it is today, especially regarding investor protections. First, both the ratio of the stock of corporate bonds to GDP and number of traded corporations per million people (a common measure of financial development) were larger before 1920 than they are today. Second, shareholder protections at the company level were stronger in the past, resulting in less concentrated ownership of large corporations before 1940 than exists today. Third, Brazil's bankruptcy laws were more protective of creditors and small shareholders at the turn of the twentieth century than is the case today.

An examination of Brazilian corporate governance practices at the end of the twentieth century reveals that controlling shareholders enjoyed the largest private benefits of control in the world as measured by the premium paid for blocks of shares with control rights (to total market value) relative to noncontrolling shares at the time control changes.[29] It is estimated that at the end of the 1990s, shareholders who controlled a Brazilian corporation could, because they had "the ability to transfer corporate assets on non-market terms [to their own businesses or families] or consume perquisites at the expense of the firm," extract in excess of 10 percent of the total value of the company for their private benefit.[30] Other frequently cited signs of

---

[29] For a general discussion of the private benefits of control in Brazil or in comparative perspective, see Luigi Zingales and Alexander Dyck, "Private Benefits of Control: An International Comparison," *Journal of Finance* 49 (April 2004): 537–600.

[30] Tatiana Nenova, "Control Values and Changes in Corporate Law in Brazil," paper presented at the European Financial Management Association Meetings, London, 2002, esp. page 1 and estimates of benefits in Section 3. For a general discussion of the private

weak investor protections in Brazilian corporations include concentrated ownership of voting shares and the existence of nonvoting shares, the latter having no representation on the board of directors and earning no compensation when the control block of the company is transferred to a new outside investor (i.e., no tag-along rights).[31]

This book shows that shareholder rights included in Brazil's national corporate laws were weak before 1940 and only a few of the shareholder protections that the law and finance literature considers relevant for the development of equity markets existed. Hence, the development of stock markets was enabled and supported by the relatively strong protections accorded to shareholders in company bylaws.[32] Financial market development also has been observed in other countries with only weak investor protections at the national level; Great Britain's stock markets evolved rapidly after 1890 and Germany developed a significant equity market after 1930.[33]

Corporate bylaws that induced investors to buy stock included provisions that protected investors' rights in shareholder meetings, limited the power of directors and insiders, and mandated voting schemes that promoted the democratization rather than concentration of control. Provisions that capped the maximum number of votes per shareholder and graduated voting schemes whereby the number of votes did not increase in direct proportion to the number of shares held, thereby limiting the power of large shareholders, were not uncommon.[34] These types of protections were simple enough that any commercial judge could have enforced them.

---

benefits of control in Brazil or in comparative perspective, see Zingales and Dyck, "Private Benefits of Control," 537–600.

[31] For a recent look at corporate governance in Brazil, see Ricardo P. C. Leal and André Carvalhal da Silva, "Corporate Governance and Value in Brazil (and in Chile)," in Alberto Chong and Florencio López-de-Silanes, *Investor Protection and Corporate Governance: Firm Level Evidence Across Latin America*, Stanford: Stanford University Press and Inter-American Development Bank, 2007, pp. 213–287, esp. p. 215.

[32] See La Porta et al., "Legal Determinants of External Finance," 1131–1150.

[33] For the case of Great Britain, see Julian Franks, Colin Mayer, and Stefano Rossi, "Ownership: Evolution and Regulation," Institute of Finance and Accounting Working Paper FIN 401, London Business School, 2004, pp. 3–4, and Pistor et al., "Innovation in Corporate Law," p. 676–694. The German case is discussed in Franks et al., "The Origins of the German Corporation," 537–585, esp. p. 2 for the argument that both the United Kingdom and Germany developed equity markets despite the lack of shareholder rights in their national company laws.

[34] Eric Hilt shows that these kinds of investor protections were common in the charters of manufacturing firms in New York in the first half of the nineteenth century. See Hilt, "When Did Ownership Separate from Control?," 645–685.

The case of Brazil is also used to demonstrate that neither the level of protection accorded shareholders in national laws nor the provisions for disclosure and protection of shareholder rights contained in private contracts
seem to be correlated in any way with the legal tradition a country follows.
Brazilian law after 1891 required that stock issuers disclose all information
that could help shareholders monitor firm activities. Investors had access
not only to detailed financial statements, but also to complete shareholders
lists detailing the voting power of each shareholder, and even precise figures
for executive compensation.

Table 1.2 summarizes some of the differences between the law and finance
approach and the approach suggested by the current book, for simplicity
called the practice and finance approach because it stems from corporate
practices rather than purely from laws and regulations. The main argument
of the law and finance literature is that investor protections matter in order
to have more savers purchasing equity and bonds. This book is in complete
agreement with that part of their argument, but suggests that most of the
protections for shareholders actually can be included in corporate statutes.
The fact that investor protections were included in corporate statutes rather
than in national laws does not mean that the mechanisms to enforce such
contracts were purely private. Brazilian courts stood ready to enforce the
rights of investors and because of this threat companies respected those
contracts.

Another key point is that this book is not a story about how the government monitored companies or about how private actors and the government
solved the "commitment problem" and "tied" the hands of the government
to prevent it from expropriating private investors. This commitment problem was solved in Brazil very early in its independent life when the constitution of 1824 created a limited government. Rather, the book is about
the emergence and demise of the institutions that allowed corporate governance and finance to protect investors against the expropriation of insiders
and managers.[35]

There was an instance, however, in which government monitoring was
particularly important to increase the trust investors had in private securities. Many companies in Brazil enjoyed government-guaranteed dividends. These guarantees generated trust by virtue of both the subsidy and

---

[35] For a good explanation of the commitment problem and how this commitment was solved
in England after the Glorious Revolution see North and Weingast, "Constitutions and
Commitment," 803–832. For an explanation of how the Brazilian government solved
the commitment problem in the 1820s see Summerhill III, "Sovereign Credibility with
Financial Underdevelopment."

Table 1.2. *Comparison of the sources of shareholder protections in law and finance vs. practice and finance*

Shareholder protections	Law and finance	Corporate practice and finance
Voting rights	National company laws should have one-share, one-vote for all companies	Company statutes include different voting provisions. The most effective provisions to reduce the power of large shareholders are those limiting the number of votes per shareholder
Minority shareholders are represented on the board of directors	National company laws	Company statutes
Right for small investors to challenge directors' decisions or allow them to leave the company and receive compensation	National company laws	Company statutes
Incumbent shareholders have the first right to buy new stock to avoid dilution of their holdings	National company laws	Company statutes
Disclosure of salaries for all directors	Not explicitly mentioned	Company statutes
Financial disclosure	National company laws	National company laws
Disclosure of deal behind the initial public offering of stock (including names of insiders and promoters)	National company laws	National company laws
Fines and criminal punishments for fraudulent practices by company insiders, founders, and promoters	National company laws	National company laws

the accompanying monitoring the federal and state governments did of the corporate accounts of the companies that enjoyed such guarantees.

Investors in corporate bonds were accorded other kinds of protections, among them strong creditor rights included in bankruptcy laws and strict enforcement of those rights by commercial courts. The cases studied in the course of documenting the evolution of creditor rights and court enforcement since 1850 reveal many instances of commercial courts enforcing bondholders' rights. That bond markets in Brazil enjoyed a historical peak in activity between the late 1880s and 1913 is largely attributable to these protections coupled with favorable economic conditions.

Just as it was shareholder and creditor rights provided at the company level and not the persistent effects of Brazil's French civil law tradition that facilitated the development of the country's prosperous stock and bond markets, so the decline of these markets after 1915 was a response not so much to any legal variable as to the rapid fall in international capital flows, which reduced the supply of funds available to Brazilian corporations and destabilized the country's monetary policy. The instability occasioned by the postwar decline in capital imports and coffee exports translated into higher inflation and lower real returns for investors. As the interests of investors in stock and bond markets declined it was easier to change national laws in a prejudicial way for investor protections, undermining the conditions that helped financial markets thrive before 1915.

The corporate landscape of Brazil changed significantly in the 1940s with the rise of state owned and controlled enterprises (SOEs) and the increasing consolidation of national corporations into business groups. Over the course of a couple of decades, widely held companies all but disappeared from the list of Brazil's largest corporations, which had become dominated by family-owned and -controlled business groups and SOEs. Concentrated ownership and weak protections for small investors became the rule in Brazil at least until the turn of the twenty-first century.

The argument I make here is not that Brazil should do whatever is necessary, including reinstating investor protections from the past, to reproduce the conditions that were responsible for the country's golden era of financial development with the expectation that that will bring it back. Rather, I suggest that the lessons taken from this historical episode can inform today's efforts to improve the state of corporate governance practices in Brazil and other countries, including the United States. Whereas in many countries, again including the United States, reform has been pursued through stronger regulation, in Brazil change mostly has taken the form of more intense monitoring by the regulatory agency, the Commisão de Valores Mobiliários (CVM), and self-regulation at the São Paulo Stock Exchange. It is generally accepted that protections for smaller shareholders need to go beyond improving disclosure requirements, assuring voting rights, and reining in abuses by insiders. What, then, might today's regulators and companies learn from this book that might help them further improve protections for small shareholders and induce larger numbers of savers to buy corporate securities?

The first lesson is about disclosure and transparency of corporate ownership. As Justice Louis Brandeis observed in his 1914 book, *Other People's Money*, "sunlight is said to be the best of disinfectants; electric light the most efficient policeman." Brazilian corporations interested in attracting larger numbers of small investors should make an effort to be transparent, not only in financial statements, but also with respect to ownership and control within the firm, right down to details of executive compensation. All of this information was required to be publicly disclosed during the pre-1950 period and was heavily relied upon by investors. Thanks to more than one hundred years of improvements in accounting, financial disclosure by publicly traded corporations today is obviously significantly more sophisticated, yet disclosure of ownership and voting power within corporations is limited to only the largest shareholders, and it can be exceedingly difficult to establish the ownership of some Brazilian corporations given the preponderance of cross-ownership structures called pyramids whereby control of a corporation is in the hands of another corporation that is, in turn, controlled by either yet another corporation or a family.[36]

The second lesson is that voting rights matter and that one-share, one-vote provisions are *not* the only way to democratize ownership. One of the most powerful explanations for why Brazil had large, widely held corporations before 1940, especially before 1910, is that many of the largest Brazilian corporations, conscious of the importance of attracting and protecting small investors, drafted corporate bylaws that included voting provisions that limited the power of large shareholders through either caps on the maximum number of votes per shareholder or graduated voting schemes that reduced the power of large investors as their shareholdings increased. In Chapter 5, I show that ownership concentration was significantly lower in corporations that had such voting provisions than it was in the average Brazilian company before 1940. A further difference is that before 1932 no shares were automatically excluded from voting (as preferred shares later were). In principle, before 1932 all the shareholders had the right to vote.

In sum, the actions of corporations matter because investor protections at the company level matter. Companies can indeed overcome some of the shortcomings of the legal systems in which they operate if they provide

---

[36] In fact, academics get credit for reconstructing some of the pyramidal ownership schemes in Brazilian corporations. See, for instance, Leal and da Silva, "Corporate Governance and Value in Brazil," pp. 213–287.

investor protections beyond what is legally mandated. This is how companies in Brazil, and in other countries such as Japan, the United States, and England, did it in the past. In fact, today an important literature published in journals of accounting and international business has been pushing the idea that it pays for companies to have better corporate governance than what is minimally mandated by the law, not only as a way to attract investors and facilitate access to foreign capital markets (a huge incentive for fast-growing firms), but also to send a signal to qualified labor that governance is relatively transparent and more democratic than the norm. According to Tarun Khanna and Krishna Palepu, this is one of the reasons Infosys, an Indian software giant, has been so successful in attracting foreign capital as well as talented and highly trained software engineers.[37]

Moreover, the findings of this book are in line with the findings of the literature of voluntary financial disclosure. For instance, Paul Healy and Krishna Palepu argue that "managers who anticipate making capital market transactions have incentives to provide voluntary disclosure to reduce the information asymmetry problem, thereby reducing the firm's cost of external financing."[38] That is, in some contexts companies are better off providing more information than what is mandated by law. In Brazil, companies in which shareholders faced a lower agency cost because of such protections attracted a large number of shareholders and ended up with lower concentration of ownership.

These lessons do not necessarily apply to all corporations at all times. They are lessons that travel and apply to corporations for which issuing equity is cheaper than obtaining a loan or using internally generated savings (retained earnings). Sharing power with more investors, of course, also poses some challenges for management, and limiting the power of large shareholders through the voting schemes referenced above is advisable only for corporations with well structured divisions of power and for which survival does not depend on rapid, consensual decision making. These are lessons that apply to a subset of corporations in Brazil and other countries of the world.

Table 1.3 summarizes the main differences between the law and finance approach and that suggested by the current book. The main differences are

---

[37] See Tarun Khanna and Krishna Palepu, "Globalization and Convergence in Corporate Governance: Evidence from Infosys and the Indian Software Industry," *Journal of International Business Studies* 35, 6 (November 2004): 484–507, esp. pp. 489–490.

[38] Paul Healy and Krishna Palepu, "Information Asymmetry, Corporate Disclosure, and the Capital Markets: A Review of the Empirical Disclosure Literature," *Journal of Accounting and Economics* 31 (2001): 420.

Table 1.3. *Main differences between the law and finance and corporate and finance approaches*

Main components	Law and finance	Corporate practice and finance
Role of company and bankruptcy laws	Central role, providing shareholder and creditor rights at the national level as well as mandating disclosure of accounts and detailed information of the activities of founders and directors. Should provide bright line rules that can facilitate enforcement by judges	Should provide a basic framework to facilitate enforcement, disclosure, and criminal trials for fraudulent practices
Role of company by laws	Do not have to provide additional protections beyond those in national laws. If they are too complex it is hard for courts to enforce investor protections	Can substitute for shortcomings of the law
Disclosure of financial information and information at the time of initial public offering of stocks (and bonds)	Central to facilitate the private enforcement of shareholder (and creditor) rights	Central to facilitate the private enforcement of shareholder (and creditor) rights
Disclosure of shareholders	Only necessary at the time of initial public offering and only if shareholders have a large stake or an interest in the offer of new securities	Regular disclosure of shareholders' identities can facilitate private monitoring of insider power
Causal mechanism	Legal traditions were inherited or adopted hundreds of years (or decades) ago and generated distinct legal systems and investor protection schemes across countries	Investor protections are determined mainly at the company level by shareholders. Creditor rights and mandatory disclosure of information regulated at the national level are determined by political interactions between interest groups and legislators
Role of history (and historical research)	Strong path-dependence. The fate of countries regarding investor protections was determined when they adopted or inherited their legal systems	The institutions of corporate governance are contingent to what companies do. That is why historical research plays a critical role in understanding the transformation of investor protections overtime

in the roles given to national company and bankruptcy laws, the causal mechanism behind investor protections, and, in general, the role of historical research. While for the law and finance approach national laws are central, I argue that while some national laws are important, especially those that mandate disclosure of financial and company information relevant to shareholders, company bylaws can substitute for some of the laws that supposedly should provide the protections that shareholders need to be encouraged to buy equity with confidence. Finally, I argue that the investor protections are not a consequence of the legal tradition countries follow, but rather are selected by shareholders or the founders of new companies when they draft the company statutes or, when included in national laws, protections are determined by the interaction of interest groups and politicians. I develop most of these arguments using the case of Brazil and, when possible, displaying comparative evidence from a variety of countries.

STRUCTURE OF THE BOOK

The second chapter presents evidence of the development of sizable stock and bond markets in Brazil between 1882 and 1915 and explains why the country's financial markets grew rapidly after 1882. By some measures Brazil's bond market was more developed in the past than today. Chapter 3 demonstrates that financial development mattered for Brazilian economic development by documenting the important role the stock markets played in the country's industrialization and urbanization. It finds significant statistical links that suggest possible causality between levels of bank credit and stock and bond issues and movements in the country's gross domestic product. Detailed data on the capitalization of the Rio de Janeiro and São Paulo stock exchanges are used to show the extent to which stock markets were used to finance the expansion of companies in all sectors of the economy. The stock markets provided capital to finance industrialization at the time when the country's GDP growth accelerated and helped to transform Brazil into a more urbanized and industrialized country by mobilizing resources for new sectors such as manufacturing and utilities, railways, banks, insurance companies, and others.

Chapter 4 examines the institutional settings that enabled corporations to induce large numbers of small investors to purchase equity. It looks at how, in the absence of regulation at the national level, Brazilian corporations interested in attracting outside investors devised statutes within their bylaws that protected small investors against the power of large shareholders who could otherwise control the company to their advantage.

The assertions made in Chapter 4 regarding the effects of voting provisions and government guarantees are empirically tested in Chapter 5, which finds that concentration of ownership (shareholdings) and control (votes) was significantly lower both in companies that had voting provisions that limited the power of large shareholders and in companies closely monitored because they had government-guaranteed dividends. Thus, in Brazil, investor protections incorporated in company bylaws seem actually to have worked in practice.

Chapter 6 continues to examine the importance of corporate bylaws, with particular emphasis on the structure of the rules and incentives that regulate directors in Brazilian corporations. Two points are made. First, corporate charters provided investors with detailed information about executive compensation including directors' fixed salaries and performance-based fees. In many instances, full compensation was determined by the shareholders at the general assembly. Second, using information from corporate charters to estimate the compensation of the presidents of the boards of directors of many of Brazil's largest corporations circa 1909 (who also acted as chief executive officers), this chapter compares average salaries (by size of the corporation) in Brazil to those in the United Kingdom and the United States (the results are hard to interpret because it is not clear that the comparison is fair). The pay of Brazilian CEOs was equivalent to directors of medium-sized companies in the United Kingdom and perhaps to directors of small to average companies in the United States. Even if Brazilian CEOs salaries were higher than those of the United States, it is not clear whether higher salaries were truly a sign of weak corporate governance or just a symptom of the scarcity of talent in this economy.

Chapter 7 examines the development of bond markets in Brazil and the institutional conditions that protected bondholders. The institutional setting for bond markets differed from that for stock markets because Brazilian bankruptcy laws provided strong protections for creditors since at least 1850. From the first commercial code, Brazilian legislation gave creditors control of corporate bankruptcies, allowed them to select trustees to run bankrupt companies, and granted them discretion to choose whether to liquidate or to negotiate a plan with incumbent management to reorganize a firm. Secured creditors (those with collateral) were always first in line to collect debts during bankruptcy, and after 1890 bondholders were accorded the status of privileged creditors. With this legislation as a backdrop, Brazilian bond market activity first peaked before 1915 while helping to finance the activities of companies in almost all of the most important industries of that time. Just as in the stock markets, the acceleration of bond financing occurred after 1900, in particular between 1906 and 1913 when coffee exports were booming because of the coffee valorization program and macroeconomic conditions were stable thanks, in part, to the institution of the gold exchange standard.

Chapter 7 also demonstrates that creditor rights were not only protected on paper, but also strongly enforced by the courts. I draw on archival records of bankruptcy cases of corporations that issued bonds to show that bondholders were, indeed, in a privileged position when bankruptcies occurred, commonly negotiating reorganizations and sometimes liquidating assets to recover their investments. If perhaps less than perfect, the process was usually brief (especially compared to today's time-consuming bankruptcy procedures). I reach conclusions: (1) the enforcement of creditor rights was strong between 1850 and the first decades of the twentieth century (i.e., strong creditor protections have been the norm for a good part of Brazil's history), (2) bankruptcy judges enforced creditor rights not only because that was their mandate, but also because they, too, were investors in the stock and bond markets, and (3) this equilibrium changed after the 1930s with the advent of a corporatist regime interested in protecting labor rights that radically changed the protection and enforcement of creditor rights.

The findings presented in Chapter 8 suggest that in Brazil the development of stock and bond markets does not seem to be explained by the dealings of banks acting as market makers. At the end of the nineteenth century, many countries achieved significant levels of financial development without necessarily providing strong protections for investors, whether in company laws, bankruptcy laws, or corporate bylaws. According to a large literature that explores the role of large investment and universal banks in countries such as the United States and Germany, the actions of banks as underwriters, promoters, and guarantors of corporate securities substituted for some of the protections investors otherwise would have expected from the legal system or from corporations themselves. Chapter 8 falsifies the hypothesis that banks were acting as market makers and intermediating between companies and investors in Brazil by pointing out that in countries in which banks played the role of market makers bankers usually sat on the boards of directors of many corporations and ended up being central actors in the network of corporate interlocks (the web of relations among corporations established through their boards of directors). I employ network analysis to show that Brazilian banks were not central actors in these networks and did not have as many interlocking boards with corporations in other industries as was commonly the case in economies that relied on bankers to play the role of market maker (e.g., Germany, Mexico, and the United States).

Taken as a whole, the first eight chapters argue that financial markets grew, in part, because of a system of investor protections that worked between 1882 and World War I. After that, evidence of financial market size shows stock and bond markets to have declined rapidly in the wake of WWI. Chapter 9 explains why financial markets in Brazil declined after 1915 by testing some of the hypotheses advanced in the literature to explain the "great reversal" in financial development worldwide in the 1920s and 1930s. The initial decline in stock and bond market activity in Brazil after 1915 coincides with diminished international capital flows consequent to the controls and instability associated with WWI. But even after international conditions improved after WWI, financial markets in Brazil did not recover because its higher inflation rates kept investors' returns negative in real terms. As support for financial markets faded away in the 1930s and 1940s, the most powerful interest groups of industrialists and labor had reached consensus around promoting a new corporate model less concerned with protecting outside investors and focused instead on preserving employment and consolidating domestic industry.

Chapter 10 shows how the system of corporate governance and finance evolved after the 1930s. It shows how the concentration of ownership increased after congress introduced preferred shares in the 1930s and as a consequence of the rise of government ownership in strategic sectors. The chapter also shows how changes in corporate governance led to change in corporate finance as well. In particular, Brazilian companies shifted their financial structure from more reliance on stocks and bonds to a system that relied more heavily on bank credit.

Chapter 11 concludes by presenting the main lessons of the book for companies and policy makers and discussing the conditions that could lead us to another great reversal in financial development, accompanied by radical changes in corporate governance.

## TWO

Financial Development in Brazil
in the Nineteenth Century

The development of stock and bond markets in Brazil started relatively late in the nineteenth century for three reasons. First, the regulation of entry constrained the creation of corporations until the 1870s. Second, basic investor protections and free incorporation were not adopted in Brazil's national company law until 1882. Third, macroeconomic instability during the first seven decades of the nineteenth century prevented the creation and expansion of banks and corporations.

This chapter argues that once entry for new corporations was liberalized (it did not depend on government approval), basic investor protections were included in a new national company law, and the economy began to grow, stock and bond markets flourished. Most of the recent literature on the development of joint stock companies and stock markets in Brazil defends the notion that regulation of entry constrained development of the country's financial system during the nineteenth century because it retarded the creation of new corporations.[1] Yet this chapter shows that the liberalization

---

[1] This has been a recurrent argument in Brazilian historiography. See, for example, Mária Bárbara Levy, *História da Bolsa de Valores do Rio de Janeiro*, Rio de Janeiro: IBMEC, 1977, p. 85, and *A Indústria do Rio de Janeiro através de suas Sociedades Anônimas*, Rio de Janeiro, UFRJ Editora, 1994, pp. 76–77. Recently, in the United States, this argument has been advanced by Anne Hanley, *Native Capital: Financial Institutions and Economic Development in São Paulo, Brazil, 1850–1920*, Stanford: Stanford University Press, 2005, Chapter 3, and William R. Summerhill III, "Sovereign Credibility with Financial Underdevelopment: The Case of Nineteenth-Century Brazil," unpublished manuscript, UCLA, 2007.

The corporate form is not the only organizational form under which capital can be raised by issuing limited liability shares. Partnerships with shares could be found in most French civil law countries (and in some parts of England). In Brazil, this organizational form has not been studied fully, and stock market data does not show that partnership shares were actively traded in stock markets. Some partnerships, mostly after 1890, took advantage of stock markets by issuing corporate bonds. The limited liability company, which existed in Germany at least since the 1890s, did not exist in Brazil at this time.

of entry in 1882 was necessary but not sufficient to promote rapid growth in stock and bond markets. This is because rapid growth in the listing of stocks and bonds in the Rio de Janeiro Stock Exchange took place only after the government pursued expansionary monetary policies and basic investor protections were set into place (for holders of both bonds and shares).

The number of companies traded in the stock market, total stock and bond market capitalization, and volume of trading of corporate securities attained levels unprecedented in the country's history after 1885. There was a doubling of the number of traded companies between the 1870s and 1880s and of the value of stock market capitalization between 1881 and 1885. Another important jump in stock and bond market capitalization took place after 1890. This jump is particularly important because, as this book argues, important protections for shareholders introduced in bankruptcy and company laws in 1890 and 1891 provided incentives for investors to participate in larger numbers in the stock markets of Brazil.

Evidence presented in this chapter suggests that before 1920 Brazil had large stock and bond markets that were, by some measures, larger even than today's markets. For instance, after peaking between 1910 and 1915, both markets entered a sustained decline from which they did not fully recover until the 1990s. In fact, in terms of the value of the total stock of bonds, Brazil has not recovered its pre-1915 level of bond market development. The size of today's market capitalization for company shares has surpassed that of the pre-World War I era, but evidence provided here shows that the number of stock-exchange listed corporations per million people still falls short of levels during the first two decades of the twentieth century.

FINANCIAL UNDERDEVELOPMENT IN NINETEENTH-CENTURY BRAZIL

Until the 1990s, the dominant view in the economic historiography of Brazil was that the country had lagged behind other economies during the nineteenth century because it had concentrated on producing primary products for export while importing most manufactures from countries such as England. According to this view, Brazil's terms of trade declined continuously during the nineteenth century; that is, the value of exports of primary products declined vis-à-vis that of imported manufactured products, preventing the country from accumulating sufficient savings to finance its own industrialization.[2]

Stephen Haber and Herbert Klein, to the contrary, maintained that the reasons for Brazil's delayed industrialization were internal rather than external.[3] They viewed the main obstacles to Brazil's development in the early nineteenth century to be the dearth of banks and stock markets needed to finance manufacturing and transportation ventures and, consequently, the absence of transportation improvements needed to facilitate the integration of an internal market. Brazil was a slave economy of small, scattered population centers focused mainly on agriculture. Even had manufacturing been technologically possible, Brazilian entrepreneurs in large cities lacked the means to transport goods at a profitable rate to the interior of the country.[4]

---

[2] This argument in Brazilian economic history is identified with Celso Furtado, *Formação econômica do Brasil,* Mexico: Fondo de Cultura Económica, 1959, but a broader view that supposedly applies to all Latin American countries was identified with the structuralist school of thought, mainly promoted by Raul Prebish from the Economic Commission for Latin America (ECLA). The idea was that Latin American exports of primary products were becoming cheaper relative to imports of manufactures, which inhibited the accumulation of capital need to support industrialization. (Also, internal markets were limited by the fact that most of the population lived at subsistence levels.) The counterfactual they had in mind was a country that did not depend on foreign manufactured products. This school of thought was highly influential in Latin America after the Great Depression, promoting import-substitution industrialization. The structuralist view was later expanded into what became known as the dependency school of thought. Dependentist authors argued that, among other problems, dependence on foreign countries was constantly increasing because the domestic exporting bourgeoisie spent their rents on imported luxury goods. This, they maintained, perpetuated underdevelopment and continued dependency on foreign powers. The most representative author of the dependency school in Brazil was Fernando Henrique Cardozo. See, for example, Fernando Henrique Cardozo and Enzo Faletto, *Dependency and Development in Latin America,* Berkeley: University of California Press, 1979. For a general reference on the logic of the arguments of the structuralist and dependency schools, see Robert Packenham, *The Dependency Movement: Scholarship and Politics in Development Studies,* Cambridge, Mass.: Harvard University Press, 1992, and the introduction in Stephen Haber, *How Latin America Fell Behind: Essays on the Economic Histories of Brazil and Mexico, 1800–1914,* Stanford: Stanford University Press, 1997.

[3] The view that internal circumstances, especially market fragmentation, had hindered Brazil's development was initially developed by Nathanial Leff in "Industrial Organization and Entrepreneurship in Developing Countries: The Economic Group," *Economic Development and Cultural Change* 26 (1978): 661–675. His work was not sufficiently popularized in Brazil to overthrow more dominant views such as that of Celso Furtado articulated in *Formação econômica do Brasil.* Haber and Klein added to this debate a channel through which the integration of the domestic market would have been feasible by focusing on financial development and the lack of infrastructure. See Stephen Haber and Herbert S. Klein, "The Economic Consequences of Brazilian Independence," in Haber, *How Latin America Fell Behind,* pp. 243–259.

[4] Haber and Klein, "The Economic Consequences of Brazilian Independence," pp. 243–259.

Throughout most of the nineteenth century, few banks were in a position to promote industrialization or the development of railway networks through the provision of long-term credit. This is because banks were, from the outset and throughout most of the nineteenth century, focused not on meeting the long-term financing needs of industrial ventures, but on discounting paper, holding treasury bills (*apólices*), and, later, extending mortgage loans for agricultural purposes. Not even this short-term mentality, however, prevented most of the banks chartered during the first part of the nineteenth century from eventually going bankrupt.[5]

But beyond some macroeconomic instability, Brazil was not in the middle of a civil war that made it virtually impossible for private finance to prosper. Instead, in 1822, right after independence, the Constitutional Congress drafted a constitution selecting a form of government that limited the power of the monarch.[6] After the approval of this new constitution in 1824, Brazil became a constitutional monarchy with an Emperor, Dom Pedro I, a two-tier parliamentary system, and a judiciary. According to William Summerhill III, the constitution of 1824 accorded the upper and lower houses of parliament sufficient power to assure the necessary institutional conditions to credibly commit the government to honor the country's foreign debts.[7]

The credible commitment established in the 1824 constitution, which endured at least until the end of the imperial period, contributed to the development of a large internal market for government debt. In the wake of Dom Pedro I's forced abdication of rule in 1831, a nine-year regency governed the country until the emperor's erstwhile son could ascend to the

[5] Gail Triner, *Banking and Economic Development: Brazil, 1889–1930*, New York: Palgrave, 2000, pp. 24–25.

[6] A short explanation of what happened in the years before independence is the following: when the army of Napoleon crossed the border between Spain and Portugal in 1807 it prompted Prince João, who had ruled over Portugal since 1792, to move the court to Brazil. The prince, after installing his son, Pedro, as the regent of Brazil in 1821 returned to Portugal and, in exchange for losing the colony, Joao demanded two million pounds sterling that Brazil had to borrow from England. See Boris Fausto, *História do Brasil*, São Paulo: Edusp, 1994, p. 122.

[7] The constitution's Article 179 established the inviolability of private property, which included debt. Article 15 assigned responsibility for budget and taxation issues, including borrowing, to the parliament. The lower house was especially protective of the interests of debt holders, the legislators having been elected by wealthy, enfranchised Brazilians (the right to vote had been conveyed by the constitution only to adult males with an income). See William R. Summerhill III, "Political Economics of the Domestic Debt in Nineteenth-Century Brazil," pp. 3–6, presented at Economics, Political Institutions, and Financial Markets II: Institutional Theory and Evidence from Europe, the United States, and Latin America, Social Science History Institute, Stanford University, February 4th and 5th, 2005.

throne. When he did so in 1840, Dom Pedro II altered neither the basic institutions nor the checks and balances established in the constitution of 1824. According to Richard Sylla, for instance, strong sovereign debt markets and government capacity to pay have been key components in promoting financial revolutions that translate into larger private financial markets. Douglass C. North and Barry Weingast go so far as to cite credible commitment in the sovereign debt market as perhaps the main reason for the development of private credit markets in England in the late seventeenth and early eighteenth centuries.[8]

Summerhill finds puzzling the fact that Brazil could develop a large market for its sovereign debt at home and in London without developing an active internal market for company stocks or corporate bonds until very late in the nineteenth century. He attributes this delay to the restrictions on entry for new corporations.[9]

Therefore, according to the recent economic historiography, financial markets did not develop in Brazil not because the conditions were not ripe for it, but because companies had to submit their statutes for government approval and entry was limited. As a result, the number of companies going public (registering in stock markets) was also constrained.

THE DEBATE AROUND REGULATION OF ENTRY

The debate around the extent to which regulations of entry restricted financial development is centered around the premise that these regulations, by lowering entry rates in general, also lowered the rate of entry into stock markets. Yet for this hypothesis to be true we would need to observe that whenever there were increases (or reductions) in the number of new corporations created in Brazil, there were also increases (or reductions) in the number of companies traded.[10]

Since independence the emperor had controlled chartering, and Decree 575 of 1849, which kept corporations under the scrutiny of the imperial

---

[8] See, for example, Richard Sylla, "Financial Systems and Economic Modernization," *Journal of Economic History* 62–2 (2002): 277–292, esp. 280. North and Weingast argued that developing a credible commitment in sovereign debt markets enabled England to secure lower interest rates at the Bank of England. See Douglass C. North and Barry Weingast, "Constitutions and Commitment: The Evolution of Institutions Governing Public Choice in Seventeenth Century England," *Journal of Economic History* 49 (1989): 803–832.

[9] William R. Summerhill, "Sovereign Credibility with Financial Underdevelopment," p. 3.

[10] Defending the view that the regulation of entry constrained financial development are Levy, *História da Bolsa de Valores do Rio de Janeiro*, p. 85; Hanley, *Native Capital*, Chapter 3; and Summerhill III, "Sovereign Credibility with Financial Underdevelopment," p. 19.

Table 2.1. *Trading and chartering requirements for corporations in Brazil,*
1850–1891

	1850	1860	1882	1890	1891
Government authorization	Y	Y	N[a]	N[a]	N[a]
Limited liability	Y[b]	Y	Y	Y[c]	Y
Deposit of initial capital			10%	10%	10%
Percentage of capital paid up before shares became tradable		25%	25%	20%	40%

Sources: Commerce Code, Law 536, June 25, 1850; Law 1083, August 22, 1860; Law 3150, November 4, 1882; Decree 164, January 17, 1890; Decree 434, July 4, 1891; and Decree 601, October 17, 1891 from Brazil, *Colecção das Leis e Decretos,* 1850, 1860, 1882, 1890–1891.
Notes:
[a] Companies with government concessions and banks still needed government approval to operate.
[b] Limited liability for shareholders of joint stock companies was included in the commerce code of 1850, but was not explained in detail, leaving it up to the company statutes to decide the extent to which the liability of the shareholders would be limited.
[c] Before 1890, if a company went bankrupt, shareholders with shares that were not fully paid were liable for the unpaid amount up to five years after selling their shares.[11]

government, required joint stock companies operating outside of the capital city of Rio de Janeiro to have the authorization of the relevant ministers and presidents of the provinces in which they were to operate. The commerce code of 1850 did not simplify things much. Its Article 295 stated that joint stock companies needed government approval, but limited the need for congressional approval to companies that required special privileges or concessions to operate (e.g., banks, railways, shipping companies). The code in Article 298 additionally provided limited liability to shareholders of joint stock companies (up to the face value of each share).[12]

Table 2.1 shows the basic chartering requirements for shareholders according to the most important company laws of Brazil between 1850 and 1891. The table also includes the limited liability provisions of each law, percentage

[11] Article 7, Law 3150, November 4, 1882, Paragraph 2. In fact, this paragraph is the reason Stephen Haber and Anne Hanley argued, in separate works, that Brazil did not have limited liability until 1890. Limited liability for shareholders was in fact explicitly included in company laws since 1850, yet shares with unpaid calls were an exception. See Stephen Haber, "The Efficiency Consequences of Institutional Change: Financial Market Regulation and Industrial Productivity Growth in Brazil, 1866–1934," in John Coatsworth and Alan Taylor (eds.), *Latin America and the World Economy Since 1800*, Cambridge, Mass.: DRCLAS and Harvard University Press, 1998, pp. 275–322 and Hanley, *Native Capital*, Chapter 3.
[12] Decree 575, January 1, 1849; for the commerce code, see Law 556, June 25, 1850.

of capital needed to secure government approval (bank deposit of the initial paid-up capital), and percentage of capital needed to trade shares in any of the local stock exchanges. This table lead us to expect that government regulation stymied the entry of new corporations until at least 1882.

The imperial government tightened control over entry in 1860 with the publication of new regulations for joint stock companies and banks. The 1860 law, also known as the *Lei dos entraves* (Law of Impediments), required that company statutes previously authorized by the Council of State (Conselho do Estado) be approved by Congress. It provided legal penalties (e.g., jail sentences and monetary fines) for companies and company promoters who failed to secure the required authorization.[13] In practice, the law had the effect of slowing the approval of company statutes. According to contemporary observers, "the norm is that the approval process takes one year or more, depending on the legislatures' recesses."[14]

The literature to date holds that the law of 1860 slowed economic growth and the development of stock markets by restricting entry of new joint stock companies and banks.[15] But the source of the data on which most studies have based this claim is the report of the number of companies registered in Brazil published by the Ministry of Justice in 1865. The data from 1851 to 1865 show a significant reduction in the number and capital of registered joint stock companies in Brazil after 1860. Moreover, this reduction does not take place in alternatives to joint stock companies such as partnerships and partnerships with shares. Unfortunately, the data end shortly after the 1860 law was passed, preventing us from tracking the evolution of the number of companies registered after 1865.[16]

Figure 2.1 shows the number of new domestic joint stock companies and new Brazilian banks chartered between 1848 and 1909 according to data compiled by the Ministry of Labor, Industry, and Commerce in 1946. We

---

[13] For more detail, see the discussion of how Brazilian laws constrained the entry of new companies and banks in Hanley, *Native Capital*, Chapter 3.

[14] Citation from Aureliano C. Tavares Bastos as quoted by Mária Bárbara Levy, *A Indústria do Rio de Janeiro através de suas Sociedades Anônimas*, p. 77 (translated into English by the author).

[15] This argument is defended in the recent studies of Anne Hanley, *Native Capital: Financial Institutions and Economic Development in São Paulo, Brazil, 1850–1920,* chapter 3, Mária Bárbara Levy, *A Indústria do Rio de Janeiro através de suas Sociedades Anônimas*, Rio de Janeiro: URFJ Editoria, 1994, Chapter 3, and Summerhill III, "Sovereign Credibility with Financial Underdevelopment."

[16] The Ministry of Justice data are used by Levy, *História da Bolsa de Valores do Rio de Janeiro*, pp. 77–80, and Summerhill III, "Sovereign Credibility with Financial Underdevelopment," Figures 10 and 11.

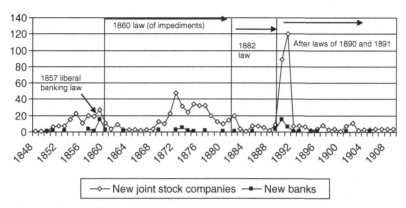

Figure 2.1. Number of new domestic joint stock companies and banks registered in Brazil, 1848–1909

Source: Compiled by the author from Brazil, Ministério do Trabalho, Indústria e Comércio. *Sociedades Mercantis autorizadas a funcionar no Brasil* (1808–1946), Rio de Janeiro, Departamento Nacional de Indústria e Comércio, 1947. The estimates for new joint stock companies added are net of reincorporations and filings to change statutes of existing corporations. The data exclude all foreign companies. The totals for New Joint Stock Companies include banks. For banks, I did not count the re-registration or rechartering of banks registered in previous periods (e.g., Banco do Brasil). The data include only companies the statutes of which were approved by the federal government or at least published in federal decrees and, hence, significantly underestimate total registration of new companies after the 1890s when state governments were accorded greater autonomy to approve charters.

see that an initial period of relatively high levels of company registrations preceded the passage of the company law of 1860. We further see a slight increase in bank registrations following passage of the law of 1857, which permitted multiple banks to issue bank notes. The number of new bank registrations reached 15 in 1859. Conflict between politicians who favored a strict gold standard with one emission bank in control of the money supply and those who favored a system with multiple banks of issue (and thus slower monetary and price adjustment under the gold standard) resulted in a series of contradictory chartering laws that ended the boom in new charters. Thus was the liberal banking law of 1857 followed by the 1860 law that sought to restrict entry and centralize the emission of bank notes in the new Banco do Brasil (created in 1853) and six closely monitored private banks.[17]

---

[17] Banco do Brasil was in fact a private bank with close links to the government. Its shares were publicly traded, but the government named the director. Moreover, the bank was in charge of managing the supply of government notes, which served as paper money

A review of the new evidence presented in Figure 2.1 reveals the effects of the 1860 law on the number of registrations of Brazilian companies to have been dramatic only during the 1860s. Although the number of new Brazilian joint stock companies registered declined from 11 in 1860 to four in 1861, in 1869 there were 13 registrations of new companies and in 1872 there were 48, more than in any other year in the country's history. Moreover, between 1872 and 1875, 11 new banks were registered.

Two factors explain the growth in the number of company registrations in the 1870s. First, as Maria Bárbara Levy emphasizes in her book on the history of the Rio de Janeiro Stock Exchange, the Paraguayan War (1864–1870) fought by Brazil, Uruguay, and Argentina against Paraguay had indirect positive consequences for the Brazilian economy. "[I]t reanimated manufacturing activities," she writes, "not only because of the increase in money issues, but also because of the increase in import duties."[18] Second, Flávio Saes, studying the evolution of railways in São Paulo, identified special conditions in the coffee market in the 1870s that benefited the chartering of new companies, in particular São Paulo's three largest railway companies. "[E]ven with the crisis of 1873," he writes, "Brasil increased its market share [in coffee] because of the failure of production in Java. Therefore, coffee export income and the profit per unit of coffee produced increased. This in part thanks to the addition of new fertile land and the decline of transportation costs as a consequence of railway development."[19]

Figure 2.1 also shows the effects of liberalization of entry following passage of the 1882 law to have been relatively minor. If regulation of entry were the only reason Brazil did not develop an active exchange before the 1880s, we would expect two things: first, an increase in the number of companies traded in stock exchanges concomitant with the increase in the number of registrations per year after 1882, and second, significant increases in the number of companies traded with every spate of company registrations (e.g., in the 1870s and early 1890s).

Yet increases in the number of companies registered in Brazil do not coincide with the movements of companies traded at the Rio de Janeiro Stock Exchange (the only organized stock exchange at the time). In Table 2.2, we can see that an initial expansion of the number of traded companies in the

before 1853. See Carlos Manuel Peláez and Wilson Suzigan, *História Monetária do Brasil*, Brasilia: Universidade de Brasília, 1976, pp. 97–104.

[18] Translated by the author from Mária Bárbara Levy, *História da Bolsa de Valores do Rio de Janeiro*, p. 94.

[19] Flávio A. M. Saes, *As Ferrovias de São Paulo, 1870–1940*, São Paulo: Editora HUCITEC, 1981, p. 171.

Table 2.2. *Number of companies registered at the exchange (per million population, averages by decade)*

	Companies/million pop.
1850s	3.4
1860s	1.3
1870s	1.9
1880s	3.8
1890s	6.4
1900s	7.1
1910s	12.4
1920s	11.1
1930s	5.9
1940s	14.8
1950s	48.7
1960s	n/a
1970	4.3
1980	4.1
1990s	5.8
2000–2003	5.6

Sources: The number of companies for the 1850s is estimated from annual summaries of the Rio de Janeiro Stock Exchange published from 1861 and 1953, taken from Mária Bárbara Levy, *História da Bolsa de Valores do Rio de Janeiro*, Tables 8, 18, 24, 38, 47, and 57. All population data are from Cláudio Contador, *Mercado de Ativos Financeiros no Brasil*, Rio de Janeiro, IBMEC, 1974, Table A.1. Data from 1991–2003 are from www. cvm.gov.br.
Note: Data for the 1860s–1950s are for the Rio de Janeiro Stock Exchange only. In the 1940s and 1950s, we observe large numbers of companies registered on the stock exchanges of Brazil because Decree-law 9,783 of 1946, intended to enable brokers to monitor corporations and facilitate the collection of dividend taxes, required that all corporations register at the local stock exchange. This artificially inflated the number of companies registered because many privately held companies (companies that did not trade their shares) were included in the lists of registered companies on the exchanges, rendering the data from the 1940s and 1950s impossible to compare with that from previous periods.

1850s was followed by a significant contraction in the 1860s and 1870s, likely a reflection of the effects of the 1860s law (i.e., the law of the impediments). But the increases in new company creations (or registrations) in Figure 2.1 do not correspond with the trends in the number of companies listed in the stock exchange (in Table 2.2). For instance, in the 1870s registrations increase and the number of traded companies increases only slightly. The big jump in the number of companies registered at the stock exchange takes place after the 1880s, even if the formation of new companies in the country does not seem to be trending upward in that decade, at least according to the data used for Figure 2.1.

Thus, there had to be another causal mechanism driving the number of companies going public and leading them to trade their securities at the stock exchange in Rio de Janeiro. One such mechanism could be that the number of companies traded does not increase when entry increases, but when the number of total outstanding companies in the country increases. That is, the number of companies traded in stock markets perhaps increases when the stock of corporations increases and not when the flow (the number of registrations) increases. But since we have no data for the stock of corporations operating in Brazil, it is hard to test this hypothesis. Another, perhaps more plausible, hypothesis is that the number of traded corporations increased because some of the outstanding companies wanted to take advantage of the opportunities generated by the law of 1882. This law established the right to charter corporations without government approval, introduced clear rules for limiting the liability of shareholders, and permitted companies to issue corporate bonds (debentures). Table 2.2 reveals that the number of joint stock companies registered at the stock exchange multiplied rapidly after 1882, from an average of 1.9 companies per million people in the 1870s to 3.9 during the 1880s.[20]

After 1890 the analysis cannot be performed in the same way. The constitution of 1891 granted state governments greater autonomy in accepting

[20] Some of the existing literature on financial development in Brazil has defended the idea that limited liability was not truly introduced in Brazil until 1890. But Article 7, Paragraph 2 of the 1882 law states that investors who originally invested in shares and sold them before the full face value had been called up by the company were liable for the portion of the capital that had not been fully paid up for up to five years after the sale. Still, these shareholders were only liable up to the amount of the face value of their shares. This liability accompanied the transfer of shares in order to avoid fraud by company founders and business promoters with bad reputations. See Law 3150, November 4, 1882, Article 7, §2. For studies that argue that limited liability was not introduced until 1890, see Hanley, *Native Capital*, pp. 66–67, and Haber "The Efficiency Consequences of Institutional Change," p. 277.

charters, and the data in Figure 2.1 capture only the registration of government approved or federally decreed company statutes. Thus, the number of registrations after 1891 must be heavily discounted.

STOCK MARKET GROWTH POST-1882

Now that we know that stock markets started to grow faster after 1882 and that this growth does not seem to be directly related to entry we can explore some of the reasons why stock and bond markets boomed in the three decades that followed. The argument of this book is that stock and bond markets experienced a major boom between the 1880s and 1915. Part of the reason investors participated actively in stock markets during this period is they were protected strongly against management abuses and mismanagement either in company bylaws or through legal protections in national laws. For instance, Chapters 4 and 5 demonstrate that shareholders were protected strongly in many companies because the bylaws included voting provisions to reduce the power of large shareholders. Additionally, shareholders of all corporations had access to detailed financial and ownership information after it became mandatory to publish all this information in 1891. Therefore, we should find that stock markets had a major boom after 1891. For bond markets we have a similar hypothesis: We should find rapid growth after the introduction of the company law of 1882 given that it allowed bond issues, but we should also find another jump after 1890 when the government reformed bankruptcy regulation and gave bondholders the statues of privileged creditors, putting them ahead of other creditors in cases of insolvency.

This section examines the boom in stock and bond market activity after 1882, looking for possible jumps in activity after the introduction of the Company Laws of 1882 and 1890. The effects of the regulatory changes to protect creditors and shareholders are not as straightforward as we would want them to be because in the late 1880s there was a radical change in monetary policy that fueled a stock market boom between 1889 and 1891. Thus, the macroeconomic changes after 1888 also coincided with some of the changes in bankruptcy and company law. It is not clear how much of the sustained change in bond and stock markets after the 1880s was due to these protections and how much is attributable to favorable macroeconomic conditions, a dilemma I will discuss in more detail. What will be clear is that they were not, by themselves, sufficient to fuel the rapid growth in stock and bond markets. For the boom to take place favorable macroeconomic conditions were needed, and these actually prevailed in Brazil after the 1890s, mostly between 1900 and 1915.

THE ANATOMY OF A BOOM: EQUITY MARKETS FROM 1882 TO 1915

The Rio de Janeiro Stock Exchange, the leading stock market in Brazil until the 1930s, at its inception in 1848 specialized in government bonds. The stock exchange had its genesis earlier in the century as informal meetings of handfuls of brokers at the Rua Direita, a street near the Imperial Palace. The legal figure of the broker (*corretor*), an agent who could facilitate the trade of anything from commodities to commercial paper, had existed since colonial times. In 1843, the government regulated the number of brokers per city and established three categories of broker according to what was traded: cargo space, commodities, and stocks and bonds. Operating as a stockbroker required a permit, the number of which was limited by law (and increased sporadically), and payment of an annual "patent" fee and security deposit. The Rio de Janeiro Stock Brokers Association was formed in 1849 in a building on the same street on which brokers earlier in the century had met informally.[21] In 1850, the profession was regulated by the commerce code.

The market for government securities having been active since the beginning of the century, stockbrokers began to report the quotes of their trades back to the treasury and to some major newspapers. Quotations for 10 or so companies were published regularly in the newspapers after 1850; by 1859, the stock exchange trading summary included 41 companies. This was the peak of stock market activity until the 1870s and 1880s, the 1864 crisis having led to the bankruptcy of many of these companies (see Table 2.2).

The real peak in stock market activity seems to have taken place after 1882. The number of traded companies doubled from the 1870s to the 1880s and stock market capitalization shows a significant jump from 1878 to 1886 (in Figure 2.2). The level of equity market capitalization rose from 10% in 1881 to in excess of 15% in 1886 and nearly 20% between 1895 and 1913.

Public and private securities traded in the stock exchanges of Brazil also increased their importance as a proportion of personal savings during the 1880s. Zephyr Frank estimates that the percentage of wealth invested in

---

[21] For more details about the history of the Rio de Janeiro Stock Exchange and Stock Brokers Association see Mária Bárbara Levy, *História da Bolsa de Valores do Rio de Janeiro*.

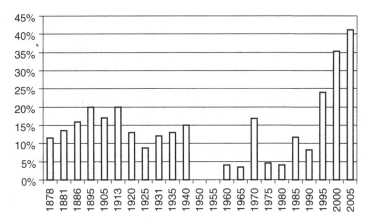

Figure 2.2. Equity market capitalization over GDP in Brazil (five-year intervals), 1878–2002

Source: See Appendix 2A.

public and private securities went from something close to 11.5% of estate valuations in Rio de Janeiro in 1868–1873, to over 32% between 1885 and 1889.[22]

As expected the boom of the 1880s in the number of stocks traded and size of the market was repeated in the 1890s. The succession of regulations that protected shareholders, bondholders, and the expansion of bank credit described in the next section provided the impetus for this latter boom. In the 1890s, the number of traded companies per million people reached, on average, 6.4. This number peaked in 1910 at 12.4 (see Table 2.2).

The rapid jump in the number of corporations registered in the Rio de Janeiro Stock Exchange at the end of the 1880s also had to do with reforms passed by the minister of finance after 1886, the Viscount of Ouro Preto, who favored a looser monetary and banking policy because the massive immigration of Europeans and end of slavery demanded that the country increase its means of payment. The end of the slave trade and pressures that had led to the abolition of slavery in 1888 prompted coffee growers in Rio de Janeiro and São Paulo to push for a massive, state-sponsored program of European immigration. According to the dominant views of the economic history of Brazil, the abolition of slavery in 1888 and wave of European immigrant workers who replaced the slaves increased the demand for cash with which to pay wages and fund transactions

---

[22] Zephyr Frank, *Dutra's World: Wealth and Family in Nineteenth-Century Rio de Janeiro*, Albuquerque: University of New Mexico Press, 2004, p. 88.

previously covered by trade credit. These pressures led the government to loosen monetary policy.[23]

Minister Ouro Preto responded in 1888 with a new banking law that simplified the process for becoming an emission bank. These banks were permitted to back 80% of their notes with internal debt bonds (*apólices*).[24] The chartering of new banks with rights to issue money led to a rapid expansion of the money supply and fueled speculation in joint stock companies accommodated by the 1888 law that permitted banks to invest in stocks and bonds. According to the figures of contemporary observer Liberato de Castro Carreira, in 1889 there were 35 banks in operation in Rio de Janeiro alone (up from 25 in the entire country in 1880).

THE REPUBLIC AND THE FIRST CRISIS OF CONFIDENCE IN STOCK MARKETS

This increase in the number of banks, amount of money issued, and level of bank involvement in stock market activities accelerated the growth of Rio de Janeiro's stock and bond market during the latter part of the 1880s. Then, following a coup that overthrew the monarchy in November 1889, a republican government was installed. Concerned with growing the financial sector to promote industrialization, the new government passed a series of laws aimed at further developing banking and the stock market. For example, in 1890, the first minister of finance under the republican government, Rui Barbosa, created new banks with the capacity to issue notes and increased the total emission limit. The effect was instantaneous: the money supply increased by nearly 100% in one year.

This rapid expansion of the money supply provided liquidity to investors willing to participate in stock markets and precipitated a sudden boom in the Rio de Janeiro Stock Exchange. Thanks to the liquidity and increase in the number of small investors, new firms had an easier time selling their shares to the public, and hundreds of companies registered in a matter of months. Corporations chartered in late 1889 and early 1890 had capital subscriptions that lasted a few days or just a few hours. The short stock boom from 1890 to 1891 was called the *encilhamento* (saddling) because

---

[23] See Gustavo Franco, "A Primeira Década Republicana," in Marcelo de Paiva Abreu (org.) (ed.), *A Ordem do Progresso: cem anos de política econômica republicana, 1889–1989*, Rio de Janeiro: Campus Editora, 1989, pp. 15–19, and Carlos Manuel Peláez and Wilson Suzigan, *História Monetária do Brasil*, p. 177.

[24] Decree 3403 of November 24, 1888. It was complemented by Decree 10,144 of January 5, 1889.

of similarities between bets placed at the Jockey Club of Rio de Janeiro on horses while they were being saddled and the purchase of stock of new companies with no clear business prospects. Before 1888, the value of all the joint stock companies established in Brazil was something on the order of 43 million pounds sterling. Between 1888 and November 1889, the capital of just the new companies was 44 million pounds. Between November 1889 and October 1890, when Barbosa presented his Ministry of Finance report, the capital of all the new companies totaled 104 million pounds.[25]

In January 1890 Barbosa also passed Law 164, which facilitated the sale of company stocks after their creation (reducing to 20% of total declared capital the amount of paid-up capital necessary to trade shares). These legal changes, together with the expansionary monetary policy, increased the rate at which new companies were created. The ease with which corporations could pursue IPOs was an incentive to create companies and trade their shares at inflated prices on the exchange.

The number of companies traded on the Rio de Janeiro Stock Exchange jumped from four to eight per million people in 1890 alone, and the number of companies registered reached record levels of more than 100 per year between 1890 and 1891 (see Table 2.2). Stock market capitalization jumped from 15% of GDP in the late 1880s to 40% during the *encilhamento,* stabilizing at around 20% of GDP after the excitement abated (see Figure 2.2).

The *encilhamento* and the investor exuberance that sustained it created incentives for corporate fraud. Many Brazilians seized the opportunity afforded by the boom to create companies that produced nothing. With an ambitious business plan and contacts with a broker or bank, these businessmen were able to sell shares in ghost companies, for the boom of 1889–1891 had also attracted many uninformed investors looking to make a quick profit.

After the excitement declined many uninformed investors in Brazil's ghost companies lost their money. Stock prices declined rapidly in 1891 and bankruptcies multiplied. The official reaction to the *encilhamento* took the form of a series of laws regulating corporations and their public offerings that were later compiled in Decree 434 in July 4, 1891 and Decree 603 in October 17, 1891. These laws were intended to forestall corporate fraud by increasing the share of fully paid-up capital necessary to trade shares from 20% to 40% of total registered capital, thereby forcing the initial subscribers to put more of their own money at risk before getting other investors

---

[25] Brazil, *Relatório do Ministro da Fazenda em Janeiro de 1891*, Rio de Janeiro: Imprensa Nacional, 1891.

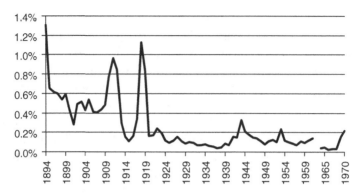

Figure 2.3. Stock turnover at the Rio de Janeiro Stock Exchange (as a % of GDP), 1894–1980

Source: See Appendix 2A.

Note: Data between 1961 and 1964 are missing.

involved in a company. These laws also increased the penalties against company founders and promoters of shares and mandated complete disclosure of information about new companies. According to Decree 603, any attempt to sell new shares required the publication in major financial newspapers of the statutes of the company, a full shareholder list, and complete information about the deal with the investment bank or broker underwriting the issue.[26] These legal proved very effective in keeping investor interest in the stock market and are discussed in more detail in Chapter 4.

TRADING AFTER THE 1890–1891 REFORMS

Figure 2.3 shows total trading of stocks relative to GDP. The trading figures mimic somewhat the findings reported in Figure 2.2. There were at least three periods of intense trading between 1890 and 1920. The first was a period of exuberance of the early 1890s (the *encilhamento* and its aftermath), and the second started after 1905 and ended in 1913. The third period was the quick recovery in trading after World War I, which declined shortly thereafter in a sustained way until at least the late 1960s.

Trading was active in the 1890s when banks were first permitted to own and manage joint stock companies and small investors increased their participation in the ownership of companies. The deflationary episode between 1898 and the first years of the twentieth century, and the banking crisis of

[26] See Decree 603, October 17, 1891, Articles 89–105.

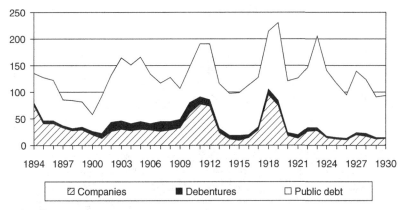

Figure 2.4. Turnover of securities in the Rio de Janeiro Stock Exchange, 1894–1930 (contos de mil reis [millions] of 1900)

Source: Maria Bárbara Levy, *História da Bolsa de Valores do Rio de Janeiro*, Tables 8, 18, 23, 24, 26, 35, 38, 41, 43, 44, 47, 57, 58, 61, and 62, and deflated using the GDP Deflator.

Note: Mortgage bonds from some banks were also traded on the Rio de Janeiro Stock Exchange, but the volume was so small as to be essentially irrelevant to the present analysis.

1900 that precipitated the bankruptcy of many companies and banks that operated in Rio de Janeiro, including the semiofficial Banco do Brasil, might have contributed to the reduction in trading. When the crisis ended, trading again picked up, reaching levels close to 1% of GDP. The volume traded increased again just before World War I and between 1919 and 1920, but these short periods of active trading were not sustained. Trading subsequently decreased to 0.1–0.2% of GDP from 1921 to 1969 (see Figure 2.3). Still, most of the trading throughout the period 1894–1930 was in Treasury bonds (see Figure 2.4).

BOND MARKETS IN BRAZIL

Bond markets, too, experienced a significant initial takeoff during the 1880s. Accounting for less than 1% of GDP in 1881, the total stock of bonds had doubled by 1882. In that year alone, the number of companies issuing bonds increased from five to eight and the number of bond issues from six to 11. This trend accelerated during the second half of the decade. In 1885, 25 companies were issuing bonds in the Rio de Janeiro Stock Exchange alone.

The market for corporate bonds had been quite thin before 1882. Three of the five companies with bonds outstanding were railways (the Leopoldina,

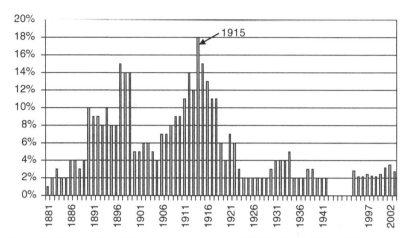

Figure 2.5. Stock of bonds (debentures) relative to GDP in Brazil, 1886–2002

Sources: Jornal do Commércio, Retrospecto Comercial do Jornal do Commércio, Câmara Sindical, *Relatorio* (1905–1926), and the *Anuário da Bolsa de Valores do Rio de Janeiro* (1926–1942). The total stock of debentures after 1990 is from *The Brazil Handbook,* 1992–2002, and the Brazilian Debenture Service. GDP data are from Raymond Goldsmith, *Brasil 1850–1984: Desenvolvimento Financeiro sob um Século de Inflação,* Rio de Janeiro: Banco Bamerindus and Editora Harper & Row do Brasil, 1986, Tables 3.1 and 4.2.

Macahé e Campos, and Sorocabana), one was a tramway (Carris Urbanos), and the other was a government-subsidized sugar mill (Engenho Central de Quisamã, in Rio de Janeiro). Railways had begun in the 1870s to trade bonds among small savers and coffee planters. In the absence of national legal provisions, the protections accorded these bondholders were detailed on the backs of their bonds. These included bondholders' rights in the event of bankruptcy, such as the right to withdraw collateral, as well as the rights to a coupon and instructions for collecting it.[27]

Figure 2.5 delineates three important jumps in total debenture capitalization, the first in the latter part of the 1880s, the second in the 1890s following the succession of laws passed in 1890, and the third in 1915 after a period of decline consequent to the wave of bankruptcies and deflation at the turn of the century. Bond market size relative to the size of the economy subsequently declined and has not been restored to its 1915 level even to this day.

---

[27] Some of these early bonds are available in the National Archive of Brazil in the bankruptcy files of railways discussed in Chapter 7.

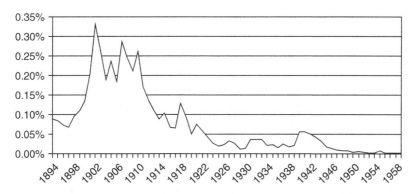

Figure 2.6. Volume of debentures traded (as a % of GDP)

Sources: The turnover of debentures is taken from Maria Bárbara Levy, *Historia da Bolsa de Valores do Rio de Janeiro*, Tables 23, 26, 35, 41, 43, 44, 58, 61, and 62. Data for the years 1934, 1935, and 1939 were corrected by the author using the reports of the stockbrokers association and the *Anuario da Bolsa de Valores do Rio de Janeiro*. GDP measures are from Raymond Goldsmith, *Brasil 1850–1984: Desenvolvimento Financeiro sob um Século de Inflação*, Tables 3.1, 4.2, and 6.2.

To measure the importance of the number of bonds issued in Brazil circa 1915 when the stock of bonds stood at 12% over GDP we could look at the size of bond markets in Brazil today. In Figure 2.5, which shows the stock of debentures from 1994 to 2003 normalized by GDP, the 1913 level of 12% looks large compared with levels of under 5% during the 1990s.[28] These latter levels seem particularly low when we take into account that the stocks of debentures in the last few years include bonds issued not only by companies but also by banks and government entities.

Figure 2.6, which plots the total volume of bonds traded relative to GDP, shows trading to have been active from 1894 through the early 1920s, but especially before World War I. The boom years in bond trading correspond with the years in which macroeconomic conditions stabilized and Brazil adopted the gold standard. The decline in bond trading and in the total stock of bonds in Brazil after 1915 is thus, as I elaborate in Chapter 9, related to increasing inflation after the 1920s and diminished capital flows following WWI.

---

[28] Debentures declined drastically throughout the twentieth century consequent to inflation increasing rapidly after 1920, and even more rapidly after 1940, and indexed debenture issues not being introduced until the last decades of the century. For an analysis of the debenture market after 1930, see Everett Santos, "Liquidez de Mercado Secundário para debêntures," unpublished manuscript, IBMEC, Rio de Janeiro, 1973.

The takeoff of debentures in Brazil followed the important reforms enacted in 1890. Legal provisions to protect small investors and the tailoring of joint stock company laws to facilitate entry by new entrepreneurs were among the reforms introduced in rapid succession by the newly established republican government's minister of finance. In particular, Minister Barbosa facilitated the rapid development of corporate bond markets between 1890 and 1915 by introducing four legal measures (see Figure 2.5). The first, a law passed in January 1890 accorded bondholders the status of secured creditors and gave them first priority during bankruptcy.[29] The second measure, also enacted in 1890, reduced from one-fifth to one-tenth of total capital the initial capital required to register a corporation. The number of joint stock companies formed and traded on the exchanges of Brazil subsequently grew rapidly, almost half issuing corporate bonds.

The third measure radically altered the incentives for companies to issue debt versus equity. Whereas chartered corporations generally could issue debentures only up to the value of their capital, after 1891 firms with government concessions (e.g., utilities) and those engaged in public services (e.g., railways, shipping companies, municipal markets) were permitted to issue debentures for more than the declared value of their paid-up capital. This provided a strong incentive to issue debentures because it facilitated the initial collection of funds for new ventures.[30]

Finally, Barbosa promoted rapid expansion of the money supply by establishing an official system of regional banks charged with expanding the emission of bank notes. Permitting a handful of banks to issue inconvertible notes backed by government bonds precipitated a doubling of the money supply from 1890 to 1891.[31] This, in turn, generated a short-term boom in securities markets. In 1895 these banking reforms were phased out, but the other three regulatory changes exerted a lasting effect on the bond markets.

---

[29] For the changes in creditor priority, see Decrees 164 of January 17 and 917 of October 24, 1890 and Decrees 434 of July 4 and 603 of October 20, 1891.

[30] Companies established before 1890 could operate with only 20% of the face value of their shares fully paid (called up), 40% if the company was established after 1890. Because bonds could be issued for up to 100% of the registered value of capital even if only 20% or 40% of equity had been called up, companies could effectively raise 1.4 times the value of capital (100% in debentures and 40% in equity) in little time and with little investment by shareholders. The process of raising capital was made even easier for many companies once the privilege of issuing more bonds than equity was extended to firms with government concessions or focused on public services. See Decrees 434 of July 4 and 603 of October 20, 1891.

[31] See Maria Bárbara Levy, *Historia da Bolsa de Valores do Rio de Janeiro*.

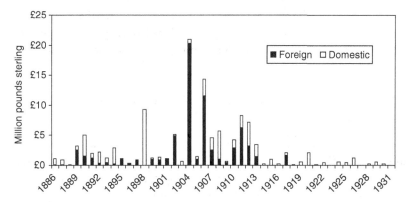

Figure 2.7. Corporate bond issues per year, Rio de Janeiro Stock Exchange, 1890–1930

Sources: Jornal do Commércio, Retrospecto Comercial do Jornal do Commércio, Câmara Sindical, *Relatorio* (1905–1926), and the *Anuário da Bolsa de Valores do Rio de Janeiro* (1926–1942). Exchange rates are from the *Brazilian Year Book 1909*.

The fact that all of these reforms were passed at the same time obscures the net effect that the changes in the priority of bondholders during bankruptcy had on the level of bond market activity. Even if we know these rights must have mattered to convince investors to buy bonds, we do not know their precise effect. Still, the golden era of corporate bond markets ushered in by the legal reforms of the early 1890s saw the largest bond issues placed in the Rio de Janeiro Stock Exchange between 1898 and 1915. This boom in bond issues is depicted in Figure 2.7, which distinguishes domestic annual bond issues denominated in domestic currency from those denominated in foreign currency and converts all figures to pounds sterling to facilitate comparisons across time.[32] It shows that most domestic bond issues during this time were denominated in sterling, francs, and other European currencies to facilitate sale to European investors. Not coincidentally, this was also the period (1906–1914) during which Brazil, to contain the appreciation of the local currency, the mil reis, first adhered strictly to the gold standard.

Among the reasons debenture issues denominated in foreign currency were so successful outside Brazil was that they had a low exchange rate risk and foreign bondholders could, in event of default, appeal to Brazilian courts (with a good chance of recouping some of their investment). After 1897, foreign bondholders could initiate bankruptcy proceedings against

---

[32] All of the bonds accounted for in my estimates were issued by companies chartered in Brazil. That is, none of my estimates include bonds issued by foreign companies operating in Brazil.

Brazilian firms in the Rio de Janeiro courts. (See The *Moniteur des Interets Materiels,* a financial newspaper published in Brussels, also lists tens of bonds and stocks with government guarantees for many countries in continental Europe.)

FINANCIAL DEVELOPMENT UNDER FAVORABLE MACROECONOMIC CONDITIONS

Again, it is hard to know precisely how much of the initial boom in bond and stock markets was due to the effects of changes in investor protections because these changes coincided with changes in macroeconomic conditions, yet using a simple counterfactual we may be able to discern better how important both the legal reforms of the early 1890s and the strong company bylaws protecting shareholders were to the stock and bond market boom in Brazil.

Important contributing factors in the growth of Brazil's equity and bond markets at the end of the 1890s were the stabilization of the exchange rate after 1898 and adoption of a gold exchange standard in 1906. In 1898, after 70 years of a relatively good administration of public debt, the central government of Brazil suffered a major setback.[33] The excessive money issues of the early 1890s increased inflation and contributed to the rapid depreciation of the currency relative to the pound sterling. Both public and private debts suffered during this period. Many private corporations defaulted on their corporate bond issues (see Chapter 7) and the denomination of a large share of public debt in foreign currency mired the government in serious financial difficulty.

In 1898, the government negotiated a debt consolidation loan, or funding loan, with the Rotschilds that included strict conditions such as a reduction of the money supply in the exact amounts of credit received. The drastic decrease in the money supply exchanged for credit and an extension on government outstanding-debt service payments occasioned a recession between 1898 and 1900, but also stabilized the exchange rate. The stability of the exchange rate from 1898 to 1913, together with the adoption of the gold standard in 1906, provided a platform for stable growth and fostered the development of active bond and equity markets.[34]

---

[33] Brazil is perhaps the only Latin American country that did not default on its debt in the nineteenth century. See Summerhill III, "Political Economics of the Domestic Debt in Nineteenth-Century Brazil," p. 3.

[34] Excellent summaries of the terms of the funding loan of 1898 and terms of the debt restructuring are provided by Marcelo de Paiva Abreu, "Os *Funding Loans* Brasileiros," *Pesquisa e Planejamento Econômico* 32–3 (2002): 515–540, esp. pp. 521–523.

The adoption of the gold standard in 1906 was a product of intense nego-
tiation between coffee exporters and the government. The government
wanted a stable exchange rate in order to be better able to service its debts;
coffee exporters wanted to stabilize their coffee export income in domestic
currency. The interests of coffee producers dominated the political scene in
Brazil during the republic, and exchange rate stability was crucial to reducing fluctuations of their incomes in domestic currency.[35]

Brazilian coffee growers faced two problems after the currency was
floated in the early 1890s. First, because Brazilian coffee exporters controlled such a large share of the world market, if too much were exported
the international price and their total export income would fall. Indeed,
the main source of price fluctuation was believed to be overproduction in
Brazil. Second, because coffee exports were the Brazilian economy's main
source of foreign exchange, higher coffee prices or higher total export
income denominated in foreign currency (price × quantity) exerted pressure on the exchange rate to appreciate, with terrible consequences for coffee growers since an increase in the exchange rate increased the price paid
by international buyers.[36]

The 1906 coffee valorization program was conceived to solve these
two problems. First, because coffee producers maximized their income
in domestic currency, the program aimed to reduce excess supply and
exchange rate fluctuation through a program based on purchasing coffee
bags to be stocked and sold only during times of short supply and keeping the price stable by regulating the international supply of coffee. The
program also involved the adoption of a gold exchange standard. The treasury was in charge of neutralizing the entrance of foreign currency (from
coffee sales) in order to keep the exchange rate from appreciating. Given
Brazilians' propensity to consume imports, a stable exchange rate also
implied lower inflation.

Together, the coffee valorization program and gold exchange standard
effectively stabilized coffee growers' real income, improved the government's ability to pay its foreign debt, facilitated the importation of industrial

---

[35] Robert Bates, *Open Economy Politics*, Princeton: Princeton University Press, 1997, Chapter 2.

[36] For details of the workings and politics of the coffee valorization program, see the clas-
sical works of Antônio Delfim Netto, "O problema do café no Brasil," in Carlos Manuel
Peláez (org.), *Ensaios sobre café e desenvolvimento econômico*, Rio de Janeiro: Instituto
Brasileiro do Café, 1973, pp. 41–160, and Carlos Manuel Peláez, "Análise Econômica do
Programa Brasileiro de Sustentação do Café, 1906–1945: Teoria, Política e Medição,"
Revsita Brasileira de Economia 25, 4 (1971): 5–211. In English, the best discussion of
the political economy of the valorization program is Bates, *Open Economy Politics*,
Chapter 2.

inputs, and benefited foreign investors into the bargain. The coffee growers' real income denominated in domestic currency was rendered more
stable and predictable. Reducing exchange rate fluctuations served the
interests of the government, which had to service its debt in pounds sterling. The stable exchange rate benefited industrialists because issuing debt
denominated in foreign currency enabled them to plan more accurately
when to import machinery and other raw materials and helped them to
issue bonds denominated in foreign currencies. This is why foreign investment increased in the period during which Brazil operated under the gold
exchange standard.

This stage of prosperity did not last long, however. World War I inter-
rupted the coffee valorization program and precipitated a permanent
decrease in the total level of foreign investment in Latin America.[37] The
decline in capital flows and coffee exports during the war disrupted the stability that had promoted the boom in stock markets. Later on, the decline in
financial market prosperity was accentuated by the post WWI world movement toward the imposition of capital controls (see Chapter 9).[38]

Does all of this evidence on the improvement of macroeconomic conditions imply that changes in company laws and having strong protections for
investors in company bylaws were relatively unimportant to fuel the stock
market boom? The answer can be elucidated if we think about a counterfactual case in which the same macroeconomic stability was achieved without
any major legal changes in company laws and with companies that did not
respect small or outside investors. The case of Mexico offers this counterfactual, even if some institutional differences complicate a perfect comparison. Mexico was industrializing rapidly after the 1890s, mostly because it
was exporting mining commodities (silver), attracting foreign capital in
large amounts and enjoying relative political and economic stability, at least
until 1910. Moreover, the Mexican government performed a series of debt
renegotiations, the last of which took place in 1899, and in 1905 adopted
the gold standard (one year earlier than Brazil). Yet the Mexican stock and
bond market did not take off as fast as did that of Brazil. In fact, no bond
market was developed in Mexico during this time, and stock markets were
relatively thin, with only a handful of industrial companies being traded

---

[37] See Barbara Stallings, *Banker to the Third World: U.S. Portfolio Investment in Latin America,*
      1900–1986 (Studies in International Political Economy), Berkeley: University of California
      Press, 1987, and my own estimates of capital flows from England reported in Chapter 9.
[38] Alan Taylor, "Foreign Capital Flows," in Victor Bulmer-Thomas, John Coatsworth, and
      Roberto Cortes-Conde (eds.), *The Cambridge Economic History of Latin America*, vol. 2,
      2006, pp. 57–100.

on the Mexico City stock exchange every year. Most stock market activity focused on mining ventures, but most of the highly traded mines were foreign companies (e.g., British) with better protections for investors than those offered by Mexican companies.[39]

In sum, if the macroeconomic conditions aided the development of Brazilian stock and bond markets, they were definitively not sufficient. Similar macroeconomic conditions existed in Mexico and the development of Mexican stock and bond markets was diametrically different. It seems that both the legal framework and the existence of bylaws protecting investors were the real triggers of investor interest in equity and bond markets. The following chapters examine in more detail the developments of stock and bond markets and the laws and company bylaws that allowed such developments.

APPENDIX 2A: SOURCES FOR ESTIMATING STOCK AND BOND MARKET DATA

METHODOLOGY FOR ESTIMATING EQUITY MARKET CAPITALIZATION

This chapter's analysis of the size of Brazil's financial system relies on estimations of equity and bond market capitalization from the Rio de Janeiro Stock Exchange annual summaries published in *Jornal do Commércio, Retrospecto do Jornal do Commércio* and the reports of the Rio de Janeiro Stock Brokers Association (*Relatorio da Câmara Sindical de Corretores Públicos da Bolsa de Valores do Rio de Janeiro*) from 1878 to 1931 and from 1944 to 1947. Additional capitalization data are from the Rio de Janeiro Stock Exchange annuals from 1932 to 1942 (*Anuário da Bolsa de Valores do Rio de Janeiro*). Information for São Paulo was added to the total estimations of stock market capitalization when available. Most of this information is from Anne Hanley, "Capital Markets in the Coffee Economy" (1995) and the *Anuário da Bolsa de Valores de São Paulo*, 1932–1950 (the 1940

---

[39] This comparison is drawn from the research done for Chapter 8, from Aldo Musacchio and Ian Read, "Bankers, Industrialists and Their Cliques: Elite Networks in Mexico and Brazil During Early Industrialization," *Enterprise and Society* 8, 4 (2007): 842–880, and from research in process co-authored with Aurora Gómez-Galvarriato. Stephen Haber developed a more detailed comparison between the development of textile corporations in Mexico and Brazil in Stephen Haber, "Industrial Concentration and the Capital Markets: A Comparative Study of Brazil, Mexico and the United States, 1830–1930," *Journal of Economic History* 51 (September 1991): 559–580.

observation is proxied with the 1939 book value observation from this publication). I did not count equity market size twice for companies that cross-listed their shares in São Paulo and Rio. Because data for the São Paulo Stock Exchange is missing for 1920, 1925, and 1935, I assume capitalization in São Paulo to have moved in line with that in Rio, which biases the estimates downward as São Paulo has grown faster than Rio since the 1920s. The data for 1947–1964 were excluded because legislation that forced all joint stock companies to register at the stock exchange rendered the data not comparable to that for other periods and other countries.

In my estimates, I use the market value of companies reflected in their last trading price, when possible, to adjust equity market size. The stock prices used to estimate registered equity at market values are from *Jornal do Commércio* and *Retrospecto do Jornal do Commércio* from 1879 to 1895 and from the annual reports of the Rio de Janeiro Stock Brokers Association (*Relatorio da Câmara Sindical de Corretores Públicos da Bolsa de Valores do Rio de Janeiro*) for 1894–1925. Stock prices for 1926 to 1942 were copied from the Rio de Janeiro Stock Exchange annuals from 1932 to 1942 (*Anuário da Bolsa de Valores do Rio de Janeiro*). This database contains thousands of trading observations with minimum and maximum prices for each year. I used the average of these prices.

The database enabled me to value companies using the last trading price for each company. I assumed the many companies for which this was not possible to have been traded at par (using the value of the fully paid up share rather than the share's registered value).[40] With the São Paulo data, I did the same for companies for which I did not have trading information. This might have caused an overestimation of the total value of some companies, but is the best that can be done with the available data. As I explain below, I made an effort to bias the estimates of stock market capitalization downward by using the largest possible GDP figures available.

Stock market capitalization data for the 1960s and 1970s are from Goldsmith (1986), Table 6.45. Stock market capitalization estimates between 1946 and 1964 were excluded from most of the graphs and tables to avoid

---

[40] Brazilian companies, following the practice in other countries, did not require that investors pay up front for their shares. Even when the full value of shares was not called up, the paid-up value up to that point was reported separately in the stock exchange annual summaries. For instance, shares usually had a face value of 200$000 (two hundred mil reis), but when only 60% of face value was fully paid (*integralizada*) the newspaper listed the face value in one column and the fully paid-up value in another (as *entradas*). Rather than use face value, I use only the paid-up value for all calculations of company capitalization when market prices are not available.

inflation of stock market capitalization occasioned by Decree-law 9,783, September 6, 1946, which mandated that all joint stock companies in Brazil register with the local stock exchange. The number of companies registered at the exchange grew rapidly after 1946 for this same reason. Between 1946 and 1947, more than 1,000 companies registered with the Rio de Janeiro Stock Exchange alone.

Finally, data for stock market capitalization after 1989 are from *The Brazil Company Handbook*, 1992–2002.

Methodology for Estimating the Stock of Bonds

To estimate the stock of bonds I used a similar methodology. I did not use market values because the companies owed the full face value of the bonds and to do so might bias my estimates upward. Instead, I estimated the stock of bonds from the Rio de Janeiro Stock Exchange annual summaries published in the *Jornal do Commércio* and the *Retrospecto Comercial do Jornal do Commércio*, the city's most important financial newspaper (see Figure 2.2). Information for São Paulo, when available, is added to the total estimations of stock market capitalization. But the source of most of the data is the Rio de Janeiro Stock Exchange, which was until the 1920s Brazil's largest financial center and the principal center for bond trading for most of the twentieth century. Data for the total stock of debentures after 1990 are from the Brazilian Debenture Service.[41]

Description of Gross Domestic Product Figures
Used to Normalize the Stock Market Data

To normalize stock market and debenture stock data over Gross Domestic Product (GDP), I used the estimates of GDP from 1861 to 1947 of Raymond Goldsmith based on the original estimates of Cláudio Contador and Cláudio Haddad.[42] I do not use the original figures published by Haddad

---

[41] São Paulo data are from Anne Hanley, "Business Finance and the São Paulo Bolsa, 1886–1917," in John Coatsworth and Alan Taylor (eds.), *Latin America and the World Economy Since 1800*, Cambridge, Mass.: DRCLAS and Harvard University Press, 1998, pp. 115–38, Table 4.4, and the *Anuário da Bolsa de Valores de São Paulo*, 1932–1950. The omission of bond data for São Paulo introduces a bias against what I am arguing (that bond markets were large before 1930 when creditor rights were stronger). I was careful not to double count equity market capitalization for companies that cross-listed in both the São Paulo and Rio exchanges.

[42] Claudio Contador and Claudio Haddad, "Produto Real, Moeda e Preços: A Experiência Brasileira no Período 1861–1970," in *Revista Brasileira de Estatística* 36, 143 (1975): 407–440,

and Contador in 1975 because their nominal values for GDP are lower than Goldsmith's. Using Goldsmith's estimates biases my normalized estimates of stock and bond market size to GDP downward. Other GDP data are taken from the web page of the Instituto de Pesquisa Econômica Aplicada (IPEA, www.ipeadata.gov.br). Whenever I had to deflate data, I used the GDP deflator used by Goldsmith, which starts in 1851, and merged it with the deflator published by IPEA in 1910.

VOLUME OF SECURITIES TRADED AND NUMBER OF COMPANIES TRADED

Information on numbers of companies traded and total volume of shares and debentures traded comes from Mária Bárbara Levy, *História da Bolsa de Valores do Rio de Janeiro* (1997), Tables 23, 26, 35, 41, 43, 44, 58, 61, and 62. Her series was incomplete for the early 1880s and for 1934, 1935, 1939, 1941, and 1946. For the 1880s, I completed the data using the annual stock market summaries published in the *Jornal do Commércio* and *Retrspecto Commércial do Jornal do Commércio*. For later periods, I used the information on traded companies published in the *Anuário da Bolsa de Valores do Rio de Janeiro*, 1932–1942, and the *Relatorio da Câmara Sindical de Corretores Públicos da Bolsa de Valores do Rio de Janeiro*, 1947. Population data used to estimate the number of traded companies per million inhabitants is from Cláudio Contador, *Mercado de Ativos Financeiros no Brasil* (1974), Table A.1, which includes estimates of population by year since 1861.

The data on total traded shares after 1939 are not comparable to earlier observations because Law 1,344 of June 13, 1939 required that companies repurchasing stocks and doing private IPOs do all trading through the stock exchange. This inflated the data on total volume traded, making comparison with pre-1939 information difficult.

Detailed Note on the Brazilian Currency

Between 1850 and 1994, Brazil changed the name of its currency and unit of account at least eight times. During the period 1833–1942 it was called mil reis (thousand kings). I generally present the data in contos of mil reis (thousand mil reis), which is equivalent to one million reis.

and Raymond Goldsmith, *Brasil 1850–1984: Desenvolvimento Financeiro sob um Século de Inflação*, Rio de Janeiro: Banco Bamerindus and Editora Harper & Row do Brasil, 1986, Tables 3.1 and 4.2.

All data in nominal terms between 1942 and 1970 were denominated in cruzeiros. One cruzeiro was equivalent to one mil reis. Accelerated inflation caused accounting problems because all figures began to include too many zeros. As part of the stabilization program of the military government (1964–1985), the currency unit was changed in 1970 to the cruzeiro novo, equivalent to 1,000 cruzeiros, and renamed cruzeiro in 1984. By the time democracy was reinstated in Brazil in 1986, the accelerated inflation necessitated changes in the unit of account.

From 1986 to 1994, struggling to stabilize inflation, the first three democratic presidents of the new republican era changed currency units repeatedly. The first change was the introduction in 1986 of the cruzado, equivalent to 1,000 cruzeiros novos. In 1989, the stabilization program based on the cruzado having failed, the first democratic government of the new republic reduced three zeros in the unit of account and called the new currency the cruzado novo. The cruzado novo was renamed the cruzeiro in 1990, and in 1993, forced by rapidly increasing inflation to again eliminate three zeros, the government created yet another new currency called the cruzeiro real. When the stabilization plan begun in 1994, the Plano Real, finally reduced inflation, the unit of account was changed again and the currency of Brazil became, after July 1, 1994, the real, equivalent to 2,750 cruzeiros reais (the plural for cruzeiro real).

Exchange Rates

Many stock and debenture and equity issues were denominated in foreign currency, and there were companies and banks with capital denominated in pounds sterling, French francs, Portuguese escudos, U.S. dollars, German marks, and even Swedish Krona. All the exchange rates needed to convert these values to mil reis are from either the *Brazilian Year Book 1909* or the reports of the brokers association, using the average of the daily quotations in the month of December of the relevant year. When exchange rates were necessary after 1942, I used the annual exchange rate to the U.S. dollar from IPEA.

THREE

The Stock Exchange and the Early Industrialization of Brazil, 1882–1930

The estimates of stock and bond market capitalization presented in the previous chapter reveal that the development of these markets enjoyed a significant period of activity during the three decades from 1882 to 1913, but not whether that development mattered for Brazil. This chapter argues that this first peak of stock market activity had a considerable impact on Brazil's transformation into a more urbanized, industrialized economy.

At the end of the nineteenth century Brazil was still predominantly an agricultural economy. Most of the population lived in rural areas and worked in agriculture or in activities related to agriculture. Therefore this chapter describes not only the rise of equity and bond markets, but also the beginning of the transformation of Brazil from an agricultural economy to a more urbanized society with a larger proportion of the population working in manufacturing and services. It shows that the stock exchange helped to mobilize resources for emerging sectors (e.g., manufacturing, utilities, and urban improvements), which accelerated the rate of urbanization, industrialization, and, ultimately, economic growth.

The last decade of the nineteenth century was particularly important for the transformation of the country into a more industrialized society. Slavery was abolished in 1888 and European immigrants were imported en masse after the 1880s. With state-sponsored programs to bring immigrants from southern Europe to work at coffee plantations and in urban manufacturing centers, wage labor markets changed significantly, especially in the intererior of the country. Thanks to the flow of European immigrants and the emergence of a large class of salaried rural and urban workers, consumption patterns changed, too. Manufacturing, transportation, and other industries responded to those needs and grew accordingly.

The data for Brazil's two most important stock exchanges reveal a rapid increase in the listing and capitalization of corporations in manufacturing, utilities, urban improvements, real estate, and other relatively new sectors after 1900. In Rio de Janeiro, acceleration begins after 1900. In the São Paulo Stock Exchange, companies in those sectors register at a more rapid pace than in Rio in a matter of five to six years (between 1907 and 1913). In the first years of the twentieth century, the capital mobilized by these new sectors also increased in importance relative to that of the sectors that had initially tapped stock markets for resources (e.g., banking, railways, and insurance).

This chapter argues that the beginning of the transformation from agriculture into manufacturing and services in Brazil was financed to a large extent through the issue of corporate equity and bonds. The rise of equity and bond finance is evident from an examination of the relative importance of the total capital corporations obtained by issuing securities vis-à-vis total bank credit in the economy. It seems that after 1882 banks played an important role in financing the agricultural export complex (especially coffee) and providing working capital for corporations, but the bulk of financing for the latter was obtained through stock and bond issues. Whereas the stock of bank credit to GDP remained at an average of 8–13 per year between 1906 and 1930 (when I have better data), the stocks of equity and bond markets were, on average, in excess of 20% of GDP per year during the same period.

The fact that Brazil was mostly an agricultural economy during the period under study does not mean that agriculture was not a dynamic sector contributing to the country's development. On the contrary, it was the savings of exporters of coffee, rubber, cotton, sugar, and cattle that fueled the demand for securities and financed the development of companies in the manufacturing and service sectors. It was also agricultural workers who initially were the main source of the increase in demand for manufactures such as textiles, shoes, hats, beer, and others.

This chapter first explains how stock markets mobilized those savings to finance industrial and services ventures, and second shows that there were some basic causal links between financial development and economic growth in Brazil. Basic Granger causality tests show measures of financial development to have preceded (Granger-caused) the movements in real GDP in Brazil. The results of this test are robust to all measures of financial development used. This result suggests that finance played a role in the larger transformation of the Brazilian economy after 1900. A simple look at growth statistics reveals that Brazil grew much faster following the revolution in financial markets that occurred in the late 1880s and early 1890s. Economists estimated that there was no growth in GDP per capita and low rates of growth for GDP throughout the nineteenth century, with a clear break after 1890 and in particular after 1900. In fact, between 1900 and 1945 the compound annual growth rate of GDP was 4%, large even when compared to more developed countries.[1]

FINANCE AND ECONOMIC GROWTH

Why not Banks?

The number of companies that listed on Brazil's stock markets increased rapidly following passage of the 1882 company law. Corporations used stock markets not only to place share issues, but increasingly to place new issues of corporate bonds (permitted for the first time). The company law also facilitated entry by new banks that were not in the business of issuing paper money. Rapid expansion in the number of total banks and in total bank credit in the economy was promoted by the minister of finance, and stock markets and a more active banking sector emerged together in the wake of the reforms enacted in the late 1880s. What roles should we attribute to banks and stock markets, respectively, in the development of the Brazilian economy during the period 1882 to 1930?

Economic historians who study the role of bank credit in financing Brazil's industrialization agree that banks did not play an active role in providing long-term financing, tending to specialize instead in discounting short-term paper and short-term credit to finance agricultural exports and provide working capital for corporations.[2] The evolution of credit

---

[1]   Nathaniel Leff's lower-bound estimate for real GDP per capita growth between 1822 and 1913 was –0.1% per year and his upper-bound estimate 0.8% per year. See Nathaniel Leff, *Underdevelopment and Development in Brazil,* Volume 1: *Economic Structure and Change, 1822–1947,* London: George Allen & Unwin, 1982, pp. 32–33. All the other GDP data comes from the estimates of Cláudio Contador and Cláudio Haddad, taken from Raymond Goldsmith, *Brasil 1850–1984: Desenvolvimento Financeiro sob um Século de Inflação,* Rio de Janeiro: Banco Bamerindus and Editora Harper & Row do Brasil, 1986,Tables 2.1, 3.1, and 4.2.

[2]   These arguments are developed in more detail in Gail Triner, *Banking and Economic Development: Brazil, 1889–1930,* New York: Palgrave, 2000; Anne Hanley, *Native Capital: Financial Institutions and Economic Development in São Paulo, Brazil, 1850–1920,* Stanford: Stanford University Press, 2005; Maria Teresa De Novaes Marques, "Bancos e desenvolvimento industrial: Uma revisão das teses de Gerschenkron à luz da história da Cervejaria Brahma, 1888/1917," *História e Economia* 1, 1 (September 2005): 87–119; and

markets in Brazil in the nineteenth century was governed by the following agreement: "[B]orrowers obtained domestic credit through personal connections. Investments requiring finance in amounts larger than what entrepreneurs could raise within their personal networks were opportunities forgone." Banking historians note that the first private banks in Brazil and elsewhere "concentrated their business in note-issuance and holding government bonds, activities not directly tied to private-sector growth." The most solid banking institutions in the long run, the British banks that operated branches in Brazil, focused mostly on trade credit and exchange transactions. Most of the domestic banks registered in the first part of the century went bankrupt soon thereafter.[3]

As mentioned Chapter 2, the development of Brazil's banking system was throughout most of the nineteenth century constrained by regulation of entry and macroeconomic instability. Only a handful of the many banks chartered between 1857 and 1859 survived the 1864 currency crisis, and from 1860 to 1882 only 21 new banks were chartered, some of which did not survive subsequent downturns in economic activity.

While the number of banks had been larger in the north and northeast of the country during the first part of the nineteenth century, the number of banks in the south and southeast grew more rapidly after the 1882 joint stock company law simplified chartering for all banks and joint stock companies, allowing all banks, except those that intended to issue notes, to file a charter without the need for government authorization. Whereas in 1880 only 25 banks operated in the entire country, by the end of the 1880s there were 35 banks in operation in Rio de Janeiro alone.[4]

The banking system further expanded with the installation of the republic, the banks listed on the Rio de Janeiro Stock Exchange alone numbering 60 by 1896. Yet, bank credit continued to be focused mostly on short-term commercial transactions. The only way banks channeled assets into long-term investments was through the purchase of corporate stocks and bonds. Gail Triner observes that banks

extended credit for commercial transactions, some financed real estate development through mortgages, and they made long-term investments by purchasing corporate bonds and equity shares. Their traditional reluctance to extend

Stephen Haber, "The Efficiency Consequences of Institutional Change: Financial Market Regulation and Industrial Productivity Growth in Brazil, 1866–1934."

[3] Triner, *Banking and Economic Development*, pp. 24–25, quotes from p. 24.

[4] Liberato de Castro Carreira, *História Financeira e Orçamentária do Império no Brasil*, Brasília: Senado Federal and Casa Rui Barbosa, 1980, p. 767.

long-term credit (in excess of a year, or often as short as six months) had not prevented banks from making significant investments in the stocks and debentures (bonds) of corporations.[5]

According to Triner, the reason banks were providers mainly of short-term capital is that they tended to make long-term loans backed by collateral only, and since collateralization was complex there were fewer of loans with long maturities.[6]

Teresa Cristina de Novaes Marques found in the archives of the Cervejaria Brahma (the second largest brewery in Brazil) no evidence that bank credit played a significant role in financing purchases of machinery. The German Brasilianische Bank für Deustchland refused even to lend on collateral to finance new machinery purchases for the company. Marques found that most of the long-term financing Brahma received from the bank was through corporate bond purchases or the bank's purchases of small lots of shares. The bank, she explains, "maintained as a priority its participation in the exchange market, extending loans to the government, and financing the export of commodities."[7]

Universal banks such as Germany's could have provided more commitment to long-term financing by acting simultaneously as underwriters, creditors, and investors in large corporations. But even if the banking reforms of 1890 gave Brazilian banks the legal right to try to play this role, actual attempts to develop universal banks failed in the long run because, according to Hanley, (1) competition among commercial banks was fierce, and (2) universal banks were overexposed to long-term loans, which put them at a disadvantage when faced with the macroeconomic contraction of 1898–1902.[8]

It was perhaps the reluctance of banks to provide long-term credit and their inclination to buy securities that afforded stock and bond markets the opportunity to play the crucial role they did in financing Brazil's industrialization. A likely scenario is that some banks provided initial funds and working capital to entrepreneurs starting new ventures, and the subsequent growth of large enterprises was financed through stock or bond issues. Supporting evidence can be found in the work of Flávio A.M. Saes and Tamás Szmrecsányi, who report that the London and Brazilian banks financed the purchase of the first flour mill of Count Francisco de Matarazzo, Brazil's most important industrial tycoon of the first half of

---

[5] Triner, *Banking and Economic Development*, p. 70.
[6] Triner, *Banking and Economic Development*.
[7] Marques, "Bancos e desenvolvimento industrial," p. 102 (quote translated by the author).
[8] See Hanley, *Native Capital*, Chapter 5.

twentieth century, and provided credit for the early development of the Companhia Nacional de Tecidos de Juta founded by another important industrialist, Jorge Street.[9] The subsequent growth of these two enterprises into dominant industrial businesses relied heavily on stock and bond issues. The Companhia Nacional de Tecidos de Juta, listed on the Rio de Janeiro Stock Exchange in 1909 with capital in the amount of 14,500 contos of mil reis (approximately $4.5 million dollars), more than doubled its stock market capitalization through new equity issues by 1930. The company had issued bonds for 8, 500 contos of mil reis ($2.5 million dollars) in 1908 and 15,000 contos of mil reis ($5 million dollars) by 1915. Matarazzo's empire also relied heavily on stock issues to finance the growth of its holding company, Indústrias Reúnidas Matarazzo, which between 1911 and 1937 tripled its capitalization (from 11,500 contos to 35,000 contos of mil reis) in nominal terms by issuing stock.

The estimates of total bank credit to GDP from 1906 to 1930 presented in Table 3.1 give a sense of the importance of bank credit and stock and bond issues relative to the size of the Brazilian economy. The first three columns report estimates of total loans using different credit categories from the aggregate banks' balance sheets. Total loans1 includes discounted paper and short term loans (*letras descontadas* and *empréstimos em conta corrente*), total loans2 adds advances on commercial paper (*letras a recever*) to total loans1, and total loans3 adds mortgage loans (*hipotecas*) to total loans2. Thus, most loans to finance the short-term needs of Brazil's manufacturing and services sectors would be portions of the amounts in total loans1 and total loans2, while total loans3 would include also mortgage loans that would have been made to the agricultural sector.

The long-term trajectory followed by total bank credit as a percentage of GDP is similar to that observed for stocks and bonds, increasing rapidly until 1915 and declining thereafter. From 1905 to 1930, a period during which better data is available for the banking system, total bank credit oscillated around 8% of GDP. From 1911 to 1915, total lending as a percentage of GDP peaked at between 18% and 28.9%, but, save for a minor blip in

---

[9]   Flávio A. M. Saes and Tamás Szmrecsányi, "El papel de los bancos extranjeros en la industrialización inicial de São Paulo," in Carlos Marichal (ed.), *Las inversiones extranjeras en América Latina, 1850–1930: Nuevos debates y problemas en historia económica comparada*, México: Fondo de Cultura Económica, 1995, pp. 230–243, esp. pp. 240–241. Stanley Stein's study of Brazil's textile manufacturing industry has many more examples of banks providing initial capital to finance the purchase of plant and equipment. See Stanley Stein, *The Brazilian Cotton Manufacture: Textile Enterprise in an Underdeveloped Area, 1850–1950*, Cambridge, Mass.: Harvard University Press, 1957, Chapter 3.

Table 3.1. *Total loans, equity, and bonds outstanding per year, 1906–1930*
(as a % of GDP)

	Total loans1	Total loans2	Total loans3	Paid-up equity	Bond issues	Stocks + bonds	Differences		
	A	B	C	D	E	F = D + E	F – A	F – B	F – C
1906	6.0	6.9	9.6	20.5	9.7	30.1	24.1	23.2	20.6
1907	7.7	8.8	12.2	18.1	9.2	27.3	19.7	18.5	15.1
1908	9.1	10.5	14.5	18.9	10.1	29.0	19.9	18.5	14.5
1909	10.4	12.0	16.6	16.6	11.6	28.2	17.8	16.2	11.6
1910	10.2	11.8	16.3	14.9	14.0	28.9	18.7	17.2	12.6
1911	12.4	14.3	19.8	14.3	16.1	30.4	18.0	16.1	10.6
1912	12.2	14.0	19.4	16.3	14.9	31.2	19.0	17.1	11.7
1913	14.8	17.0	23.5	17.6	11.8	29.4	14.7	12.4	5.9
1914	18.2	20.9	28.9	22.2	14.5	36.7	18.5	15.8	7.8
1915	12.7	14.6	20.2	20.2	13.7	33.9	21.3	19.3	13.7
1916	10.3	14.8	16.4	17.1	11.5	28.6	18.3	13.8	12.2
1917	7.6	8.8	12.2	14.7	9.9	24.6	17.0	15.8	12.4
1918	12.6	14.5	20.1	14.3	9.3	23.5	10.9	9.0	3.5
1919	8.3	9.6	13.3	12.4	7.2	19.6	11.3	10.0	6.3
1920	6.3	7.3	10.1	9.2	4.9	14.1	7.8	6.9	4.1
1921	9.1	10.5	14.6	12.6	7.5	20.1	11.0	9.6	5.5
1922	7.9	9.1	12.6	11.8	6.4	18.3	10.4	9.2	5.7
1923	5.5	6.3	8.7	9.1	3.1	12.2	6.8	5.9	3.5
1924	3.5	4.1	5.6	7.1	2.6	9.6	6.1	5.5	4.0
1925	2.8	3.2	4.4	6.6	1.9	8.5	5.8	5.3	4.1
1926	3.0	3.4	4.8	8.1	2.2	10.3	7.3	6.8	5.5
1927	2.8	3.3	4.5	8.3	2.4	10.6	7.8	7.4	6.1
1928	2.8	3.2	4.4	6.7	2.0	8.7	5.9	5.5	4.2
1929	3.5	4.1	5.6	7.1	2.1	9.2	5.7	5.1	3.6
1930	4.4	5.0	7.0	8.4	2.6	11.0	6.6	6.0	4.1
Avg.	8.2	9.5	13.0	13.3	8.0	21.4	13.2	11.8	8.4

Sources: See text for differences across total loan estimates. I used the *Retrospecto Comercial do Jornal do Comércio 1916* figures of total bank credit for Brazil as the basis for my estimates (according to this source total loans1 were 794,002 contos of mil reis, while total loans2 and total loans3 were 1,145,489 and 1,266,021 contos respectively). I then computed the amounts for other years using the growth rates of bank credit from Table A.2 in Triner, *Banking and Economic Development: Brazil, 1889–1930.* According to Triner, these growth rates were estimated with a sample that represents 90–95 of total bank credit in Brazil (using the *Retrospecto Comercial* aggregates). All stock and bond figures are at face value and are from the Rio de Janeiro Stock Exchange annual summaries published in the *Jornal do Commércio.* GDP figures are from Goldsmith, *Brasil 1850–1984: Desenvolvimento Financeiro sob um Século de Inflação,* Tables 3.1, 4.2, 6.2.

1918, declined rapidly thereafter. Finally, total credit to GDP stabilized at around 5% of GDP in the 1920s.

Total bank loans between 1906 and 1930 were never as high as a percentage of GDP as corporations' stock and bond issues during that period (see Table 3.1). The outstanding amount of stocks and bonds represented, on average, approximately 20% of GDP, whereas bank loans fluctuated at around 8%. This is certainly not to say that bank credit was irrelevant. Banks mobilized considerable resources in order to be able to lend to the agriculture export sector (mostly coffee and rubber) and provide working capital for industries. But the bulk of the funds that fueled the takeoff of industrialization in Brazil flowed from the country's stock markets.

The gap between bank credit and securities issues closed rapidly during the first two decades of the twentieth century. The flow of new loans into the Brazilian economy accelerated after 1907, and by the 1920s, when stock and bond markets went into in decline, the amount of stocks and bonds outstanding was about 8–10%, and total bank credit about 4–6%, of GDP.

Notwithstanding that the figures show the stock of total bank loans to have been smaller than the stock of total securities issues of Brazilian corporations, we can see in Figure 3.1 that for the period 1906–1930 net flows of bank credit per year are quite similar to the net amounts mobilized in the stock and bond markets. Before 1915, banks and securities issuers added approximately 2% per year in new loans or securities issues (net figures).

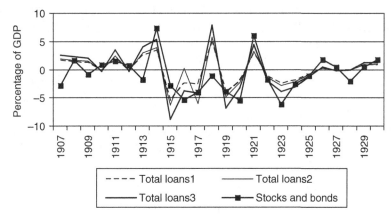

Figure 3.1. Net flows of bank credit and net changes in private securities outstanding, 1906–1930

Source: Table 3.5. The flow figures are estimated by subtracting the stock figures in year t from those in year $t-1$.

Table 3.2. *Total loans to GDP in selected countries, 1895–1929*

	1895 (%)	1900 (%)	1913 (%)	1929 (%)
Belgium	66		75	64
Brazil			**24**	**6**
Denmark		184	220	183
France			112	71
Germany	124		159	73
Great Britain	54		52	52
India	2		3	5
Italy	51		43	5
Japan		28	56	94
South Africa			36	43
Switzerland		50	70	66
United States		61	60	86

Source: Estimated from data in Goldsmith, *Comparative National Balance Sheets*, pp. 199, 209, 216, 225, 232, 241, 249, 256, 280, 290, and 300. Total loans includes mortgage loans.

These flows declined during World War I, then jumped up and down in one- or two-year periods before stabilizing, after 1925, at a level close to zero percent of GDP per year.

Even if the amounts of resources banks and stock markets added per year before 1915 were quite similar, the total stock of loans to GDP was comparatively small. Table 3.2 compares the Brazilian figures with the level of total loans (including mortgages) to GDP in seven European countries as well as India, Japan, South Africa, and the United States. Circa 1913, Brazil's estimates of total credit seem large only relative to India's, but the gap between the two nations almost disappears in the 1920s. Figures for Brazil and South Africa are also close in 1913, but then diverge widely. In general, Brazil's total credit to GDP seems to have been small relative to the figures recorded for more industrialized countries and even some of the world's largest colonies.

Finance and Development

Economists and economic historians have been able to demonstrate some significant causal links between financial development and economic growth across countries. For instance, Robert G. King and Ross Levine show that the level of financial intermediation is a good predictor of long-run economic growth, and Ross Levine and Sarah Zervos show stock market liquidity and banking development to predict growth positively. There is also evidence that firms that rely more strongly on external sources of finance to expand operations have grown disproportionately faster in countries that have more developed financial markets. More recently, Peter L. Rousseau and Richard Sylla showed that development of a sophisticated financial system in the wake of independence caused some of the rapid growth in the United States during the first part of the nineteenth century.[10]

How can we know that having relatively developed stock and bond markets and a banking system that provided short-term capital were important factors in Brazil's industrialization? What evidence do we have that the level of financial development, in particular of stock and bond market development, mattered for Brazil's economic performance? Detailed evidence from the textile industry suggests that companies that could issue bonds and stocks had faster (total factor) productivity growth than unlisted competitors, mainly because they were able to adopt the latest technology. Then there is statistical evidence, using Granger causality tests, suggesting the precedence of financial development over GDP growth.

Stephen Haber's study of Brazil's textile industry yields robust econometric evidence that mills listed on the country's stock exchanges had higher total factor productivity growth than their unlisted competitors (both partnerships and corporations). Haber argues that accessing capital through stocks and bonds afforded firms greater flexibility in choosing the capital-labor ratio, which enabled them to develop into larger, more productive companies. When he compares Brazilian textile mills to their capital-constrained counterparts in Mexico, the results are even more striking. Not only were Brazilian firms more productive, but fewer restrictions

[10] See, Robert G. King and Ross Levine, "Finance and Growth: Schumpeter Might Be Right," *Quarterly Journal of Economics* 108, 3 (1993): 717–737; Ross Levine and Sara Zervos, "Stock Markets, Banks, and Economic Growth," *American Economic Review* 88 (June 1998): 537–558; Raghuram G. Rajan and Luigi Zingales, "Financial Dependence and Growth," *American Economic Review* 88 (June 1998): 559–586; and Peter L. Rousseau and Richard Sylla, "Emerging Financial Markets and Early U.S. Growth," *Explorations in Economic History* 42, 1 (2005): 1–26. A good survey of the works that link finance to growth can be found in Peter L. Rousseau and Richard Sylla, "Financial Revolutions and Economic Growth: Introducing this EEH Symposium," *Explorations in Economic History* 43, 1 (2006): 1–12.

gave rise to a less concentrated textile sector by facilitating the entry of new companies.[11]

Further evidence of the importance of financial development to Brazil's industrialization is the rapid growth of the Brazilian economy in the wake of the revolution in financial markets that occurred in the late 1880s and early 1890s. The most conservative estimates show no growth for GDP per capita and low rates of growth for GDP throughout the nineteenth century (e.g., 2.6% per year).[12] Yet, between 1890 and 1945, the compound annual growth rate of GDP nearly doubled to 4%. The greatest acceleration occurred after 1900, as reflected in the 5% compound annual growth rate of GDP recorded from 1900 to 1945.[13]

In fact, simple Granger causality tests show causality between financial development and GDP growth (but not the other way around). The test results suggest not that growth occurred only because of financial development, but rather that there is sufficient statistical evidence that financial development took precedence over growth for one or two years (the test uses a two-year lag).

The Granger causality tests I present are based on simple regressions of the following form:

$$y_t = \alpha + \alpha_1 y_{t-1} + \alpha_2 y_{t-2} + \beta_1 x_{t-1} + \beta_2 x_{t-2} + e_t$$

which means that we are trying to explain the current levels of a variable (y_t) using its past values $(t-1, t-2)$, the past values of another variable (x_t), and a residual e_t. I then test whether adding past values of x_t help to explain more of the variation in y_t in a significant way (using a simple F-test). The null hypothesis of the F-test is that $\beta_1 = \beta_2 = 0$, that is, that x_t does not explain much of the variation in y_t (lags of x do not Granger-cause y_t). When past values of x_t explain a significant part of the variation of y_t, we would find a large F-statistic (significant at the 5% level) and would reject the null hypothesis of no causation. Then we can repeat the exercise using x_t as the dependent variable and the former dependent variables (y_t) as explanatory variables. To sustain causality from either x_t to y_t or vice versa, we need the test to prove causality only in one direction.

---

[11] Haber, "The Efficiency Consequences of Institutional Change," pp. 298–311. The comparisons with Mexico were published in Stephen Haber, "Industrial Concentration and the Capital Markets: A Comparative Study of Brazil, Mexico and the United States, 1830–1930," *Journal of Economic History* 51 (September 1991): 559–580.

[12] Leff, *Underdevelopment and Development in Brazil*, pp. 32–33.

[13] Goldsmith, *Brasil 1850–1984*, Tables 2.1, 3.1, and 4.2.

Table 3.3. *Granger causality tests of financial development and real GDP levels,*
1906–1930 and 1896–1930

Null hypothesis	Obs	F-statistic	Probability
1906–1930 sample			
REALGDP does not Granger cause LOANS2	23	5.849	0.011
LOANS2 does not Granger cause REALGDP		0.498	0.616
REALGDP does not Granger cause LOANS3	23	4.780	0.022
LOANS3 does not Granger cause REALGDP		0.694	0.513
TOTCREDIT does not Granger cause REALGDP	23	1.179	0.330
REALGDP does not Granger cause TOTCREDIT		5.689	0.012
TOTSECURITIES does not Granger cause REALGDP	23	0.395	0.680
REALGDP does not Granger cause TOTSECURITIES		8.246	0.003
1896–1930 sample			
TOTSEC does not Granger cause REALGDP	33	3.382	0.048
REALGDP does not Granger cause TOTSEC		2.880	0.073

Source: Test performed using data from Table 3.8.

Table 3.3 shows the results of the Granger causality test of financial development and real GDP levels using two samples, one from 1906 to 1930, the other from 1896 to 1930. Given the limited sample, it should be taken as a low-power test that suggests precedence rather than causality. To test the robustness of its results to the measures used, the test uses two measures of bank credit (total loans1 and total loans2), a measure of total private credit (total loans3 plus bond issues), and a measure of stock market development (stock issues plus bond issues). In all tests using the sample from 1906 to 1930, we reject the hypothesis of no causation from financial development variables (we find that financial development Granger-causes real GDP) and accept the null hypothesis of no causation from real GDP to financial development.

That this one-way causation works is evidence that the changes in financial development between 1906 and 1930 preceded and caused some of the movements in GDP. Using the sample from 1896 to 1930, we can test whether stock and bond issues Granger-caused real GDP. Here the results (presented in the bottom rows of Table 3.3) are weaker, but we still find causation from financial development to real GDP (at the 0.05 significance level). Inverse causation from real GDP to financial development is weakly rejected because the F-statistic is significant at a probability of 0.073 (quite close to the 0.05 threshold to accept causality).

THE STOCK MARKET AND THE EARLY INDUSTRIALIZATION OF BRAZIL

Having determined that its stock markets very likely played an important role in accelerating Brazil's economic growth, this section examines how the process played out within the stock markets and the sectors that were spun out of the development of equity markets. It first looks at the relationship between the evolution of the Rio de Janeiro Stock Exchange and the modernization of the Brazilian economy, and then examines the parallels in the evolution of the São Paulo Stock Exchange.

The Size and Importance of the Rio de Janeiro Stock Exchange

Table 3.4 clearly shows that the takeoff of the equity and bond markets in the late 1880s and early 1890s helped to attract a massive amount of foreign and domestic savings. When we look at the value of all the public and private securities traded on the Rio de Janeiro Stock Exchange from 1895 to 1931, we find two things.

First, since the nineteenth century public debt represented the largest part of total capitalization (public and private).[14] The federal government and state and municipal governments placed large issues of debt that were actively negotiated on the Rio de Janeiro Stock Exchange (as well as in other markets). Public debt took over the stock exchange in the late 1920s, when most of the federal, state, and municipal debts were sold in domestic markets.

Second, between the 1890s and the first two decades of the twentieth century, corporations captured a large share of the total savings invested in Brazilian securities. In 1895, the face value of all paid-up capital registered in the Rio de Janeiro Stock Exchange, a measure of the accumulated amounts received from investors, represented 38% of GDP. In the following

---

[14] As mentioned in Chapter, William R. Summerhill III argues that it is striking how long it took for the market of private securities to take off given how big and successful was the market for sovereign bonds since the early part of the nineteenth century. See William R. Summerhill III, "Sovereign Credibility with Financial Underdevelopment: The Case of Nineteenth-Century Brazil," unpublished manuscript, University of California, Los Angeles, May 2007.

Table 3.4. *Capitalization of the Rio de Janeiro Stock Exchange by type of security (at face value, in thousand contos of mil reis of 1900)*

	1895	1905	1913	1920	1925	1931
Public debt	590	1,724	3,745	2,249	1,008	10,005
Banks	439	289	293	142	100	161
Other corporations	898	601	688	938	746	568
Partnerships			24	18	9	8
Debenture issues	392	300	1,003	957	1,142	562
Mortgage bonds	62	15	17	11	0	17
Total capitalization	2,381	2,930	5,769	4,314	3,004	11,321
As a % of GDP	*51%*	*52%*	*71%*	*38%*	*21%*	*107%*
All private issues	1,791	1,206	2,024	2,065	1,996	1,316
As a % of GDP	*38%*	*21%*	*25%*	*18%*	*14%*	*12%*

Sources: Estimated by the author from the annual reports in Camara Sindical de Corretores de Fundos Públicos da Bolsa de Valores do Rio de Janeiro, *Relatorio da Câmara Sindical de Corretores de Fundos Públicos da Bolsa de Valores do Rio de Janeiro.* The GDP deflator is from Goldsmith, *Brasil 1850–1984,* Tables 3.1, 4.2, 6.2.

Note: This table includes only the securities approved by the Rio de Janeiro Stock Brokers Association. Government bonds include federal, state, and municipal debt traded on this stock exchange. Actual capitalization of the companies traded in Rio de Janeiro differs from that reported in this table because there were more companies and securities traded than were on the official list and because the figures in the table are estimated using face value rather than market prices (paid-up capital being what companies actually receive) to facilitate comparisons with public debt and bond issues.

two decades, private issues were in excess of 20% of GDP. These figures would be even higher were we to take into account the private capitalization of the São Paulo Stock Exchange, which added another 6% or so of GDP in 1913 and about 4% in 1930.

Although the exchange accommodated the trading of partnership shares (shares of Sociedades em Comandita Simples) and mortgage bonds as well as corporate stocks and bonds, the former securities did not represent a large share of capitalization and were not actively traded on the stock market. Most partnerships only registered at the stock exchange in order to be able to issue bonds.[15]

---

[15] Partnerships with shares were allowed to trade those shares on Brazil's stock exchanges. There were as many as 13 limited partnerships (*sociedades em comandita*) registered in the Rio de Janeiro Stock Exchange after 1890. Many of these owned or controlled corporations that were also listed. For instance, the partnership Crissuma Filho & Comp. controlled

The transformation of Brazil from a primarily agricultural country into one with a larger share of manufacturing and services was abetted by the stock markets in an important way. The evolution of the number of companies traded on the Rio de Janeiro Stock Exchange tells the story (see Table 3.5). During the initial period of transformation, railways and domestic shipping lines helped to integrate Brazil's internal markets. These transportation improvements also benefited the export complex, which was financed by the joint stock banks that sold their shares on the country's stock exchanges. More financing and better infrastructure pushed the coffee export economy to record output levels in the 1890s. The integration of internal markets, tariff protection afforded after 1900, success of the coffee export economy, and large inflows of immigrants from Europe over the last two decades of the nineteenth century provided ideal conditions for the development of textile mills, food processing companies, breweries, glass factories, urban development companies, tramways, and utilities companies.

The expansion of textile companies and other manufacturing firms, utilities companies, and urban development companies occured after the initial rapid expansion of railways. The length of railways open to traffic went from nine miles in 1854 to 628 miles in 1872. After 1872, railway mileage tripled every decade, reaching 2,115.6 miles in 1880 and nearly 6,000 miles in 1890 before the rate of construction per year slowed down (still, another

the clinic Casa de Saude Crissiuma Filho; Alencar Lima & Comp. controlled the construction company Construtora Brasileira; Rodriges & Comp. and Marques, Marinho & Co. controlled the newspapers *Jornal do Commércio* and *A Noite*, respectively; Gonçalves Ramos & Co. was listed as controlling the mining company Minas de Manganez; Oetterer Soeers & Co. controlled the textile mill Tecidos Santa Rosalia; and D. Da Silva & Comp. controlled The Red Star Company (shipping?). Other partnerships registered at the exchange to secure the right to trade debentures or for other purposes not clearly disclosed in the stock exchange documents. For example, the Sociedade em Commandita Paulo Zsigsmond & Comp. and the Sociedade em Commandita Trajano de Medeiros & Comp. issued bonds, and Francisco Graell & Comp. and Sampaio Correa & Comp. were apparently listed just to have their shares traded. Of the 13 partnerships listed, only three ever had their shares traded: Marques, Marinho & Co., Paulo Zsigsmond & Comp., and Trajano de Medeiros & Comp. All of this information is from Câmara Sindical de Corretores de Fundos Públicos da Bolsa de Valores do Rio de Janeiro, *Relatorio da Câmara Sindical de Corretores de Fundos Públicos da Bolsa de Valores do Rio de Janeiro*, Rio de Janeiro: Imprensa Nacional, 1894–1947. For a good discussion of the differences between partnerships with shares and other organizational forms in French civil law countries and a comparison to the organizational forms of the United States and England see Naomi Lamoreaux and Jean-Laurent Rosenthal, "Legal Regime and Contractual Flexibility: A Comparison of Business's Organizational Choices in France and the United States during the Era of Industrialization," *American Law and Economics Review* 7 (Spring 2005): 28–61.

Table 3.5. *Number of companies traded on the Rio de Janeiro Stock Exchange, 1896–1930*

	1896	1900	1905	1913	1920	1925	1930
Total number of traded companies	**343**	**208**	**199**	**335**	**453**	**444**	**465**
Agricultural	39	22	22	18	25	26	27
Banks	60	38	28	26	28	28	29
Insurance	23	21	18	22	22	26	24
Manufacturing	36	22	22	40	56	58	68
Ports	2	2	2	5	5	6	6
Railways	36	29	22	30	31	27	28
Shipping	16	10	9	8	12	13	13
Telegraph & telephone	1			1	2	2	2
Textiles	35	29	30	50	48	50	51
Utilities	9	7	11	27	35	36	39
Other	86	28	35	108	189	172	178

Source: *Jornal do Commércio and Retrospecto Commercial do Jornal do Commércio, Rio de Janeiro, 1895–1931.*

8,000 miles were built over the following 20 years).[16] In 1896, railways, agricultural companies, banks, and shipping companies accounted for almost half of the total number of companies traded. This changed rapidly after the 1890s, as industrial companies (in manufacturing and textiles) and utilities and other services companies came to account for more than half of the total. In 1913, of the 335 companies traded, 50 were textile mills and at least 40 clearly identified as manufacturing businesses, 27 were utilities companies, and 108 fell into diverse categories such as construction, urban development, and other services.

Its stock market also helped to accelerate Brazil's urbanization. Even though the majority of Brazilians continued to live in rural areas until 1970, the urbanization rate accelerated during the first republican period (1889–1930). An imperfect sign of this transformation is that from 1872 to 1920 the population of Brazil grew at a compound annual growth rate of 2.3%, while the city of Rio de Janeiro grew at 3%. Just from 1872 to 1900 the population of the country grew at approximatly of 2% per year, while

---

[16] *Brazilian Year Book 1909*, London: McCorquodale & Co., 1910, p. 612.

the population of the cities of Rio de Janeiro and São Paulo grew at 3.6% and 8%, respectively.[17] The stock markets aided the urbanization process by funding companies that specialized in real estate, municipal works, and construction (all under the "other" category in the tables) as well as tramways and utilities (these last two included under "utilities" in all tables). The Rio de Janeiro Stock Exchange listed many such companies operating not only in Rio de Janeiro and São Paulo, but also in other relatively rich cities in Brazil. Construction and improvement companies, for example, operated in the municipalities of Riberão Preto in São Paulo, São Luiz de Maranhão in the northern state of Maranhão, and Recife in the northeastern state of Pernambuco, and port and construction companies operated in the northeastern state of Bahia.

The transformation of the economy is clearly in evidence in the evolution of electric power generators installed between 1890 and 1920. Before 1890, Brazil hosted two generators with a total capacity of 10,400 horsepower (h.p.). Even with the installation of six more generators between 1891 and 1900, total capacity declined to 7,091 h.p. as one of the old generators was taken out of service. Then, between 1901 and 1910, 69 new power generators were installed, boosting capacity to 186,460 h.p. Companies in the states of Rio de Janeiro and São Paulo alone installed 74% of the new capacity (78,150 h.p. and 59, 745 h.p., respectively).[18] Most of the new capacity was installed by companies issuing stocks and bonds in either Brazil or Canada. The two largest power plants in Brazil, São Paulo Tramway, Light and Power Co. (21,500 h.p.) and Rio de Janeiro Tramway, Light and Power Co. (60,000 h.p.), were controlled by a group of Canadian and American investors led by Percival Farquhar (American) and F. S. Pearson (Canadian). But Brazilian corporations that traded stocks and bonds domestically also

---

[17] At the same time, the populations of the richest states in Brazil more than doubled. For example, between 1890 and 1920, the populations of São Paulo increased from 1.38 to 4.6 million, Rio de Janeiro from 926,000 to 1.6 million, the Federal District (Rio de Janeiro City) from 522,000 to 1.16 million, and Minas Gerais from 3.1 million to 5.88 million. For population figures, see Brazil, *Anuário Estatístico do Brasil*, Rio de Janeiro: Instituto Brasileiro de Geografia e Estatística, Ano 5, 1939/1940, p. 1302. For data on labor force participation by sector, see Goldsmith, *Brasil 1850–1984*, Table 1.4.

[18] The special report on utilities of the 1920 census is the source of all data on the installed capacity of power generators. See Brazil, Ministério de Agricultura, Indústria e Comércio, *Recenseamento do Brasil Realizado em 1 de Setembro de 1920*, Rio de Janeiro: Typografia da Estatística, 1929, vol. 5, pp. xv–xviii. Studies that have examined the centrality of company directors in the networks of corporate interlocks find both Farquhar and Pearson to have been the most central directors in Brazil. See Aldo Musacchio and Ian Read, "Bankers, Industrialists and their Cliques: Elite Networks in Mexico and Brazil, 1909," *Enterprise and Society* 8, 4 (December 2007): 842–880.

Table 3.6. *Stock market capitalization by industry, Rio de Janeiro Stock Exchange, 1896–1930 (thousand contos of 1900)*

	1896	1900	1905	1913	1920	1925	1930
Agricultural	34	15	17	13	13	11	15
Banks	273	127	120	199	201	265	303
Insurance	7	5	12	14	17	38	33
Manufacturing	25	45	59	74	60	43	82
Ports	15	101	135	50	125	82	110
Railways	83	106	104	221	111	127	221
Shipping	13	8	23	32	33	21	24
Telephones	0.15			0.15	0.21	0.13	0.13
Textiles	43	40	90	141	138	115	85
Utilities	29	19	58	69	43	28	39
Other	52	17	32	97	90	114	134
Total market cap	575	482	651	909	833	843	1,046
Deflator	0.98	1.00	0.73	0.82	1.32	2.09	2.13

Sources: Estimated by the author using the Rio de Janeiro Stock Exchange annual summaries published in *Jornal do Commércio*, Rio de Janeiro, 1897–1931. The GDP deflator is from Goldsmith, *Brasil 1850–1984*, Tables 3.1, 4.2, 6.2.

installed a good share of the total capacity. By 1920, companies listed on the Rio de Janeiro and São Paulo stock exchanges had installed some of the largest power generators in the country (e.g., the Port of Santos [Docas de Santos], 20,000 h.p.; the Companhia Brasileira de Energia Elétrica, 20,000 h.p. and 18,000 h.p.; the Cia. Brasileira Carbureto de Calcio, 7,800 h.p.; and the Empresa de Força e Luz de Jaú, 6,000 h.p).[19]

An examination of the composition of the stock market capitalization of the Rio de Janeiro Stock Exchange in Table 3.6 reveals a similar pattern for the sequencing of Brazil's economic transformation. Capitalization was initially dominated by bank and railway issues, but manufacturing, utilities, and other industries gained importance after 1900.[20] The estimates of stock

[19] See Brazil, Ministério de Agricultura, Indústria e Comércio, *Recenseamento do Brasil Realizado em 1 de Setembro de 1920*, vol. 5, pp. xvii–xviii.

[20] Banks and railways dominate total capitalization in real terms throughout the Republican period and end up increasing their size by 1930 because Banco do Brasil, the main quasi-government bank, doubles its capitalization between 1921 and 1925 and the Rio de Janeiro Stock Broker's Association decides to cross-list the shares of Brazil's largest railway

market capitalization presented in Table 3.6 value each company's capital at market prices (and assume a price of 50% of face value for all non-traded shares), deflating all values using the GDP deflator (1900=100).[21] Brazil's turn of the century transformation is also reflected in the capitalization of manufacturing, textile, and utilities companies throughout the period. The capitalization of manufacturing firms (including textiles) tripled in real terms from 1896 to 1913, while that of utilities doubled between 1896 and 1905.

In fact, the capital of industrial securities traded on the Rio de Janeiro Stock Exchange alone represented a large share of the country's total capital. There were, for example, according to the 1907 industrial survey, 3,258 industrial establishments with total capital of 666,000 mil reis, but the combined capital of the 52 industrial companies (approximately 1% of Brazil's total) registered at the stock exchange represented between 15% and 30% of the country's total industrial capital. Comparable figures from the 1912 survey show the industrial firms registered at the Rio de Janeiro stock exchange to have represented between 30% and 57% of the country's total industrial capital. Clearly, the largest industrial firms in the country were registered at this stock exchange.[22]

Perhaps more important than the stock of total capital is the degree to which companies in different industries used stock issues to obtain capital on a regular basis. In Table 3.7, which shows the value of new share issues by industry between 1896 and 1930, we can see that banks were heavy users of stock markets, selling between 10% and 20% of total new issues. Railways followed the same pattern, with equity issues of around 20% for most periods. Manufacturing and textiles together account for a stable 20% to 30% of total issues. Companies in the service sector (in the "other" category) appear to have been the third largest sellers of stock between 1910 and 1920. These figures would be higher and more biased toward banks and railways if the table started in 1890, but studying stock issues after 1896 enables us to avoid adding the many companies created in the early 1890s that ended up disappearing after a couple of years.

---

company, the Companhia Paulista, in São Paulo (where it had traded shares since 1890) and Rio de Janeiro.

[21] For the methodology, see Appendix 2A.

[22] Brazil, *Annuario Estatístico do Brasil (1908–1912)*, 1917. This evidence coincides with some of the results of Haber's study of the textile industry. He finds that firms financed through the stock exchange were significantly larger than partnerships and sole proprietorships operating in the textile sector.

Table 3.7. *New equity issues by industry in the Rio de Janeiro Stock Exchange, 1896–1930*

	1896–1900	1900–1905	1905–1910	1910–1915	1915–1920	1920–1925	1925–1930
Total new equity issues (thousand contos of 1900)							
Total	250.1	359.2	240.0	846.1	255.2	401.4	335.5
Percentage per industry							
Agricultural	5.3	4.7	4.4	2.0	3.6	1.6	3.8
Banks	22.8	16.1	3.8	19.3	21.6	44.3	9.5
Insurance	4.0	3.3	0.6	1.5	1.8	2.8	1.5
Manufacturing	5.7	29.0	7.5	14.7	10.5	8.3	13.7
Ports	19.7	5.9	7.1	7.1	0.0	7.0	12.6
Railways	23.5	13.8	21.0	20.9	9.9	3.3	25.1
Shipping	2.6	4.8	2.9	6.2	6.1	5.0	4.8
Textiles	5.1	3.9	21.6	7.6	12.5	5.4	3.4
Utilities	0.8	2.3	19.5	3.6	4.8	1.4	17.0
Other	10.7	16.2	11.7	17.1	29.2	20.8	8.6

Sources: Estimated by the author using the Rio de Janeiro Stock Exchange annual summaries published in *Jornal do Commércio*, 1897–1931. The GDP deflator is from Goldsmith, *Brasil 1850–1984*, Tables 3.1, 4.2, 6.2.

Once companies traded on the Rio de Janeiro Stock Exchange obtained the capital from their initial public offerings, turnover rates for existing shares were quite low. As I discussed in Chapter 2, the volume of trading was relatively low when normalized by either GDP or stock market capitalization. Table 3.5 shows that, on average, 5% (with a standard deviation of 2%) of the total capital of the companies that were actively traded on this market was traded per year. For most industries, we find turnover rates lower than 10% of paid-up capital per year. Given that all stock of Brazilian companies had voting rights (there were no nonvoting shares until 1932), this result means that 10% of the total votes could change hands in one year. This figure is quite impressive if we consider that today voting shares are practically never traded in stock markets, while the trading of nonvoting shares represents "practically the entire trading volume."[23]

---

[23] See Tatiana Nenova, "Control Values and Changes in Corporate Law in Brazil," paper presented at the European Financial Management Association Meetings, London, 2002, p. 2.

Table 3.8. *Average turnover rates per year for traded companies, Rio de Janeiro Stock Exchange, 1896–1930*

	Turnover rates as a % of paid-up capital			
	Mean	Max	Min	Standard deviation
All companies	5.08	13.34	2.06	2.62
Agricultural	6.28	28.82	0.02	7.88
Automobiles	2.47	2.63	2.31	0.22
Banks	6.46	12.61	1.78	2.91
Insurance	2.82	6.14	0.94	1.43
Manufacturing	3.59	32.13	0.10	5.88
Ports	6.92	34.54	0.03	8.95
Railways	2.32	15.71	0.02	3.45
Shipping	5.10	57.85	0.01	13.59
Textiles	3.56	9.13	0.48	2.04
Utilities	3.40	19.88	0.10	4.87
Other	9.60	50.83	0.96	11.26

Sources: Estimated by the author by combining two datasets, one on average stock prices and total trading per company compiled from Câmara Sindical de Corretores de Fundos Públicos da Bolsa de Valores do Rio de Janeiro, *Relatorio da Câmara Sindical de Corretores de Fundos Públicos da Bolsa de Valores do Rio de Janeiro*, 1890–1930, and the database of total paid-up capital by company from *Jornal do Commércio*, 1896–1930.

Note: Turnover rates are for companies that actually had their shares traded (all companies with turnover rates of zero were excluded).

From the third column of Table 3.8, which shows maximum turnover in one year, we can see that in some sectors, in some years, large portions of total equity changed hands. This reflects either years in which companies made initial public offerings of new shares, or years in which there were changes in the control of a company. I identified at least 10 cases in which more than 40% of a company's capital was sold on the exchange in a given year, very likely accompanied by transfers of control to new groups of investors. This is a sign that the market, even if shallow in terms of turnover rates, had spurts of activity that involved mergers and/or acquisitions.

The São Paulo Stock Exchange

The general patterns of the Rio de Janeiro Stock Exchange are consistent with the findings of Anne Hanley's study of the São Paulo Stock Exchange. She finds that manufacturing firms, particularly textile and machinery companies, become increasingly important during the "particularly dynamic period of expansion between 1909 and 1913." According to her estimates for the period 1886–1917, "between 65% and 70% of the public utilities companies, textile firms, and other industrial and commercial firms [were] founded during this booming five-year period [1909–1913]." In fact, her findings paint a more striking picture of the economic transformation of the economy inasmuch as in São Paulo railways, banks, and insurance companies constitute a minority of the companies listed on the stock exchange, even if São Paulo had the most densely developed railway network. Finally, Hanley also found that the São Paulo Stock Exchange's "vigor disappeared after 1913."[24]

Unfortunately, the stock exchanges of São Paulo and Rio de Janeiro cannot be compared for the entire period because data for the former are incomplete, making it difficult to construct a series of stock market capitalization, number of firms traded, and turnover rates. Moreover, the São Paulo Stock Exchange was organized in August of 1890, much later than the Rio de Janeiro Stock Exchange. Because most trading took place in private brokering houses, good data for the first years of operation are lacking. In fact, the São Paulo Stock Exchange was closed in 1891. "Its demise appears to have been due to the drop in the volume of trading from the euphoric levels of the previous year" to almost no trading at all. The São Paulo Stock Exchange was not opened again until 1895.[25] Because of these complications there are no detailed reports of the sort that were published by the Rio de Janeiro Stock Exchange until 1905. Table 3.9 reproduces some of the data for the São Paulo Stock Exchange that is comparable to that presented in the tables for the Rio de Janeiro Stock Exchange.[26]

São Paulo experienced an initial boom in stock market activity in the early 1890s, but peaked in 1913. The number of companies traded exceeded 100 in 1890, but rapidly declined thereafter, to 57 in 1898, 34 in 1900, and 20 in 1902.[27] Table 3.9 shows the rapid expansion of the number

[24] Hanley, *Native Capital*, pp. 99, 100, 111.
[25] Hanley, *Native Capital*, p. 89.
[26] Hanley, *Native Capital*, pp. 87–90.
[27] From Hanley, *Native Capital*, Table 4.2.

Table 3.9. *Number of companies traded on the São Paulo Stock Exchange,*
1902–1917

	1902	1905	1907	1909	1911	1913	1917
Number of companies by industry							
Agricultural			4	4	11	17	16
Banks	9	8	18	14	15	18	17
Insurance			1	1	1	3	2
Manufacturing	2	6	9	14	27	34	31
Ports			1	1	1	1	1
Railways	5	5	8	10	10	11	8
Shipping					1		1
Telephones	1	1	1	2	2	4	3
Textiles		2	5	10	19	25	21
Utilities		4	9	11	26	34	38
Other	3	3	6	15	25	47	39
Companies listed in São Paulo	**17**	**26**	**56**	**67**	**113**	**147**	**138**
Cross-listed in Rio de Janeiro	1	2	11	9	15	15	18

Source: Estimated by the author from the annual summaries published in *O Estado de São Paulo*, São Paulo, 1903–1918.

of companies traded between 1909 and 1913. The 82 companies traded in 1909 had more than doubled by 1913. According to Hanley, this "renaissance of the São Paulo Bolsa [the stock exchange] was directly related to new macroeconomic vigor produced by government policy after 1906." The period of prosperity for both the Rio de Janeiro and São Paulo stock markets coincides with the government's stabilization of coffee prices and adoption of the gold standard to control the appreciation of the exchange rate and follows the legal reforms enacted in joint stock company laws of 1882 and 1890.

Table 3.9 (bottom row) shows that the number of companies that cross-listed on the stock exchanges of São Paulo and Rio de Janeiro were initially few, but increased over time. That the companies that cross-listed tended to be large corporations or banks, whether chartered domestically (e.g., Docas de Santos [Port of Santos] or the Paulista Railway) or abroad (e.g., three British banks or the Brasilianische Bank für Deustchland), accounts for

Table 3.10. *Stock market capitalization by industry, São Paulo Stock Exchange,*
1902–1917

	1902	1905	1907	1909	1911	1913	1917
Stock market capitalization							
Thousand contos of 1900	371.4	314.8	661.0	668.2	891.7	777.8	854.6
As a % of GDP	6.8%	5.6%	9.9%	10.0%	12.4%	9.6%	8.7%
Equity not cross-listed in Rio as a % of GDP	6.6%	5.5%	6.0%	3.3%	7.6%	4.3%	3.6%
Percentage by sector							
Agricultural			1.1	1.0	1.8	2.6	2.1
Banks	13.3	15.1	27.4	50.2	38.5	28.6	32.8
Insurance			0.2	0.2	0.1	0.4	0.2
Manufacturing	4.3	4.0	3.2	4.0	4.4	6.1	4.4
Ports			19.9	21.7	4.7	8.1	16.5
Railways	81.7	78.0	45.8	18.4	43.6	43.2	35.2
Shipping					0.02		0.1
Telephones	0.2	0.2	0.2	0.4	0.7	1.2	0.7
Textiles		0.8	0.8	1.5	2.1	3.2	2.6
Utilities		1.7	1.2	1.8	1.8	2.7	2.9
Other	0.5	0.2	0.3	0.9	2.3	3.8	2.7

Source: Estimated by the author from the annual summaries published in *O Estado de São Paulo*, São Paulo, 1903–1918. The GDP and GDP deflator are from Goldsmith, *Brasil 1850–1984*, Tables 3.1, 4.2, 6.2.

why approximately 50% of total capitalization was cross-listed in Rio de Janeiro during its peak years (see Table 3.6).[28]

Tables 3.9 and 3.10 show for the São Paulo Stock Exchange the same striking pattern of rapid growth in the importance of listings from relatively new sectors that the Rio de Janeiro Stock Exchange experienced. Between 1907 and 1913, the number of utilities companies tripled, the number of textile mills grew fivefold, and the number of manufacturing establishments (other than textiles) grew fourfold. Other urban improvement companies

[28] Anne Hanley suggests that most companies traded in São Paulo did not cross-list on the Rio de Janeiro Stock Exchange, with the notable exception of Docas de Santos. In number, the cross-listed firms represented a small proportion (about 10%), but when measured by market value, both stock markets (São Paulo and Rio de Janeiro) had an important share of companies cross-listed. See Hanley, *Native Capital*, p. 104.

also almost tripled during this period. In contrast to the Rio de Janeiro Stock Exchange, though, by 1913 "railways were a minority of the firms listed."[29]

Finally, the São Paulo Stock Exchange also shows signs of decline after 1913 (see Table 3.10). There are no available figures for stock market capitalization during the 1920s, but estimates using data for 1932 show that it declined in São Paulo from 12.4% of GDP in 1911 to less than 4% in 1932. Of course, 1932 might not be the best year for comparison, but it gives an idea of the sharpness of the decline in the size of the São Paulo stock market after World War I.[30]

Conclusion

The stock exchange system in Brazil, and the stock market in Rio de Janeiro in particular, was used by all sectors of the economy to obtain resources and expand operations. Its evolution explains, in part, Brazil's accelerated urbanization and industrialization rates, especially at the turn of the twentieth century. After 1900, the stock exchange was more actively used by manufacturing companies, textile mills, and utilities companies to obtain resources through either the listing of new companies or the sale of new share issues by existing companies.

This chapter provides evidence that links financial development to economic growth in Brazil. The figures for stock and bond market issues as well as the stock of bank loans, in fact, Granger-cause real GDP. The results are consistent to all measures of financial development as well as to the size of the sample over time (even if longer samples weaken the results of the test).

This chapter presents evidence that the resources mobilized by financial markets abetted the transformation of Brazil from an agricultural society into an industrializing economy. Urbanization rates and the importance of manufacturing to total GDP increased rapidly after 1900, and much of the capital used to establish the companies that made this transformation possible was raised on the Rio de Janeiro and the São Paulo stock exchanges. Corporations used stock markets mainly to obtain long-term financing, relying on banks to provide short-term financing and finance the export of agricultural products. The stock of total securities issued by Brazilian

---

[29] Hanley, *Native Capital*, p. 100.
[30] *Anuário da Bolsa de Valores do Rio de Janeiro*, 1932. The capitalization estimates for 1932 are at face value, given that this publication listed no quotations for the São Paulo stock market.

companies was nearly 30% of GDP in 1913 if we add stocks and bonds traded in Rio de Janeiro and São Paulo.

How corporations were able to interest savers in Brazil and other countries in buying their stock and bonds is an important question, the answer to which will inform our understanding of the rapid changes in financial development after the 1880s. Whether investors were protected by national laws, courts, or the corporations themselves is discussed in the following two chapters.

## FOUR

The Foundations of Financial Democracy

Disclosure Laws and Shareholder Protections in Corporate Bylaws

Corporations are republics. The ultimate authority rests with voters (shareholders).
Paul Gompers et al., "Corporate Governance and Equity Prices," 2003.[1]

That Brazil had relatively large equity markets before 1915 should make us wonder what institutional system was in place in this country that provided national and foreign investors enough securities to buy equity issued by local companies. One possibility is that Company Laws passed in 1882, 1890, and 1891 provided strong protections for investors. In particular we would want to know if small investors were protected against the power or abuses of managers or insiders (e.g., large shareholders).

Some works in the law and finance literature argues that protection for minority shareholders is afforded by a basic set of principles, or rights, embodied in corporate laws with which companies are obliged to comply. Smaller investors are presumed to be encouraged by these protections to participate in the ownership of corporations, thereby deepening equity markets. Evidence for the 1990s reveals that equity markets tended to be larger and more corporations tended to be traded on the stock exchanges of countries in which small shareholders were accorded greater protection in national company laws.[2] Thus, this chapter first explores whether the set of investor protections La Porta et al. consider relevant for the protection of small shareholders was present during the first boom in stock market development in Brazil.

In other countries there is evidence that these protections were not necessary for the development of equity markets. Julian Franks, Colin Mayer,

[1] Paul Gompers, Joy Ishii, and Andrew Metrick, "Corporate Governance and Equity Prices," *Quarterly Journal of Economics* 118, 1 (February 2003): 107–155, quote from p. 107.
[2] See Rafael La Porta, Florencio Lopes-de-Silanes, Andrei Shleifer, and Robert Vishny, "Legal Determinants of External Finance," *Journal of Finance* 52, 3 (1997): 1131–1150.

and Stefano Rossi found that in Great Britain stock markets evolved rapidly after 1890, even if the national laws also lacked shareholder protections. In their work on Germany, Franks, Mayer, and Hannes Wagner also find that Germany developed a significant equity market after 1930 without having to protect shareholders on its national laws. In the case of Germany, explicit legal protections were not necessary because banks worked as intermediaries between investors and companies, thus providing the protection and trust investors required to overcome the fear of fraud by company directors, founders, or individuals promoting company shares.[3]

Second, the chapter suggests that perhaps the protections for shareholders in national laws are not necessary for the development of equity markets, but companies have to find ways to commit to respect the rights and claims of outside investors. For instance, Eric Hilt, in his research on early American corporations, finds that corporate bylaws frequently provided important protections to small investors in the form of voting provisions that limited the power of large shareholders.[4] The last part of this chapter shows that beyond national laws the bylaws of Brazilian corporations included important protections for small shareholders. Companies induced small investors to buy securities by protecting their rights in shareholder meetings, limiting the power of directors and insiders, and offering voting schemes that promoted the democratization rather than concentration of control. A significant share of Brazilian corporations capped the maximum number of votes per shareholder, while others limited the power of large shareholders through graduated voting scales, giving them fewer votes as their shareholdings increased.

The Brazilian government also provided important protections that encouraged more investors to participate in the ownership of corporate

---

[3] For the case of Great Britain see Julian Franks, Colin Mayer, and Stefano Rossi, "Ownership: Evolution and Regulation," Institute of Finance and Accounting Working Paper FIN 401, London Business School, 2004, pp. 3–4, and Katharina Pistor, Yoram Keinan, Jan Kleinheisterkamp, and Mark West, "Innovation in Corporate Law," *Journal of Comparative Economics* 31, 4 (2003): 676–694. The German case is discussed in Julian Franks, Colin Mayer, and Hannes F. Wagner, "The Origins of the German Corporation: Finance, Ownership and Control," *Review of Finance* 10, 4 (2006): 537–585, see esp. p. 2 for the argument that both the United Kingdom and Germany developed equity markets despite the lack of shareholder rights in their company laws. The idea that banks, acting as intermediaries, facilitated investor trust to buy equity and other securities in Germany is also discussed by Caroline Fohlin, "Does Civil Law Tradition and Universal Banking Crowd out Securities Markets?: Pre–World War I Germany as a Counter-Example," *Enterprise and Society* 8-3 (September 2007): 602–641.

[4] Eric Hilt, "When Did Ownership Separate from Control?: Corporate Governance in the Early Nineteenth Century," *Journal of Economic History* 68, 3 (September 2008): 645–685.

stock. These protections mostly took the form of government-guaranteed dividends. The argument defended in this chapter is that investors trusted guaranteed companies not only because of their safer stream of dividends, but also because the government guarantee came accompanied by stronger monitoring of the corporate accounts and an implicit bailout safeguard.

INVESTOR PROTECTIONS IN BRAZIL'S COMPANY LAWS, 1882–2001

La Porta et al. suggest that the basic set of protections for small investors should include voting rights for all shareholders (one-share, one-vote provisions) and other six protections. Leaving the study of voting rights for the latter part of the chapter, I created an index of shareholder rights following the methodology of La Porta et al. is created by determining how many of the following six shareholder protections were included in specific national company laws:[5] First was whether shareholders absent from shareholder meetings were permitted to vote (proxy voting). Second was whether shares had to be deposited before shareholder meetings (some companies required this to prevent shareholders from selling their equity for several days after the meeting). Third was whether there was cumulative voting or proportional representation whereby minority shareholders elected board members. Fourth was whether minority shareholders had the right to challenge directors and assembly decisions in court, or the option to sell their holdings to the firm and end their participation in the event of disagreement with a managerial or assembly decision. Fifth was whether shareholders had first right to purchase new stock to prevent their share of the company from being diluted in the event that the assembly decided to expand total equity. Sixth was whether the percentage of capital needed to call an extraordinary meeting was less than or equal to 10%, was added.

Table 4.1 displays the rights embodied in Brazil's joint-stock company laws between 1882 and 2001. The index of shareholder rights on paper (the antidirector rights index in the bottom row) indicates that Brazilian shareholders enjoyed little protection against directors' abuses before 1940. Only two relevant shareholder protections were binding on all corporations in Brazil until 1940. From 1882 to 1891, all corporations were required to allow proxy voting and were not permitted to require shareholders to deposit

---

[5] The argument that shareholder protections in national laws matter for equity market development are made in at least two papers: La Porta et al., "Legal Determinants of External Finance," and "Law and Finance."

Table 4.1. *Shareholder rights in Brazil and England, 1882–2001*

	Brazil							England		
	1882	1890	1891	1940	1976	1995[a]	2001	1908	1948	1995
Proxy voting	1	1	1	1	1	0	1	0	1	1
Shares not blocked before meeting	1	1	0	1	1	1	1	1	1	1
Cumulative voting or proportional representation	0	0	0	1	1	0	1	0	0	0
Provision for minorities to challenge directors' decisions[b]	0	0	1	1	1	1	1	0	1	1
Shareholders have first right to buy new stock	0	0	0	1	1	0	1	0	0	1
Capital needed to call an extraordinary meeting is less than or equal to 10%	0	0	0	0	1	1	1	0	1	1
Antidirector rights index[c]	2	2	2	5	6	3	6	1	3	5

Sources: Law 3150, November 4, 1882; Decree 164, January 17, 1890; Decree 434, July 4, 1891; and Decree 603, October 17, 1891, Decree-Law 2627, September 26, 1940, Laws 6404, December 15, 1976, and 10,303, October 31, 2001, available from www2.senado.gov.br (last accessed 05/05/09). Shareholder rights for England from Franks, Mayer, and Rossi, "Ownership: Evolution and Regulation," Table 1, Panel C.

Notes:

[a] 1995 rights follow the classification of La Porta et al., "Law and Finance," Table 4.

[b] Withdrawal rights (right of a shareholder to walk away with a fair share of total equity) were temporarily suspended between 1997 and 1999.

[c] The antidirector rights index adds up the number of shareholder rights included in the existing company laws by period.

their shares before assemblies. The latter right was withdrawn in 1891; subsequently, shareholders in possession of bearer shares were required to deposit them with the company and register their names in order to vote in shareholder meetings. This provision was not properly against shareholders, but rather just a way to maintain a registry of who was to vote in share-holder assemblies.

Shareholder rights on paper were strengthened in 1891 when the new company law introduced the right to challenge in court directors' decisions that contradicted any company statute. After 1882, moreover, shareholders could, individually or as a group (class action), sue and hold directors per-sonally liable for decisions that caused them a loss.[6]

Even with few shareholder protections on paper, Brazil had its first peak in stock market activity between the late 1880s and 1915. In fact, there seems to be a tenuous relation between shareholder protections in national laws and stock market development. For instance, by the time additional protections for minority shareholders were written into law in 1940, stock markets were already in decline.[7] Moreover, following the liter-ature that relates equity market size to shareholder rights on paper, Brazil's equity markets should have prospered between 1940 and the 1990s, when investor protections were strong (in Table 4.1), and jumped significantly in size after 2001 (after laws provided even more protections). But this is clearly not the evolution we observe in the long run. Figure 4.1 shows that the first peak in Brazil's stock market development occurred before 1920. A nearly half-century period of relatively small equity markets ensued, followed by a decline in the 1980s and then rapid expansion since 1994. There is some correlation between the level of stock market development and investor protections on paper, but between 1940 and 1976 there is none at all. Moreover, the period of relatively strong shareholder rights after 1976 (excluding the 1995 survey of La Porta et al., which probably missed some rights) is precisely the period during which Brazil has been portrayed as one of the worst countries in which to be a small investor.[8]

These results mimic the evolution of equity markets in Germany and the United Kingdom (data for the latter are included in Table 4.1). Both countries' financial markets developed rapidly at the end of the nineteenth

---

[6]   See Law 3150, November 4, 1882, esp. Article 11 and Decree 603, October 17, 1891, Article 189, blocking shares before meeting, and Article 209, allowing legal action against directors.

[7]   See Decree-Law 2627, 1940. Articles 17 and 107 permitted shareholders who disagreed with directors or assembly decisions to walk away from the company with the share of net worth that corresponded to the lot of shares held. The 1940 law included the right of minority shareholders to elect members of the board of overseers. Any group of share-holders, ordinary or preferred, that represented at least 20% of capital that disagreed with the election of a member of that board (*conselho fiscal*) could name one member of its preference.

[8]   See Franks et al., "Ownership," pp. 3–4, and "The Origins of the German Corporation," p. 2.

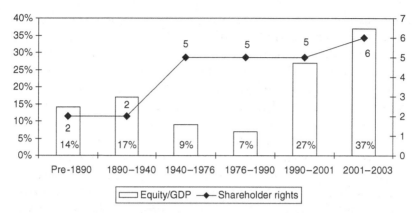

Figure 4.1. Shareholder rights and average stock market capitalization to GDP, 1890–2003

Sources: Table 4.1 and average stock market capitalization to GDP from Figure 2.2.

century despite the lack of shareholder protections in national laws. Until 1948 England had one of the six shareholder protections included in Table 4.1, while Germany has had only the last one from 1861 until today.[9] This is why I look at protections at the company level instead.

The organization of voting rights also has been advanced as an important incentive (or disincentive) to participate in stock markets. The econometric results of La Porta et al. show countries in which national laws mandate one-share, one-vote provisions to have larger financial markets.[10] But few countries' national laws incorporate this provision; in most countries, corporations decide individually how many shares are required for one vote. In fact, a review of company bylaws in Brazil at the end of this chapter reveals significant variation in voting schemes.

WHAT NATIONAL LAWS MATTER FOR THE PROTECTION OF SHAREHOLDERS?

If provisions in national laws are not really what drove investors to participate in financial markets, what protections did? The growth of stock markets from 1882 to 1915 should attest that investors trusted the issuers of securities for some reason, but the episode of fraudulent stock issues between 1889 and 1891 should have deterred further purchases of equity

[9] Franks et al., "Ownership," p. 2.
[10] La Porta et al., "Legal Determinants of External Finance."

in the absence of protections for investors. In an environment with low public monitoring of corporate activities, investors need to have access to accurate financial information of the company, they need to know who is running the company, how powerful the largest shareholders are, and who can manipulate directors or name managers, and they need to have powers to check and counterbalance the influence of large shareholders and managers.

In Brazil, shareholders have had two important protections in national laws since 1882: limited liability and financial disclosure. These were perhaps the two of the most important national regulations to protect investors in Brazil not included in the antidirector rights index of Table 4.1. Limited liability provisions were explicitly included in national laws since at least the commerce code of 1850, and Brazilian corporations have been required to disclose financial statements before annual shareholders' meetings at least since 1882. Obviously these laws were familiar only to a small elite of middle to upper class Brazilians (and to foreign investors).[11]

The company law of 1882 mandated that all corporations have at least one general shareholder meeting per year. Shareholders were permitted to examine their companies' books one month before the annual meeting. Following the meeting, and after company financial statements were approved by the overseeing board, a balance sheet with additional details on profits, reserves, and dividends paid as well as a full disclosure of transfers of shares that occurred during the year was required to be published.[12] Although companies published the transfers of shares only in official annual reports and not in the financial press, they published balance sheets once or twice per year in newspapers with wide circulation in the state in which they operated. From these balance sheets it was easy to infer net profits (as dividends + change in reserves + changes in other retained earnings), and after 1891 corporations operating in Brazil also were required to publish profit and loss statements.[13]

The sophistication and regularity of Brazilian financial statements seem to be no better or worse than those of British companies of the time, but

---

[11] See Law 556, June 25, 1850, Article 298.

[12] Law 3150, November 4, 1882, Articles 15 and 16. The overseeing board was composed of three shareholders elected at the shareholders meeting to a term usually of three years. Most of the provisions that regulated the overseeing board were mandated by law.

[13] Decree 603, October 20, 1891, Article 211 required directors to prepare a balance sheet and a profit and loss statement one month before the annual general shareholder meeting. Those financial statements had to be published, together with the minutes of the meeting, one month after the meeting, both in a newspaper with wide circulation and in the official gazette of the state where the company operated.

whereas Brazilian legislation since 1882 had required that *all* companies publish financial statements, similar British legislation did not appear until around 1900. In England, disclosure of financial statements was required for railways in 1868, insurance companies in 1870, gas utilities in 1871, and electricity utilities in 1882, but other industries had to await subsequent legislation. At the New York Stock Exchange, disclosure was not required for domestic listed companies until 1895.[14]

Of course, financial disclosure in Brazil was far from perfect. Just as in England, "depreciation accounting rules were not well developed" and "directors could create secret reserves by understating profits in good years, raiding them – without disclosing this – in bad." The advantage of Brazil's civil law system, like those of many European nations, was perhaps that corporate responsibilities, including disclosure, were clearly spelled out. Disclosure in England, in contrast, "was not a world of rigorously prescribed *rules*," but "a world of shared *values* or *standards*."[15]

The existence of mandatory disclosure and limited liability since 1882 did not prevent a major crisis of investor confidence in Brazil. After 1888, when the rules constraining banks from issuing bearer notes were relaxed, there was a rapid increase in the money supply. This was intensified when, in November 1889, a republican movement took over the government. As soon as the republic was established, the new minister of finance, Rui Barbosa, increased the issue of bank notes by creating a national system of reserve banks with the right to issue notes (on top of the banks that had authorization to issue notes). The result was a rapid increase in the money supply of almost 100% in one year and a consequent increase in bank loans that fueled a boom in stock market activity and inflation in general.

According to the accounts of a contemporary observer, the increase in bank loans:

Initially financed legitimate operations, targeting profitable enterprises and reasonable commercial transactions, but corruption could not wait to take place... and enterprises of pure and audacious speculative nature became mere gambling... shares [in initial public offerings] were sold immediately as subscribers used the lines of credit banks provided.... In many of those companies the founders or incorporators collected special fees from the initial subscription.[16]

[14] See Leslie Hannah, "Pioneering Modern Corporate Governance: A View from London in 1900," *Enterprise and Society* 8 (September 2007): 15–17.

[15] See Hannah, "Pioneering Modern Corporate Governance," pp. 19–20 (italics original).

[16] Carlos Riberiro de Andrada, *Bancos de Emissão no Brasil*, Rio de Janeiro: Leite de Ribeiro, 1923, p. 240.

This speculative fever, called the *encilhamento,* had perverse effects on the wealth of some of the shareholders of ghost companies or of the companies that went bust in 1891. Investor confidence in joint stock corporations would have been decimated for a long time if it had not been for the legislative reaction to the crisis. The Ministry of Justice reacted by asking Dídimo Agapito Veiga Júnior, an expert in company law, to draft a new law that would prevent further corporate fraud. His approach to company law was in agreement with the liberal tradition permeating the ideology of the new republican government. He believed that "the interested parties [shareholders] are the ones concerned about protecting their rights through clear and protective bylaws." This is why he admitted that "it was appropriate for the law-makers to acknowledge that they [the shareholders] are the most suitable ones to monitor the use of their capital."[17] With this ideology in mind Veiga Júnior drafted a law that gave shareholders most of the responsibility for the monitoring of company founders, managers, and other shareholders.

Legal expert Veiga Júnior recommended, among other things, protections for investors against the fraudulent practices of company promoters or deceiving prospectuses published by issuers of securities. For instance, this decree required that the prospectus for a new share issue should have names of the company founders, a detailed explanation of the contracts with the bankers or financiers involved in the operation, AND the amounts that company was paying to these intermediaries in the form of commissions or fees. More importantly, the prospectus had to be accompanied by a copy of the company statutes after their publication in a newspaper of wide circulation.[18] In fact, since 1882, all new corporations were required to publish the statutes before starting their operations or before trading their shares. Decree 603 of October 20, 1891 not only regulated the issuing of shares in a more stringent way, but also provided criminal penalties (including jail sentences and monetary fees) for directors or promoters of new companies who provided false information or violated the bylaws of the corporations they worked for. Similar penalties (without the jail sentences) were included for members of the overseeing board of directors (*conselho fiscal*) who approved fraudulent practices during their terms (the overseeing board was part of the two-tier board system mandated by law since 1882).

---

[17] Quotes taken from Mária Bárbara Levy, *A Indústria do Rio de Janeiro através de suas Sociedades Anônimas*, Rio de Janeiro, UFRJ Editora, 1994, p. 179 (translated by the author).

[18] See Decree 603, October 20, 1891, Articles 89, 90, and 105. See also, Law 3150, November 4, 1882, Article 3.

These provisions imply that what the law included were not direct protections for shareholders, but a system of laws mandating private disclosure so that investors could monitor managers and insiders themselves. By forcing the founders and promoters of a corporation to publish and publicize the statutes of all new corporations, the law made precious information available to interested buyers. Statutes included the bylaws to regulate the governance of the corporation and detailed information about executive compensation, voting rights, and share ownership. For instance, a small investor interested in buying shares in a company could see how powerful large shareholders were (by examining the size of their shareholdings and the voting power they had) and know, right from the beginning, who the directors were, how many shares and votes they controlled, and how high their fixed and performance-based compensation was.

Most other protections for shareholders were left up to the founders and shareholders of a corporation to decide when drafting statutes. Yet, some important provisions to protect small shareholders were still included. For instance, minorities opposed to a merger had the right to walk away from the corporation and get a payment equivalent to the higher of either their share of the total net worth of the corporation or their share of the value of the company according to the merger offer. Additionally, family members were prohibited from serving on any of the boards of directors (the managing board and the overseeing board) simultaneously and managers were prohibited from engaging in business deals with any family member or with related firms without informing the corporation about it.[19]

Coincidentally, these kinds of disclosure requirements included in Brazilian law after 1891 recently have been linked to the development of equity markets around the world. According to recent revisions to the rights that should *really* matter for financial development Rafael La Porta, Florencio Lopez-de-Silanes, and Andrei Shleifer create, among other indicators, what they call an "index of disclosure requirements" that is highly correlated with different measures of stock market size. Even though the calculation of this index is not as straightforward as that for shareholder rights, the index is higher if (1) the law prohibits the sale of shares without issuing a prospectus, (2) the prospectus discloses the compensation of directors and key officers, (3) the prospectus discloses the name and ownership stake of shareholders who, directly or indirectly, control 10% or more

---

[19] See Decree 603, October 20, 1891, Article 282 for shareholder rights in mergers, Article 148 for restrictions on transactions with family members, and Article 165 for constraints on family members serving on any of the boards simultaneously.

of the voting shares, (4) the prospectus discloses the share ownership of directors and key officers, (5) the prospectus discloses the contracts of the company issuing the shares outside of the ordinary course of business, and (6) the prospectus discloses transactions between the company issuing the securities and its directors, officers, or large shareholders. The index is estimated by averaging how many of these protections are present (the presence of these provisions in the law are not recorded as 1 and 0; in some cases fractions can be added according to how strict the law is mandating the disclosure of some of the items).[20] In any case, after 1891 Brazil had at least the first four provisions of this index, which would yield an estimated index of 0.66 (or 4/6).

The level of mandatory disclosure of information was higher in Brazil than in Germany or England at least until 1929. For instance, Franks, Mayer, and Rossi estimate that England only had the first right (the requirement of issuing a prospectus), while Franks, Mayer, and Wagner estimate that Germany had none of these disclosure requirements.[21] To gauge how significant these provisions would be in comparison to today's standards, we could imagine that if Brazil today had these same provisions (with an index of 0.66), it would be one of the three French civil law countries with the strongest disclosure requirements (together with Italy, Jordan, and the Philippines) and would have requirements similar to those of Ireland, Israel, and New Zealand among common law countries.[22]

In sum, Brazil company law preferred to leave it up to investors to regulate financial markets and company law included provisions to help them to gather the necessary information to do this job. Beyond the information investors had, perhaps most of the *actual* protections to induce shareholders to buy equity were in the form of bylaws included in corporate statutes. The next section explores some of these protections in company bylaws.

INVESTOR PROTECTIONS IN COMPANY BYLAWS

It is generalize about the kinds of protections included in corporate bylaws in Brazil between 1882 and 1940 because of the variation across industries

---

[20] Rafael La Porta, Florencio Lopez-de-Silanes, and Andrei Shleifer, "What Works in Securities Laws?," *Journal of Finance* 61, 1 (February 2006): 1–32, for the methodology of the index see Table 1.

[21] See Franks et al., "Ownership," Table 1, Panel D, and "The Origins of the German Corporation," Table 3, Panel B.

[22] See La Porta et al., "What Works in Securities Laws?," Table 2.

and companies. This section examines the provisions that might have induced investors to buy securities in some corporations, focusing on two important provisions: government guarantees and voting provisions to protect small shareholders.

Government Guarantees

Federal and state government subsidies for corporations also translated into protections or incentives for shareholders. These usually took one of two forms. One, usually associated with railway corporations, banks, and some utilities, was a guaranteed minimum dividend paid directly to shareholders through a transfer from the government. The second consisted privileges granted to companies such as the right to collect special taxes or duties, or simply of a direct government subvention awarded to companies each year. Shareholders benefited, of course, from reduced uncertainty about the performance of companies and whether or not a dividend would be paid. Moreover, most companies with government guarantees operated in sectors that were subject to government regulation and the guarantees also compensated shareholders for regulatory uncertainty or for the restrictions companies in such sectors had to charge the prices or tariffs that maximized shareholder value. For instance, railways and utilities companies had natural or near natural monopolies and, thus, the optimal pricing strategy would have been to charge monopoly prices. Since the Brazilian government had the right to regulate such tariffs, subsidizing or guaranteeing dividends for shareholders compensated for the limitations these regulations imposed.

Shareholders of companies with guaranteed dividends also benefitted from government monitoring over the firm's activities. One of the most important features of the companies receiving government guarantees is that they were subject to more intense monitoring by government officials. By law, the government had the right to send a representative to audit shareholder meetings and to revise their financial statements. Therefore, these companies published complete financial statements twice per year, with balance sheets and profit and loss statements. In the case of banks balance sheets were published monthly.[23]

Government-guaranteed dividends were probably copied from other countries. There is evidence that the governments of France, the United States, the United Kingdom, and Canada guaranteed dividends or bond

[23] See, for example, see Decree 603, October 20, 1891, Articles 125 and 126.

coupons.[24] In Brazil, the dividend guarantees the government provided to shareholders of railway companies helped close important information asymmetries that prevailed during the initial stage of railway development. There were not many takers when the government began in 1852 to offer concessions to build railroads in different parts of the territory.[25] Even into the 1860s and 1870s, Brazilian stock markets were not yet sufficiently deep to finance such large ventures, and foreign investors wanted more guarantees before putting money into businesses with unproven results.

The Brazilian government compensated for an unstable macroeconomic environment and regulatory uncertainty by establishing a subsidy system that assured returns to foreign and domestic shareholders. Most of the subsidies were structured as follows. The imperial government guaranteed an annual dividend of approximately 5% per company. Provinces could complement this with additional subsidies of 2%. If net profits exceeded the government-guaranteed amounts, the surplus was required to be divided between the company and the government.[26] These subsidies proved to be a powerful incentive, facilitating the rapid development of railway companies in Brazil.

The government-guaranteed dividend contract was to benefit poorly performing companies and did not necessarily help successful ones. The

[24] The *Investor's Monthly Manual* lists tens, perhaps hundreds, of corporations with guaranteed dividends or coupons, which implies that the practice was common in Great Britain. The *Moniteur des Interets Materiels*, a financial newspaper published in Brussels, also lists tens of bonds and stocks with government guarantees for many countries in continental Europe. For government guarantees in Canada see Anne Carlos and Frank D. Lewis, "Foreign Financing of Canadian Railroads: The Role of Information," in Michael Bordo and Richard Sylla (eds.), *Anglo-American Financial Systems: Institutions and Markets in the Twentieth Century*, New York and Burr Ridge, Illinois: New York University Press and Irwin Press, 1995, pp. 383–414. For government guarantees for railway securities in France see Jim Cohen, "Divergent Paths: How Capital Market Development Affected Differentiation in Transportation Structures, U.S. and France, 1840–1940," Paper presented at Financer le Entreprises face aux Mutations Économiques do XX Siècle, Institut de la Gestion Publique et du Dévelopment Économique, Paris, France, March 2007.

[25] Some of the earliest railroad companies were not particularly successful, a number of them failing altogether. The railroad Dom Pedro II, for example, established to transport coffee from the Paraiba Valley to the port of Rio de Janeiro, had to be bailed out in 1865 when it ran out of funds to complete construction. Flávio A. M. Saes, *A Grande Empresa de Serviços Públicos na Economia Cafeeira*, São Paulo: HUCITEC, 1986, pp. 37–38.

[26] For details of the history of the expansion of railroads and subsidy policies, see William R. Summerhill III, *Order Against Progress: Government, Foreign Investment, and Railroads in Brazil, 1854–1913*, Stanford: Stanford University Press, 2003, Chapter 3, and Flávio A. M. Saes, *As Ferrovias de São Paulo, 1870–1940*, São Paulo: HUCITEC, 1981, pp. 151–154. An even more detailed contemporary account is provided by Chrockatt de Sá, *Brazilian Railways; Their History, Legislation and Development*, Rio de Janeiro: Typografia de C. Leuzinger & filhos, 1893.

stipulation that profits in excess of the percentage of guaranteed dividends be split between the company and the government was a way for the latter to recover the capital invested in the guarantees. Thus, for companies earning profits in excess of 10–14% before dividends (a common occurrence after the 1880s), the government contract effectively constituted a tax on good performance. Some companies cancelled their contracts with the government when their situation implied they were better off paying the dividend themselves and keeping the extra profits for the company, rather than sharing them with the government.[27]

Since the subsidies also provided incentives for excessive risk taking on the part of managers and founders, the government regulated and monitored the business of some of these companies rigorously in at least three ways. First, the government had complete control over the tariffs companies with such guarantees could charge for their services (sometimes tariffs were determined on a case-by-case basis).[28] Second, these companies were required to publish complete financial statements (with profit and loss statements) earlier than the rest of Brazilian corporations. Additionally, most of the companies that received these subsidies operated government concessions for railway lines, utilities, ports, or waterworks and in the event the contract was violated or the company was driven into insolvency, the concession reverted to the government. The government usually would rehabilitate, for instance, railways, after buying the assets of a liquidated company.[29]

In sum, the government, by guaranteeing payment of a minimum dividend, reduced information asymmetries with respect to future streams of cash flow to investors and provided close monitoring of company activities. Mitigating risks should have induced more investors to buy shares of guaranteed companies and thereby, perhaps, reduced concentration of ownership and control. Investors trusted these guarantees because they were backed by the same level of commitment with which the federal and state governments honored their debts. William Summerhill III has argued that the Brazilian government created a political structure that forced the

---

[27] See Saes, *As Ferrovias de São Paulo*, pp. 151–152.

[28] William Summerhill III examines how the regulation of railway tariffs worked before 1914. See Summerhill III, *Order Against Progress*, Chapter 7.

[29] This was the case of the Sorocabana Railway in 1902 and the E. F. Dom Pedro II in 1865. See Estrada de Ferro Sorocabana, *Relatório: Anno de 1904*. São Paulo: Typografia A Vap. Rosehan & Meyer, 1905 for a description of the acquisition of the assets of the Soroбana by the federal government and Saes, *A Grande Empresa de Serviços Públicos na Economia Cafeeira*, p. 36 for the story of the E. F. Dom Pedro II.

imperial governments before 1889 to credibly to commit to honor the country's sovereign debt. With such a strong credit record, the Brazilian government's reputation as a good payer was well established by the 1890s and, even if it almost defaulted on dividend guarantees in 1898, a funding loan from the House of Rotschild kept the government in good standing.[30]

Voting Rights

More important than many of the disclosure requirements were the provisions that divided power among shareholders. The bylaws governing the voting rights of shareholders were the key determinant of the participation of small investors in the ownership of equity. There are only a few scenarios in which small investors would want to participate in the ownership of a corporation in which the voting power is concentrated in the hands of a large shareholder.[31] We could think that most investors preferred the certainty of knowing the balance of power within the corporation was not tilted toward insiders, directors, or large shareholders. This is why a significant share of early Brazilian corporations (mostly before 1910) used voting rights to distribute power more evenly among shareholders.[32] Before 1932, there were no shares without voting rights in Brazilian corporations. Any shareholder who held the number of shares required to get one vote could participate in a company's decision-making process. About a third of Brazilian corporations capped the maximum number of votes to limit the power of large shareholders, and many large corporations employed graduated voting schemes that restricted the number of votes that accompanied increases in shareholdings.

---

[30] Summerhill further argues that the credible commitment of the Brazilian government to honor its sovereign debt did not translate into either stock market or banking sector development before 1889. His story, however, is that powerful groups of bankers and others captured the government and complicated entry from the middle of the nineteenth century. I thus argue that once restrictions to free incorporation were eliminated in 1882, Brazilian corporations with guaranteed dividends could piggyback on the good reputation of the state and federal governments in order to induce investors to buy their securities. See William R. Summerhill III, "Sovereign Credibility with Financial Underdevelopment: The Case of Nineteenth-Century Brazil," unpublished manuscript, University of California, Los Angeles, May 2007, esp. pp. 26–33 on financial development before 1889.

[31] This would be the case when there are two rival groups with large shareholdings monitoring one another or when a large shareholder with good reputation monitors the actions of directors or founders. In both cases small shareholders would buy equity as a way to free ride on the monitoring effort of these large shareholders.

[32] Article 15 of Law 3150, November 4, 1882, stated that voting rights were to be established by each company in its bylaws.

Table 4.2 presents data on voting rights by company derived from a survey of companies published in the *Brazilian Year Book 1909* (a handbook of Brazilian corporations published in London). It shows that the average number of shares necessary to get the right to vote was relatively low in most industries surveyed in 1909. On average, corporations from all over Brazil required investors to hold between five and ten shares to vote at shareholder meetings. Approximately 20% of the companies in the sample had one-share, one-vote provisions; the percentage was higher for some industries. Banks seem to have been particularly democratic: 46% of domestic banks had a one-share, one-vote provision. Utilities, ports, and mining companies were not far behind at 30%. Other companies chose mostly the five shares per vote (37% of firms) or ten shares per vote (34%) provision; only 7% of companies required 20 to 25 shares to one vote.

That Brazilian companies, on average, had relatively low ratios of shares per vote does not translate, however, into worker participation in the ownership and control of corporations. Data on average annual salaries by profession in Rio de Janeiro in 1909 show the cost of a single share (with face value of 200 mil reis) to have equaled the entire *annual* salary of a cook, carpenter, or messenger, and other, relatively unskilled workers earned less per year than the face value of one share (normally either 100 or 200 mil reis), most jobs at the time paid an average wage of between 100 and 200 mil reis per year.[33] Thus the "democratic" corporate practices described in this book were exclusive to landowners, professionals (e.g., lawyers, accountants, bankers, dentists, and engineers), widows, urban landlords, and other citizens with relatively high incomes or sizable inheritances. This is not, however, to imply that shareholder rights (and creditor rights discussed in subsequent chapters) were enforced by networks of elites making sure their rights were protected against one another through informal means. The system of investor protections in place in Brazil at this time was relatively impersonal and relied on the threat of court enforcement.

The bottom row of Table 4.2 gauges the importance of voting provisions that limited the power of large shareholders by showing that more than a quarter of the companies in the 1909 sample limited the maximum number of votes a single shareholder could cast during a given meeting. On average, 26% capped the maximum number of votes, and in industries such as utilities and shipping more than 38% did so. Although in services and mining and some other industries no companies seemed to use this voting scheme, the sample size is small for those sectors.

[33] For salary data, see Mária Eulália Lahmeyer Lobo, *História do Rio de Janeiro: do capital comercial ao capital industrial e financeiro*, Rio de Janeiro: IBMEC, 1978, Table 4.44.

Table 4.2. *Voting rights in Brazilian corporations, c. 1909*

	Agriculture	Banks	Insurance	Manufacturing	Mining	Services	Utilities	Shipping	Ports	Railways	Full sample
	N=11	N=23	N=14	N=44	N=3	N=8	N=17	N=7	N=2	N=6	N=135
Avg. shares to get one vote	7	6	7	7	12	15	20	5	5	6	7
Percentage of companies with											
One-share, one-vote	20%	46%	13%	15%	33%		33%	13%	30%	21%	23%
Five shares to one vote	20	19	44	37			50	75	40	53	37
Ten shares to one vote	50	23	44	46	33	50		13	30	16	34
>10 shares to one vote	10	12		2	33	50	17			11	7
Percentage of companies with maximum votes	20%	27%	25%	29%			50%	38%	10%	21%	26%

Source: Compiled by the author from information in *Brazilian Year Book 1909.*
Note: Includes only companies the original bylaws of which were chartered in Brazil. Companies with graduated voting schemes are assumed to use only one scheme of shares per votes (usually five shares per vote).

Capping the maximum number of votes protected smaller shareholders in two ways. First, it limited the power large shareholders could exert during shareholder meetings. Second, it encouraged the formation of large voting blocks that included smaller shareholders as a way to reach consensus on important assembly resolutions including the election of directors. The decision-making process was thereby rendered more democratic and smaller investors were encouraged either to participate more actively in shareholder assemblies or at least to decide which voting blocks to join.

Anne Hanley's observation that "while the stock market was expanding [in São Paulo], a sort of democratization was taking place within the market" was playing out as a more even distribution of power among existing shareholders was taking place in large corporations. Provisions to protect investors attracted new investors and "the growth in the number of outstanding shares listed on the exchange was accompanied by an increase in the number of individuals investing in the stock market."[34]

Many corporations also adopted graduated voting rights as a way of limiting the number of additional votes that accompanied increases in shareholdings. Companies such as Antarctica, Estrada de Ferro (E. F.) Paulista, E. F. Mogyana, and Banespa exemplify how binding graduated voting rights and maximum vote provisions were. The percentage of shares controlled by the largest shareholders was higher than the percentage of votes those shareholders controlled. Why some shareholders with large equity holdings might have been willing to settle for control rights that were proportionally less that their cash flow rights is open to conjecture. It may be that there was among many Brazilian investors a "democratic" attitude toward corporate governance consistent with the broader democratization of the country's financial markets. A democratic attitude, in this context, would mean the intention or agreement to share power within corporations more equally among shareholders.

Some corporations included in their bylaws provisions to limit the abuses of large shareholders or of families with significant shareholdings. For instance, the Antarctica Brewery, the textile mill São Paulo Fabril, and the railway E. F. do Dourado included provisions that prohibited two family members from holding board positions during the same term.[35] The São

---

[34] See Anne Hanley, *Native Capital: Financial Institutions and Economic Development in São Paulo, Brazil, 1850–1920*, Stanford: Stanford University Press, 2005, p. 96.
[35] See Cia. Antarctica, *Atas da Assembléia de Acionistas da…*, São Paulo, 1891–1927 (São Paulo State Archive); "Estrada de Ferro do Dourado," Bolsa de Valores do Rio de Janeiro, Sociedades Anônimas, Transportes, Caixa 2166; and *Estatutos da Companhia São Paulo Fabril*, São Paulo: Companhia Impressora Paulista, 1890.

Paulo Fabril and the Mogyana Railway capped not only the number of votes per shareholder, but also the maximum number of votes that any single shareholder could represent as a proxy.[36]

An obvious question with respect to the bylaws of Brazilian corporations is: How did Brazilian investors and entrepreneurs decide to include such bylaws in their companies' charters?

WHERE DID THESE BYLAWS COME FROM?

The kind of corporate governance practices just explained were imported to Brazil around the middle of the nineteen century by foreign capitalists, immigrants, and Brazilians educated abroad. The first Brazilian corporations most likely sketched their statutes or charters by copying what was common practice in Europe. Railway companies followed the practices of companies in France, Belgium, and the United Kingdom. Insurance and harbor companies had strong British influence and British capital. Finally, not only were Brazilian banks modelled after British banks, but also some of the first Brazilian bankers had close connections with British bankers (the best known example is that of the Viscount of Mauá, who developed a long-lasting partnership with British merchants and bankers).

With the flows of foreign capital and trade to Brazil came capitalism as well. Foreign investors looking for standard practices and Brazilian entrepreneurs importing European practices led the way to creating the corporate governance practices described in this chapter. Even if we know little about transnational investors outside of the United Kingdom and the United States, there is scattered evidence that investors in Europe crossed national boundaries and even served on the boards of directors of many companies in different countries.[37] Therefore one can speculate that Brazilian entrepreneurs interested in attracting foreign investors designed corporate charters that provided assurances to foreign investors (e.g., maximum vote provisions, disclosure requirements, etc). This, in fact, happened before Brazilian corporate law included such provisions.

---

[36] See Cia. Mogyana (Mojiana) de Estradas de Ferro, *Relatório da Diretoria em Assembléia Geral...* 1878–1922 and *Estatutos da Companhia São Paulo Fabril*, São Paulo: Companhia Impressora Paulista, 1890.

[37] This was the case of S. Wellhoff, documented in a book that shows the differences in corporate governance practices across countries. What is perhaps more impressive about this book are the few differences in investor protections in the countries he compares (in continental Europe, Egypt, and the United Kingdom). See S. Wellhoff, *Sociétés par Actions*, Alexandria: Société de Publications Égyptiennes, 1917.

The first Brazilian railway concessions intended to attract domestic as well as foreign investors. Their charters included government-guaranteed dividends of 7% per year and a series of bylaws protecting shareholders from possible abuses by managers and insiders. For instance, the statutes of the E. F. Dom Pedro II, the first railway company in Brazil, already included many of the bylaws discussed in this chapter. For instance, the company had to disclose every year a balance sheet and profit and loss statement and gave shareholders a vote for every five shares. What is more impressive is that the company had a maximum vote provision, capping shareholder power at 20 votes, either per shareholder or per proxy. In other words, shareholders who owned or represented more than 100 shares could not exercise more than 20 votes in the shareholders' assembly. This is an extremely low cap considering that the railway was established with a capital of 60,000 shares of 200$ (with total capital of 12,000,000$ mil reis or about £1,350,000).[38]

Shareholder lists of some of the first Brazilian railways include British and German investors as well as recent immigrants from Germany and Italy. In 1869, the shareholder list of the E. F. Paulista shows that British merchants and financiers owned 6% of the total shares, while German investors or recent immigrants from that country controlled another 1%.[39] The E. F. São Paulo e Rio also shows that British investors controlled 4% of the shares in 1876.[40]

Later, foreign influence actually translated into law in Brazil. According to Richard Graham in 1968 the liberal minister of justice, Nabuco de Araújo, "inspired by the British and French laws of 1862 and 1863... decided to... free limited liability companies from the requirement of prior authorization" of entry. He drafted a project following the British company law of 1862, which was not approved until almost two decades later. In 1877 a report of a congressional committee proposed a new law that closely followed British law and argued that the effects of the law of 1862 had resulted in a "new order of things" in Britain. According to this report, "the spirit of association...grew prodigiously. The number of companies organized rose to an elevated figure." This committee ended up proposing a new law, which after a few modifications was approved as the company law of 1882 (discussed previously in this chapter).[41]

---

[38] See the statutes of the Estrada de Ferro Dom Pedro II in Decree 1,500, May 9, 1855, esp. Articles 39, 45, and 46.

[39] See Companhia Paulista de Estradas de Ferro, *Presença de Acionistas em Assembléia* ... São Paulo, 1869.

[40] See Estrada de Ferro São Paulo e Rio, *Relatório da diretoria, 1876*, São Paulo, 1877.

[41] Richard Graham, *Britain and the Onset of Modernization in Brazil, 1850–1914*, London: Cambridge University Press, 1968, p. 228.

CONCLUSION

This chapter shows that Brazilian company laws did not directly include many of the protections shareholders would want to trust equity issuers. Instead, the 1891 company law was strict in mandating the disclosure of detailed information about a company's owners, directors, and contracts when issuing new shares (or debt). The disclosure of information was so detailed that investors interested in buying equity could know even how much directors were getting paid (something I explore in more detail in Chapter 6). Therefore, the law mandated the disclosure of information that facilitated private enforcement of investor protections and helped investors to do this job by providing criminal penalties for directors and company founders who violated these provisions.

Yet, the main argument of this chapter is that these disclosure provisions and penalties might not have been enough to encourage the participation of small investors. For instance, today Brazil has strict penalties against insiders and provides conditions that allow minority shareholders to take them to litigation, but disclosure of the ownership of the corporation is limited and small shareholders have almost no power when it comes to voting rights. This is why I argue that small investors need assurances that the possible abuses of large shareholders and founders will be counterbalanced by other shareholders with perhaps smaller holdings. The early development of stock markets in Brazil was accompanied by relatively strong investor protections in the bylaws of many midsized and larger corporations. These ranged from government-guaranteed dividends to voting provisions that limited the power of large shareholders. Although it is hard to make a direct link between shareholder rights and stock market development (e.g., statistically), we know that protections such as maximum vote provisions and government-guaranteed dividends should have induced more shareholders to buy equity in Brazilian corporations, probably yielding lower ownership concentration. In fact, the next chapter shows that both maximum vote provisions and government guarantees were correlated with less concentration of ownership and voting power among shareholders.

## FIVE

Voting Rights, Government Guarantees, and
Ownership Concentration, 1890–1950

The degree to which shareholder protections mattered in practice to smaller investors should be reflected in tangible outcomes such as low levels of concentration in ownership and control in large Brazilian corporations. Ownership concentration is a good indication of the state of shareholder protections for at least two reasons. One, smaller investors unsure of the degree to which they are protected against the abuses of managers or other shareholders would be unlikely to participate actively in equity markets. Two, in the presence of weak shareholder protections there would be little to stop managers from pilfering company resources. Ownership concentration would compensate for inadequate shareholder protections because large shareholders with large blocks of votes would have more incentive to monitor managers and the power to dismiss and name new ones to replace any who committed abuses.

This chapter uses data on ownership concentration for a sample of some of the largest Brazilian corporations between 1890 and 1940 to show that corporations with more protective shareholder rights in their bylaws had lower concentration of ownership than the average company. Statistical analysis of the data on ownership concentration reveals that in companies that limited the power of large shareholders through voting provisions, such as maximum votes, the concentration of ownership and control rights (votes) was significantly lower than for the average Brazilian company.

The fact that bylaws protective of small shareholders might have reduced ownership concentration in some of the largest corporations in Brazil helps to explain why there was lower concentration of voting power in the hands of large shareholders of publicly traded corporations in the past than today. In Brazilian corporations today, on average, the largest three shareholders own 70% of equity and control about 90% of the votes in shareholders meetings. The equivalent percentage for both stock and votes in Brazil before 1910 was 53%.

THE DATA TO STUDY OWNERSHIP CONCENTRATION BEFORE 1950

Because few Brazilian corporations have archives, and the state and national archives gathered only scattered documents and shareholder meeting minutes, it is hard to find complete shareholder lists and shareholder meeting minutes for a large number of corporations over a long period of time. I compiled shareholder lists for some of the largest Brazilian corporations from data available at the Rio de Janeiro Stock Exchange Archive in Rio de Janeiro and the São Paulo State Archive in São Paulo.[1] Most were part of published annual reports of a sample of corporations. I was able to consult, for some companies, the entry books in which shares were registered before shareholder meetings.

When possible, concentration of ownership and voting rights are estimated directly from these shareholder lists, some of which include detailed data on votes per shareholder from which I was able to derive the data on concentration of control. In other cases, I examined the voting rights included in the company statutes and applied the rules to the shareholder lists at hand. For statutes that had to be approved by the government, I looked in the collection of national laws. For others, I looked in the *Official Gazette of the State of São Paulo* (*Diário Oficial do Estado de São Paulo*) or the *Federal Official Gazette* (*Diário Oficial da União*). For some companies, I used the same sources to estimate the share of votes controlled by the directors.

The data for the study of the correlation between ownership concentration and voting provisions is in Table 5.6 (in Appendix 5A). This table presents disaggregated data on ownership concentration, the concentration of control, and voting rights for a sample of 57 Brazilian corporations between the 1870s and 1950 (with multiple observations for some companies, thus yielding a sample of 84 observations). Panel A includes large corporations with somewhat dispersed ownership and the same data for some companies that were not controlled by a single family. Panel B shows companies

---

[1] Both archives have special sections on Sociedades Anônimas with files for each company that usually include company statutes, shareholder lists, and changes of statutes every time there was a bond or new share issue. See, for example, the collection of documents for *Sociedades Anônimas* in the National Archive of Brazil, Rio de Janeiro.

that were controlled by the federal government or the São Paulo state government (controlling the Banco do Estado de São Paulo, Banespa). Panel C shows family-owned and controlled corporations. Since this database was constructed using ownership for many companies at the time of their initial charter (coded as IPO in Table 5.6), the information for these companies most likely exaggerates the extent of ownership concentration in Brazil. This is somewhat compensated by the fact that for some companies with dispersed ownership I have more observations over time.

VOTING AND CONCENTRATION OF OWNERSHIP AND CONTROL, 1890–1940

How do we know if voting provisions that aimed to distribute concentration control rights were binding and whether such provisions induced more investors to buy stock? One way to address these questions is to examine the correlation of voting provisions and other investment protections with ownership concentration in large corporations. Eric Hilt, following this procedure in his study of the charters of corporations in New York in the early part of the nineteenth century, found concentration of control to be lower in companies that had maximum and graduated voting provisions.[2] I follow Hilt's methodology to explore the effects of some of these governance provisions on the concentration of ownership and control in Brazilian corporations.

Pooling all data on ownership concentration and company characteristics for the period 1890–1950 I run either a Tobit estimate or an ordinary least squares estimate (OLS) of the following form:

$$y_i = \beta_0 + \beta_1 \log (capital\ 1900) + \beta_2 (maxvote/graduated\ voting)$$
$$+ \beta_3 (gov't\ guarantee) + \beta_4 New + \sum_z^Z \theta_z\ industry_{iz}$$
$$+ \sum_k^K \gamma_k\ SP\ \&\ Rio_{jk} + \sum_w^W \theta_w\ decade_{iw} + e_i$$

where y_i is a measure of the concentration of ownership or control for firm i. The concentration of ownership is measured as the percentage of shares controlled by the three largest shareholders. The concentration of control is estimated using the Herfindahl-Hirschman Index (HHI) of concentration

---

[2] Eric Hilt, "When Did Ownership Separate from Control? Corporate Governance in the Early Nineteenth Century," *Journal of Economic History* 68, 3 (September 2008): 645–685.

of control (sum of the squared share of votes of each shareholder) and the percentage of votes controlled by the three largest shareholders.[3] Two coefficients, β_2 and β_3, capture the differences in the concentration of ownership and control between the average Brazilian company and those with a voting cap, graduated voting, or government-guaranteed dividends. If these protections do have an effect on ownership concentration, we would expect the coefficients β_2 and β_3, to be large and negative. I also control for size (using the deflated capital in mil reis of 1900),[4] industry, whether the company is from São Paulo or Rio, whether the shareholder list is from the original charter (a control for new companies), and dummies that capture the decade in which the shareholder list was reported (the sample size is too small to use shorter time periods). The São Paulo and Rio dummies do not yield significant results and thus are not reported.

Table 5.1 presents summary statistics for the pooled data on ownership concentration for the sample of 57 companies (I have repeated observations for some, generating a total sample of 84 observations). In particular, it shows significant differences in the average HHI and the concentration of equity and votes controlled by the three largest shareholders in companies with and without voting caps and with graduated voting. Companies with voting caps had an HHI, on average, 0.19 points lower than companies without this provision. This is a significant reduction because the mean of this index for the entire sample is 0.20 points (standard deviation of 0.24), which would be the equivalent of having a corporation with only five shareholders with equal holdings. In companies with maximum voting rights, the HHI is close to 0.01, the equivalent of a company with 100 shareholders holding equal shares of the total capital.[5]

According to the simple difference of means in Table 5.1, there are significant differences in the percentage of shares and votes controlled by the top three shareholders in companies with voting caps. In these companies the percentage of votes controlled by the three largest shareholders is 0.36 lower, while the percentage of shares controlled by these shareholders drops to 0.21,

---

[3]   On the Herfindahl-Hirschman Index of concentration and some of its interpretations, see Albert O. Hirschman, "The Paternity of an Index," *American Economic Review* 54, 5 (September 1964): 761, and M. A. Adelman, "Comment on the 'H' Concentration Measure as a Numbers-Equivalent," *Review of Economics and Statistics* 51, 1 (February 1969): 99–101.

[4]   Data deflated using the GDP deflator of Raymond Goldsmith and merged with the deflator of IPEA, www.ipeadata.gov.br. See Raymond Goldsmith, *Brasil1850–1984: Desenvolvimento Financeiro sob um Século de Inflação*, Rio de Janeiro: Banco Bamerindus and Editora Harper & Row do Brasil, 1986, Tables 3.1 and 4.2.

[5]   See Adelman, "Comment on the 'H' Concentration Measure as a Numbers-Equivalent," pp. 99–101, for interpretations of the HHI.

Table 5.1. *Summary statistics: ownership data, Brazil, 1890–1950*

Variable	Full sample			Without max votes			With max votes		
	Obs	Mean	Std. dev.	Obs	Mean	Std. dev.	Obs	Mean	Std. dev.
HHI	81	0.20	0.24	57	0.25	0.25	24	0.06	0.11
Votes by top 3 sh.	82	0.47	0.32	58	0.58	0.29	24	0.21	0.22
Shares by top 3 sh.	84	0.51	0.30	60	0.57	0.28	24	0.35	0.28
Capital (million US$ 1900)	76	2.79	6.90	52	1.27	3.30	24	1.90	4.25
Max vote	84	0.29	0.45						
Government guarantee	84	0.14	0.35						
Graduated voting	84	0.25	0.44						

	Difference of means (t-statistics)		
	By maximum votes	By government guarantees	By graduated voting (dummy)
hhi	3.51***	0.06	2.69***
votes3	3.14***	2.36**	4.08***
shares3	5.58***	1.18+	4.18***

Source: Aldo Musacchio, "Laws versus Contracts: Legal Origins, Shareholder Protections, and Ownership Concentration in Brazil, 1890–1950," *Business History Review* 82, 3 (Fall 2008): 445–473.
Notes:
+ *significant at 10%,* ** *significant at 5%,* *** *significant at 1%.*

on average. This last result implies not only that caps on voting limited the power of large shareholders in the assemblies, but also that it encouraged more shareholders to buy equity in those companies (or alternatively that in companies with these voting provisions each shareholder bought a large share of equity in equal proportion, generating lower inequality in ownership).

Government-guaranteed dividends might also be expected to have affected ownership concentration (of votes and equity, but not differences in the HHI). About one-fifth of the companies in the sample enjoyed this investor protection. As shown in Table 5.1, companies with government guarantees seem to have had lower concentration of ownership (shares) and especially of control rights (votes). On average, government guarantees reduced the percentage of shares controlled by the three largest shareholders by 21%.

Finally, results of the difference of means test reported in Table 5.1 show that companies with graduated voting schemes had significantly lower concentration of ownership and control. To give an idea of the differences between the average Brazilian company and those with graduated voting scales, the HHI is only 0.06 for the latter, with the three largest shareholders controlling, on average, 21% of the votes and 35% of the shares. These effects are almost equivalent to a reduction by a half in the level of concentration of ownership and control relative to the average company in Brazil.

The inherent difficulty of analyzing the effects of these three governance provisions on ownership concentration is that they overlap significantly. For example, Banespa had government guaranteed dividends and graduated voting; some of the railway companies had graduated voting and maximum votes. Also, once we control for industry the effects of graduated voting will fade away since most companies with these provisions are in the railway sector and there is not enough variation within this industry to sustain a significant coefficient.[6]

Most of the differences in ownership concentration are confirmed in the multivariate setting except for the effects of graduated voting scheme, which are statistically insignificant. When we control for size or age, industry dummies, and other company characteristics, we find that maximum vote provisions and government guarantees had the largest effects. Table 5.2 presents the correlates of the concentration of ownership and control in a simple Tobit model. Companies with maximum votes per shareholder seem to have lower concentration of ownership and control rights. In specifications 1–5 of Table 5.2 we can see that having maximum votes reduced the HHI of voting concentration by approximately 0.15, even after controlling for size, industry, time period in which the company data were reported, whether the company was new, and whether it had government guarantees. Companies with caps on voting had a lower percentage of votes controlled by the three largest shareholders, on average 0.30–0.31. This coefficient is very large if we take into account the fact that the average for the concentration of votes is 0.51. Finally, maximum votes are also correlated with

---

[6]   For more details on the governance of Banespa see Banco do Estado de São Paulo, *Atas da Assembléia de Acionistas do Banco do Estado de São Paulo,* Museu Banespa, São Paulo, Brazil, 1889–1950.

lower concentration of ownership. This implies that in companies with this provision we usually find more shareholders with smaller equity shares. These results are robust to different controls and when the estimation is done using OLS rather than a Tobit model. Table 5.3 confirms the results of Table 5.2, but using OLS estimates of the same specifications.

Government guarantees enter the specifications of Tables 5.2 and 5.3 with significant coefficients. Guaranteed dividends are more weakly correlated with lower HHI, but still reduce it by around 0.20. This dummy has stronger coefficients in the specifications that examine the concentration of voting and ownership. Government guarantees reduce the concentration of ownership and control even more than maximum vote provisions, but there are only five companies with such guarantees.

As the previous chapter suggests, the reason government-guaranteed dividends would be so strongly correlated with lower ownership concentration is not only the more steady flow of dividends, but also that guarantees on dividends came together with stricter monitoring by the government, including semiannual financial disclosure and direct inspections by government officials. This made it harder for company directors and insiders to cheat or steal from shareholders.

In specifications 3, 5, 7, 8, 10, 12, 13, and 15, of Tables 5.2 and 5.3 I add dummies to control for the three companies that have more observations and maximum vote provisions: Antarctica Brewery and the railways E. F. Paulista and E. F. Mogyana (these dummies are referred to as "multiple obs. dummy"). Because several observations of these companies are included, we would expect them to be averaged out by the regression, but we might also expect them, because they have low concentration of ownership and control, to bias the coefficients of the maximum vote and government guarantees upward. Yet, the addition of these dummies still yields significant coefficients for the maximum vote and the government-guaranteed dividend dummies.

Since the voting provisions usually were selected by shareholders and government guarantees could be selected for companies in which shareholders asked for protection one could argue that there is a severe endogeneity problem with the estimates in Tables 5.2 and 5.3. For instance, coffee planters who wanted to own and operate a railway that would cross through their region could lobby the government to provide a dividend guarantee for their enterprise. The larger the group of coffee planters, the easier it would be to get the government to provide the guarantee. Yet, there is no reason why the lobbying efforts would benefit only companies with dispersed ownership. The same argument could be made about powerful planters who wanted to keep tight control of a railway company and

Table 5.2. *Correlates of governance and ownership concentration using a Tobit estimate, Brazil, 1890–1950*

	HHI (1)	HHI (2)	HHI (3)	HHI (4)	HHI (5)	Votes by top 3 (6)	Votes by top 3 (7)
Constant	0.123 [0.290]	−0.096 [0.291]	−0.105 [0.296]	0.095 [0.318]	−0.071 [0.314]	0.951 [0.378]**	0.582 [0.352]
Ln(cap1900)	0.002 [0.019]	0.022 [0.020]	0.023 [0.020]	0.004 [0.021]	0.014 [0.021]	−0.035 [0.025]	−0.003 [0.024]
Maxvoted	−0.187 [0.051]***	−0.146 [0.060]**	−0.145 [0.060]**			−0.402 [0.066]***	−0.312 [0.074]***
Gov't guarantee		−0.256 [0.124]**	−0.252 [0.126]+				−0.418 [0.145]***
Graduated voting				−0.053 [0.089]	0.05 [0.096]		
New company			0.009 [0.051]		0.027 [0.053]		
Industry dummies	Y	Y	Y	Y	Y	Y	Y
Time period dummy	Y	Y	Y	Y	Y	Y	Y
Multiple obs. dummy	N	Y	Y	N	Y	N	Y
Observations	73	73	73	73	73	74	74
Log likelihood	18.62	22.21	22.23	12.54	17.72	−2.03	6.59
Pseudo R²	−1.23	−1.65	−1.66	−0.5	−1.12	0.92	1.26

Notes: Depedendent variables measure ownership and voting power concentration using the Herfindahl-Hirschman Index (HHI) of voting power concentration, the percentage of total votes controlled by the top three shareholders, and the percentage of total equity controlled by the top three shareholders. The hypothesis tested is that either a limit on the maximum number of votes, graduated voting, or government guarantees would be correlated with lower concentration of ownership and control. In specifications 3, 5, 7, 8, 10, 12, 13, and 15 I add dummies for the three

Votes by top 3 (8)	Votes by top 3 (9)	Votes by top 3 (10)	Equity of top 3 (11)	Equity of top 3 (12)	Equity of top 3 (13)	Equity of top 3 (14)	Equity of top 3 (15)
0.497	0.871	0.517	0.486	0.433	0.329	0.431	0.22
[0.353]	[0.463]+	[0.410]	[0.346]	[0.307]	[0.303]	[0.376]	[0.342]
0.001	−0.029	−0.008	0	0.011	0.015	0.004	0.013
[0.024]	[0.031]	[0.027]	[0.023]	[0.020]	[0.020]	[0.025]	[0.023]
−0.309			−0.222	−0.181	−0.18		
[0.073]***			[0.067]***	[0.072]**	[0.070]**		
−0.389				−0.483	−0.43		
[0.145]***				[0.125]***	[0.124]***		
	−0.16	0.076				−0.158	0.087
	[0.130]	[0.127]				[0.112]	[0.115]
0.08		0.106			0.117		0.155
[0.060]		[0.069]			[0.058]**		[0.063]**
Y	Y	Y	Y	Y	Y	Y	Y
Y	Y	Y	Y	Y	Y	Y	Y
Y	N	Y	N	Y	Y	N	Y
74	74	74	76	76	76	76	76
7.47	−16.24	−3.41	−0.5	12.55	14.57	−4.66	6.53
1.3	0.35	0.86	0.96	1.95	2.1	0.65	1.49

Notes: (continued)
companies that have multiple observations and more dispersion of ownership, just to see if those observations were driving the results. This table uses the log of a firm's paid up capital (in mil reis of 1900) as the main control of firm characteristics (as well as industry dummies). Standard errors are in brackets.

+ *significant at 10%,* ** *significant at 5%,* *** *significant at 1%.*

Table 5.3. *Correlates of governance and ownership concentration using OLS, Brazil, 1890–1950*

	HHI (1)	HHI (2)	HHI (3)	HHI (4)	HHI (5)	Votes by top 3 (6)	Votes by top 3 (7)
Constant	0.131 [0.271]	0.016 [0.271]	−0.099 [0.276]	0.104 [0.285]	−0.064 [0.278]	0.993 [0.378]**	0.615 [0.340]+
Ln(cap1900)	0.002 [0.018]	0.013 [0.018]	0.022 [0.019]	0.003 [0.019]	0.013 [0.019]	−0.037 [0.024]	−0.005 [0.023]
Maxvoted	−0.186 [0.045]***	−0.204 [0.046]***	−0.145 [0.060]**			−0.396 [0.069]***	−0.305 [0.084]***
Gov't guarantee		−0.18 [0.051]***	−0.251 [0.071]***				−0.419 [0.099]***
Graduated vote				−0.052 [0.104]	0.051 [0.094]		
New company			0.01 [0.063]		0.029 [0.061]		
Dummies							
Industry	Y	Y	Y	Y	Y	Y	Y
Time period	Y	Y	Y	Y	Y	Y	Y
Multiple obs.	N	N	Y	N	Y	N	Y
Observations	73	73	73	73	73	74	74
R-squared	0.096	0.097	0.116	0.069	0.092	0.264	0.288

Notes: Depedendent variables measure ownership and voting power concentration using the Herfindahl-Hirschman Index (HHI) of voting power concentration, the percentage of total votes controlled by the top three shareholders, and the percentage of total equity controlled by the top three shareholders. The hypothesis tested is that either a limit on the maximum number of votes, graduated voting, or government guarantees would be correlated with lower concentration of ownership and control. In specifications 3, 5, 7, 8, 10, 12, 13, and 15 I add dummies for the three

Votes by top 3 (8)	Votes by top 3 (9)	Votes by top 3 (10)	Equity of top 3 (11)	Equity of top 3 (12)	Equity of top 3 (13)	Equity of top 3 (14)	Equity of top 3 (15)
0.52	0.907	0.535	0.486	0.433	0.329	0.431	0.22
[0.328]	[0.430]**	[0.386]	[0.342]	[0.288]	[0.278]	[0.350]	[0.368]
−0.001	−0.031	−0.009	0	0.011	0.015	0.004	0.013
[0.022]	[0.029]	[0.026]	[0.022]	[0.018]	[0.018]	[0.024]	[0.024]
−0.303			−0.222	−0.181	−0.18		
[0.080]***			[0.077]***	[0.093]+	[0.087]**		
−0.388				−0.483	−0.43		
[0.102]***				[0.083]***	[0.083]***		
	−0.18	0.049				−0.158	0.087
	[0.211]	[0.161]				[0.177]	[0.154]
0.087		0.115			0.117		0.155
[0.077]		[0.080]			[0.071]		[0.073]**
Y	Y	Y	Y	Y	Y	Y	Y
Y	Y	Y	Y	Y	Y	Y	Y
Y	N	Y	N	Y	Y	N	Y
74	74	74	76	76	76	76	76
0.29	0.136	0.206	0.261	0.392	0.397	0.179	0.285

Notes: (continued)
companies that have multiple observations and more dispersion of ownership, just to see if those observations were driving the results. This table uses the log of a firm's paid up capital (in mil reis of 1900) as the main control of firm characteristics (as well as industry dummies). Robust standard errors are in brackets.

+ *significant at 10%,* ** *significant at 5%,* *** *significant at 1%.*

simultaneously lobbied to get government subsidies. In any case, if there were a selection problem it would exist only in certain industries, such as railways or banks. Therefore, part of the endogeneity problem should be captured by the industry dummies.

The endogeneity problem could also come from a large number of shareholders with equal holdings selecting limits on voting. In industries in which we would expect ownership to be more democratic, for example textiles, we would find companies with a large number of shareholders with relatively equal holdings of shares selecting democratic voting provisions too. But, again, part of this problem would be corrected with the industry dummies.

Another problem with the analysis is that there were no enduring maximum vote provisions or graduated voting rights. These provisions tended to disappear from company bylaws over time. Two examples from the sample of companies used in this chapter attest to that. First, Banespa, the largest bank in São Paulo, as soon as the government became a large shareholder in 1926, abandoned graduated voting rights. The second example, and even more extreme, is that of the Matarazzo family businesses. This family eliminated the voting cap included in the original bylaws of the holding company Indústrias Reunidas Matarazzo in 1916 and increased its control from 10% of the votes to a majority position by diluting the voting power of smaller shareholders through changes in the minimum share requirement to get one vote. By 1934, the family had full control of the company.[7]

Perhaps the democratic impulses in the investment community were strong only during the financial markets' boom years (from the 1880s to 1915). However, the coefficient that captures time period in which the shareholder's list was collected shows significant coefficient for the dummy "before 1910" only in a couple of specifications.

IMPLICATIONS OF THE STATISTICAL RELATIONS BETWEEN SHAREHOLDER PROTECTIONS AND OWNERSHIP CONCENTRATION

Do these results imply that most corporations in Brazil were widely held before the 1920s? Not really. The corporate landscape of Brazil was more

---

[7] See the changes in statutes made in the extraordinary shareholders' meeting of May 29, 1926 in "Decreto n. 17544 – de 10 de Novembro de 1926" in *Diario Oficial do Estado de São Paulo,* January 4, 1927 and the shareholder list and voting count of the extraordinary shareholder meeting of October 11, 1933 in "Decreto N. 2 – de 25 de Julho de 1934" in *Diario Oficial do Estado de São Paulo,* August 15, 1934.

complex than that. Given the data presented in Panels A and B of Table 5.6 (Appendix 5A), more than 50% of Brazilian companies must have been controlled by families. Yet among the largest corporations many were relatively widely held before 1940. I argue that Brazil had two dominant ownership schemes before the 1940: large, widely held corporations, predominantly railways, banks, and textile mills; and family-owned and -controlled firms with relatively concentrated ownership that tended to be more abusive toward outside shareholders (when they had them).

Widely-held Corporations in Brazil

Panel A of Table 5.6 shows that before 1940 some of Brazil's largest corporations had dispersed ownership and even more dispersed control rights a consequence of the voting schemes that had been adopted. The simplest was a cap on the number of votes available to any single shareholder. The Antarctica Brewery, a company dominated by a few families of German immigrants with large shareholdings, employed this practice. In fact, the concentration of share ownership was quite large (the top three shareholders controlled 62% of the equity). Thanks to the maximum votes per shareholder restriction (of 40 votes) these families had to broker deals to share power. For instance, in 1913, the top three shareholders controlled 58% of total equity, but only 12% of the votes. As an additional check for possible abuses by a single family, the company bylaws included a provision prohibiting two members of the same family from serving on the board simultaneously.[8]

Both voting caps and graduated voting rights reduced the concentration of control significantly in companies such as E. F. Paulista and E. F. Mogyana. In the 1890s, the largest three shareholders of the Paulista and Mogyana owned 10% and 13% of the total shares, but in most shareholder meetings controlled only 7% and 10% of the votes, respectively. The cap on the maximum number of votes was increased as the capital of these companies expanded, and disappeared altogether in some companies as share issues accelerated during the boom years of stock market activity (1890–1913). For E. F. Paulista, dispersion of ownership continued until the company was bailed out by the government in the 1960s.

The reasons railways ended up with such dispersed ownership vary. First, there is obviously an element of magnitude. Railways required a lot

---

[8] See *Estatutos da Companhia Antarctica Paulista*, 1891–1913, published in Decree 217, May 2, 1891; Decree 3348, July 17 1899; Decree 10,036, February 6, 1913; and Cia. Antarctica, *Atas da Assambléia de Acionistas da…*, São Paulo, 1891–1927.

of capital, and thus were more likely to have larger numbers of shareholders. Second, railways' dividends were guaranteed by the federal and state governments, which would be expected to encourage the participation of small shareholders in the companies. Finally, just as in the United States, railways were owned by their main beneficiaries, in this case coffee planters. The shareholder lists of the most important lines of São Paulo represent the elite of coffee plantations.[9] According to William R. Summerhill, railways such as the E. F. Paulista, "tapped mainly rural investors in the interior of São Paulo. Shares of stock for the Paulista were peddled virtually door to door in the interior of the province ... The very *fazendeiros* [coffee planters] who stood to gain so much from the reduction in transport costs were prominent among the company's investors."[10]

In smaller firms such as Companhia Petropolitana, a textile mill, a similar voting rights structure mitigated against concentration of control. This company had begun as a family business outside of Rio in the 1890s. The shareholder list when it was chartered showed somewhat concentrated ownership in the hands of the few founders, who likely introduced the cap on the maximum number of votes as a check against one another's power. But as the company expanded and began to rely on equity issues to finance its growth, the number of shareholders increased. Although ownership was relatively dispersed by 1928, voting caps reduced the voting power of some of the largest shareholders even more. The top three shareholders controlled 20% of equity but only 12% of votes.[11]

Caps on the number of votes available to any single shareholder and graduated voting rights made it difficult for a single group of shareholders to obtain the majority of votes needed to pass resolutions in large, widely held corporations. The 1935 shareholder list of E. F. Paulista affords a detailed look at the size of shareholder blocks that were created by proxy voters. Table 5.4 summarizes the number of shares, number of votes controlled, number of shareholders, and proxy representative for each block of shares that participated in the shareholder meeting of 1935. We can see

[9]   See Anne Hanley, "Is It Who You Know?: Entrepreneurs and Bankers in São Paulo, Brazil, at the Turn of the Twentieth Century," *Enterprise and Society* 5, 2 (2004): 187–225, for a description of some of the relations among these coffee planters and their role in the network of investors and directors in São Paulo.

[10] William R. Summerhill III, *Order Against Progress: Government, Foreign Investment, and Railroads in Brazil, 1854–1913*, Stanford: Stanford University Press, 2003, p. 45.

[11] See "Companhia Petropolitana" in *Diario Oficial*, April 16, 1898 and Companhia Petropolitana, *Relatorio da directoria da Companhia Petropolitana apresentado à Assembléa Geral Ordinaria dos Snrs. Accionistas*, Rio de Janeiro: Typografia Do jornal do Commércio, 1928 and 1929.

Table 5.4. *Voting groups at the E. F. Paulista shareholder meeting, 1935*

Proxy for the group	Number of shares	Votes controlled	% votes	Number of shareholders
Luiz Carneiro	189,524	17,456	30	392
Banco de Comércio e Indústria de S. Paulo	123,038	11,248	19	167
Companhia Prado Chavez	65,386	6,245	11	125
Olympio Félix de Araújo Cintra	67,668	4,157	7	28
Antonio Aymore P. Lima	30,538	3,061	5	49
Banco Francez e Italiano para a America do Sul	43,142	2,330	4	3
C. Paes de Barros Júnior	27,859	1,653	3	3
Banco de Londres e America do Sul	27,347	1,367	2	2
Jose Federico de Souza Martins	8,973	896	2	4
Oscar A. do Nascimento	5,600	560	1	2
João Rodriguez Macedo	10,320	536	1	2
Not in any proxy block	118,429	8,320	14	68
TOTAL	717,824	57,829	100	845

Sources: Cia. Paulista de Estradas de Ferro, "Presença de acionistas em assembléia geral extraordinária de 25 de junho de 1935" and voting rights from *Estatutos da Companhia Paulista de Estradas de Ferro reformados em assembléa geral extraordinária celebrada a 25 de junho de 1926.*

that only one group had more than 20% of the votes. Organizing this group required the cooperation of 392 shareholders who held nearly 190,000 shares. Moreover, to obtain a majority required that at least three groups of proxy voters be in agreement.

Of course, E. F. Paulista is an extreme case of dispersed ownership (with graduated voting and maximum vote provisions). But large blocks of shares represented by proxy voters were not a common occurrence in large Brazilian corporations, at least not in the sample of companies used for the analysis of this chapter. Proxy voting was more commonly found in family companies, where husbands usually represented their wives in shareholder meetings.[12]

---

[12] This was the case in the shareholder meetings of the Matarazzo family companies, the businesses of the family of Puglise Carbone, and others. See the changes in statutes made

Voting Caps in Other Countries

It is important to note that Brazil was not the only country in the world where large corporations had voting caps constraining the power of large shareholders. Consider the United Kingdom, which had one of the largest stock markets in the world (perhaps the largest if cross-listed corporations are counted), yet did not have strong protections for investors in its national laws. Julien Franks, Colin Mayer, and Stefano Rossi suggest that this was possible because "firms upheld the interests of minority shareholders by convention rather than regulation." They describe managers "behaving like gentlemen" owing to directors "concerned to sustain their reputation and the value of their securities" because "equity was primarily issued for and traded by local shareholders with good knowledge of the firms in which they were investing."[13]

There were, however, other protections that mattered for the development of equity markets in the United Kingdom at the end of the nineteenth century. Leslie Hannah argues that the London Stock Exchange, by requiring external auditing of accounts and mandatory disclosure, contributed to the improvement of corporate governance after 1900.[14] Campbell and Turner find this account insufficient to explain the sustained growth in stock markets, noting that local stock exchanges "simply performed a screening function for initial public offerings" and that companies had dispersed ownership that included investors well beyond the geographical location of the company.[15] Their research suggests that perhaps more important for attracting shareholders than either national laws or the regulation of local

in the extraordinary shareholders' meeting of Indústrias Reúnidas Matarazzo of May 29, 1926 in "Decreto n. 17544 – de 10 de Novembro de 1926" in *Diario Oficial do Estado de São Paulo,* January 4, 1927 and the shareholder list and voting count of the extraordinary shareholder meeting of October 11, 1933 in "Decreto N. 2 – de 25 de Julho de 1934" in *Diario Oficial do Estado de São Paulo,* August 15, 1934. For the practices of the Puglise Carbone see "Companhia Puglise" in *Diário Oficial do Estado de São Paulo,* August 9, 1922, and September 23, 1923.

[13] Julian Franks, Colin Mayer, and Stefano Rossi, "Ownership: Evolution and Regulation," Institute of Finance and Accounting Working Paper FIN 401, London Business School, 2004, pp. 32–33.
[14] External auditing of corporate accounts, a British innovation, was the "work of professional accountants under the self-regulating auspices of the Institute for Chartered Accountants of England and Wales." See Leslie Hannah, "Pioneering Modern Corporate Governance: A View from London in 1900," CIRJE Discussion Papers, University of Tokyo, Japan, March 2007, pp. 15–18, quote from p. 15.
[15] Gareth Campbell and John D. Turner, "Protecting Outside Investors in a Laissez-faire Legal Environment: Corporate Governance in Victorian Britain," paper presented at the Business History Conference, Cleveland, June 2007, for quotes see pp. 9–10. Most of the data are from Table 2. Results of the dividend regressions are presented in Tables 8 to 10.

stock exchanges were the protections afforded shareholders at the company level. They note that in 1883, 43% of the 716 companies for which they have data had graduated voting scales and 23% had maximum vote provisions. In the aggregate, 52% of corporations had caps on voting, graduated voting schemes, or a combination thereof. The percentage of companies with graduated voting was even higher for railways (88%), banks (59%), insurance companies (49%), and docks (67%). In banking, textiles, insurance, and canals, approximately 40% of companies had maximum vote provisions. Such provisions, even if they did not yield higher dividend payments or returns, must have provided sufficient assurances to induce investors to purchase equity rather than invest in other securities or activities.[16]

The situation was not different on the other side of the Atlantic, where protections for outside investors also tended to be stronger in companies' bylaws than in national laws. Gonzalo Islas Rojas shows that, notwithstanding the lack of protections for shareholders in Chile's national laws, by the 1870s the Chilean stock market represented 17% of GDP (more than any other Latin American market at the time). Using all of the corporate charters issued in Chile from the 1850s to 1902, he shows that the majority of companies had relatively diffused ownership and strong firm-level protections for shareholders. Forty-five percent of the population of Chilean corporations chartered in the second half of the twentieth century had maximum vote provisions and almost 10% graduated voting scales. Islas Rojas estimates that most companies' bylaws included about four of the protections for shareholders identified by La Porta et al. when they created their shareholder protections indices. It is perhaps because of these protections on company statutes that ownership dispersion was common in Chilean corporations.[17]

Yoshiro Miwa and J. Mark Ramseyer's study of cotton textile corporations in Meiji, Japan, reveals remarkable parallels between corporate governance in Japanese and Brazilian companies. They show that in contrast to the concentrated ownership that today characterizes Japan, the cotton industry between the 1880s and the 1890s had diffused ownership. On average, firms had 331 shareholders. "[T]he largest investors held about 8 percent of the stock, the five largest together held 24 percent, and the 10 largest held 33 percent.... [I]n no firm did the largest shareholder hold 50 percent or more of the stock, and in only three firms did a shareholder hold 20 percent." These corporations,

---

[16] Campbell and Turner, "Protecting Outside Investors in a Laissez-faire Legal Environment," Table 2. Results of the dividend regressions are presented in Tables 8 to 15.

[17] Gonzalo Islas Rojas, "Does Regulation Matter?: An Analysis of Corporate Charters in a Laissez-faire Environment," unpublished manuscript, University of California Los Angeles, September 2007, see pp. 15 and 48.

according to the authors, attracted investors through charter provisions that aligned the incentives of managers with their firms (as by tying managerial pay to profits) by restricting managerial discretion "by charter and statute" and by hiring reputable industrialists to their boards of directors. For example, even though "the Commercial Code provided a one-share-one-vote default rule, firms could legally reduce the voting power of the largest shareholders" by, for example, adopting graduated voting scales. Miwa and Ramseyer estimate that before 1893 112 out of 134 companies used some form of voting rights that restricted the power of large shareholders. This number decreased after 1893, but still 20% of companies used graduated voting between 1893 and 1900. Finally, companies hired reputable industrialists to monitor their managers, knowing that the reputations of these distinguished gentlemen were too valuable for them to do a poor job.[18]

Finally, Eric Hilt's research on early New York corporations reveals that corporate bylaws often gave critical protection to small investors in the form of voting provisions that limited the power of large shareholders. Colleen Dunlavy also argues that voting rights mattered in the nineteenth century; she points out that company laws in certain U.S. states protected shareholders more strongly when they included mandatory graduated voting scales (owners had fewer votes per share as their shares increased). Yet those protections disappeared after the 1880s as many of the most industrialized U.S. states began to mandate one-share, one-vote provisions. In fact, even though the United States had some relatively good practices in the earlier part of the nineteenth century, and while it offers strong shareholder protections today, according to Naomi Lamoreaux and Jean-Laurent Rosenthal, protections for minority U.S. shareholders were relatively weak during the late nineteenth and early twentieth centuries. Their findings are based on an extensive set of court cases that show directors and large shareholders to have been "engaged in a variety of ... actions from which they benefited at the expense of their associates."[19]

---

[18] Yoshiro Miwa and J. Mark Ramseyer, "Corporate Governance in Transitional Economies: Lessons from the Prewar Japanese Cotton Textile Industry," *Journal of Legal Studies* 29, 1 (January 2000): 171–203, quotes from pp. 180, 192, 198–199.

[19] See Hilt, "When Did Ownership Separate from Control?," 645–685; Colleen Dunlavy, "Corporate Governance in Late 19th-Century Europe and the U.S.: The Case of Shareholder Voting Rights," In Klaus J. Hopt, H. Kanda, Mark J. Roe, E. Wymeersch, and S. Prigge (eds.), *Corporate Governance: The State of the Art of Emerging Research*, Oxford: Clarendon Press, 1998, p. 28; and Naomi Lamoreaux and Jean-Laurent Rosenthal, "Corporate Governance and the Plight of Minority Shareholders in the United States before the Great Depression," in Edward Glaeser and Claudia Goldin (eds.), *Corruption and Reform*, Chicago: University of Chicago Press, 2006, 147.

Family-owned Corporations in Brazil

The other ownership pattern that prevailed in Brazil after 1890, which stood in contrast to companies that adopted rules to prevent control by a few shareholders, was the family-controlled corporation in which family members held large blocks of shares and occupied most managerial positions. An example of a family-owned corporation was the Companhia Fabricadora de Papel (Klabin) controlled by the Klabin family (see Panel B in Table 5.6), members of which occupied three of five directorships from the company's beginnings. Eight of the 36 shareholders of the company were part of this family, and only one of the top five shareholders was not an immediate family member, the other four being three brothers and the partnership Klabin Irmãos & Comp. (a firm of the Klabin brothers). The top five shareholders controlled 75% of the firm's equity.

In fact, the corporation was organized somewhat like a partnership. All shareholders had one vote per share, and the directors did not have a fixed salary until 1937. Profits were divided among the directors and shareholders following a formula that guaranteed 10% of profits to directors plus an extra 20% of any amount after paying a 12% dividend. In 1937, the company gave the partnership Klabin Irmãos & Comp. control of 75% of total equity in exchange for forgiving accumulated debt. The Klabin family continued to expand its empire, and by the 1970s controlled one of the largest business conglomerates of Brazil, making the list of the top 100 business groups every year.[20]

No family was more prominent in business in Brazil during the early part of the twentieth century than the Matarazzo family (see the bottom of Panel C in Table 5.6). In the 1890s, Count Francisco de Matarazzo and his family started a trading business selling staples and imported goods to coffee plantations in the interior of São Paulo.[21] Importing know-how and resources from Europe, this Italian family expanded rapidly into the processing of sugar, wheat, and pork lard, and within a few years was running a diversified business that operated everything from textile mills to commercial houses. By 1911, the business was so large that the family created the first conglomerate in Brazil, the Indústrias Reunidas Fábricas Matarazzo, opening up the

---

[20] See "Estatutos da Companhia Fabricadora de Papel (Klabin)" in *Diário Oficial do Estado de São Paulo*, June 15, 1909 and "Cia. Fabricadora de Papel (Klabin)" in *Diário Oficial do Estado de São Paulo*, May 8, 1937.

[21] In 1891 the Matarazzo family chartered their first corporation, the Companhia Matarazzo. The main objective of this company was to process and sell pork lard in the states of São Paulo and Rio Grande do Sul. This company required 10 shares to get one vote and capped the number of votes at 50. See "Cia. Matarrazo" in *Diario Oficial do Estado de São Paulo*, June 2, 1891.

capital to subscription by friends and other family members. The statutes were, by design, somewhat democratic, incorporating in 1911, for example, ten shares for one vote and maximum of 50 votes rules. This voting scheme restricted the top three, five, and ten shareholders, who controlled most of the equity, to 10%, 17%, and 34% of total votes, respectively. But the scheme lasted only a few years. By the 1920s, the Matarazzo family had purchased back most of the equity held by nonfamily members and changed the voting rights, first pulverizing share ownership by issuing thousands of small-denomination shares, then altering the statutes to restrict the right to vote to only those with holdings of 1,000$ (a thousand mil-reis). In 1934, only four or five shareholders held enough shares to vote. From that time on, the family purchased most shares and held them tightly.[22]

The Matarazzo family controlled a variety of businesses including the Banco Italiano del Brasile, the complete shareholder lists of which help illuminate its approach to corporate governance (see Panel B of Table 5.6). The bank originally had a relatively large number of shareholders from the Italian community, though the Matarazzos controlled most of the equity and shares. Then, in 1907, the family used its voting power to dissolve the firm and sell its assets to another bank that it controlled.

This model of concentrated ownership under family control is stereotypical for Brazil, though it has not always been the dominant model. Many of the family businesses before the 1930s were relatively small enterprises compared to railways and large banks. But by the 1980s, family-controlled conglomerates had become the dominant corporate form (see Chapter 10).

There were thus two dominant ownership structures in Brazil before the 1940s: companies in which families controlled a large part of the shares and supplied most of the managers, and corporations with dispersed ownership that included in their bylaws such strong protections for smaller shareholders as caps on the number of votes available to individual shareholders.

THE AGGREGATE EVIDENCE ON OWNERSHIP CONCENTRATION IN THE LONG RUN

Concentration of ownership in Brazil seems to have been lower between 1890 and 1910 than afterward. Table 5.5 displays mean and median ownership

---

[22] See the changes in statutes made in the extraordinary shareholders' meeting of May 29, 1926 in "Decreto n. 17544 – de 10 de Novembro de 1926" in *Diario Oficial do Estado de São Paulo*, January 4, 1927 and the shareholder list and voting count of the extraordinary shareholder meeting of October 11, 1933 in "Decreto N. 2 – de 25 de Julho de 1934" in *Diario Oficial do Estado de São Paulo*, August 15, 1934.

Table 5.5. *Evolution of ownership concentration and control in Brazil, 1890–2004*

	Before 1910	1910–1920	1920–1957	1998	1998	2004	2004
Sample size	23	24	14	All traded	20 largest	All traded	20 largest
Shares owned by top 3 shareholders							
Mean	0.53	0.59	0.53	59.6	52.2	66.5	51.2
Median	0.46	0.63	0.55	57.6	51.8	69.4	46.5
Votes controlled by top 3 shareholders							
Mean	0.53	0.52	0.55	81.5	74.7	84.9	76.6
Median	0.47	0.55	0.59	86.3	83.9	90.2	83.4

Sources: Estimated by the author using data in Appendix 5A. The table excludes repeated observations for the same company (takes the average by company in the time period). Data for 1998 and 2004 created by the author using the database of Economatica. Top 20 companies selected on the basis of total assets as reported by Bovespa (São Paulo's Stock Exchange).

concentration for all companies for which I have information. Before 1910 the three largest shareholders controlled between 46% and 53% of shares and between 47% and 53% of total votes. These figures are not so high relative to the average ownership concentration in England during the same period. In a sample of 40 British firms between 1900 and 1910, the largest shareholders were estimated to have controlled between 52.86% and 64.39% of total equity, slightly higher than the average for Brazil. This is impressive if we take into account the fact that London was the most developed financial center.[23] After the 1920s, Brazilian corporations exhibited more concentrated ownership, the three largest shareholders holding between 59% and 63% of the shares and controlling between 52% and 55% of the votes. Still, these figures are slightly biased upward by the fact that most of the sample comes from companies before they were traded in stock markets.

Even if the data before the 1940s is slightly biased upward there are significant differences in the concentration of control in Brazil before 1910 and during the period 1998–2004 (see Table 5.5). Whereas before 1910 the three largest shareholders controlled approximately 47% of the votes, they controlled, on average, between 82% and 84% of the votes in 1998 and 2004 (the standard deviation being only 16% in both cases). Even in the sample between 1910 and 1957 the three largest shareholders controlled less than 60% of the votes.

[23] See Franks et al., "Ownership," Table 4.

In sum, the evidence presented in this chapter suggests an increase in ownership concentration over the twentieth century, particularly steep in the second half of this century. Given the statistical findings of this chapter, voting provisions distributing the power of shareholders in a more even way might have been an important reason why ownership and control were less concentrated in the past than today.

CONCLUSION

This chapter argues that investor protections did matter for the development of equity markets and democratization of stock ownership in Brazil. Protections such as maximum vote provisions and government-guaranteed dividends induced more shareholders to buy equity in Brazilian corporations, thereby reducing concentration of ownership and control.

What is striking about the effects of voting provisions is that they were so binding. For instance, in companies that included maximum vote provisions or graduated voting schemes large shareholders were willing to hold a large proportion of shares, even if they gave them less than proportional voting power. Though in some of those companies cash flows in the form of dividends were higher, the difference between the holdings of cash flow rights (shares) and control rights (votes) seems disproportionate in some cases. This truly speaks of a democratic attitude on the part of these large shareholders. Perhaps company founders and insiders understood well that the only way to attract outside shareholders was to share power with them. In other cases, when the statutes were designed by a large group of initial shareholders, they intentionally promoted this even distribution of power among themselves.

The initial period of stock market development also coincided with what appears to have been a period of lower concentration of ownership and control (mainly before 1910), implying that most of the concentration of ownership and control rights that we find in Brazil today is a product of the twentieth century rather than a direct consequence of the country's French civil law heritage. How ownership and control ended up so concentrated is also related to the fact that family firms, not widely held corporations, prevailed and became in the long term the dominant corporate form. This evolution is explored further in Chapter 8. But before exploring how investor protections came to decline, the book examines, in the next two chapters, their consequences. Chapter 6 examines executive compensation and Chapter 7 looks at creditor rights.

APPENDIX 5A

Table 5.6. *Ownership concentration in some of Brazil's largest corporations*

Panel A. Multiple corporations with relatively dispersed ownership

Year	Company	Sector	Capital in million US$ of 1900	Grad. voting	Max votes	No. of shareholders	Shares of top 3 sh.	Votes of top 3 sh.	HHI	IPO	Est.
1869	E. F. Paulista	Railway	2.50	Y	Y	64	0.02	0.03	0.00	N	1869
1872	E. F. Paulista	Railway	2.59	Y	Y	654	0.10	0.05	0.00	N	1869
1873	E. F. Mogyana	Railway	1.49	Y	Y	350	0.13	0.06	0.01	N	1872
1883	E. F. Paulista	Railway	2.40	Y	Y	153	0.13	0.02	0.01	N	1869
1883	E. F. Mogyana	Railway	4.79	Y	Y	395	0.13	0.04	0.00	N	1872
1889	Tecidos D. Isabel	Textiles	0.10	N	Y	13	0.36	0.36	0.09	Y	1889
1889	Banespa	Bank		Y	N	150	0.14	0.13	0.02	N	1889
1890	São Paulo Fabril	Manuf.	0.08	N	Y	37	0.30	0.30	0.05	Y	1890
1890	Banespa	Bank		Y	N	135	0.13	0.11	0.02	N	1889
1891	São Paulo Industrial	Multiple	0.03	N	Y	51	0.40	0.38	0.07	Y	1891
1891	Industrial Rodovalho	Multiple	0.62	N	Y	30	0.05	0.15	0.07	Y	1891
1892	Antarctica Paulista	Beer	0.71	N	Y	57	0.62	0.14	0.03	Y	1891
1892	Tecidos Esperança	Textiles	0.31	N	N	52	0.26	0.26	0.04	N	1892
1892	E. F. Mogyana	Railway	7.08	Y	N	168	0.13	0.10	0.01	N	1872

(continued)

Table 5.6 *(continued)*

			Capital in million US\$ of 1900	Grad. voting	Max votes	No. of shareholders	Shares of top 3 sh.	Votes of top 3 sh.	HHI	IPO	Est.
			Panel A. Multiple corporations with relatively dispersed ownership								
Year	Company	Sector									
1898	Petropolitana	Textiles	0.71	N	Y	43	0.44	0.27	0.06	N	1898
1898	E. F. Paulista	Railway	0.89	Y	Y	514	0.10	0.07	0.00	N	1869
1899	Banespa	Bank		Y	N	48	0.57	0.49	0.11	N	1889
1899	Viação Férrea Sapucaí	Railway	0.03	N	N	217	0.22			N	1891
1900	Nacional de Tec. de Linho	Textiles	0.38	N	N	41	0.46	0.46	0.11	Y	1900
1903	Tecidos Cometa	Textiles	0.64	N	Y	46	0.36	0.36	0.09	N	1903
1904	Dos Funccionarios Publicos	Bank	0.48	N	N		0.39	0.39		N	1891
1905	Fiação e Tecidos Santa Maria	Textiles	0.08	N	N	27	0.33	0.34	0.07	Y	1905
1906	E.F. do Dourado	Railways	0.77	Y	N	36	0.92	0.84	0.37	Y	1899
1907	Brasileira de Alpargatas	Shoes	0.21	N	N	41	0.45		0.09	N	1907
1908	E. F. Mogyana	Railway	16.67	Y	N	461	0.08	0.06	0.00	N	1872
1910	Banespa	Bank	1.39	Y	N	58	0.18	0.15	0.04	N	1889
1911	Usinas Nacionais	Agriculture	0.26	N	N	35	0.50	0.50	0.12	N	1911

1911	Mercantil do Rio de Janeiro	Bank	1.10	N	N		0.14	0.12		N	1911
1912	Petropolis Industrial	Textiles	0.11	N	N	50	0.30	0.30	0.06	N	1912
1912	Paulista de Forçae Luz	Utilities	0.44	N	N	63	0.23	0.23	0.04	N	1912
1913	Antarctica Paulista	Beer	1.97	Y	N	80	0.58	0.12	0.03	N	1891
1913	Telefonica do Est. de S. Paulo	Utilities	1.16	N	N	48	0.39	0.40	0.10	Y	1884
1918	E. F. Mogyana	Railway	13.60	N	Y	433	0.36	0.27	0.06	N	1872
1918	Banespa	Bank		N	Y	71	0.34	0.33	0.06	N	1889
1922	E. F. Paulista	Railway	2.86	Y	Y	268	0.21	0.15	0.02	N	1869
1926	Antarctica Paulista	Beer	0.98	Y	N	65	0.80	0.13	0.03	N	1891
1926	Santa Luzia Industrial	Textiles	0.04	N	N	63	0.41	0.41	0.08	N	1926
1926	Banespa	Bank	2.30	N	N	217	0.14	0.14	0.02	N	1889
1928	Petropolitana	Textiles	0.67	Y	N	227	0.20	0.12	0.02	N	1898
1932	Banespa	Bank		N	N	217	0.20	0.20	0.03	N	1889
1935	E. F. Paulista	Railway	37.76	Y	Y	845	0.14	0.09	0.01	N	1869
1937	Cimento Portland	Cement	0.71	N	N	81	0.34	0.34	0.06	Y	1937
1942	Tecelagem Divinópolis	Textiles		N	N	247	0.25	0.25	0.03	N	1942
1943	Panair do Brasil S. A.	Airline	5.15	N	N	1238	0.61	0.61	0.33	N	1943

(continued)

Table 5.6 (continued)

Panel A. Multiple corporations with relatively dispersed ownership

Year	Company	Sector	Capital in million US$ of 1900	Grad. voting	Max votes	No. of shareholders	Shares of top 3 sh.	Votes of top 3 sh.	HHI	IPO	Est.
1946	Refinaria de Petróleos (D. F.)	Oil refining	2.39	N	N	75	0.36	0.36	0.08	Y	1946
1947	Refrigerantes Guanabara	Soft drinks	0.26	N	N	220	0.34	0.34	0.04	Y	1947
1947	E. F. Paulista	Railway	17.39	Y	Y	267	0.31	0.03	0.05	N	1869
1951	Lanari Engenharia	Services	0.51	N	N	44	0.35	0.35	0.08	Y	1945
1957	E. F. Paulista	Railway	4.97	Y	Y	487	0.17	0.14	0.01	N	1869

Panel B. Ownership concentration in government-controlled corporations

Year	Company	Sector	Capital in million US$ of 1900	Grad. voting	Max votes	Num. of shareholders	Shares of top 3 sh.	Votes of top 3 sh.	HHI	IPO	Est.
1941	Banespa	Bank		N	N	17	0.98	0.98	0.93	N	1889
1941	Cia Siderurgica Nacional	Steel	41.24	N	N	129	0.73	0.73	0.25	N	1941
1944	Cia Nacional de Alcalis	Chemicals	2.76	N	N	630	0.52	1.00	1.00	N	1944
1950	Banespa	Bank		N	N		1.00	1.00	0.97	N	1889

Panel C. Family-controlled corporations

Year	Company	Sector	Capital in million US$ of 1900	Grad. voting	Max votes	No. of shareholders	Shares of top 3 sh.	Votes of top 3 sh.	HHI	IPO	Est.
1890	Industrial de São Paulo	Multiple	0.24	N	N	53	0.60	0.60	0.24	N	1890
1890	Fiação e Tecidos Santa Barbara	Textiles	1.62	N	N	8	0.59	0.60	0.18	Y	1890
1891	Cia de Tecelagem Santa Luiza	Textiles	0.11	N	Y	8	0.80	0.59	0.43	Y	1891
1901	Lloyd Brazileiro	Shipping	6.76	N	N	9	0.75	0.75	0.22	N	1890
1905	Fiação e Tecidos Sacramento	Textiles	0.10	N	Y	9	1.00	0.99	0.37	Y	1905
1905	Banco Italiano del Brasile	Bank	0.65	N	N	195	0.68	0.68	0.21	N	1905
1907	Tecelagem Italo-Brasileira	Textiles	0.08	N	N	13	0.82	0.82	0.39	N	1907
1907	Cia. Puglise	Multiple	0.51	N	N	12	0.80	0.80	0.31	Y	1907
1907	Banco Italiano del Brasile	Bank	0.64	N	N	40	0.74	0.73	0.25	N	1905
1908	Sao Bernardo Fabril	Textiles	0.48	Y	N	8	1.00	1.00	0.40	Y	1908
1909	Cotonificio Rodolfo Crespi	Textiles	0.72	N	N	20	0.92	0.92	0.71	N	1909

(continued)

Table 5.6 (continued)

Year	Company	Sector	Capital in million US$ of 1900	Grad. voting	Max votes	No. of shareholders	Shares of top 3 sh.	Votes of top 3 sh.	HHI	IPO	Est.
						Panel C. Family-controlled corporations					
1909	Força e Luz de Santa Cruz	Utilities	0.12	N	N	13	0.83	0.83	0.27	N	1909
1909	Fabricadora de Papel (Klabin)	Manuf.	0.36	N	N	36	0.49	0.49	0.11	N	1909
1911	Ind. Reunidas Fab. Matarazzo	Multiple	2.31	N	Y	74	0.83	0.10	0.03	N	1891
1912	Brasileira de Ar Liquido	Manuf.	0.06	N	N	14	0.73	0.73	0.26	N	1912
1912	E. F. Paracatu	Railroads	2.21	N	N	14	1.00	1.00	0.39	Y	1912
1912	Sao Bernardo Fabril	Textiles	0.77	Y	N	11	0.94	0.88	0.54	Y	1908
1912	Industrial Fluminense	Construction	0.11	N	N	12	0.81	0.82	0.24	Y	1912
1912	Quimica Brasileira	Manuf.	0.02	N	N	14	0.55	0.55	0.13	N	1912
1913	Tecidos Santa Rosa	Textiles	0.12	N	N	34	0.57	0.58	0.20	N	1913
1919	Lanificio Petropolis	Textiles	0.19	N	N	10	0.95	0.95	0.58	Y	1919
1919	Cia. Fiação e Tecelagem Alegria	Textiles	0.16	N	N	18	0.63	0.63	0.21	N	1919

1922	Lanifício Minerva	Textiles	0.43	N	15	0.98	0.98	0.93	N	1922
1923	Cia. Puglise	Multiple	1.97	N	12	0.96	0.96	0.38	Y	1907
1923	Energia Eletrica Rio Grandense	Utilities	0.39	N	17	0.65	0.65	0.28	Y	1923
1924	Carbonifera Prospera	Mining	0.35	N	14	0.74	0.74	0.27	Y	1924
1931	Cia. Ferro Brasileiro	Manuf.	0.25	N	18	0.93	0.93	0.34	Y	1931
1934	Ind. Reunidas Fab. Matarazzo	Multiple	2.41	N	13	0.95	1.00	0.51	N	1891
1937	Renascença Industrial	Textiles	0.61	N	78	0.59	0.59	0.16	N	1937
1937	Ind. Reunidas Fab. Matarazzo	Multiple	3.55	N	14	0.53	0.65	0.21	N	1891
1949	Cia. Lancaster	Textiles	0.30	N	15	0.80	0.80	0.34	Y	1949

Sources: "Panair do Brasil, S. A." in *Diário Oficial*, December 27, 1943; "Sociedade Anonyma Fabrica de Tecidos Esperança" in Diario Official, julho 16, 1919; "Companhia Fiação e Tecelagem Alegria," in *Diário Oficial*, 12/06/1919; "Companhia Luz e Força de Santa Cruz," in *Diário Oficial*, 10/23/1909; "Companhia Paulista de Força e Luz" in *Diário Oficial do Estado de São Paulo*, 16 de novembro de 1912; "Companhia Petropolis Industrial," *Diário Oficial*, 30/11/1912; "Companhia Petropolis Industrial," *Diário Oficial*, 30/11/1912; "Companhia Puglise" in *Diário Oficial do Estado de São Paulo*, 10/17/1907 and 9/23/1923; "Companhia Renascença Industrial" in *Diário Oficial do Estado de Minas Gerais*, 3/19/1937; "Companhia S. Bernardo Fabril" in *Diário Oficial do Estado de São Paulo*, 2/7/1908 and 2/7/1915; "Companhia Telephonica do Estado de São Paulo" in *Diário Oficial do Estado de São Paulo*, 1/30/1913; "Cotonifício Rodolpho Crespi" in *Diário Oficial do Estado de São Paulo*, 4/1/1909; "Estatutos da Companhia S. Paulo Industrial" in *Diário Oficial do Estado de São Paulo*, 10/21/1891; "Estatutos da Sociedade Anônyma Lanifícios Minerva" in *Diário Oficial*, January 6, 1922; "Estatutos da Sociedade Anônyma Tecelagem Italo-Brazileira" in *Diário Oficial do Estado de São Paulo*, 4/25/1907; "Estrada de Ferro do Dourado," Bolsa de Valores do Rio de Janeiro, Sociedades Anônimas, Transportes, Caixa 2166; "Fiação e Tecelagem Divinopolis S.A., Extraordinária," in *Diário Oficial do Estado de Minas Gerais*, 22/03/1942; "Lanari Engenharia, Industria e Comercio,"in *Diário Oficial do Estado de São Paulo*, 08/12/1951; "Publica Forma. Primero Traslado de Escriptura de Constituição de Sociedade Anônyma (Comp. Brasileira de Ar Liquido)" in *Diário Oficial do Estado de São Paulo*, 9/3/1912; "Santa Luzia Industrial S.A." in *Diário Oficial do Estado de Minas Gerais*, 2/23/1926; "Sociedade Anonyma Companhia Chimica Brazileira" in i, 8/20/1912; "Tecidos Cometa" in *Diário Oficial*, May 12, 1903; "Usinas Nacionais" in *Diário Oficial*, 6/3/1911.

(*continued*)

133

Table 5.6 (continued)

Banco do Estado de São Paulo, *Atas da Assembléia de Acionistas do Banco do Estado de São Paulo*, Museu Banespa, São Paulo, Brazil, 1889–1950. Antarctica Paulista, Cia. *Atas da Assembléia de Acionistas da* . . ., São Paulo, 1891–1927 (São Paulo State Archive); Antarctica Paulista, Cia. *Estatutos da Companhia Antarctica Paulista*, 1891–1913, published in Decree 217, May 2, 1891, Decree 3348, July 17 1899, Decree 10,036, February 6, 1913; Banco Dos Funcionarios Públicos. *Relatório apresentado pelo presidente do Banco dos Funcionarios Públicos*. Rio de Janeiro: Typographia Leuzinger, 1904; Banco Mercantil do Rio de Janeiro, *Lista dos Acionistas do Banco Mercantil do Rio de Janeiro em 31 de Julho de 1911*, Rio de Janeiro: typ. Leuzinger, 1911; *Estatutos da Companhia Industrial de São Paulo*, São Paulo: Typographia a Vapor de Jorge Seckler & Comp., 1891 (São Paulo State Archive); *Estatutos da Companhia Industrial Rodovalho*, São Paulo: Companhia Impressora Paulista, 1891 (São Paulo State Archive); *Estatutos da Companhia São Paulo Fabril*, São Paulo: Companhia Impressora Paulista, 1890 (São Paulo State Archive); Fiação e Tecidos Santa Rosa, Cia. *Estatutos*, 07/09/1913 (São Paulo State Archive); Mogyana (Mojiana) de Estradas de Ferro, Cia. *Relatório da Diretoria em Assembléia Geral* . . . 1878–1922 (São Paulo State Archive); Paulista de Estradas de Ferro, Cia. *Presença de Acionistas em Assembléia* . . . São Paulo, 1869–1957 (São Paulo State Archive); Petropolitana, Companhia. *Relatorio da directoria da Companhia Petropolitana apresentado à Assembléa Geral Ordinaria dos Snrs. Accionistas*, Rio de Janeiro: Typ. Do jornal do Commércio, 1928 and 1929

Notes: Panel A: Under the voting scheme used by E.F. Paulista and E.F. Mogyana, five shares were required for each additional vote up to 50 votes, 10 shares for each additional vote from 51 up to 150 votes, and 20 shares for each additional vote thereafter. These maximum vote numbers changed over time. The scheme employed by The Banco do Estado de Sao Paulo required 20 shares for each additional vote up to 50 votes and 40 shares per vote thereafter until the 1920s, after which only 10 shares were required for each vote. The Estrada de Ferro do Dourado required five to get one vote until a limit of 50 votes. After that 20 shares were required to get one vote. Panel C: The São Bernardo Fabril had a graduated voting system that required five shares to vote up to 10 votes. Then for shareholdings between 50 and 100 it required 10 shares per vote. For shareholdings between 100 and 1000 shares it required 20 shares per vote, and 30 shares per vote thereafter.

SIX

Directors, Corporate Governance, and Executive
Compensation in Brazil, c. 1909

Shareholder abuse today is commonly associated with excessively large
executive compensation packages or outright fraud. Directors extract value,
for example, through compensation packages that pay large fixed salaries
and provide significant additional payments or fees if a company meets or
exceeds performance goals. But many of these concerns are related to the
secrecy of executive compensation. Both in Brazil and in other places such
as the United States, shareholders in large corporations have no clear idea
of how much the CEO makes after stock options and other fees and benefits
are taken into account.

During the period under study in this book, Brazilian companies exhibited a very different approach to executive compensation. The statutes of
all corporations had to be published in newspapers with wide circulation
(in the state where the company was going to operate) and these statutes
included valuable information for shareholders, including the fixed salary
of all of the directors and the percentage of profits that they would receive
as performance-based compensation.

The company statutes of Brazilian corporations typically included three
provisions to keep directors' incentives aligned with those of shareholders.
First, most company bylaws required that directors be shareholders. On
average, corporations required that directors own at least 1.2% (standard
deviation 2.5%) of total paid-up capital and keep their shares on deposit
with the company throughout their tenure, a provision referred to as directors' "qualifications" in company statutes. Second, corporate statutes typically required that directors' annual or monthly fixed salaries be disclosed.
Third, shareholders often used additional performance-based compensation to align directors' interests with their own.

Although the structure of incentives was similar between companies in
Brazil, Great Britain, and other countries at the time, Brazilian companies

were unique in that executive compensation and fees were determined at annual shareholder meetings and published in the company statutes. It was possible for any shareholder to know precisely the annual fixed salary and estimate the end-of-year bonus to which each of the directors of the company were entitled.

This chapter uses that information to estimate the salaries of the presidents of the boards of managing directors of a sample of 116 corporations from all around Brazil circa 1909. A comparison of these figures to the salaries of companies in the United States and England shows that the presidents of the boards of directors, who usually also acted as CEOs, were relatively large. It is hard to disentangle whether these high salaries should have been expected because, on the one hand, in a talent-scarce economy qualified work should be highly compensated, especially relative to the salaries of countries where talent was more abundant; on the other hand, large salaries could be a sign that directors were abusing shareholders by obtaining large compensation packages.

The last section of this chapter examines the hypothesis that large salaries were a sign of shareholder abuse by exploring the correlation between executive compensation and governance provisions. In particular, the premise of the test is that one way to see if high salaries are a sign of extraction of shareholder value would be to see if companies with provisions limiting the power of large shareholders (e.g., caps on voting) or those with lower requirements to vote (e.g., one-share, one-vote) paid their directors lower salaries (after controlling for industry, size, and other factors). In companies in which shareholders had more power vis-à-vis directors it should have been be harder for directors to get a salary above the rates that prevailed in the market. Since the evidence does not yield any significant relation between governance measures and director salaries, the chapter concludes by arguing that perhaps the high salaries were just a reflection of the "talent premium" (the premium companies have to pay to have talented managers) or a sign that in some companies there was some extraction of shareholder value.

BOARDS OF DIRECTORS, INCENTIVE STRUCTURE, AND DIRECTOR COMPENSATION

One of the most striking features of the system of corporate governance in Brazil before 1940 was that company statutes were publicly available and contained detailed information on the compensation of directors. Most of the data used in the analyses performed here are from the compilation of company statutes published in the *Brazilian Year Book 1909*, a document that contains firm-level data on many variables including the number of shares required to be deposited with the company during executives' terms, executives' annual salaries, and the structure of performance-based fees (e.g., as a percentage of net profits or dividend payouts).

Brazilian companies had a two-tier board system consisting of a three- to four-member board of managing directors and a three-member oversight board charged with auditing the companies' financial statements (the term, size, and duties of the oversight board were regulated by national company laws). All directors were elected by shareholders, and the president or chairman of the board of directors usually served as well as CEO with the help of superintendents in each factory or division.

Most companies had, on average, three managing directors who were usually elected from among the shareholders at the annual shareholder meeting. Directors' terms of service varied across corporations, but ranged from three to six years (the average for 1909 was four years; see Table 6.1). To be named director, one had to deposit a certain number of shares at the company. The size of this deposit or qualification was 1.2% of paid-up capital, on average.

Executive compensation in Brazil circa 1909 was structured in much the same way as in, for instance, contemporaneous British firms.[1] Total executive compensation was divided into two parts, a fixed, monetary salary (on average about US$2,725, or 15,000 mil reis) and, often, a performance-based component that was a percentage of either total profits or total dividend payments. The performance-based portion of executives' salaries was usually 5–10% of net profits after deducting dividends and reserve funds. Most companies deducted 10% of profits for the reserve fund, but some "careful" companies deducted an additional 5% for depreciation of machinery. Many companies less strict with their reserve funds, however, deducted only the 5% mandated by law.[2] Sometimes, performance-based fees were a percentage of the total dividend payout. In those cases the fees were usually 5–10% of dividends (mean = 6.33%).

---

[1] British firms paid director fees following a similar scheme. For a sketch of how corporate governance and executive compensation worked in England, see Leslie Hannah, "Pioneering Modern Corporate Governance: A View from London in 1900," CIRJE Discussion Papers, University of Tokyo, Japan, March 2007, p. 26.

[2] The amount deducted varied across companies. In cases in which this provision was not explicit, the law mandated that a minimum of 5% of net profits be deducted for a reserve fund up to a maximum of 25% of total paid-up capital. See Article 324, Law 603, October 20, 1891.

Table 6.1. *Management composition and incentive structure in Brazilian corporations (by industry), c. 1909*

	Agriculture	Banks	Insurance	Manufacturing	Mining	Railways	Shipping & ports	Services	Utilities	Total sample
	N = 11	N = 23	N = 19	N = 57	N = 4	N = 10	N = 10	N = 111	N = 15	N = 160
Management										
Number of managing directors	2.6	3.6	3.0	2.7	2.8	3.2	3.3	2.4	2.8	2.9
Directors' term (years)	3.6	3.5	4.0	3.9	2.0	3.9	5.0	3.5	6.0	3.9
Executive incentive structure										
Qualifications as a % of equity[a]	0.86	0.54	0.76	1.63	1.42	0.36	0.48	2.28	1.44	1.19
Fixed salary per year (avg. in US$)[b]	4,170	5,713	4,700	4,344	4,690	3,173	4,015	3,189	3,242	4,313
Performance-based portion										
% companies with % of profits	36.4	43.5	63.2	54.4	50.0	10.0	50.0	36.4	46.7	47.5
% companies with % of dividends	9.1	13.0	26.3	10.5		10.0			13.3	11.3

% of companies that determine it at meeting	21.4		8.7		16.1	25.0	25.0	60.0		15.3
% of companies with fixed salaries only	33.1	34.8	10.5	50.0	19.0	55.0	25.0	3.6	40.0	26.0
Executive compensation estimates (mean values)										
Total annual compensation (in US$)	8,945	11,964	10,736	9,864	10,307	9,591	8,285	9,535	6,743	9,918
Total compensation to capital (%)	2.8	0.9	2.7	2.4	3.3	0.5	2.8	3.2	1.9	2.5
Performance-based/total (PBCI)	0.5	0.5	0.6	0.5	0.6	0.6	0.5	0.6	0.5	0.5

Source: Compiled by the author from information in the *Brazilian Year Book 1909.*

Notes:

[a] The qualifications represent the percentage of equity that directors had to own in order to be elected.

[b] The fixed salary per year is the dollar amount directors received as part of their compensation according to their contracts. Directors also received a performance-based portion that was a percentage either of (net) profits or of dividends.

Estimates of average fixed salaries, performance-based salaries, and total CEO compensation are presented in Table 6.1. On average, total CEO compensation was roughly half fixed salary (mean = US$4,313) and half performance-based salary (the mean is 50%). Estimated total compensation of CEOs of Brazilian corporations was, on average, US$9,828 per year, with significant variation by industry (for directors of utilities companies about US$6,743 per year, directors of manufacturing and insurance companies a little over US$10,000, and bank directors nearly US$12,000).

According to the sample of statues compiled in the *Brazilian Year Book 1909* and presented in Table 6.1, 15.3% of companies determined total executive compensation at the annual shareholders meeting. While 26% of the companies paid only a fixed salary, almost 50% paid managing directors a fee as a percentage of profits and 11.3% paid them a fee as a percent of the total dividend payout of the year.

Estimating total executive compensation for the entire sample requires two steps and a few assumptions. For each company, I first took the fixed salary portion of compensation as reported in the *Brazilian Year Book* or from the last company statutes before 1909, then estimated the performance-based portion of the salary. With respect to the latter step, because I have profit and loss statements for only 60 companies, only 23 of which paid performance-based fees, some assumptions were required to construct the absent figures.

To estimate monetary amounts for the performance-based fees of a larger sample of companies, I assumed that all firms earned the median profit level for their industries (profits to paid-up capital). Table 6.2 presents the median profit rates (to paid-up capital) per industry that were used. I estimated directors' fees according to the compensation scheme of each company by taking the median profit level, subtracting the average dividend payment reported in the yearbook (between 1905 and 1909), and subtracting a 10% deduction for reserve funds. I then multiplied the net profit after dividend payments and reserve fund deductions by the percentage fee that each company paid its managing director.

Any bias in the estimates of executive compensation most likely derives from the assumption that all companies had profits. Because 1908 and 1909 were average years for the Brazilian economy, any such bias is probably not great. In any case, because I apply the profit assumption to all companies, any bias will be systematic and should not alter much the comparisons of executive compensation contracts across firms.

The estimates of total CEO compensation by region and industry are presented in Table 6.3. The salaries of directors in companies in the southeast

Table 6.2. *Median profit rates (to capital) by*
industry, Brazil, c. 1909

Sector	Median profits/capital
Agriculture	0.06
Banking	0.04
Insurance	0.17
Manufacturing	0.13
Mining	0.26
Railways	0.13
Shipping and ports	0.08
Other services	0.11
Utilities	0.15

Source: Estimated by the author using figures
reported in the *Brazilian Year Book 1909.*

(São Paulo, Rio de Janeiro, and Minas Gerais) were on average over $10,000, while the average salary for the other regions was below $7,000. There was an agglomeration effect in the most industrialized areas, with a higher demand for talent helping to push directors' salaries up. When we look at the totals by industry we see that there is less variation in average salaries; in most industries CEO salaries were above $9,000 per year (except in agriculture and utilities). Even if most of these averages are biased upward by the salaries of directors in São Paulo and Rio de Janeiro, there seems to be low variation within industries in Brazil.

DIRECTORS' COMPENSATION IN BRAZIL, THE UNITED STATES, AND ENGLAND

One way to see how high the salaries of Brazilian directors were is to compare them the salaries of directors in other countries. If the Brazilian estimates were out of line with international standards, we would expect the salaries of Brazilian managing directors to have been higher than those of their American and British counterparts. For instance, we can compare the pre-tax CEO compensation in these three countries using the work of F. W. Taussig and W. S. Barker for the United States and of Guy Routh for Great Britain. In 1925, Taussig and Barker asked 400 U.S. manufacturing corporations to disclose executive compensation during the period 1904–1910 and

Table 6.3. *Estimated CEO total compensation by industry and region, Brazil, c. 1909 (current US$)*

	Agriculture	Banking	Insurance	Manufacturing	Mining	Railways	Shipping & ports	Other services	Utilities	Full sample
Northeast										
# of obs	2	2		5			2		5	16
Average	6,875	2,605		10,898			2,934		5,699	6,738
Median	6,875	2,605		6,773			2,934		4,939	4,647
North										
# of obs		1	1	2			1			5
Average		4,647	4,999	7,557			3,312			5,614
Median		4,647	4,999	7,557			3,312			4,939
Southeast										
# of obs	6	11	14	38	2	6	1	5	6	89
Average	9,526	14,372	11,040	10,478	9,774	9,504	25,327	9,448	8,137	10,853
Median	9,294	14,871	9,980	9,294	9,774	5,254	25,327	8,855	7,821	9,294
South										
# of obs		1		2			1		2	6
Average		9,861		6,130			6,538		4,772	6,367
Median		9,861		6,130			6,538		4,772	6,562
By industry										
# of obs	8	15	15	47	2	6	5	5	13	116
Average	8,863	11,854	10,638	10,213	9,774	9,504	9,433	9,448	6,681	9,828
Median	9,294	13,239	9,926	9,294	9,774	5,254	5,056	8,855	5,021	4,937

Source: Estimated by the author from the *Brazilian Year Book 1909*. See the text for the assumptions used to estimate total compensation.

Table 6.4. *Total executive compensation in manufacturing companies in Brazil, c. 1909, and the United States, 1904–1914 (annual salary in current US$)*

Company size (paid-up capital)	CEO compensation, Brazil		Executive compensation, U.S.	Salary differential
	Median	N	Mean	U.S./Brazil
>$1.5 Million	$13,942	25	$9,958	71%
750,000–1,500,000	$12,491	17	$6,897	55%
250,000–750,000	$9,294	45	$5,195	56%
<250,000	$7,199	29	$3,885	54%

Sources: Author's estimates for Brazil; U.S. estimates from Taussig and Barker, "American Corporations and Their Executives," p. 19. Data converted to US$ at the exchange rate of 3.28 mil reis per dollar.

averaged the results according to the size of the corporation.[3] Routh's estimates of average salaries of managers in Great Britain, which came from the surveys of the Ministry of Labor and Inland Revenue Service, tend to give a better picture of aggregate salaries than Taussig and Barker's study, which relied on voluntary responses to mailed questionnaires and so is subject to underreporting and self-selection of respondents (e.g., perhaps only companies with lower executive salaries responded).[4] Moreover, in the Taussig-Barker study, neither the size of the sample used to estimate the average salaries nor the regions in which the companies operated are disclosed. Table 6.4 compares the executive compensation packages of Brazilian corporations with those of corporations in other countries.

Brazilian managing directors of manufacturing companies were, according to my estimates for Brazilian corporations and those of Taussig and Barker for U.S. corporations, earning 30–45% more than their American counterparts (assuming that all Brazilian companies in the manufacturing sector had a gross profit rate of 13% of paid-up capital). Because the representativeness of the sample on which the Taussig-Barker study derives its estimates is questionable, the salary differentials could be much narrower. Another reason the estimates of compensation should be expected

[3] See F. W. Taussig and W. S. Barker, "American Corporations and Their Executives: A Statistical Inquiry," *Quarterly Journal of Economics* 40, 1 (November 1925): 19.
[4] Guy Routh, *Occupation and Pay in Great Britain, 1906–60*, Cambridge, U.K.: Cambridge University Press, 1965, Chapter 2, p. 51, describes the sources of the salary estimates.

to differ in these two countries is that whereas 1905 through 1909 were mostly normal years for Brazilian firms because of the prosperity afforded by control of the world coffee supply, in the United States the post-1907 period was one of crisis and depression during which U.S. salaries can be expected to have been lower. Moreover, adjusting for purchasing power differences across countries should not yield significantly different results because a large part of the consumption baskets of executives in both countries consisted of imported luxury goods and, although the cost of services was lower in Brazil, tariffs on imported luxury items were higher.

We should not draw any strong conclusion from these comparisons because we may be comparing apples and oranges. Data for Brazilian companies represents the best and largest companies in the country, which had to pay a talent premium and probably had the best performance and compensation. Thus, ideally we would want to compare the salaries of directors of these companies in Brazil to the salaries of the directors of the top 500 U.S. companies. Since the data for salaries in the United States comes from a survey, we do not even know how representative the companies are in relation to the top American corporations. We could be comparing small manufacturing companies in New England with the most sophisticated factories in Brazil.

Comparisons with the salaries of directors in the United Kingdom are perhaps more illustrative because the data was collected in a systematic way. Routh's estimate of the average annual salaries of the 212 managers with the highest pay (pre-tax) in Great Britain circa 1913 was £4,321 (or US$21,000), 50% higher than my estimates of executive compensation in large Brazilian companies. If we consider, though, the salaries of individual British directors' recorded by Routh – of between £2,000 ($9,720) and £500 ($2,430) per year – and the £200 ($972) per year median income of lower level management, Brazilian directors, with an average or median salary of about $6,000, were making as much as executives in mid-sized British companies and much more than the average lower-level manager in a British firm.[5]

These results should not be surprising given that I have made assumptions that should bias Brazilian CEO average pay upward. Moreover, most of the directors of large corporations in Brazil were either Brazilians educated in Europe (most of whom had earned engineering degrees) or European or North American immigrants, many with previous experience managing large corporations. Higher salaries are to be expected for such individuals to compensate for the risk and opportunity costs of working in South America.

---

[5]   Routh, *Occupation and Pay in Great Britain*, pp. 71–72.

IMPLICATIONS OF THESE FINDINGS

How are we to interpret the results reported in this chapter? First, the estimated average CEO compensation in Brazil was nearly US$10,000 per year, relatively high compared to salaries in the United States and close to the average for salaries paid by large corporations in Britain. This is difficult to interpret in the abstract because some companies might have been paying higher salaries to attract more sought after directors or to compensate the directors' opportunity costs. Higher salaries might simply have been the premium Brazilian companies had to pay to get directors to work in a distant location. Taking recourse, in the absence of a systematic study of manager careers, to the work of historians of the textile industry and of railways, we find that the CEOs of large corporations were often North American or European immigrants with engineering and management backgrounds, many of whom had run companies in other countries.[6]

This is not to suggest that the high salaries were a reflection of an active market for CEOs equivalent to today's market for talent across companies and countries. Executives' compensation packages in Brazil were largely determined by the shareholders and most company directors came from the rank and file of the shareholders. Nevertheless, because many CEOs were European entrepreneurs working in Brazil, compensation in Brazilian companies sought equilibrium with that in European companies (plus a premium).[7]

Average compensation was nevertheless so much higher in Brazil than in the United States as to lend merit to the assumption that Brazilian directors were extracting value from shareholders. Does that mean that directors of Brazilian corporations were abusing shareholders across the board? This is difficult to answer because some companies with more "democratic" governance provisions might have restricted the salaries of their directors to the market average, while in family firms the salary for directors might have been the way to insure family members of a regular source of income. Recalling from the previous chapter the two basic ownership forms in Brazil circa 1909,

---

[6] Examples of the backgrounds of some of Brazil's most influential directors can be found in Warren Dean, *The Industrialization of São Paulo, 1880–1945*, Austin: University of Texas Press, 1969, esp. Chapter 4; Stanley Stein, *The Brazilian Cotton Manufacture: Textile Enterprise in an Underdeveloped Area, 1850–1950*, Cambridge, Mass.: Harvard University Press, 1957, Chapter 3; and Aldo Musacchio and Ian Read, "Bankers, Industrialists and their Cliques: Elite Networks in Mexico and Brazil, 1909," *Enterprise and Society* 8, 4 (December 2007): 842–880.

[7] It is clear from my reading of meeting minutes for most of the corporations for which I have shareholder lists that directors were elected from among the shareholders who had been at the firm for a while.

widely held corporations and family-controlled companies, it might have been the case that family-controlled companies were inclined to pay high salaries to family members serving as directors and widely held corporations to pay lower salaries consequent to their adoption of provisions to protect smaller shareholders, which rendered their governance more "democratic." By way of an example of the former, family patriarch Francisco Matarazzo, who owned a significant share of equity in the Matarazzo family holding company, managed in every shareholder meeting between 1891 and 1934 to convince shareholders to increase his salary. His fixed salary by 1916 was 24,000 mil reis, or almost US$7,500, nearly three times the national average in 1909 (see Table 6.1).[8]

Take also the example of Rodolfo Crespi, another eminent Italian immigrant who turned into an influential textile entrepreneur in São Paulo. Originally from Piedmont, Italy, he immigrated to Brazil as a salesman for a Milanese textile firm. He and his brother, Giuseppe, later created a partnership to operate a small textile mill and an Italian restaurant. By 1903 the textile mill had over three million dollars in sales.[9] In 1909 they filed a charter to incorporate the business as a joint stock company. What is peculiar about Rodolfo Crespi's rather egocentric company, Cotonifício Rodolfo Crespi, is that the director's salary depended only on a performance-based fee. According to the statutes of the company, the managing director – Rodolfo Crespi – collected 40% of profits as a managing fee after deducting a modest amount for depreciation, 6% for the shareholders, 10% for the reserve fund, 1% for an employee fund, and a fee for his brother, who also acted as a second managing director.[10]

DIRECTOR COMPENSATION AND CORPORATE GOVERNANCE

Research on corporate governance insists that there is a clear agency problem in any corporation in which ownership and control are separated, specifically that directors have incentives to shirk or extract value that should accrue to shareholders (either in the form of dividends or as higher net worth).[11] Opportunities to extract value, in large salaries or any other form,

---

[8] See "Indústrias Reunidas Fábrica Matarazzo" in *Diário Oficial do Estado de São Paulo*, December 14, 1911, and "Sociedade Anônima Indústrias Reunidas Fábrica Matarazzo" in *Diario Oficial do Estado de São Paulo*, July 12, 1916.

[9] See Dean, *The Industrialization of São Paulo*, pp. 59–60.

[10] See "Cotonifício Rodolpho Crespi" in *Diário Oficial do Estado de São Paulo*, April 1, 1909.

[11] Michael C. Jensen and William H. Meckling, "Theory of the Firm: Managerial Behavior, Agency Costs and Ownership Structure," *Journal of Financial Economics* 3, 4 (October 1976): 305–360, and see, for instance, p. 309 for an explanation of the agency costs

are generally limited by imposing "checks and balances" on the actions of directors or through provisions that attempt to achieve a balance of power between smaller and larger shareholders. Although ownership was probably separated from control to a lesser extent in Brazilian corporations given that managers were usually elected from among their number, investors still are likely to have been concerned that the largest shareholders could exploit their power to secure director positions and vote themselves extravagant salaries.[12]

One way to determine whether if the level of compensation directors received in Brazilian corporations represents an extraction of value rather than just a premium for talent in an economy with a scarcity of educated managers is to look at the correlation among governance provisions and executive pay. The hypothesis is that if the provisions that limit the power of managers or insiders (e.g., maximum vote provisions) or that try to align the incentives of managers (e.g., higher share qualifications) are correlated with lower executive pay, then compensation in the companies that paid higher salaries reflects an extraction of value resulting from the lack of checks and balances on the power of managers and insiders. If there is no clear correlation between these governance variables and executive compensation then the evidence is inconclusive and we might want to argue that high salaries in Brazil were a sign that there was a talent premium and some extraction of value.

If governance somehow mattered, we would expect to find significant correlations of executive compensation with voting rights, maximum votes, and of director qualifications. In particular, one could argue that voting provisions that were more democratic – that is, that fostered voting by more shareholders by requiring fewer shares for one vote or by distributing votes more evenly by capping the maximum number of votes available to any individual – would make it harder for powerful shareholders to be elected as directors and pay themselves high salaries. We thus would expect companies with these provisions to have paid lower executive salaries. Obviously, these companies could still pay high executive salaries to attract top talent to meet a particular set of challenges or for other reasons that cannot be controlled for. But if we start from the premise that directors were trying to extract value, we can determine whether or not governance was correlated with executive compensation.

---

associated with management being separated from and imperfectly monitored by a corporation's principal(s).

[12] Technically, managers could not use their voting power when the shareholder assembly was deciding their salaries or any other issue(s) related to them, but a large shareholder could, in anticipation of becoming a director, have voted the position a large salary the year prior, or name as director, and vote excessive perquisites and a high salary for, an associate.

For instance, using multivariate analysis we would expect a positive sign for the coefficient that measures the correlation between director qualifications (the percentage of total capital required to be deposited with the company during their tenure) and executive compensation for two reasons. First, we expect that companies that required directors to deposit a large share of capital would compensate them for the low diversification risk (because their career, salary, and investments all would depend on the performance of that one company).[13] Second, higher qualifications would commit directors to put the interests of the firm over their private interests because their claims on their companies' cash flows would be higher. The higher the qualifications, the higher we would expect performance-based fees and, for the same reasons, total compensation, to be.

Table 6.5 presents the summary statistics for the Brazilian data and the difference of means of total pay (normalized by size) according to relevant governance provisions. At the bottom of the table we can see that the one-share one-vote and maximum vote provisions yield no significant difference of means for any of the compensation variables (normalized by capital). We also see significant differences in total compensation, fixed salary, and performance-based salary between companies with a large qualifications requirement (over the mean) and companies with a low qualifications requirement (less than 1.1% of equity). We thus do not see a clear difference in executive compensation relative to variation in governance provisions.

To gauge any effects of governance provisions on four variables related to executive compensation in a multivariate setting, I use OLS estimation techniques to explore the correlation of governance variables with total CEO compensation, fixed salary, and performance-based salary, controlling for some firm characteristics. I focus on CEO compensation because the data were more comprehensive than for the salaries of directors or board members.

I examine the correlates of governance provisions (maximum votes, one-share one-vote, and CEO qualifications) and executive pay with OLS estimates of the following form:

$$y_i = \beta_0 + \beta_1 \log{(age)} + \beta_2 \, (governance\ provision) + \sum_{z}^{Z} \gamma_z \, industry\ z_{zi}$$
$$+ \sum_{k}^{K} \theta_k \, region_{ki} + e_i$$

---

[13] I owe this insight to Claudia Goldin.

Table 6.5. *Summary statistics and difference of means for CEO compensation variables, Brazil, c. 1909*

	Panel A: Summary statistics				
	Observations	Mean	Std. dev.	Min	Max
Compensation in US$					
Total compensation (US$)	188	9,828	6,043	387	28,594
Fixed salary (US$)	116	4,274	2,567	194	13,942
Performance-based salary (US$)	116	5,179	4,237	45	24,977
Normalized measures					
Total compensation to capital	114	0.025	0.025	0.001	0.128
Fixed salary to capital	114	0.011	0.012	0.0004	0.061
Performance-based salary to capital	136	0.013	0.014	0.0004	0.071
Salary index (PBCI)[b]	116	0.550	0.078	0.500	0.915
Other					
Compensation determined at meeting	157	0.15	0.36	0	1
Capital (in million US$)	188	1.41	3.33	0.02	22.90
Age	189	18.58	14.54	1	102
Governance variables					
Maximum vote dummy[a]	139	0.27	0.45	0	1
Qualif. as a % of total equity	160	0.01	0.03	0.0002	0.30
One-share, one-vote dummy	139	0.17	0.37	0	1

(continued)

Table 6.5 *(continued)*

	Panel B: Difference of means (t-statistics)			
	Compensation to capital	Fixed salary to capital	Performance-based salary to capital	Salary index
By maximum vote	0.92	0.76	0.83	-0.32
By qualifications/ equity > 0.011	5.35***	5.06***	5.04***	0.57
By one-share, one-vote dummy	1.17	1.01	1.44	1.50

Notes:
[a] Assumes companies with no explicit limit on votes had a maximum of 100% of total votes.
[b] PBCI is the Performance-based Compensation Index, estimated as the share of total compensation paid in performance-based fees.
[+] significant at 10%, ** significant at 5%, *** significant at 1%.

where y is a normalized measure of total executive salary, fixed salary, or performance-based salary over capital, or the performance-based compensation index (PBCI). The PBCI simply measures the share of total compensation represented by performance-based fees (estimated as fees/total compensation). The estimation controls for the log of age, dummies for each industry z, and dummies for each region k where the company headquarters are located.

We do find variation associated with differences in governance provisions when we control for company characteristics such as industry, age, and region. Table 6.6 presents the correlations between one-share one-vote provisions and level of qualifications (as a % of capital) and the different measures of executive compensation. One-share one-vote provisions are significantly correlated with lower performance-based compensation indices (PBCI) and lower total executive compensation (in Panel A), as well as with lower fixed salary and lower performance-based salary (but with weaker significance – see Panel B). The one-share one-vote provision (with coefficient around –0.011 to –0.014 in Specifications 1 and 2) is correlated with having almost half of the full sample average compensation to capital (0.025 of paid-up capital). This voting provision would also reduce the PBCI from its mean value of 0.55 to between 0.40 and 0.50, which means that performance-based compensation in companies that included this voting provision in their statutes was about 40% of total compensation instead of the 50% paid by the average Brazilian firm.

Table 6.6. *Regressions CEO compensation estimates (normalized by size), Brazil, c. 1909*

Panel A: Dependent variables are CEO total pay to capital and the performance-based compensation index (PBCI)

	OLS	OLS	OLS	OLS	OLS	OLS	OLS	OLS
	CEO pay to capital (1)	CEO pay to capital (2)	CEO pay to capital (3)	CEO pay to capital (4)	PBCI (5)	PBCI (6)	PBCI (7)	PBCI (8)
Constant	0.03 [0.003]***	0.035 [0.014]**	0.038 [0.015]**	0.031 [0.010]***	0.563 [0.011]***	0.541 [0.063]***	0.544 [0.067]***	0.535 [0.056]***
One-share, one-vote	−0.011 [0.005]+	−0.014 [0.006]**			−0.042 [0.016]***	−0.087 [0.024]***		
Max. votes dummy			−0.004 [0.007]				0.01 [0.020]	
Qualif % of capital				0.142 [0.112]				−0.051 [0.133]
Industry dummies	N	Y	Y	Y	N	Y	Y	Y
Regional dummies	N	Y	Y	Y	N	Y	Y	Y
Observations	78	78	78	106	79	79	79	106
Adjusted R^2	0.02	0.20	0.18	0.22	0.03	0.26	0.17	0.12

(continued)

Table 6.6 (*continued*)

	OLS	OLS	OLS	OLS	OLS	OLS	OLS	OLS
Panel B: Dependent variables are fixed salary to capital and performance-based fees to capital								
	Fixed salary to capital (9)	Fixed salary to capital (10)	Fixed salary to capita (11)	Fixed salary to capital (12)	Perf. fees to capital (13)	Perf. fees to capital (14)	CEO pay to capital (15)	Perf. fees to capital (16)
Constant	0.013 [0.002]***	0.014 [0.007]**	0.015 [0.007]**	0.012 [0.004]***	0.015 [0.002]***	0.017 [0.008]**	0.018 [0.008]**	0.016 [0.007]**
One-share, one-vote	−0.004 [0.003]+	−0.005 [0.003]+			−0.006 [0.003]**	−0.005 [0.003]+		
Max. votes dummy			−0.002 [0.003]				−0.001 [0.003]	
Qualif. % of capital				0.062 [0.052]				0.086 [0.061]
Industry dummies	N	Y	Y	Y	N	Y	Y	Y
Regional dummies	N	Y	Y	Y	N	Y	Y	Y
Observations	78	78	78	106	98	98	98	128
Adjusted R²	0.01	0.17	0.16	0.020	0.02	0.23	0.22	0.24

Notes: This OLS model tests whether having one-share one-vote, maximum vote provisions, or higher qualifications is correlated with lower or higher CEO compensation. Robust standard errors are in brackets.

+ *significant at 10%,* ** *significant at 5%,* *** *significant at 1%.*

I do not find significant correlations with other governance provisions, though. Maximum vote provisions were not significantly correlated with CEO compensation in any specification (in both Panels A and B). And, contrary to what we expected from the difference of means test, the qualifications of directors also is not correlated to executive compensation.

These results are rather weak and the only conclusive correlation between executive compensation and governance provisions is that one-share, one-vote provisions seem to be related to significantly lower pay. Yet, this result is hard to interpret because even if this voting provision makes it easier for any shareholder to vote in the shareholders meeting, a shareholder holding a large portion of total shares can act like an autocrat and devise for herself a sizable compensation package.

In sum, what the results imply is that there is only weak evidence to support the hypothesis that director salaries were high only in the companies with weak corporate governance. It seems that salaries were relatively high across the board either because of the biases in the estimation or because educated immigrants and Brazilians educated in Europe received a talent premium for working in a relatively inhospitable location. But the evidence does not allow us to discard the hypothesis that some excessively large salaries did denote some extraction of value. It is improbable that this occurred in companies with many outside shareholders because no investors with access to this (public) information would retain their shares in a venture in which salaries reached abusive levels. Most likely companies in which the abuses were allowed were family-owned corporations in which it did not make much of a difference for shareholders if large salaries were paid to the patriarch(s) of the family.

CONCLUSION

This chapter presented estimates of the salaries of managing directors of Brazilian corporations circa 1909. The fact that these salaries could be estimated for the present chapter is in and of itself an important indicator of the quality of information at the disposal of the average Brazilian investor in that period. Executive salaries were fully disclosed and were determined by the shareholders during the shareholder meetings (at least the fixed part and the size of the performance-based fees).

The comparison data presented here, albeit not optimal, reveals that executive compensation paid by Brazilian corporations circa 1909 was high relative to that paid by the American corporations in the Taussig and Barker survey and lower than that paid by the largest British corporations. This denotes that Brazilian CEOs were paid like directors of medium-sized companies in the United Kingdom and perhaps like directors of small to average companies in the United States. Even if Brazilian CEOs salaries were higher than those of U.S. CEOs, it is not clear whether higher salaries were truly a sign of weak corporate governance or just a symptom of the scarcity of talent in this economy. If some directors, such as Francisco de Matarazzo or Rodolfo Crespi, had enough power to pay themselves large compensation packages, it does not mean that this was common practice across the board. Family corporations, in which these practices were common, usually had very few shareholders. Because the information on director salaries was public, shareholders who felt salaries were abusive would very likely leave those companies and buy shares in other companies with less abusive practices.

So far we have seen evidence of the emergence of a structure of corporate governance wherein provisions to protect smaller shareholders were enforced at the company level, and of a distinct division between companies that protected shareholders strongly and companies that did not. But with the exception of disclosure, discussed in the previous chapter, we have not yet examined the laws and principles whereby investors were protected in the same way across corporations, states, and industries. We begin this exploration in Chapter 7, which examines the protections creditors were accorded by bankruptcy laws and their enforcement in Brazilian courts.

## SEVEN

Bond Markets and Creditor Rights
in Brazil, 1850–1945

Corporate bond markets in Brazil grew to historical levels at the same time stock markets peaked. This chapter shows that the development of corporate bond markets was, to a large extent, linked to the protections for creditors in national bankruptcy laws. This chapter discusses the importance of the bond market and explains the evolution of the protections for creditors both on paper and by the courts between 1850 and 1945.

Beyond sheer size relative to GDP, the scale of development of Brazil's bond markets before 1920 is impressive in two respects. First, corporations in all sectors of the economy issued bonds to obtain funds. In fact, bond markets were among the most important sources of new funds for corporations (issuing companies secured approximately 30% of their capital through this channel). Second, the scale of Brazil's bond markets relative to the size of Brazil's economy suggests that a strong formal institutional system was in place to enforce bondholder rights (e.g., in the event of bankruptcy).

But although size should attest to the existence of an institutional framework for protecting creditors, the strength of creditor protections was called into question by research such as Gail Triner's influential study of Brazilian banking. Arguing that the "insufficient protection for the recovery of debt was a serious problem throughout the First Republic [1889–1930]," Triner maintained that the main problem for banks trying to recover unpaid debts was that "the laws and Commercial Code simply did not address issues involving financial property," making it difficult for them to take possession of debtors' bank accounts and other financial assets.[1] Triner concluded that "the law protected the role and the interests of the bankrupt party, sometimes

---

[1] Gail Triner, *Banking and Economic Development: Brazil, 1889–1930*, New York: Palgrave, 2000, p. 96.

in prefcrcncc to those of creditors," and that their resulting "weak position in bankruptcy procedures" reduced banks' incentives to lend.[2]

This raises an interesting historical puzzle: if the property rights framework constrained the development of banking intermediation, how is it that we find such large bond markets before 1915? This chapter attempts to solve this puzzle by examining in detail the creditor property rights accorded by Brazil's bankruptcy laws.

The right of secured creditors to recover collateral in case of default, priority during bankruptcy according to the seniority of the debts, the right to control its assets during a company's bankruptcy, and the right to nominate new managers are among the creditor rights deemed to be important to the development of credit markets by La Porta et al., whose methodology I follow in collecting indices of creditor rights protection and tracking changes in Brazil's bankruptcy laws from 1850 to 2005.[3] My evidence suggests that between 1850 and 1945 Brazil had relatively strong creditor rights, including first priority among creditors to bondholders. Moreover, between 1890 and 1908 Brazil instituted the four protections for creditors that La Porta et al. consider relevant for the development of a bond market, and Brazilian bankruptcy legislation included three of these four protections from 1908 to 1945.[4]

It could still be the case, notwithstanding strong creditor protections on paper, that Brazil's bond markets developed to a significant degree through the agency of formal and informal arrangements whereby investment and commercial banks underwrite bond issues. Banks could, for example, pressure companies to pay their coupons on time and not default on their debts, a role J. P. Morgan and his executives are widely acknowledged to have played in the United States in the late nineteenth century. Morgan and other bankers in the United States sat on the boards of directors of large corporations and from there influenced the behavior of managers and protected their reputations with investors.[5]

---

[2]   Triner, *Banking and Economic Development*, pp. 142–143.

[3]   Rafael La Porta, Florencio Lopez-de-Silanes, Andrei Shleifer, and Robert Vishny, "Law and Finance," *Journal of Political Economy* 106, 6 (1998): 1113–1155.

[4]   Rafael La Porta, Florencio Lopez-de-Silanes, Andrei Shleifer, and Robert Vishny, "Legal Determinants of External Finance," *Journal of Finance* 52, 3 (1997): 1131–1150.

[5]   This view of the role of bankers is mainly from Vincent P. Carosso, *Investment Banking in America: A History*, Cambridge, Mass.: Harvard University Press, 1970 (e.g., p.38), and Brad De Long, "Did J. P. Morgan's Men Add Value?: An Economist's Perspective on Financial Capitalism," in Peter Temin (ed.), *Inside the Business Enterprise: Historical Perspectives on the Use of Information*, Chicago and London: NBER, 1991, pp. 205–250.

I find no evidence that Brazil's bond markets were sustained by these kinds of network arrangements between bankers and corporations, the evidence from bankruptcy court cases instead revealing strong enforcement of creditor rights. The cases show that bondholders had first priority to recover their claims when a court declared a company bankrupt. Trustees who took charge of reorganizing or liquidating the company were chosen from among the creditors.

THE SCOPE OF CORPORATE BOND MARKETS

Brazil's bond markets played an important role in the financing of corporations after the 1880s. The combined effects of the regulatory changes of the 1880s and 1890s can be seen in Table 7.1, which shows the enormous growth of the market for corporate bonds with real assets as collateral (referred to as debentures). The table also shows the magnitude of debenture issues relative to the total capitalization of the exchange. Comparing the size of bond markets, at face value, with the total declared capital of corporations in the Rio de Janeiro Stock Exchange, also at face value, we can see in column 5 that by 1913 the total bond issue represented 60% of the total capital of the stock exchange, then declined to around 35% during the 1920s. We can also see in Table 7.1 that the ratios of the capital of debenture issues to registered capital for issuing companies exceeded 100% in some years (column 4), which implies that some companies obtained more funds from bond than from equity issues.[6]

In Brazil as in other countries, railway bond issues represented a large share of total bond issues. From Table 7.2, which reports total capitalization of bond issue by industry, we can see that railways always had the largest share of total bond issues by value. Before 1890, railway bonds represented 80% of the total stock of bonds. The importance of railway bonds was reduced when (after 1890) manufacturing and textile companies began to make more intensive use of bond issues, coming to represent, collectively, 12–18% of the total stock of bonds. The utilities sector, which includes tramways, waterworks, and gas and electricity companies, also became a more prominent bond issuer after 1890, accounting for 7% of bond issues that year and 15% in 1900 and 1905.

Adoption of the gold standard, stabilization of the coffee price, and the end of regulated tariffs for railways at the turn of the century provided new

---

[6]   This table is constructed using face value rather than market prices to avoid the bias of ratios downward or upward by swings in market prices.

Table 7.1. *Debentures relative to capitalization*

	(Thousand contos of mil reis of 1900)				
	Capitalization of debenture issues	Paid-up capital of issuing companies	Stock market capitalization	Debentures to capital of issuers	Debentures to total stock market capitalization
	1	2	3	4	5
1895	261	671	2,683	39%	10%
1905	360	474	1,316	76%	27%
1913	1,150	899	1,843	128%	62%
1920	645	679	1,514	95%	43%
1925	306	422	877	72%	35%
1931	455	427	1,179	106%	39%

Source: Estimated by the author using the face values (not market values, with equity not fully paid in some cases) from the Annual Reports of the Rio de Janeiro Stock Brokers Association, Camara Sindical de Corretores de Fundos Públicos da Bolsa de Valores do Rio de Janeiro, *Relatorio da Câmara Sindical de Corretores de Fundos Públicos da Bolsa de Valores do Rio de Janeiro*, 1896, 1906, 1914, 1921, 1926, 1932.

impetus for bond issues circa 1905. This was especially the case for railways; in 1905 alone, three new Brazilian railway bonds began to be traded in Rio de Janeiro and Europe. The Noroeste do Brazil, São Paulo-Rio Grande, and Victoria-Minas railways issued bonds worth in excess of 120,000 contos of mil reis (about £8 million or 117.2 million francs), accounting for the jump, shown in Table 7.2, from 40% to 60% from 1900 to 1905.[7]

We can see from Table 7.3, which reports the number of issuing firms as well as percentages by sector, that firms in all sectors used debentures. More than half of the port, railroad, textile, and utilities companies registered on the stock exchange, and more than one-third of firms aggregated in the "other" category, used debentures during the period 1895–1931.

That bonds were widely issued does not, however, imply that trading in domestic exchanges was particularly active. Investors usually purchased

[7] The expansion of the share of railway issues is even more impressive because the largest bond issuer in the Rio de Janeiro market, the Railway Sorocabana e Ituana, went bankrupt and was purchased by the federal government at the turn of the century. Thus, its bonds had stopped being traded on the exchange by 1905. For details of the bankruptcy of the Sorocabana, see Flávio A. M. Saes, *As Ferrovias de São Paulo, 1870–1940*, São Paulo: HUCITEC, 1981, pp. 158–160.

Table 7.2. *Total debenture stock by industry, Brazil, 1881–1925*

	1881	1885	1890	1895	1900	1905	1910	1915	1920	1925
Debenture stock[a]	37.3	177.0	640.6	520.2	232.6	306.9	1097.6	1155.8	538.2	257.3
Bond stock/GDP	2%	3%	10%	8%	5%	5%	14%	14%	5%	2%
Percentages of total bond stock by sector										
Agricultural	14.1	5.7	3.2	4.3	2.7	1.8	0.4	0.5	0.9	0.7
Banks			27.2	4.6	0.8	2.2	5.6	9.1	7.3	7.9
Manufacturing			7.5	5.4	4.7	6.4	1.4	5.1	6.2	5.7
Ports		0.7	0.2	0.1	0.5	0.3	10.8	5.3	6.7	9.7
Railways	81.2	80.7	39.5	48.5	40.4	60.8	60.9	55.0	44.8	30.8
Shipping		2.7	8.2	16.3	20.2	0.7	1.0	3.4	4.1	4.0
Telecomm.		0.8	0.2							
Textiles		3.7	9.4	6.9	7.3	7.8	5.5	7.9	11.8	14.8
Utilities	4.7	3.9	2.5	7.6	15.3	13.3	10.6	10.6	12.7	15.3
Other		1.8	2.1	6.3	8.0	6.7	3.8	3.1	5.5	10.9

Sources: Estimated by the author from data in the *Jornal do Commércio* and *Retrospecto Commércial do Jornal do Commércio*, 1882–1926. GDP data and the deflator are from Goldsmith, *Brasil 1850–1984*, Tables 3.1 and 4.2.
Note:
[a] Data in thousand contos of mil reis of 1900.

bonds and held them for a few years or sold them back to the issuing company when they were "recalled" for amortization.[8] Between 1894 and 1925, for example, 273 companies issued debentures, but only the bonds of 143 of those companies were traded.

The importance of debentures as a source of capital for Brazil's corporations can be gauged from the two estimates of the proportion of total equity raised through bond issues presented in Table 7.4. On average, 40–60% of capital (excluding short-term credit) was obtained through bond issues. At the peak of bond markets circa 1910, these ratios are, on average, 0.61–0.78. By 1925, we observe across the board a trend toward less reliance on bonds. Bonds were a particularly important source of financing for railways and utilities, although during the peak years companies in most industries financed 30–40% (or more) of their total capital through bond issues.

[8] Newspapers of the time would publish notices with the bond numbers that were to be sold back to the company at par. These numbers were selected randomly in raffles. Many examples appear in the ad sections of the *Jornal do Commércio* and *O Estado de São Paulo*.

Table 7.3. *Percentage of firms that issued debentures by sector, 1881–1931*

	1881	1885	1890	1895	1900	1905	1910	1915	1920	1925	1931
Percentage by sector											
Agricultural	20%	15%	15%	16%	12%	6%	2%	4%	6%	5%	5%
Banks		5	6	3	3	2	4	4	4		
Manufacturing			15	10	10	12	10	17	18	18	24
Ports		4	1	1	1	2	1	1	1	2	5
Railways	60	35	16	17	20	21	14	13	12	6	12
Shipping		4	5	5	4	2	6	5	5	4	5
Telephones		4	1								
Textiles		15	19	22	17	24	28	28	25	25	41
Utilities	20	12	6	4	9	9	12	13	14	15	7
Other		12	17	18	23	21	24	15	16	22	
Number of companies issuing bonds	5	26	81	93	69	66	86	134	141	106	41

Sources: Estimated by the author from data in the *Jornal do Commércio* and *Retrospecto Commércial do Jornal do Commércio*, 1882–1926, and the Bolsa de Valores do Rio de Janeiro, *Anuário da Bolsa de Valores do Rio de Janeiro*, 1932.

In his study of Brazil's textile industry, Stephen Haber observes that "the use of long-term bond debt and the high percentages of capital coming from debt issues were quite remarkable by the standards of other countries." He estimates the bond-to-equity ratio (calculated in the same manner as estimate 1 in Table 7.4) at between 0. 11 and 0.29 (my estimates are around 0.30, but Haber has more complete information on reserves and retained earnings). Adding other short-term debt to the numerator pushes Haber's estimates to 0.50–0.60 between 1895 and 1940. These figures become even more impressive when compared to those of other countries. Haber points out, for example, that the 0.20 observed for Brazil's textile manufacturers circa 1860 compares with 0.18 in Mexico during its early industrialization circa 1910.[9]

---

[9]   Total debt-equity ratios in the United States increased to 0.40 by 1910, but still this figure would be relatively low compared to Brazilian figures. For instance, Haber estimates total debt-equity ratios of 0.50 to 0.60 during this time, half of which came from bond issues. See Stephen Haber, "The Efficiency Consequences of Institutional Change: Financial Market

Table 7.4. *Bond-equity ratios for debenture-issuing companies*

	1896	1900	1905	1910	1915	1920	1925
Debt equity ratio estimates 1							
Agricultural	0.60	0.66	0.52	0.47	0.47	0.49	0.35
Manufacturing	0.22	0.16	0.37	0.49	0.39	0.30	0.30
Other	0.25	0.25	0.29	0.42	0.44	0.35	0.38
Ports							0.56
Railways	0.70	0.65	0.63	0.95	0.83	0.84	0.85
Shipping	0.91	0.75	0.22	0.34	0.37	0.28	0.31
Textiles	0.40	0.33	0.30	0.37	0.34	0.30	0.25
Utilities	0.45	0.42	0.45	0.50	0.51	0.52	0.49
Average	**0.62**	**0.54**	**0.55**	**0.78**	**0.65**	**0.58**	**0.49**
Debt equity ratio estimates 2							
Agricultural	0.47	0.44	0.40	0.43	0.42	0.40	0.34
Manufacturing	0.22	0.15	0.36	0.43	0.32	0.26	0.26
Other	0.23	0.23	0.25	0.34	0.31	0.30	0.34
Ports	0.32	0.23	0.29	0.60	0.52	0.54	0.46
Railways	0.55	0.50	0.50	0.76	0.70	0.72	0.77
Shipping	0.58	0.55	0.21	0.32	0.37	0.28	0.31
Textiles	0.38	0.33	0.28	0.32	0.32	0.28	0.24
Utilities	0.45	0.42	0.42	0.44	0.44	0.40	0.35
Average	**0.48**	**0.42**	**0.42**	**0.61**	**0.52**	**0.48**	**0.44**

Source: Estimated by the author from data in the *Jornal do Commércio* and *Retrospecto Commércial do Jornal do Commércio*, 1882–1926. Estimate 1 takes into account only companies that reported their reserve funds and paid up capital in the Stock Exchange Annual Summaries. The bond-equity ratio is estimated as the sum of the stock of debentures by sector over the sum of paid-up capital + reserves + debenture issues, but only for companies that report reserves. For estimate 2, I follow the same procedure but include the paid-up capital of companies that did not report reserves. The second estimates should yield higher bond-equity ratios given that the denominator is underestimated, but the fact that the second estimates are lower implies that the companies that issued more bonds were also the ones reporting reserves to the stock exchange. The ratios tell us the percentage of total funding that came from bonds (as opposed to equity and retained earnings).

The next section considers how such a large and important bond market emerged in Brazil and what kinds of institutional systems were necessary to induce domestic and foreign investors to buy corporate bonds.

CREDITOR RIGHTS IN BRAZIL, 1850–2001

Measuring Creditor Rights in Brazil

To assess the degree to which creditors were protected on paper, I created indices of creditor rights following the methodology of La Porta et al., which facilitates comparisons across time and countries.[10] I identified the following rights of secured (collateralized) creditors: to repossess collateral in the event of default (no automatic stay on debtors' assets); to be paid first; to approve firm reorganization or rescheduling of debt service; and to replace original managers during reorganization (no debtor-in-possession reorganization). According to La Porta et al., the more of these rights are embodied in a country's bankruptcy law, the larger the expected size of its debt markets.[11]

I read and coded the bankruptcy legislation included in the commerce code of 1850, Joint Stock Company Laws of 1882, 1890, and 1891, and Bankruptcy Laws of 1902, 1908, 1929, 1945, and 2005, then added the number of rights written into each of these bankruptcy laws (see the compilation of rights in Table 7.5) and used the sum of these rights to create a creditor-rights index (bottom row of Table 7.5).

Bankruptcy laws that strongly protect creditors earn countries high scores according to the following logic. In countries in which legislation does not accord secured creditors (among them, bondholders) priority or the right to repossess collateral (in many countries, companies are permitted to keep assets pledged as collateral until their fate is decided by a judge, and workers' compensation and unpaid taxes are given priority over bonds and secured debts), investors and banks expect a high premium to compensate for the uncertainty they face in the event of

---

Regulation and Industrial Productivity Growth in Brazil, 1866–1934," in John Coatsworth and Alan Taylor (eds.), *Latin America and the World Economy Since 1800*, Cambridge, Mass.: DRCLAS and Harvard University Press, 1998, pp. 289–291.

[10] See La Porta et al., "Legal Determinants of External Finance," La Porta et al., "Law and Finance," and Rafael La Porta, Florencio Lopes-de-Silanes Andrei Shleifer, and Robert Vishny, "Investor Protection and Corporate Governance," *Journal of Financial Economics* 58, 1 (2000): 1–25.

[11] La Porta et al., "Law and Finance."

Table 7.5. *Creditor rights in Brazil since 1850*

Source:	C. Code of 1850	Law 3150, 12/04/1882	Dec. 917, 01/17/1890	Dec. 603, 10/20/1891	Law 859, 8/16/1902	Law 2024, 12/17/1908	Dec. 5746, 9/12/1929	Dec.-Law 7661, 6/21/1945	La Porta et al. 1995	Law 11,101, 2/9/2005
1. Secured creditors can repossess collateral (no automatic stay)	1	1	1	1[a]	1	1	1	0	0	1
2. Secured creditors have first priority[b]	1	1	1	1	1	0	0	0	0	0
3. Approval of creditors for reorganization	1	1	1	1	1	1	1	1	1	1
4. Management does not automatically stay for reorganization	1	1	1	1	1	1	1	0	0	0
Index	4	4	4	4	4	3	3	1	1	2

Sources: Brazil, *Coleção das Leis e Decretos*. For Decree Law 7661, June, 1945, see Bevilaqua, *Falência Dec.-lei n. 7661, de 21 de junho de 1945*, 1958. For 1995, coding is not with respect to a law, but corresponds to that of La Porta et al., "Law and Finance." For the 2005 Law (Law 11,101 February 9, 2005), see www.planalto.gov.br (last accessed 05/05/09).

Notes:
[a] Although not explicit in the decree, this right was included in an earlier law that remained in force.
[b] Bondholders did not have first priority until 1890.

bankruptcy.[12] In addition, "lenient" bankruptcy laws that permit company reorganizations without creditor approval and under the direction of incumbent management effectively reward, with more time to try to undo their actions, and against the interests and at the expense of creditors, managers who have made bad decisions or taken ill-advised risks.[13] This reduces incentives for investors to buy corporate bonds and banks to lend to companies.[14]

Financial contracts such as corporate bonds reflect high costs and uncertainty in higher risk premiums. In the world of corporate debt, higher risk is associated with higher cost of capital and the cost of capital is an important determinant of investment. Reducing uncertainty during bankruptcy can thus reduce the effect of unforeseen insolvency on the risk attributed to long-term debt contracts. Uncertainty can to some degree be legislated away by clearly defining creditors' property rights in case of bankruptcy and providing a mechanism, generally a judiciary system, to enforce those rights.[15]

---

[12] Whether bankruptcy laws that are tougher on debtors or those that emphasize their rehabilitation are better is today a subject of debate. On bankruptcy practices around the world, see Stijn Claessens and Leora Klapper, "Bankruptcy Around the World: Explanations of its Relative Use," *American Law and Economics Review* 7, 1 (June 2005): 253–283.

[13] According to Joseph Stiglitz, managers and shareholders of firms forced into insolvency by a crisis such as affects the entire economy – a currency crisis, for example – and that could neither have been anticipated nor planned for, are treated too harshly by bankruptcy laws that are highly protective of creditors. See Joseph Stiglitz, "Bankruptcy Laws: Basic Economic Principles," in Stijn Claessens, Simeon Djankov and Ashoka Mody (eds.), *Resolution of Financial Distress: An International Perspective on the Design of Bankruptcy Laws*, Washington, D.C.: The World Bank, 2001, pp. 1–24. During the economic downturn of the late 1890s caused by the stabilization of the exchange rate, companies frequently had to negotiate with their creditors for more time to make payments, continuation rather than liquidation of a business usually being preferred.

[14] That Brazil's banks typically preferred negotiating terms of payment or forgiving a debtor over repossessing collateral (for evidence, see Triner, *Banking and Economic Development*) is understandable if we consider that unfortunate financial circumstances are sometimes a consequence of forces outside of a company's control and that continuation of a debtor's business and relationship with a creditor can yield a higher expected discounted return than the value that might be obtained by auctioning repossessed collateral.

[15] Bankruptcy laws are also important to resolve or generate insolvency crises that could affect the financial system. For instance, the inability of lenders to repossess collateral (the guarantees they ask in order to lend) could trigger a cascade of debtor defaults because lenders may be borrowers themselves and may need the money they collect to pay their creditors.

Evidence of Creditor Rights in Bankruptcy Laws

Brazil had strong creditor rights from 1850 until at least 1945, the Commercial Code of 1850 having established a bankruptcy procedure that incorporated the four provisions deemed by La Porta et al. to be important for the development of debt markets.

First priority for bondholders was introduced in 1890 in some of the first laws passed by the republican government. Although the Bankruptcy Law of 1908 reduced the number of basic creditor protections from four to three and moved unpaid taxes and some workers' compensations to the top of the priority list, and Decree 10,902 of May 20, 1914 again put taxes ahead of creditors, these changes occurred only on paper; in practice, judges persisted in favoring secured creditors throughout this period.[16] Even the reform of bankruptcy law in 1929 was mostly cosmetic, leaving the basic creditor protections unchanged. From 1850 until 1929, Brazil thus accorded creditors all the legal protections La Porta et al. consider important for the expansion of credit markets.

If Triner found there to be an institutional obstacle to the expansion of bank credit during the republic (1889–1930), it is not that creditors lacked protections, but precisely the opposite, that they were strongly protected by law. Triner found that banks preferred to lend on collateral because creditors were permitted by law to take possession of that collateral and accorded first priority in bankruptcy proceedings. Banks were not so advantageously positioned to recover loans made without collateral to corporations or partnerships with previous mortgages or collateralized credit. Banks thus had incentives either to ask for collateral or to minimize the risk associated with their lending portfolios by lending only small amounts to diversified sets of borrowers.

Studying creditor protections historically thus reveals that, if today relatively weak, creditor protections in Brazil were strong in the past, at least on paper. If a necessary condition for bond market development is a creditor protection index of four, then the legal provisions of bankruptcy laws before 1945 might explain, in part, the success of Brazil's bond markets. But the variation in creditor rights over time makes us wonder to what

---

[16] Although this decree stated, in articles 139 and 240, that if a bankrupt debtor was found to owe overdue taxes the trial would become federal with the Ministry of Finance as prosecutor, in practice, the ministry was not involved in bankruptcy cases and usually did not follow the judiciary papers that published bankruptcy notices. An example of the enforcement of creditor priority after the 1908 law can be found in Corte de Apelação, "Companhia Nacional Mineira," 1916.

degree legal measures enacted to protect investors are determined by time-invariant factors such as a country's legal traditions, a notion advanced by the law and finance literature. Were such theories to hold, Brazil's creditor protections should have been weak not just today, but throughout its history. Examination of the creditor rights index in Table 7.5 suggests that a better explanation of the evolution of creditor protections is in the perhaps wanted in the long run. The following section will review the evolution of bankruptcy laws in Brazil, both following domestic political interests and mimicking the evolution of these laws in other countries.

International Influences and the Politics behind Creditor Rights
The creditor rights incorporated in Brazil's bankruptcy laws and commerce code were products of the interaction of interest groups and lawmakers, but in every case they followed international practices in bankruptcy. In fact, Brazil's bankruptcy practices were constrained from deviating from the laws of other countries by the Lei da Boa Razão, enacted in 1769, which authorized lawyers and judges to cite in their legal arguments the laws and jurisprudence of other prospering (mostly European) "Christian, illuminated and civilized nations."[17]

Having been granted independence in 1821, Brazil adopted in 1824 a constitution that established a parliamentarian regime. The emperor was responsible for naming the ministers and prime minister, and all economic activity was regulated by Congress, which was divided into a senate and lower house, both elected (until 1881) through indirect vote.[18] The Napoleonic commerce code of 1807, which Brazil adopted, was widely applied during the first years of the century by most of the countries from which Brazil drew inspiration in drafting its own laws (mainly Portugal,

---

[17] The literal translation from Portuguese would be "Christian, illuminated and polished nations," but I took polish as meaning civilized. See Mária Bárbara Levy, *A Indústria do Rio de Janeiro através de suas Sociedades Anônimas*, Rio de Janeiro: UFRJ Editora, 1994, p. 34.

[18] Voters chose electors who, in turn, chose legislators by participating in state electoral colleges. Voting was restricted to Brazilian males 21 years of age and older who had an income of 100$000 (one hundred mi-reis) or more (the income requirement was doubled in 1846). Members of the lower house were elected to four-year terms and senators for life. The number of senators was equal to half the number of lower chamber representatives per state. The electoral colleges made lists of the three most-voted candidates for each seat in the senate. The emperor had the right to choose one of the three candidates. Electors and congressmen were required to have an income of more than 200$000 (400$000 after 1846). See, for example, Jairo Nicolau, *História do voto no Brasil*, Rio de Janeiro: Jorge Zahar, 2002, pp. 10–12.

Spain, Italy, Belgium, and France). The bankruptcy provisions excluded merchants and were strict with debtors, deeming them criminals and prescribing jail sentences for some forms of default.

A commission established early in 1850 was charged by Minister of Justice Eusébio de Queiroz with drafting a Brazilian commerce code in close consultation with businessmen. Committee members included congressional specialists in commercial legislation and the Viscount of Mauá, the most prolific Brazilian businessman of the nineteenth century, who had built the first railroad from the interior to the coast, owned several banking houses, and developed infrastructure and utility projects in Rio de Janeiro. The commerce code drafted by the commission included a section that followed Napoleonic strictness with respect to the treatment of debtors.

A procreditor bias continued to characterize bankruptcy laws drafted during the republican period. In 1890, bondholders were accorded first priority during bankruptcy and the company laws of 1890 and 1891 afforded debtors who got into financial difficulties little breathing room. All of the bankruptcy procedures granted creditors control of insolvent businesses. This procreditor bias in bankruptcy procedures was also common outside Brazil during the nineteenth century, especially in countries that followed the French civil law tradition. For instance, Jerôme Sgard, who studied the evolution of bankruptcy laws in Europe, observes: "[N]ineteenth-century laws emphatically protected their [creditor] rights during bankruptcy."[19]

Reforms to the bankruptcy law during the republican period were subject both to foreign influence and to Congress's fraternization with business associations. The republican system intensified political competition and encouraged congressmen to court interest groups that could influence large numbers of voters. Commercial associations, because they had a strong political voice and a large base of literate, male voters, were natural targets for politicians. Powerful businessmen and associations could, moreover, finance political campaigns and political parties. When these associations were consulted, their lawyers would review the practices of bankruptcy law in other countries and suggest reforms accordingly.

The 1902 law that changed bankruptcy procedures mimicked Italian laws of the time in changing the possibility of having creditors elected as trustees and accorded judges the right to choose trustees from lists of reputable merchants and businessmen compiled by the commercial associations of each city. These reforms were not passed until the draft had been

---

[19] Jérôme Sgard, "Do Legal Origins Matter? Bankruptcy Laws in Europe (1808–1914)," *European Review of Economic History* 10, 3 (December 2006): 389–419, esp. pp. 397–398.

circulated among "justice tribunals, the Lawyers Institute, the law schools, the commercial associations of the largest cities, and a great number of legal specialists."[20] When, in 1928, the congressional commission charged with drafting a new bankruptcy law asked the stock brokers associations of Rio de Janeiro and São Paulo and the Commercial Association of São Paulo to propose a new law, the lawyer for the latter suggested only minor edits to the 1908 law and hinted at complete satisfaction with the current state of the law.[21]

Getúlio Vargas, upon securing the presidency of Brazil in 1930 following a brief civil war, immediately installed a provisional government and dismissed Congress. After a two-year interim government, Vargas was elected president in 1934 under a new constitution that restored the secret ballot and introduced mandatory voting for all male and female Brazilians of 18 years and older. Yet the improved democratic system was short lived. In 1937, Vargas established an authoritarian regime that gave unrestricted power to the executive without any oversight from Congress. In order to build a large base of political support, Vargas began to build a new social pact much in the spirit of Mussolini's corporatist state.

Vargas had an implicit contract with labor unions whereby he exchanged political support for labor protections. Vargas drew his main base of support from labor unions, especially those he artificially created in the first years of his presidency. Since the early 1930s, his government had promoted labor legislation that introduced such basic protections for workers as a minimum wage, paid vacations, and pension funds.[22] An effort to consolidate labor laws initiated in 1943 yielded the Consolidation of Labor Laws

---

[20] "A novísima lei de fallencias," *São Paulo Judiciário*, October 2003, p. 157.

[21] Courting the votes and political support of these associations was important because after 1891 only literate males could vote and these associations represented a mass of literate males who also could provide financing for political parties (the 1890 census estimated that only 19.1% of the population was literate, while the 1920 census estimated this figure was 28.9%). For a better description of how Congress consulted with the lawyers of these associations see Adamastor Lima, *Nova lei das fallencias: decreto n. 5.746 de 9 de dezembro de 1929, comparada com a lei n. 2.024 de 1908*, Rio de Janeiro: Coelho Branco, 1929, pp. 11.

[22] The constitution drafted by Vargas in 1937 respected labor rights that had been included in the 1934 constitution. Specific labor protections were legislated thereafter. A minimum wage was established in 1938, unions were transformed into state and national unions by profession in 1939, union contributions were made mandatory in 1940, and the Justiça do Trabalho (Justice of Labor) was regulated in 1941 by a law that introduced an arbitration panel to resolve all labor disputes. For more information on the Consolidation of Labor Laws legislation that compiled previously legislated labor rights, see CLT in Decree-Law 5,452, May 1, 1943.

(*Consolidação das Leis do Trabalho* or CLT). Most of the changes in labor laws were promoted by the Ministry of Labor under Minister Alexandre Marcondes Filho, whom Vargas had also appointed minister of justice. The new bankruptcy law passed by Marcondes Filho in 1945 as part of legal reforms to put in place the CLT radically altered creditor protections. Drafted by a committee of lawyers loyal to Vargas, it was passed as presidential decree-law (a presidential decree that automatically became law) without congressional approval.[23]

The bankruptcy law of 1945 protected incumbent management and labor and eliminated many important creditor protections. Debtors could avoid liquidation by filing for a composition scheme called *concordata preventiva*, which gave debtors two years to reorganize and pay all debts. Creditor approval was not required if the debtor paid 50% of unsecured debts up front or promised to pay more than 60% of debts over two years.[24] Secured creditors, in theory, could opt out of the deal and collect collateral, but in practice they rarely recovered anything as credits owed in the form of social security payments and labor injury compensation took precedence over other creditors and the process whereby collateral was collected lengthened over time.

The legal figure of the *concordata preventiva* was copied from European bankruptcy laws after some delay. According to Paolo Di Martino, the *concordato preventivo* (its name in Italian) introduced in Italy in 1903 was an attempt to avoid unnecessary liquidations by extending the possibility of reaching an agreement before bankruptcy procedures were initiated. Although not particularly successful in Italy in providing for the continuation of businesses because it required of debtors an upfront payment of 40% of total debt as a prerequisite for reaching an agreement with creditors, in Brazil, *concordatas preventivas* were less problematic because debtors were offered the possibility of paying off most of their debts over time.[25]

---

[23] Information on Alexandre Marcondes Filho is from Fundação Getúlio Vargas, CPDOC, "A Era Vargas – 1º tempo – dos anos 20 a 1945," available at www.cpdoc.fgv.br.

[24] Article 156 of Decree-Law 7661, June 21, 1945 specified that debtors could retain control of their assets by agreeing to pay 50% of debts up front, or 60%, 70%, 90%, or 100% of their debts in six, 12, 18, or 24 months, respectively. Debtors were required to pay two-fifths of their total debts during the first year.

[25] The lower the up-front payment a debtor offered, the greater the proportion of creditors whose support was needed to make the proposal legally binding. This was the case not only in the *concordata preventiva*, but also in all concordata arrangements. For the history of bankruptcy in Italy, see Paolo Di Martino, "Approaching Disaster: Personal Bankruptcy Legislation in Italy and England, c. 1880–1939," *Business History* 47, 1 (January 2005):

In fact, delays in bankruptcy cases afforded debtors even more time and reduced creditors' expected recovery rates. After 1945, bankruptcy became a slow judicial process, tending to last, on average, five to ten years. Delays and the post-1940s high-inflation scenario lowered secured creditors' real expected recovery rate to zero, and when, after a few years, creditors repossessed the collateral, the assets collected tended to be worthless.[26]

Brazil did not see another bankruptcy law with less prodebtor bias until 2005, following ten years of congressional negotiations during which congressmen from leftist parties tried to protect the priority of labor and the national treasury fought to preserve its priority over secured creditors. In the end, an agreement among congressmen limited the maximum amount labor could claim as privileged credits and gave secured creditors priority over debts owed to the treasury.

AN EXPLORATION OF COURT ENFORCEMENT OF CREDITOR RIGHTS IN BRAZIL, 1850–1945

Thus far, this chapter has presented evidence of the extent of creditor protections on paper. A common concern in developing countries is whether courts enforce contracts following the letter of the law or deviate to follow personal biases or the customs of a country. This section recounts evidence of bankruptcy court cases to show how Brazil's bankruptcy law was, in practice, enforced by judges, at least in Rio de Janeiro.

The section is divided into four parts. The first part explains the bankruptcy procedures for corporations as enforced by the commercial courts of Rio de Janeiro. They uncover a strong protection for bondholders and show that the process tended to be relatively quick, in many cases yielding good recovery rates. The second section examines the enforcement of creditor rights between 1850 and 1889, demonstrating that Brazil had a long tradition of strong court enforcement of creditor rights since at least the drafting

---

22–43, esp. p. 28, and "Bankruptcy Law and Banking Crises in Italy (c. 1890–1938)," *Revista di Storia Economica* 20, 1 (April 2004): 65–85.

[26] On the actual law, see Brasil, Decree-Law 7661, June 21, 1945, and on the history of bankruptcy law, see Paulo Penalva Santos, "Brevíssima notícia sobre a recuperação extrajudicial," *Revista do Advogado* 25, 83, (September 2005): 107–115. Inflation correction for assets and liabilities of bankrupt firms was forbidden by law until 1984. The changes in foreclosures are based on the experiences of bankruptcy lawyers in São Paulo. Among others, I interviewed Luis Fernando de Paiva and Giuliano Colombo, bankruptcy specialists from Pinheiro Neto Advogados; Thomas Felsberg, of Felsberg & Associados; and Jairo Saddi, of Saddi Advogados. All of the interviews were conducted in São Paulo, Brazil, November 11, 2005.

of the commerce code in 1850. This means that by the time bondholders got priority during bankruptcy, in the bankruptcy law of 1890, the courts already had been enforcing the rights of creditors (and secured creditors in particular) for decades. The third part examines the evidence of the most controversial scandal of corporate governance and creditor protections of the period, which is the fraudulent issues of bonds of the Estrada de Ferro (E. F.) Sorocabana. The evidence shows that the controversy was solved in court and in favor of creditors. Finally, the last section studies the motivation of judges for protecting bondholder rights. It looks at the life of two judges who commonly presided over the cases found at the National Archive in Brazil. The argument of this section is that they had a strong motivation to enforce creditor rights, not only because that was mandated by law, but also because they and their families were investors and were part of the Brazilian elite who had access to securities markets.

Bankruptcy Procedures and Court Enforcement of Creditor Rights in Brazil, 1850–1945

There were three main bankruptcy arrangements in Brazil between 1850 and 1945. The first was the *liquidação forçada*, or forced liquidation, after 1908 called simply bankruptcy (*falência*).[27] This process was like the United States' Chapter 7 arrangement, also called, in English legislation, simply bankruptcy.[28] In fact, the Brazilian procedure was quite similar to the English one. Creditors first had to ask the tribunals to declare a company bankrupt, then prove that the company was insolvent or had stopped servicing its debts. This was the most common way for creditors to protect their interests against managers. Once forced liquidation was declared by a judge (who had 24 hours to check creditor allegations before declaring bankruptcy), the process of handing over management to trustees began, and the debtor was required to submit a list of creditors to be called by the courts to initiate the liquidation.

---

[27] This was more clearly typified in the compilation of decrees related to Joint Stock Company Laws, Decree 603, October 17, 1891. See articles 233, 234, and 235 on forced liquidation. In the commerce code of 1850, this type of bankruptcy was called simply *quebra* (bankruptcy). See Brazil, *Coleção das Leis e Decretos*, Rio de Janeiro: Imprensa Nacional, 1890–1930.

[28] For American bankruptcy procedures, see Margaret Howard and Peter A. Alces, *Cases and Materials on Bankruptcy*, St. Paul, Minn.: West Group, 2001, and for English procedures see *English Statutes: The Bankruptcy Act, 1969* (32 & 33 Vict., c. 71, 1869) and *The Companies (Consolidation) Act 1908* (8 Edw. VII, c. 69, 1908).

The second, probably more common, arrangement, called *concordata* (composition), was an agreement to reschedule or pay with equity debts to creditors.[29] Unlike the modern American Chapter 11 arrangement, whereby managers are protected from creditors and given time to reorganize, in Brazil the *concordata* reorganization plan proposed by debtors, before or after the bankruptcy was initiated, was subject to creditors' approval.[30] Until 1902, to be approved, a reorganization agreement required a majority vote by a sufficient number of creditors to represent three-quarters of all credits. Beginning in 1902, the proportion of the total debt a company committed as a down payment began to determine the number of creditors needed to approve a reorganization. The more a firm paid up front, the fewer creditors were needed to approve the deal.[31] Small creditors opposed to the plan had three days to contest it.[32]

A third type of bankruptcy arrangement, not explicitly included in the bankruptcy codes until 1890–1902, was called *liquidação amigável*.[33] Bankruptcy in this case was filed by managers, as in Chapter 11 arrangements, but the judge was required, if agreement was not reached, to deliver control of the company to the creditors.[34] The attractiveness of this procedure was that it made it less likely for managers to face jail sentences,

---

[29] *Concordata* schemes appeared in the Commerce Code of 1850, articles 842–854. See Brazil, *Coleção das Leis e Decretos*, Rio de Janeiro: Imprensa Nacional, 1890–1930.

[30] The Brazilian *concordata* was exactly the same procedure that American bankruptcy law included in Chapter 10 of the 1898 Bankruptcy Law. This receivership scheme only survived until the 1978 law merged the old Chapter 10 with the old Chapter 11 into the modern Chapter 11. The modern Chapter 11 permits management to stay while the firm is reorganized. See Howard and Alces, *Cases and Materials on Bankruptcy*.

[31] See article 260 of Decree 603, October 20, 1891; Article 54 of Law 859, August 16, 1902; Law 2024, December 17, 1908; and Article 106 of Decree 5746, September 12, 1929 in Brazil, *Colecção das Leis e Decretos*, Rio de Janeiro: Imprensa Nacional, 1888–1930. All the details of the size of the down payment needed to get the reorganization approved and the size of the majority needed to approve it (e.g., simple majority vs. super majority) are in Aldo Musacchio, "Law and Finance in Historical Perspective: Politics, Bankruptcy Law, and Corporate Governance in Brazil, 1850–2002," unpublished Ph.D. dissertation, Stanford University, 2005, Appendix A.

[32] See, for example, Antônio Bento de Faria, *Das Fallencias (Lei n. 859 de 16 de agosto de 1902), Annotada de Accordo com a doutrina, a legislação e a jurisprudencia e seguida de um formulário por Antonio Bento de Faria, Bacharel em sciencias jurídicas e sociais*, Rio de Janeiro: Jacintho Ribeiro dos Santos, 1902, p. 146, and other annotated bankruptcy laws. The most cited work on *concordatas preventivas* was by the legal specialist (*jurisconsulto*) Dr. Carvalho de Mendoça called *Fallencias*.

[33] Decree 603, October 17, 1891 included this provision in articles 214, 221, and 224.

[34] There are in Brazil court cases that show that this practice existed before 1890. See, for example, Corte de Apelação, A. A. Figueira e Companhia, 1879.

which was a normal punishment for negligence when creditors filed for bankruptcy.

How a company declared bankrupt was run varied with the bankruptcy laws that prevailed. For example, before 1890, an official trustee, the *curador da massa falida*, was appointed by the courts to take charge of the reorganization or liquidation of the company. This system was much like the English trustee system in which professional officials ran bankrupt companies. After Brazil's bankruptcy laws were reformed in 1890, bankrupt companies were run by two trustees selected by a judge from among the largest creditors (usually banks). In 1902 the system was changed again and the judge had to nominate trustees from within lists of reputable banks, companies, and merchants by town. Finally, in 1908, the system returned again to one in which the judge selected trustees from the largest creditors.[35]

The 1908 bankruptcy law again modified the manner in which trustees were selected, assigning to the presiding judge responsibility for choosing from among the largest creditors of a bankrupt company one to three trustees. The "liquidating" trustees were retained as a way for creditors democratically to elect representatives who could monitor the trustees' activities.[36]

Bankruptcy court cases available at Brazil's national archive show that bankruptcy was usually solved in one of three ways. If a bankrupt company's current accounts or liquid assets yielded sufficient cash, this was used by the trustees to pay its creditors. If a bankrupt company lacked sufficient cash to pay its outstanding debt and an agreement could not be reached between its shareholders and creditors, the trustees would sell some or all of its assets, usually through public auction. But the *concordata*, which employed receivership or reorganization and arranged for creditors to be paid either in installments or with equity, was the recourse to bankruptcy perhaps most commonly invoked in Brazil during this period.

Bankruptcy Cases in the National Archive of Brazil

This section uses a sample of approximately 40 bankruptcy court cases (some companies have more than one case) from the national archive in Rio de Janeiro. Albeit relatively small, this sample, being representative of the

---

[35] See the changes in the selection criteria to elect trustees in Adamastor Lima, *Nova lei das fallencias: decreto n. 5.746 de 9 de dezembro de 1929, comparada com a lei n. 2.024 de 1908.*

[36] See Musacchio, "Law and Finance in Historical Perspective, Appendix A, for a detailed list of changes in this law.

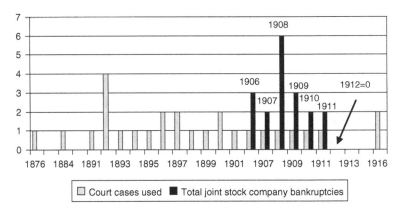

Figure 7.1. Total corporate bankruptcies and cases used
Source: *Retrospecto Comercial do Jornal do Commércio*, 1906–1916.

different types of joint stock companies that issued bonds, likely reflects with reasonable fidelity the workings of Brazil's bankruptcy procedures during the period 1850–1945. Most of the cases are from the Civil and Commercial Tribunal of Rio de Janeiro (in particular the archive of the court of appeal in Rio de Janeiro). Companies referenced in the cases were mostly chartered in Rio de Janeiro, although some cases involving corporations operating in other states reached the Rio courts, and corporations chose to establish their headquarters there because it was the capital of Brazil until 1967 and the country's main financial center until at least the 1930s.[37]

To determine how representative the offset of 40 sampled cases is would require knowing the total number of joint stock company bankruptcies, but accurate bankruptcy statistics for this period are imprecise. The only reliable source available to me was the financial newspaper, *Jornal do Commércio*, which published annual summaries of bankruptcy proceedings of the Rio de Janeiro Civil and Criminal Tribunals for the period 1906–1916.[38] Figure 7.1 compares the number of cases I examined to the total number of

---

[37]　A review of the books of the first two civil courts in the state of São Paulo, which cover most commercial cases until the first decades of the twentieth century, yielded not a single case of a corporation filing for bankruptcy. The books can be consulted at the Museu da Justiça in São Paulo.

[38]　Annual summaries of the number of bankruptcy cases published in Brazil, Ministério da Justiça, *Relatório do Ministério da Justiça*, Rio de Janeiro: Typografia Universal de Laemmert, 1866 were not separated by type of firm (joint stock company vs. partnership) and the method of reporting was changed several times during this period, making comparisons across time difficult.

cases for those years, which, after the turn of the twentieth century, is not high, ranging from two to three per year except in 1908, when it reached six. The cases I examined represent 30–50% of the total cases between 1906 and 1911. The cases I examined for the period 1895–1900. Even if during this period many companies declared bankruptcy, my sample is not that large. Yet the sample is representative of how courts operated because it includes small and unknown cases as well as some of the largest and most controversial cases of the time (e.g., those of the large railroad companies).

Court Enforcement of Creditor Rights

The *concordatas* (compositions) commonly employed to resolve bankruptcy disputes involving companies with substantial cash flows were the preferred means for human capital intensive companies and those for which the creation of value relied to a greater degree on intangible than on fixed assets. For example, a railroad was worth more as a going concern than were its constituent pieces to be sold. Creditors preferred reorganization to liquidation as well for companies that had fallen on difficult times as the result of an external shock rather than ineffective or irresponsible management.

The Leopoldina Railway Company is a case in point in the enforcement of creditor protections during the bankruptcy of a large company. One of the largest joint stock companies in Brazil, the Leopoldina stopped paying the coupons on its pound sterling bonds in 1895. The company was declared bankrupt in 1897 after Edward Herdman, representing its British debenture holders, showed proof of suspension of payments for two years (the minimum to request bankruptcy was six months). Because he represented a significant portion of the company's debts, Herdman became, together with the Banco da República (Brazil's largest bank), a trustee of the company's receivership. The trustees serviced the company's debt with its profits and later mediated an agreement between bondholders and shareholders whereby, instead of liquidating the company, the former swapped their bonds for equity. The bankruptcy process was initiated in 1897; by the summer of 1898, the company had swapped its former gold-denominated bonds for ordinary shares and made a new issue of 4% bonds, which traded at 83% of par in their first year.[39] It began paying coupons in January 1899.

Creditor rights were accorded strong protection not only by judges' strict adherence to the provisions of Brazil's bankruptcy law, but also by

---

[39] Corte de Apelação, "Estrada de Ferro Leopoldina," 1897, and *Investor's Monthly Manual*, foreign railways section, 1894–1898.

precedents that were thereby established. Foreign creditors of the railroad company Sapucaí were among the beneficiaries of the precedents set by the Leopoldina case, in the wake of which the jurisprudence stated that "the foreign creditor with an address outside of the country can request a bankruptcy procedure for a debtor established here [in Brazil], without having to file a charter in the local registry." Thus, when in 1899 management of the Sapucaí Railway stopped servicing the company's bonds in pounds sterling, the firm's shareholders and exdirectors proposed to the English bondholders, who had created a bondholders' association and sent a representative to Rio de Janeiro, a swap of debt for equity, a sweet deal for bondholders because the Minas Gerais state government had guaranteed a dividend of at least 6% on the company's shares. Moreover, the government had made the concession of a new line conditional on reorganization. Bondholders accepted the deal and ended up owning 80% of total equity.[40]

Such reorganizations, common for railways, were also undertaken in the cases of smaller companies. In the 1915 reorganization of the Companhia Industrial e de Construções Prediais "O Prédio" (a construction company), for example, privileged creditors took control of the company and scheduled payments for the other creditors.[41]

Companies with less certain cash flows were more likely to have their assets liquidated to pay creditors. Creditors of the Companhia Vidraria "Carmita" recovered 25% of their debts from liquidation of the glass factory's assets, the same percentage recovered by even nonpriveleged creditors of the Companhia Anonyma Coudelaria Cruzeiro after the horse breeding farm's assets were liquidated and bondholders were repaid. Some assets of the E. F. Leopoldina were liquidated to pay some of its creditors, and trustees of the bankrupt textile mill Santa Maria auctioned all of its assets to pay its debts.[42]

In liquidation, assets of other firms that belonged to the same organization could be used to pay creditors of companies that were part of a holding. The 1894 case of the Companhia Geral de Estradas de Ferro do Brasil, a

---

[40] For jurisprudence see *Revista de Jurisprudencia*, vol. 2, 1897, pp. 84–86,. For bankruptcy case see Corte de Apelação, "Viação Férrea Sapucahy," 1899 and Viação Férrea Sapucahy, "Various," 1899–1900.

[41] See Corte de Apelação, "O Prédio," 1915.

[42] See Corte de Apelação, "Carmita," 1916; Corte de Apelação, Companhia Anonyma Coudelaria Cruzeira, 1892; Corte de Apelação, Estrada de Ferro Leopoldina, 1897; and Corte de Apelação, Companhia de Fiação e Tecidos Santa Maria, 1909.

holding group that had shares in some major railways and at least one bank, the Banco de Crédito Universal, became famous in this regard. Because it had issued debentures for more than its capital, the Companhia Geral de Estradas de Ferro do Brasil, in bankruptcy, used assets of the Banco de Crédito Universal to pay creditors before ultimately being sold to the Leopoldina Railway.[43]

Judges played an important role in monitoring creditors' running of bankrupt companies or taking them to liquidation. They monitored the work of trustees and paid them a fee proportional to the value of the assets under management (the fees had to be approved by creditors). Day-to-day costs of administration were charged against the assets to be distributed among creditors. An example of how judges' monitoring of trustees contributed to successful outcomes in bankruptcies is provided by case of Companhia Nacional Mineira. When a group of creditors of the failed mining concern complained that the liquidating expenses declared by the trustees were excessive, the court readjusted the expense statement and reduced the payments requested by the trustees.[44]

Creditors could only appropriate the operating capital of companies that had sufficient liquid assets to repay them through the liquidation procedure (bankruptcy or *falência*). Thus, in 1916, the trustees of the textile mill Companhia de Tecidos e Fiação Santo Aleixo, after gathering the funds available from different bank accounts, paid the firm's debenture holders. Similarly, when Cervejaria Bavaria, a beer brewing company, was forced into liquidation in 1898, the trustees assumed control of the firm and used available cash to pay debenture holders their titles, including late payment of the last two coupons.[45]

Albeit far from perfect, tending to last more than a year and frequently uncovering other problems such as poor accounting procedures, Brazil's bankruptcy procedures nevertheless worked well enough to contribute to the development in the early 1900s of a large bond market. By comparison, bankruptcy procedures in Brazil in 1990 tended to last, on average, from four to six years.[46]

---

[43] See Corte de Apelação, Companhia Geral de Estradas de Ferro do Brasil, 1894.
[44] See Corte de Apelação, Companhia Nacional Mineira, 1916.
[45] See Corte de Apelação, Companhia de Tecidos e Fiação Santo Aleixo, 1916, and Corte de Apelação, Cervejaria Bavaria, 1900.
[46] See Doing Business Reports by the World Bank, 2006, especially the "closing a business" reports at www.doingbusiness.org.

The Sorocabana Railway Scandal

Few if any countries' corporate histories are without scandals, and Brazil is not the exception. But in Brazil, corporate scandals that involved abuse of bondholders generally ended in court procedures that protected the rights of creditors.

At the turn of the twentieth century, in fact, Brazil was the locus of one of the most noted corporate scandals in the world, involving the bond issues and accounting procedures of one of the country's largest railway companies, the E. F. Sorocabana e Ituana. The E. F. Sorocabana e Ituana was the product of the 1892 merger of the E. F. Sorocabana and E. F. Ituana railways. The company tried to consolidate the debenture issues of the merged railways by inviting bondholders voluntarily to swap their old bonds for two new issues of the merged company. In 1901, harsh criticism from the Rio de Janeiro Stock Brokers Association alerted the public that the company had issued a larger number of new bonds than was necessary to swap the old issues. Because accounting irregularities made it difficult to track how many bonds were actually swapped, the scandal only began to unravel when the company was declared bankrupt and the trustees began to examine the books.[47]

The court was asked to initiate bankruptcy procedures by Doctor João Caldas, owner of 569 of the company's debentures, who maintained that coupon payments were three months late and other of the company's debts were in default. The E. F. Sorocabana was declared bankrupt in 1901 by a court in Rio de Janeiro and liquidated. Most of the company's creditors were paid with the proceeds of the auction of its assets.[48]

The liquidation ended in 1904 when the federal government purchased the company's assets and concession for 60 thousand contos of mil reis (approximately £3,000,000). By January 1905, the government had transferred the railway to the Sao Paulo State government, which had offered £3,250,000. The state government, in turn, leased the railway for 60 years to railway and port entrepreneur Percival Farquhar, under whose management it adopted the name Sorocabana Railway Co. and issued new debentures.[49]

---

[47] Camara Sindical de Corretores de Fundos Públicos da Bolsa de Valores do Rio de Janeiro, *Relatorio da Câmara Sindical de Corretores de Fundos Públicos da Bolsa de Valores do Rio de Janeiro 1904–1905*, Rio de Janeiro: Imprensa Nacional, 1905, pp. 19–26.

[48] Corte de Apelação, "Companhia União Sorocabana e Ituana," 1901. The case folder is incomplete. I deduce that creditors were paid because we know the company's assets were auctioned for 60,000 contos or three million pounds sterling. The next footnote further contributes to our understanding of this episode.

[49] Percival Farquhar became a railway tycoon in Brazil, leasing, with his partners, some of the largest lines in the country (e.g., the Sorocabana e Ituana and Mojiana [Mogyana]) and

In the notarial records of the company's first bond issue, Farquhar commits the company to honor the bonds of certain British investors who had apparently not taken part in the liquidation a couple of years earlier or had cut a deal with the federal or state government to have their bonds honored in full. This group of British bondholders, represented by the London Country and Westminster Bank Ltd., received new bonds in 1907.[50]

The Long Tradition of Court Enforcement of Creditor Rights, 1850–1889

Two further questions regarding the enforcement of creditor rights in Brazil emerge at this point. First, were courts enforcing creditor rights strongly only after 1890 or was there a longer tradition of court enforcement of credit contracts? Second, why were Brazilian judges eager to enforce creditor rights so strongly before 1945 and not willing to protect creditors after that?

What is perhaps most interesting about bankruptcy court cases in Brazil is that from the empire to the early republic there were no notable changes in the way courts enforced the law. There is a demarcation in judicial practice circa 1889, after which emerged the provision that accorded first priority to bondholders in bankruptcy procedures and the reorganization of the justice system that decentralized the judiciary and rendered it more independent of the executive. This section explains how bankruptcy institutions operated before 1889 and provides evidence that judges' eagerness to enforce creditor rights derived from their own cognitive bias and the fact that they also were investors in securities.

A representative case of how bankruptcy disputes were resolved before 1889 is that of João Monteiro Ornellas. The tobacco planter and cigar producer filed for bankruptcy in 1863 at the 1a Vara do Comércio of Rio de Janeiro (the First Commercial District Court of Rio de Janeiro). The judge first declared the process to be open and requested a list of creditors. A notice calling the creditors was subsequently published in the major

---

buying or building other important lines. Researchers using network analysis techniques have argued that Farquhar might have been the most central and influential businessman in Brazil circa 1910. See Aldo Musacchio and Ian Read, "Bankers, Industrialists, and their Cliques: Elite Networks in Mexico and Brazil during Early Industrialization," *Enterprise and Society* 8, 4 (December 2007): 842–880.

[50] For the sale of the Sorocabana, see Saes, *As Ferrovias de São Paulo*, pp. 159–160. The notarial records of the bond issues of the company come from Primeiro Cartório de Notas da Capital, "Sorocabana Railway Co.," 1907.

ncwspapcrs and the judge, once proof of their credits was presented, selected from among the major creditors a trustee to run the liquidation (called *curador fiscal da massa falida*). Much the same procedure was followed during the republic, save that during the empire a judge had been obliged to call eight witnesses together with the debtor and affected creditors to declare the type of bankruptcy (whether fraudulent or not).

When debtors committed fraud that led to their bankruptcy, judges usually punished them with prison sentences. This was more common during the imperial period. For instance, Alberto da Fonseca, partner of Alberto da Fonseca & Cia, was sent to prison in 1859 for having been discovered by the judge and trustees handling the firm's bankruptcy to have intentionally overstated the value of the firm's assets. Antonio José da Cunha, sole partner of A.J. da Cunha & Cia, in 1882 earned a similar fate because important ledgers, mainly "one ledger book where the credits and debits (should have been) carefully registered," went missing.[51] Debtors who committed fraudulent actions were treated as criminals during the republic as well. One was Vicente Lattuga, sentenced to prison for trying to remove "objects" from his company during the bankruptcy process.[52]

The evidence available for the period 1859–1888 suggests that during this time creditors could expect to recover some of their investments through either *concordatas* or liquidation. In the *concordata* case of Aguiar & Cunha circa 1861, creditors agreed to receive 30% of debts upfront and the rest in installments. Creditors in the case of João Monetiro Ornelas were similarly repaid in installments. Liquidation of all the merchandise in the bankrupt tailoring shop Camacho & Cia, in 1887, brought sufficient cash to pay the company's bankruptcy expenses and fully repay the debts contracted with privileged creditors (those with collateralized loans). Similarly, creditors of the bankrupt A. Gomes & Cia were able to recover 53% of their debts through liquidation of the firm's assets in 1888.

How strongly the courts enforced creditors' rights is illustrated by the case of Azevedo Lima & Cia circa 1874, the assets of which were permitted by the judge to be liquidated by the creditors when the partners in the firm failed to comply with their *concordata* to repay 15% of the creditors' debts in cash and the rest in installments, and perhaps even more dramatically in the case of A. Guimarães & Cia, in which the widow of one of the partners

---

[51] I do not have the final sentence for the case of Alberto da Fonseca because the firm's creditors abandoned the process because it was becoming too costly to pay the lawyers. See Processos Comerciais, Alberto da Fonseca & Cia, 1859 and Processos Comerciais, A. J. da Cunha & Cia, 1882.

[52] See Brazil, "Vicente Lattuga," *Diario Oficial da União*, April 10, 1896.

was made to give up her inheritance in order to repay debts her deceased husband had contracted in the name of the firm.[53]

In sum, the tradition of strongly enforcing creditor rights was established before the republic. Therefore, when other legal changes and policies facilitated the expansion of bond markets (e.g., when bondholders got first priority), the institutional settings in which the expansion of bond markets could be sustained were already in place and functioning.

Explaining Judges Attitudes toward Creditors

What disposed Brazil's judges to protect creditors' rights before 1945, and what could have changed such attitudes over the long run? That many of the judges before the 1930s were progeny of Brazil's wealthy families (in many cases of imperial nobility) and generally graduates of the law school of the University of São Paulo, and their families and friends of their families often wealthy creditors and shareholders, suggests the possibility of a cognitive bias toward the enforcement of laws enacted to protect investors.[54]

Researching the lives and backgrounds of the republican judges of the Civil and Commercial Tribunal of Rio de Janeiro proved difficult; probate records after 1900 are hard to locate in the archives and few judges made it into the encyclopedias of Brazil. Information was available, however, on Caetano Pinto de Miranda Montenegro and Pedro de Alcântara Nabuco de Abreu, two judges who frequently led corporate bankruptcies.

Judge Caetano Pinto de Miranda Montenegro was born into a wealthy Rio de Janeiro family; his father, according to probate records, owned buildings on some of the main streets in the commercial district (including three houses on Rua do Ouvidor) and had approximately 10% of his wealth in government bonds at the time of his death in 1852. The inheritance of Judge Montenegro (two years old at the time) was 13.798$881, the mean

---

[53] See Processos Comerciais, Aguiar & Cunha, 1861; Processos Comerciais, Aguiar & Cunha, 1861; Processos Comerciais, A. Gomes & Cia, 1888; Processos Comerciais, A. Guimarães, 1881; Processos Comerciais, Camacho & Cia, 1887; Processos Comerciais, Azevedo Lima & Cia, 1874; and Processos Comerciais, João Monteiro Ornelas, 1863.

[54] By cognitive bias I mean that judges make rulings and issue sentences based on what they believe to be right in accordance with what they have seen in the courts and studied in law school and their knowledge of the world. For an appraisal of how cognitive bias changed in the twentieth century in civil law countries, see Benito Arruñada and Veneta Andonova, "Market Institutions and Judicial Rulemaking," in Claude Menard and Mary Shirley (eds.), *The Handbook of New Institutional Economics*, Dordrecht, The Netherlands: Springer, 2005, pp. 229–250.

value of an urban property in Rio de Janeiro between 1850 and 1860.[55] If we take into account that the probate records from which these averages were obtained were those of relatively wealthy people, we can assume Judge Montenegro started life relatively well off. The trustee of his inheritance was his grandmother, the Viscount of Praia Grande.

The probate record for the judge's wife, who died in 1875, shows her estate, which included three houses, jewelry, and cash, to have been divided between the judge and his daughter. The total inheritance of approximately 43 contos (43.000$000), 21.000$000 for Judge Montenegro and an equal share for his daughter, represented a substantial amount of money in the 1870s; it would have put the judge and his family at the top 15–20% of probated wealth, or in the top 5–10% of all households, in Rio de Janeiro, even without taking into account the judge's own wealth.[56]

Being rich, of itself, was not necessarily an incentive for judges to protect creditors, but judges in Rio de Janeiro at the turn of the twentieth century tended to be investors as well, and thus creditors and shareholders, and therein lay the incentive to enforce the law pertaining to creditors' rights strongly. Judge Montenegro was a shareholder in one of the most prosperous textile mills in Rio de Janeiro, and indeed, appears to have been an original subscriber in the charter of the Companhia Petropolitana in Petropolis. His share was relatively small, 100 out of 15,000 shares originally sold, and the judge did not participate in shareholder meetings directly, relying instead on his proxy, the wealthy Baron of Vidal, the second-largest owner of the industrial venture with the second largest block of shares (11% of total shares) at the time of subscription.[57]

Judge Pedro de Alcântara Nabuco de Abreu, who graduated from the University of São Paulo law school toward the end of the 1880s, also came from one of the wealthiest families in Rio de Janeiro. His father, a doctor and an honorary member of the Imperial Academy of Medicine, was also part of the Imperial House in the 1850s and was named Knight of the Order

[55] Arquivo Nacional, Juizo de Orfãos, *Caetano Pinto de Miranda Montenegro,* Inventário, caixa 1385, no. 149. The mean value of urban property comes from Zephyr Frank, *Dutra's World: Wealth and Family in Nineteenth-Century Rio de Janeiro,* Albuquerque: University of New Mexico Press, 2004, p. 73.
[56] Arquivo Nacional, Juizo de Orfãos, *Michaella de Paula Costa Montenegro,* Inventário, caixa 4256, No 2466. Wealth comparisons to a more general sample of probate records are from personal communications with Zephyr Frank. See Frank, *Dutra's World* for references and methodologies.
[57] This information is from "Companhia Petropolitana," in Brazil, *Diario Oficial da União,* April 16, 1898.

of the Rose, one of the highest titles granted a nonnoble.[58] Like many rich doctors of the time, his father and other family members were probably investors in Brazilian corporations.

What could have changed the attitudes of such judges or shifted their cognitive bias over time to favor labor protections over creditor rights? This part of the story is more difficult to reconstruct, but we do know that the 1930s saw major changes in the way Supreme Court judges were named. During the Old Republic (1890–1930) the process was internal – judges of the Supreme Federal Tribunal (the Supreme Court) were nominated and elected by its members.

During his authoritarian regime, Getulio Vargas (1937–1945) passed decree-law 2,770, November 11, 1940, which called for Brazil's president to name the president and vice presidents of the courts. Also during his first regime in the 1930s, Vargas forced some of the judges of the Supreme Court into retirement and battled with the lawyers of the law school of the University of São Paulo, finding it difficult to find judges who would support him.

In fact, Vargas made a complete sweep of the Supreme Court during his first 15 years as president. Whereas most presidents named, on average, two or three Supreme Court judges (*ministros*), Vargas named 21 judges during this time, a number that becomes even more impressive when one takes into account that the Supreme Federal Tribunal, or Corte Suprema, had only 11 judges total. Moreover, not one of Mr. Vargas's nominations to the Supreme Court had to be approved by the Senate.[59]

In the span of a few decades after the Vargas regime, judges' attitudes and the laws changed significantly to favor labor and the government over creditors, with long-term negative consequences for the development of the country's private debt markets and the rule of law. At the turn of the twenty-first century a survey of Brazilian judges indicated that the majority of them

---

[58] See Carlos Eduardo de Almeida Barata and Antonio Henrique da Cunha Bueno (org.), *Dicionário das Famílias Brasileiras,* vol. 2, São Paulo: Ibero América, 2000, p. 1596.

[59] The Supreme Court judges named by the provisional government of Getúlio Vargas (November 2, 1930 to July 20, 1934) were Eduardo Espinola, Carvalho Mourão, Plínio Casado, Laudo De Camargo, Costa Manso, Octavio Kelly, and Ataulpho De Paiva. During his regime (1937–1945), Vargas named Armando De Alencar, Cunha Mello, José Linhares, Washington De Oliveira, Barros Barreto, Annibal Freire, Castro Nunes, Orosimbo Nonato, Waldemar Falcão, Goulart De Oliveira, Philadelpho Azevedo, Lafayette De Andrada, Edgard Costa, and Ribeiro Da Costa. See the text on the history of the Supreme Federal Tribunal on the tribunal's Web page, written by Ministro Celso Mello, "algumas notas informativas (e curiosas) sobre o Supremo Tribunal (Império e República)," at www.stf.jus.br/bicentenario/publicacao/arquivo/notasInformativas.pdf accessed 5/15/2009.

felt their judgements should directly pursue social justice or fight poverty rather than to protect creditor rights during a bankruptcy case.[60]

CONCLUSIONS

From the 1880s until 1920, Brazil's bond markets were not only large, but, as revealed by evidence presented here, relied upon by corporations in all sectors to obtain funds. Although the bulk of bond issues were by railway companies, smaller enterprises such as textile and other manufacturers and utilities companies were also important bond issuers. Many of the industries that relied on bonds to obtain funds beyond retained earnings and bank credit secured approximately 30% of their funds from debenture and about 70% from equity issues.

Evidence presented in this chapter also reveals the success of Brazil's bond markets to have been sustained by a legal framework that strongly protected creditors' rights. Creditor rights in Brazil were strong on paper and enforced by the courts of Rio de Janeiro at least between 1850 and 1916. Bondholders were accorded first priority over other creditors and were often intimately involved in the bankruptcy process. The extent of creditor rights and their enforcement seems to have changed during the Getúlio Vargas government. Between 1930 and 1945, bankruptcy laws were changed in a way that favored labor and the government over creditors (e.g., by giving them priority over most creditors or by favoring the continuation of business over liquidation). No only did the codification of laws change, but also the enforcement of the new laws was different, particularly because Vargas forced many judges into retirement and shuffled the courts as he pleased. Some of the effects of these changes persist to the present day. As noted previously, by 2006, the average bankruptcy case in Brazil took from four to six years to conclude with uncertain returns for creditors.

Finally, this chapter provides detailed evidence of how both creditor rights and court enforcement of bankruptcy law can change over time and in significant ways. I suggest that this evidence calls into question the notion propounded in the law and finance literature that legal traditions have a deterministic effect, across countries, on the legal environment that imparts protection to investors. Before 1908, all four of the protections this

---

[60] Armando Castelar Pinheiro presents the results of the opinion survey among judges in "Judiciário, reforma e economia: a visão dos magistrados," in Armando Castelar Pinheiro (ed.), *Reforma do Judiciário: Problemas, Desafios, Perspectivas*, Rio de Janeiro: IDESP and BookLink, 2003, pp. 138–206; the results of the survey asking judges whether they prefer to enforce contracts or seek social justice are presented on pp.172–173.

literature deems relevant to the development of debt markets were incorporated in Brazil's bankruptcy laws; today, only two are. More would seem to change over time than this literature assumes, but we still do not know with certainty whether such changes are country-specific or might be explained across many countries by international shocks or other events. I return to these issues in Chapter 9.

EIGHT

Were Bankers Acting as Market Makers?

The evidence presented thus far of relatively developed equity and debt markets in Brazil at the turn of the twentieth century, with a bonanza between 1890 and 1920 when the stock exchange's capitalization fluctuated between 40% (1895) and 20% (1920) of GDP and the stock of private bond issues amounted to 15% of GDP, has indicated that financial market development was sustained by institutional settings that afforded ample investor protections.[1] In this context we would not expect to find intermediaries such as universal or commercial banks playing the role of market makers. That is, we would not expect bankers to have played an important role in brokering information, relations, and long-term credit. Does history meet this expectation?

In more developed economies during this period, commercial and investment banks did play the role of market makers, "replacing" shareholder and creditor protections and providing "housekeeping seals of approval" for corporations subject, through their management teams, to the banks' influence. In the United States investment bankers played the role of market makers by underwriting securities for companies that they could monitor and influence through interlocking boards of directors.[2] German banks also played an important role as intermediaries between investors and companies, purchasing stocks (and bonds) of German corporations in blocks and then selling them to their accountholders through a system of intrabank

---

[1] These values of the stock of private issues of corporate bonds (debentures) are higher than the average capitalization for the 1990s, which fluctuated at levels lower than 10% of GDP.

[2] See, for instance, Bradford DeLong, "Did J. P. Morgan's Men Add Value?: An Economist's Perspective on Financial Capitalism," In Peter Temin (ed.) *Inside the Business Enterprise: Historical Perspectives on the Use of Information*, Chicago: University of Chicago Press, 1991, pp. 205–250.

trading. These banks also acted as proxies for their accountholders in share-holder meetings and influenced corporate direction by naming directors to the board. These directors often were also on the boards of directors of banks and, thus, interlocking boards of directors have been identified as a sign of the banks' power to act as market makers in this country too.[3]

Universal banks clearly did not play the role of market makers in Brazil as they did in continental Europe or the United States; attempts to develop them met with little success and most were abandoned by 1905.[4] But the tens of commercial banks operating throughout the country could have done so. One way to establish whether banks played a role as market makers or brokers of information and influence between depositors and corporations is to examine their position within the network of corporate board interlocks. A large literature has shown that banks that act as market makers tend to have many representatives on the boards of directors of companies for which they underwrite securities or over which they desire to have influence, the idea being that bankers, by exerting influence over boards, can, for instance, guarantee investors that companies will pay dividends or coupons on time. Banks acting as market makers therefore would be expected to occupy seats on the boards of multiple corporations, becoming central actors in the corporate network of board interlocks.

The hypothesis that it was banks acting as market makers that sustained the development of Brazil's financial markets is effectively discredited by the three pieces of evidence: (1) Brazil's banks had fewer interlocks with corporations than did banks in countries where banks have been identified as having played the role of market makers, (2) banks were less central in the web of corporate board interlocks in Brazil than in both Mexico and the United States, and (3) the correlates of bank interlocks in a multivariate set-ting using basic regression analysis on a sample that includes Brazilian and

---

[3] See Mary O'Sullivan, *Contests for Corporate Control: Corporate Governance and Economic Performance in the United States and Germany*, Oxford: Oxford University Press, 2000, Chapter 7, esp. pp. 237–238; Caroline Fohlin, "Does Civil Law Tradition and Universal Banking Crowd out Securities Markets?: Pre–World War I Germany as a Counter-Example," *Enterprise and Society* 8, 3 (September 2007): 602–641; Jeffrey Fear and Christopher Kobrak, "Banks on Board: Banks in German and American Corporate Governance, 1870–1914," unpublished manuscript, Harvard Business School and European School of Management, May 2007; and Paul Windolf, "The Emergence of Corporate Networks in the United States and Germany, 1896–1938," paper presented at the annual meeting of the American Sociological Association, Philadelphia, Penn., August 2005.

[4] The evolution of universal banks in São Paulo is discussed in detail by Anne Hanley, *Native Capital: Financial Institutions and Economic Development in São Paulo, Brazil, 1850–1920*, Stanford: Stanford University Press, 2005, Chapter 5.

Mexican companies shows that in Brazil interlocks were less common than in Mexico, even after controlling for basic company characteristics.

Mexico and the United States circa 1910 are useful for purposes of comparison because in both countries at that time bankers have been identified as important actors. In the United States, there is evidence that banks, especially investment banks, were central in the network of corporate interlocks that served as signalling and monitoring mechanisms on which shareholders and bondholders relied for assurance that their investments were protected.[5] In Mexico, the evidence suggests that banks tended to lend to related parties because of extreme information asymmetries and the discretionary nature of the legal mechanisms by which contracts were enforced.[6]

BANK-CORPORATE INTERLOCKS:
THEORY AND EVIDENCE

Bankers sit on corporate boards of directors largely for three reasons. One, interlocking boards of directors can enhance firms' access to capital and reduce banks' monitoring costs. Where contract enforcement is poor and obtaining information about borrowers too costly, banks prefer to lend to companies related to them. When credit is scarce and substitutes for it are limited, corporations might seek out board interlocks with banks.[7]

Two, having bankers on boards of directors might constitute a certification mechanism that serves to guarantee performance and on time payment of dividends or bond coupons. It was common practice in the United States

---

[5] See Vincent P. Carosso, *Investment Banking in America: A History*, Cambridge, Mass: Harvard University Press, 2007, p. 32, 38–39; and Mark Mizruchi, *The American Corporate Network: 1904–1974*, Beverly Hills, Calif.: Sage, 1982, Chapters 2 and 3.

[6] The importance of networks to improving contract enforcement and monitoring has been explored for the period 1876–1910 by Noel Maurer and for 1940–1980 by Gustavo Del Angel. See Noel Maurer, *The Power and the Money: Credible Commitments and the Financial System in Mexico, 1876–1934*, Stanford: Stanford University Press, 2003; and Gustavo Del Angel, "Paradoxes of Financial Development: The Construction of the Mexican Banking System, 1941–1982," unpublished Ph.D. dissertation, Stanford University, 2002.

[7] See Mitchell A. Petersen and Raghuram G. Rajan, "The Benefits of Lending Relationships: Evidence from Small Business Data," *Journal of Finance* 49, 1 (March 1994): 3–37; Masahiko Aoki, "Toward an Economic Model of the Japanese Firm," *Journal of Economic Literature* 28, 1 (March 1990): 1–27; Douglas W. Diamond, "Financial Intermediation and Delegated Monitoring," *Review of Economic Studies* 51, 3 (July 1984): 393–414; Naomi Lamoreaux, *Insider Lending*, Cambridge: Cambridge University Press, 1994; Randall S. Kroszner and Philip E. Strahan, "Bankers on Boards: Monitoring, Conflicts of Interest, and Lender Liability," *Journal of Financial Economics* 62, 3 (December 2001): 415–452; and Daniel Byrd and Mark S. Mizruchi, "Bankers on the Board and the Debt Ratio of Firms," *Journal of Corporate Finance* 11 (September 2005): 129–173.

at the turn of the twentieth century for investment bankers to sit on the boards of companies for which they underwrote securities.[8] A banker on the board might also signal a company's creditworthiness to other lenders.[9]

Three, bankers are a source of financial advice. Instances of commercial bankers sitting on boards of corporations that needed to restructure debt or change their financial structure substantiated the suggestion that "bankers are invited onto the boards of highly indebted nonfinancial firms to ensure continuing flows of capital as well as to allow banks to influence the firm's decision-making structure."[10] Close ties to a bank, moreover, might guarantee access to funds during a crisis.[11]

But opening a corporate board to outsiders is not always beneficial. Banks that develop close ties to firms, to the extent that they become more intimately acquainted with their past behavior as borrowers and the cash flows of their customers, can, on the basis of this private information, "extract the rents attributable to knowing that the borrower is less risky."[12] In other words, related banks, if they are better able than distant lenders to evaluate risky projects, have an incentive to capture "most of the rents that client firms may enjoy due to their access to capital and thereby push down firm profits."[13] Moreover, banks' interests are not necessarily in harmony with those of corporate shareholders. Banks, for example, "prefer that the firm undertakes actions that maximize the probability of their repayment rather than maximize the expected return of shareholders."[14]

In some institutional settings, companies might thus be well advised to distance themselves from bankers. If, for example, financial markets are developed and other financing options are available, there is less reason

---

[8] See Carosso, *Investment Banking in America,* pp. 32–33.

[9] See Kroszner and Strahan, "Bankers on Boards:," p. 419.

[10] Quote from Byrd and Mizruchi, "Bankers on the Board and the Debt Ratio of Firms," p. 131. For more on how banks have acted as advisers of companies in the United States see Gerald Davis and Mark S. Mizruchi, "The Money Center Cannot Hold: Commercial Banks in the U.S. System of Corporate Governance," *Administrative Science Quarterly* 44, 2 (1999): 224.

[11] See Takeo Hoshi, Anil Kashyap and David Scharfstein, "The Role of Banks in Reducing the Costs of Financial Distress in Japan," NBER Working Paper 3435, 1990; Raghuram G. Rajan and Luigi Zingales, "Financial Systems, Industrial Structure, and Growth," *Oxford Review of Economic Policy* 17, 4 (2001): 467–482, esp. p. 473; and Kroszner and Strahan, "Bankers on Boards," p. 419.

[12] Petersen and Rajan, "The Benefits of Lending Relationships," 3–37, quote from p. 6.

[13] Quote from David E. Weinstein and Yishay Yafeh, "On the Costs of Bank-centered Financial System: Evidence from the Changing Main Bank Relations in Japan," *Journal of Finance* 53, 2 (April 1998): 635–672, esp. p. 639.

[14] See Kroszner and Strahan, "Bankers on Boards," p. 420.

to maintain relationships with banks for purposes of accessing capital. Similarly, if open disclosure rules make it relatively easy for lenders and investors to obtain information about companies, there will be less need to establish interlocking boards of directors between banks and corporations in order to reduce information asymmetries. In these environments, the role of bankers might be reduced to certification or advice.

There have been since the late 1980s at least two documented cases in which the development of more financial options for corporations reduced the importance of interlocks between banks and corporations. In Japan, where close bank-firm relations have been pervasive since World War II, the opening of financial markets at the end of the 1980s afforded companies access to other sources of funds such as uncollateralized bonds, which enabled risk-taking companies to grow faster than those that stayed linked to banks.[15] Close relations between banks and companies had been a common feature of the U.S. economy as well since at least 1904. There, the financial liberalization of the late 1980s, in giving rise to additional financing options such as commercial paper, rendered relationships with banks less necessary as evidenced in the decline in number of corporate board interlocks with banks from 1980 to 1994.[16]

BANKERS AND THE FINANCIAL SYSTEM IN BRAZIL, MEXICO, AND THE UNITED STATES CIRCA 1909

Bankers as Market Makers: The Case of the United States

Financial markets in the United States at the turn of the twentieth century were relatively developed by international standards, but large corporations did not access capital on an impersonal basis.[17] One characteristic of large corporations during this period, commonly termed the era of the robber barons or financial capitalism, is that they shared their boards of directors

---

[15] Weinstein and Yafeh, "On the Costs of Bank-Centered Financial System."
[16] Davis and Mizruchi, "The Money Center Cannot Hold," 215–239.
[17] See Raymond W. Goldsmith, *Comparative National Balance Sheets: A Study of Twenty Countries, 1688–1978*, Chicago: University of Chicago Press, 1985, pp. 291–301; Raghuram Rajan and Luigi Zingales, "The Great Reversals: The Politics of Financial Development in the 20th Century," *Journal of Financial Economics* 69 (2003): 5–50 (in several tables they present comparative figures of the levels of financial development since 1913); and Richard Sylla, "Schumpeter Redux: A Review of Raghuram G. Rajan and Luigi Zingales, 'Saving Capitalism from the Capitalists,' *Journal of Economic Literature* 44 (June 2006): 391–404 (esp. pp. 401–402 on which he argues that the U.S. stock market was larger than Rajan and Zingales estimated).

with investment bankers as a way to access external financing.[18] These bankers had the capacity to sell large amounts of equity and bonds to customers in Europe and the United States. The guarantee investment banks offered bond and equity buyers was that they would be closely involved in the businesses they underwrote, monitoring and directing managerial decisions through positions on their boards of directors.

In most deals, investment bankers such as J. P. Morgan had as their primary concern the protection of "the interests of investors and [their] own." In the case of railroads, for example, the investors of J. P. Morgan "held him accountable for the prosperity of the roads he endorsed, an obligation that Morgan accepted seriously, and he expected the managers of these lines to exercise a similar responsibility toward him." The way to achieve this was by naming a "man he considered prudent" as director of the venture for which he was selling securities.[19] Bradford J. DeLong even shows that companies that had this kind of relations with J. P. Morgan usually had higher market valuations and paid investors higher returns.[20]

Also problematic for investors in the United States during the era of the robber barons was that manufacturing companies did not commonly disclose financial information. According to a study of company disclosure practices at the turn of the twentieth century, "so secretive were some manufacturing companies that even into the twentieth century they failed to make available to investors any financial information other than the company's capitalization and dividend records."[21] Another source reported, "[f]ew manufacturers before 1900 considered it necessary or advisable to issue regular operating statements and balance sheets; and, those that did, too often published reports that either were incomplete or, because of the absence of standard accounting practices, were of 'dubious value.'"[22] The study of company disclosure practices found further that, "not only was there inadequate financial disclosure, but some companies were irregular in the frequency with which they issued reports." In fact, "between 1897

---

[18] Carosso, *Investment Banking in America*, pp. 33–35.

[19] Carosso, *Investment Banking in America*, p. 38.

[20] See DeLong, "Did J. P. Morgan's Men Add Value?," pp. 205–250. Carlos D. Ramirez also shows that companies that had close relations with J. P. Morgan (e.g., through interlocking directorates) also had higher liquidity. See Carlos D. Ramirez, "Did J. P. Morgan's Men Add Liquidity?: Corporate Investment, Cash Flow, and Financial Structure at the Turn of the Twentieth Century," *Journal of Finance* 50, 2 (1995): 661–678.

[21] David F. Hawkins, "The Development of Modern Financial Reporting Practices Among American Manufacturing Corporations," *Business History Review* 37 (1963): 135–168, esp. p. 135.

[22] Carosso, *Investment Banking in America*, p. 44.

and 1905, the Westinghouse Electric and Manufacturing Company neither published an annual financial report to its stockholders, nor held an annual meeting."[23]

Investment bankers helped to resolve many of these information problems. Most companies controlled by investment bankers or that wanted to trade securities, for example, developed better financial disclosure systems. Some of the most detailed reports after 1900 emanated from companies such as American Tobacco, Continental Tobacco, General Electric, National Biscuit Company, and Federal Steel Company, some of which were under the control of investment bankers.[24]

With the prevailing lack of financial information, promoters of securities relied on strong reputations in order to sell. Many investors in the United States bought securities based on their confidence in the promoters or investment bankers that offered the issue, believing that investment bankers endorsed, only after investigating, issues of securities that they then guaranteed through their control of the company. Interlocks between investment bankers and corporations in this context also enabled the former to access financial information to which the public did not have access and thereby helped to resolve information asymmetries. It was reported that "few buyers and apparently fewer sellers [of securities] were disturbed by the absence of financial statements."[25]

Investment bankers having clearly played the role of market makers in the United States, we would expect banks to have been central to the network of corporate board interlocks there, and, indeed, Mark S. Mizruchi undertook to map the network of corporate interlocks circa 1904 founding, among the most central companies, many banks.[26]

---

[23] Hawkins, "The Development of Modern Financial Reporting Practices Among American Manufacturing Corporations," p. 137.

[24] Interestingly, many of these companies became active in trading securities at the turn of the century and had close relationships with investment bankers. J. P. Morgan & Co. was behind the consolidation of General Electric. For balance sheet comparisons, see David F. Hawkins, "The Development of Modern Financial Reporting Practices Among American Manufacturing Corporations"; for J. P. Morgan's deals, see Vincent P. Carosso, *Investment Banking in America, A History*, pp. 37–42.

[25] Secrecy in company accounts also stemmed from a long tradition of family ownership in the United States as a result of the belief that firms under family or close ownership by revealing "financial information they would unwittingly assist their competitors." See Hawkins, "The Development of Modern Financial Reporting Practices Among American Manufacturing Corporations," p. 143.

[26] Mizruchi, *The American Corporate Network*, p. 99.

Bank Ties to Corporations in Mexico: Market
Makers and Insider Lending

In this period in Mexico, too, economic historians agree, close relationships between banks and corporations facilitated access to capital for the latter and helped the former reduce information asymmetries and enforce credit contracts. In part, this was a way to compensate for poor protection of property rights. For instance, Noel Maurer and Tridib Sharma argue that, given the difficulty of repossessing collateral in Mexico in the event of default, banks and firms developed business groups that enabled close monitoring of corporate activities and afforded some leverage with respect to credit contracts.[27]

But perhaps more important was that market entry for banks was complicated, which further limited financing options. Haber, Razo, and Maurer documented during the Porfirian period (1876–1910) in Mexico five main obstacles:[28] (1) Bankers needed charter approval by the minister of finance (who was at the same time a stockholder in and director of the Banco Internacional e Hipotecario); (2) a high minimum capitalization (approximately US $125,000, later raised to US $250,000) was required to obtain a charter; (3) given prohibitive taxes on notes issued by second-comer banks, only the first state banks to charter were able to issue notes successfully, which limited competition; (4) only the Banco Nacional de Mexico and the Banco de Londres y Mexico could establish branches in all states; And (5) only the Banco Nacional de Mexico and the Banco de Londres y Mexico could issue notes for three times their reserves (other banks could issue notes for only two times their reserves) and only the notes of these two banks were considered legal tender nationwide.

By 1909, the Mexican banking system consisted of a handful of national and approximately 40 state banks. Banco Nacional de Mexico (Banamex), Banco Central (Mexican Central Bank), Banco de Londres y Mexico (Bank of London and Mexico), Mexican Bank of Commerce and Industry, the Banco Internacional e Hipotecario (International Mortgage Bank), and the Mortgage and Credit Foncier Bank of Mexico were the national banks.

[27] Noel Maurer and Tridib Sharma, "Enforcing Property Rights Through Reputation: Mexico's Early Industrialization, 1878–1913," *Journal of Economic History* 61, 4 (2001): 950–973.
[28] Stephen Haber, Noel Maurer, and Armando Razo, *The Politics of Property Rights: Political Instability, Credible Commitments, and Economic Growth in Mexico, 1876–1929,* Cambridge: Cambridge University Press, 2003, p. 87.

Connections were needed to access credit, so the limited number of banks in Mexico presented a problem for companies seeking financing.[29] Companies most commonly secured capital from banks by prevailing on connections to help roll over short-term loans.[30] Gomez-Galvarriato, in her study of CIVSA, one the largest cotton mills in Mexico during the Porfirian period, found that "reports given in the board meeting's minutes indicate that bank credit was … provided through short-term loans, [thus] it did not appear in the annual balance sheets."[31]

Protection of property rights in Mexico circa 1909 also relied on connections, specifically on the "vertical political integration" of the government and investors.[32] Government officials and businessmen partnered to distribute privileges and enforce property rights by selectively granting concessions to and protecting the property of parties that shared rents with the political brokers. That contract enforcement in Mexico depended more on connections than on the general application of legal principles affected in dramatic ways how companies related to the financial system.

Foreign companies that operated in Mexico, although part of the network of relations, did not depend as heavily on domestic banks. They established partnerships with Mexican political operators to gain concessions to do business in Mexico, but they had access to foreign capital markets, issuing equity and bonds in their countries of origin. Only two Mexican companies had bonds outstanding in 1909, both railroad companies bought by the government from foreign investors between 1903 and 1907 that, in 1909, still had outstanding debts in other countries.

We thus expect to find that banks were central actors in the network of corporate interlocks in Mexico and, given corporations' limited options for obtaining financing, to find many companies establishing interlocks with banks.

---

[29] For examples of the difficulty even large corporations had obtaining bank loans, see Aurora Gomez-Galvarriato, "The Impact of the Revolution: Business and Labor in the Mexican Textile Industry, Orizaba, Veracruz, 1900–1930," Ph.D. dissertation, Harvard University, 1999, Chapter 2. For a general description of the inadequacy of its banking system relative to Mexico's industrialization, see Stephen Haber, *Industry and Underdevelopment*, Stanford: Stanford University Press, 1989, Chapter 5.

[30] This has been extensively researched in Mexican economic historiography. See, for instance, the compilation of articles on banking in Leonor Ludlow and Carlos Marichal, *Banca y poder en México, 1800–1925*, 1st ed., Historia: Colección Enlace, México: Grijalbo, 1986.

[31] See Gomez-Galvarriato, "The Impact of the Revolution," p. 121.

[32] Haber et al., *The Politics of Property Rights*, Chapter 2.

Reasons to Compare Brazil with Mexico and the United States

It is useful to compare Brazil and the United States for two reasons: First, corporations in Brazil had options other than banks for obtaining financing in the domestic market, which was not as much the case in Mexico. Second, ownership of large corporations, in Brazil as in the United States, was either highly concentrated (e.g., in family firms) or relatively dispersed (e.g., in railway companies), but there is evidence showing that in the U.S. shareholder rights were weak, even compared to Brazil. While this book makes the argument that Brazil had strong shareholder rights at the company level, recent work by Naomi Lamoreaux and Jean-Laurent Rosenthal finds that in the United States shareholder rights were relatively weak and declining after the turn of the twentieth century.[33]

In Brazil, the participation of investors who held small lots of stock was fostered by institutions, including a system of financial information disclosure arguably more complete than the one operating in the United States at that time. Brazilian laws required corporations that issued debentures to file semiannually, and all companies to issue reports annually. Also, as I explained in Chapter 4, issuers of new shares and bonds in Brazil had to issue prospectuses that included the statutes of the corporation, the shareholder list, and financial information.

Comparing Brazil and Mexico is informative because, similarities in their development and growth rates notwithstanding, they ended up exhibiting significant differences in investor protections, financial market

---

[33] The division of corporations along the lines of concentrated and dispersed ownership in the United States is clear in the case of railways. The ownership of small railways in the South tending to be more concentrated than the ownership of their New England counterparts. Also, larger railways tended to have more dispersed ownership than smaller railroads. See Salomon Huebner, "The Distribution of Stockholdings in American Railways," *Annals of the American Academy of Political and Social Science* 22 (November 1903): 63–78, esp. pp. 72–73. Kenneth Lipartito and Yumiko Morii claim that most of the 200 largest corporations in the United States in the 1930s had concentrated ownership, arguing that examples of extreme ownership dispersion found in companies such as AT&T, and used in Berle and Means' seminal study of the separation of ownership and control, were an exception rather than the rule. See Kenneth Lipartito and Yumiko Morii, "Rethinking the Separation of Ownership from Management in American History," unpublished manuscript, Johns Hopkins University, 2007.

Naomi Lamoreaux and Jean-Laurent Rosenthal use court cases to make the argument that shareholder rights in the United States were weak and declining at the turn of the twentieth century. See Naomi Lamoreaux and Jean-Laurent Rosenthal, "Corporate Governance and the Plight of Minority Shareholders in the United States before the Great Depression," in Edward Glaeser and Claudia Goldin (eds.), *Corruption and Reform*, Chicago: University of Chicago Press, 2006, pp. 125–152.

development, and the rule of law in general. Three common features of Mexico and Brazil account for their striking similarity circa 1910. First, they were two of the richest and most populous countries in Latin America. Second, both adhered to the civil law tradition, had been colonized by Catholic countries, and had a low ratio of colonizers to indigenous and slave populations.[34] And third, when the British company that edited the year books used for this analysis compiled the data, both countries were undergoing an industrial transition at a accelerated pace, with similar GDP per capita levels circa 1900 and real GDP growth of 3–4% per year fueled, in part, by the onset of industrialization.

But significant differences existed in the two countries' financial development circa 1909. Because Brazil's capital markets were much more integrated than Mexico's with the world market, Brazilian companies could also issue bonds and stocks and sell them in foreign markets. Few Mexican companies had access to foreign markets, and domestic markets for stocks and bonds were relatively shallow. Brazil also differed from Mexico in having widely operational branch banking and no major legal obstacles to the entry of new banks. To open a new bank or corporation merely entailed an administrative procedure, and charters were approved upon presenting the required documents (charter, bank deposit slip, and list of at least seven subscribers) to the local Junta Comercial (commercial registry). Ministry of Finance approval was needed only by banks that were to issue notes, and only until 1893 when the government established a monopoly on note issuance.[35] Banco do Brasil, Brasilianische Bank für Deutschland, the London and Brazilian Bank, and the British Bank of South America were among the

---

[34] That the process of colonial settlement determined the subsequent institutional development of former colonies has been argued by Stanley Engerman and Kenneth Sokoloff, "Factor Endowments, Institutions, and Differential Paths of Growth Among the New World Economies: A View from Economic Historians of the United States," in Stephen Haber (ed.), *How Latin America Fell Behind*, Stanford: Stanford University Press, 1997, pp. 260–304, and Daron Acemoglu, Simon Johnson, and James A. Robinson, "The Colonial Origins of Comparative Development: An Empirical Investigation," *American Economic Review* 91 (December 2001): 1370. According to these theories, we would expect Mexico and Brazil to have had similar institutional structures by 1913. Moreover, the law and finance literature would lead us to expect civil law countries to have afforded similar protections to investors throughout history, which would have occasioned greater similarity in the development of financial markets. See, for example, Rafael La Porta, Florencio Lopes-de-Silanes, Andrei Shleifer, and Robert Vishny, "Legal Determinants of External Finance," *Journal of Finance* 52 (July 1997): 1131–1150; and Rafael La Porta, Florencio Lopes-de-Silanes, Andrei Shleifer, and Robert Vishny. "Law and Finance," *Journal of Political Economy* 106 (December 1998): 1113–1155.

[35] Triner, *Banking and Economic Development*, pp. 42–46.

domestic and foreign banks with branches throughout the country. Most states had more than two large banks; Rio de Janeiro, Rio Grande do Sul, and São Paulo each had more than ten.

Because Brazilian companies had many options for obtaining credit, and lenders and investors relatively easy access to good financial information, we might expect Brazilian banks to have been less central than Mexican banks in networks of corporate interlocks. Differences in disclosure rules and investor protections between Brazil and the United States lead us to expect banks to have been less central in the former's networks.

EXAMINING THE ROLE OF BANKS IN THE CORPORATE NETWORKS OF BRAZIL, MEXICO, AND THE UNITED STATES

The Number of Connections between Banks and Corporations

The role of banks in the networks established among corporations can be assessed by the frequency and extent of the sharing of directors on corporate boards. If each board interlock establishes a connection between two corporations, the web of corporate relations can be mapped using these interlocks as links. The network is the total "web" of relationships between these actors (companies or directors). Having created relational matrices that tell us how many connections a company has with the other companies in the network, we can apply quantitative techniques to determine the frequency of interlocking boards among companies and the centrality of each company.

My first step in examining the number of relations between banks and corporations in Mexico and Brazil was to create a database of corporate relations. I then assembled a data set of 98 Mexican firms and 371 Brazilian firms that shared board members in 1909. The data set yields Mexican and Brazilian networks of 1,206 and 1,039 connections, respectively, with 92 companies in Mexico and 298 in Brazil linked to a main network. Next I created a database of director names and company information for 1909 from that year's *Mexican Year Book* and *Brazilian Year Book*, which list joint-stock companies, their boards of directors, capital, industry, age, stock prices (for some companies), and size of debenture issues.

Tables 8.1 and 8.2, which map the network of corporate interlocks in Brazil and Mexico in terms of the number of connections between banks and companies in other industries and within industries, yield two important findings. One is that the number of interlocks per industry, especially in banking, is higher in Mexico than in Brazil, even though the number

Table 8.1. *Number of interlocking boards of directors by industry in Brazil, c. 1909*

	BAN	AGR	INS	MAN	MIN	Other	Rail	SVCs	SHIP	T&T	TEX	UT
Banking	**10**											
Agriculture	21	**24**										
Insurance	27	8	**20**									
Manufacturing	13	9	9	**10**								
Mining	1		3	3	**38**							
Other	3	4	1		2							
Railways	6	6	1	4	1		**54**					
Services		5	3	5			2					
Shipping and ports	8	7	8	2			18	1	**14**			
Telephone and telegraph	1			2			2					
Textiles	26	9	30	12	3	1	4	3	15		**80**	
Utilities	19	6	12	2	3	1	21	4	23	1	18	**36**
Total connections by industry	135	78	87	40	47	2	101	8	52	1	98	36
As a % of total network connections[a]	20	11	13	6	7	0.3	15	1	8	0.1	14	5
Connections with other industries	104	54	67	30	9	2	47	8	38	1	18	0
Number of companies with interlocks	31	23	25	24	14	4	24	8	17	2	51	36
Average interlocks per company (total)	4.4	3.4	3.5	1.7	3.4	0.5	4.2	1.0	3.1	0.5	1.9	1.0
Average interlocks with other industries	3.4	2.3	2.7	1.3	0.6	0.5	2.0	1.0	2.2	0.5	0.4	0.0

Note:
[a] The network has 685 connections in total.

Table 8.2. *Number of interlocking boards of directors by industry in Mexico, c. 1909*

	BAN	AGR	MAN	MIN	OIL	PORT	Rail	TEL	TEX	UT
Banking	**180**									
Agriculture		1								
Manufacturing	**52**		**12**							
Mining	39		8	**42**						
Oil	20		18	4	1					
Ports	4		3	1	1					
Railways	**62**		18	35	19	8	**78**			
Telegraph and telephone	1									
Textiles	21		19	1	5	1	7		**12**	
Utilities	25		19	3	8	1	37		7	**30**
Total connections by industry	405	2	97	133	67	16	259	2	68	125
As a % of total network connections[a]	34.5	0.2	8.3	11.3	5.7	1.4	22.1	0.2	5.8	10.6
Connections with other industries	225	2	85	91	67	16	181	2	56	95
Number of companies with interlocks	28	1	6	23	1	1	18	1	7	6
Average interlocks per company (total)	14.5	2.0	16.2	5.8	67.0	16.0	14.4	2.0	9.7	20.8
Average interlocks with other industries	8.0	2.0	14.2	4.0	67.0	16.0	10.1	2.0	8.0	15.8

Note:
[a] The network has 1174 connections in total.

199

of companies in the network is smaller. Mexico, with 92 companies in the network, averages 12.8 interlocks per company, a large number considering that boards in Mexico at that time consisted, on average, of four members, many of whom sat on the boards of more than three companies. Contemporaneous boards of directors in Brazil averaged three members who sat on the boards of 2.6 companies. Brazil also has fewer interlocks within a larger network of 259 connected companies.

The other important finding is that in both countries the banking sector has significant connections with corporations in other industries, but the average number of these is higher in Mexico, with eight interlocks per bank compared to Brazil's 3.4. One interpretation of this finding is that the directors on the boards of Mexico's banks, being more influential, were able to obtain information and resources from companies in other industries. Or perhaps, as Maurer and Sharma argue, directors were dispatched by banks to monitor their borrowers.[36]

The number of connections between Brazil's banks and corporations is low relative not just to Mexico, but to other countries as well. Table 8.3 presents data on the number of interlocks between banks and other banks and between banks and nonfinancial corporations in Brazil, Mexico, the United States, and Germany circa 1910. The number of interlocks within Brazil's banking sector was, on average, lower than those in Mexico and the United States (in 1914), if slightly higher than in Germany from 1896 to 1914, but the average number of interlocks with other industries in Brazil was among the lowest in the sample.

Table 8.3 also displays two important figures that demonstrate that banks were not as important in the Brazilian corporate network as were their counterparts in other countries' corporate networks. Brazil's corporations did not rely heavily on connections with banks, at least not in the form of corporate interlocks. Only 22.9% of the country's corporations had bankers on their boards, compared to more than 30% of U.S. corporations, 25.3–40.9% of German corporations, and 61.1% of Mexican corporations. What's more, only 2.43% of Brazilian corporations had more than three bankers on their boards compared to 6.9–8.3% of U.S. corporations, 3.8–7.2% of German corporations, and 17.7% of Mexican corporations.

Methodologies for collecting the data across these four countries varied little, and for Brazil and Mexico, for which the year book series was used, they were identical. Windolf's study, which was the source of the data for U.S. and German networks between 1896 and 1938, fortunately followed

---

[36] See Maurer and Sharma, "Enforcing Property Rights Through Reputation," pp. 950–952.

Table 8.3. *Bankers in the networks of corporate interlocks in Brazil, Mexico, the United States, and Germany, c. 1910*

	Brazil	Mexico	United States		Germany	
	1909	1909	1900	1914	1896	1914
Number of banks in network	31	28	46	49	30	47
Banks to banks	10	180	41	65	10	41
Interlocks bank to banks (avg.)	1	6.4	0.89	1.33	0.33	0.87
Interlocks bank to other industries (avg.)	3.4	8.0	4.1	4.2	2.9	5.03
Nonfinancial corp. with a banker on board (%)	22.9	61.1	32.5	36.2	25.3	40.9
Non-financial corp. with 3+ bankers (%)	2.43	17.7	6.9	8.3	3.8	7.2

Sources: Data for Mexico and Brazil are estimated by the author from data in *Mexican Year Book 1909–1910* and *Brazilian Year Book 1909.* Data for the United States and Germany are from Windolf, "The Emergence of Corporate Networks in the United States and Germany 1896–1938," Table 4. Interlocks between banks and other industries for the United States and Germany are estimated by adding Windolf's indegree and outdegree figures.

a similar methodology, using the handbook of joint stock companies for Germany, and for the United States *The Manual of Statistics* (Stock Exchange Handbook), Moody's and Poor's manuals of investment, and *Rand McNally's Bankers' Almanac.*[37] Thanks to the globalization of securities markets, all of these publications have similar formats and tend to include the largest publicly traded companies in each country.[38]

Still, one could argue that, notwithstanding the low number of connections between Brazil's banks and corporations, the few banks that had connections might have been extremely central to the network of corporate

[37] Paul Windolf, "The Emergence of Corporate Networks in the United States and Germany 1896–1938," paper presented at the annual meeting of the American Sociological Association, Philadelphia, Penn,, August 2005. His data are summarized in Table 4 and the sources identified in Appendix II.
[38] The network of corporate interlocks in the United States includes 226 companies in 1900 and 193 companies in 1914; in Germany, 156 companies in 1896 and 292 companies in 1914. Windolf, "The Emergence of Corporate Networks in the United States and Germany," Table 1.

relations, perhaps intermediating information and resources among, or otherwise linking, important companies in different parts of the country. I analyze this hypothesis in the following section.

Measuring the Centrality of Banks in the Networks of Corporate Interlocks

The relative importance of bankers in the networks of corporate connections (corporate interlocks) in Brazil, Mexico, and the United States can also be gauged by examining the centrality of banks in these networks. This can be measured in a number of ways. One, termed "degree," which is simply a given company's total number of interlocks, is an imperfect measure of centrality for several reasons. A company can, for example, have many connections without necessarily being central to the network, or have connections with many companies disconnected from the network and be central within this group but isolated from most of the network. Consequently, I employed two other measures of centrality: betweenness and Bonacich. Betweenness, which measures the brokerage power of an actor in terms of how often the actor is in the path that links two other actors in the network is not always optimal because it weights too heavily the bridging power of actors who might be unconnected to important people or even to many people directly. Bonacich is perhaps the more informative measure of centrality because it "weights interlock ties according to the interlock partner's number of ties such that sharing a director with a firm whose other directors serve on many boards is weighted more heavily that sharing a director with a firm with few ties."[39]

The betweenness and Bonacich measures of bank centrality are used to compare for Brazil, Mexico, and the United States the top 15 most central corporations in their respective networks of corporate interlocks. For Mexico and Brazil they are presented for the entire networks. All estimates were generated by the UCINET program.[40] Bonacich and degree centrality data are presented for the United States using data obtained from the studies of Windolf and Mizruchi, specifically Mizruchi's study of the network

---

[39] See Davis and Mizruchi, "The Money Center Cannot Hold," p. 227. More detailed explanations of these centrality measures and their estimation procedure can be found in Stanley Wasserman and Katherine Faust, *Social Network Analysis: Methods and Applications*, Cambridge: Cambridge University Press, 1997, and John Scott, *Social Network Analysis: A handbook*, London: Sage, 1991.

[40] S. P. Borgatti, M. G. Everett, and L. C. Freeman, *UCINET 6.0 Version 1.00*, Natick: Analytic Technologies, 1999.

of corporate interlocks in the United States in different years during the twentieth century.[41]

Examining Table 8.4, which presents the top central companies in the United States according to degree and Bonacich centrality in 1904 and 1928, we find National Bank of Commerce, National City Bank, First National Bank, and New York Trust among the 10 most central corporations in 1904, and the number of interlocks between these banks and other corporations to be quite high. Top-ranked National Bank of Commerce had 153 interlocks; the other banks had between 45 and 75. The most central banks' numbers of interlocks was still impressive in 1928, with more than 45 connections each for Guaranty Trust, Chase National Bank, and Bankers Trust. These results bespeak a system in which interlocks with banks were quite important.[42]

The literature that reports studies of banking during Mexico's Porfirian period has attributed a central role to bankers in the network of corporate relations. Recent work suggests that close relations between banks and manufacturing companies facilitated the resolution of information asymmetries and monitoring of borrowers.[43]

In Table 8.5, which lists Mexico's top companies in terms of Bonacich centrality, six of the top 15 actors were banks. Most of Mexico's top central banks have been identified by the literature as having been important brokers of relations with corporations. The National Bank of Mexico (Banamex) in Mexico City was, for example, connected to manufacturing groups and the government and had been granted special privileges to establish national branches, issue more notes relative to reserves, and have its notes considered legal tender nationally.[44]

---

[41] Mizruchi, *The American Corporate Network.*

[42] An in-depth analysis of bankers on the boards of directors of corporations in the United States by Mark S. Mizruchi revealed the importance of the J. P. Morgan house in sending directors to the boards of different companies. Mizruchi undertook to identify instances in which a director of a corporation was actually an officer of a bank sent to monitor and control the activities of the company. Unfortunately, this type of analysis cannot be performed for Mexico and Brazil. But for the United States, it shows J. P. Morgan to have been the most central actor in the network of corporate interlocks, followed by many other banks. Mizruchi found the top 10 corporations to be: J. P. Morgan & Co., Great Northern, New York Life, First National Bank (New York), International Harvester, National City Bank, U.S. Trust, New York Trust, Standard Oil, and U.S. Steel. See Mizruchi, *The American Corporate Network*, p. 66.

[43] Maurer and Sharma, "Enforcing Property Rights Through Reputation" and Maurer, *The Power and the Money.*

[44] Aldo Musacchio and Ian Read, "Bankers, Industrialists and their Cliques: Elite Networks in Mexico and Brazil During Early Industrialization," *Enterprise and Society* 8, 4 (December 2007): 864–865.

Table 8.4. *Most central corporations in the United States, degree and Bonacich centrality, 1904 and 1928*

	Mizruchi's study, 1904			Windolf's study, 1928		
Company name	Sector	Degree[a]	Bonacich rank	Company name	Sector	Degree
Erie	Transportation	76	1	**Guaranty Trust**	**Bank**	51
New York Central	Transportation	68	2	**Chase National Bank**	**Bank**	49
U.S. Steel	Industrial	88	3	**Bankers Trust**	**Bank**	46
Baltimore & Ohio	Transportation	76	4	General Electric	Electrical industry	45
Great Northern	Transportation	58	5	Western Union Tel.	Communication	41
National Bank of Commerce	**Bank**	153	6	**New York Trust**	**Bank**	38
National City Bank	**Bank**	69	7	Mutual Life of NY	Insurance	37
First National Bank (N.Y.)	**Bank**	45	8	Brooklyn, Manhattan Transit	Public transp.	34
New York Trust	**Bank**	75	9	**Equitable Trust**	**Bank**	33
New York Life	Insurance	62	10	Metropolitan Life	Insurance	33
International Harvester	Industrial	44	11			
Union Pacific	Transportation	71	12			
Chicago & Alton	Transportation	56	13			
Lehigh & Wilkes-Barre Coal	Industrial	N.A.	14			
U.S. Trust	**Bank**	58	15			

Source: Adapted from Mizruchi, *The American Corporate Network: 1904–1974*, p. 64, and Windolf, "The Emergence of Corporate Networks in the United States and Germany, 1896–1938," Table 2.

Note:

[a] Degree represents the number of board interlocks of each company, which matters to determine centrality in the network. Yet in this table centrality is determined using the eigenvalue or Bonacich centrality measure. This latter measure of centrality takes into account not only the degree centrality of the company, but also the centrality of the companies to which it is linked.

Table 8.5. *Most central corporations in Mexico, Bonacich centrality, 1909*

Company name	Sector	Degree[a]
1. Mexican Eagle Oil Co	Oil	67
2. Fundidora de Fierro y Acero de Monterrey	Manuf.	46
3. Caja de Prestamos	**Bank**	42
4. General Bonded Warehouses of Mexico	**Bank**	50
5. National Bank of Mexico	**Bank**	47
6. Chapala Hydro-Electric And Irrigation Co	Utilities	37
7. Buen Tono Cigarette Factory	Manuf.	39
8. Mexican Bank of Commerce and Industry	**Bank**	47
9. National Railways of Mexico	Railroad	50
10. Mortgage and Credit Foncier Bank of Mexico	**Bank**	36
11. Pan-American Railway	Railroad	39
12. Dos Estrellas Mining Co	Mining	21
13. Mexican Central Bank	**Bank**	31
14. Agujita Coal Co	Mining	18
15. Fabricas de Papel de San Rafael y Anexas	Manuf.	24

Sources: The network of corporate interlocks was generated by the author from lists of directors by company in *Mexican Year Book 1909*. Bonacich centrality was estimated by the author using Borgatti, Everett, and Freeman, UCINET 6.0 Version 1.00.

Note:

[a] Degree represents the number of board interlocks of each company, which matters to determine centrality in the network. Yet in this table centrality is determined using the eigenvalue or Bonacich centrality measure. This latter measure of centrality takes into account not only the degree centrality of the company, but also the centrality of the companies to which it is linked.

Table 8.6 presents Mexico's top companies in terms of betweenness centrality. Banks in Mexico City tended to be important brokers of information, credit, and influence within the system, and seven of the 15 most central corporations were banks. In terms of degree (number of interlocks), of each of these top actors had 30 or more interlocks with other banks and corporations. In both Mexico and the United States, we find among the most central corporations a large proportion of banks. The number of interlocks of the top-connected banks is also impressive at more than 150 in the United States and, on average, 30 in Mexico.

The Brazilian case differs from that of Mexico and the United States in two ways: (1) the absence of a large proportion of banks among the most central corporations in the network, and (2) the lesser importance of interlocks to Brazilian corporations. Table 8.7 shows that when the 15 most central

Table 8.6. *Most central corporations in Mexico, betweenness centrality, 1909*

Company name	Sector	Degree[a]
1. Mexican Eagle Oil Co	Oil	67
2. Mexico Tramways Co	Utilities	32
3. Fundidora de Fierro y Acero de Monterrey	Capital goods	46
4. Mexican Northern Railway	Railroad	11
5. **General Bonded Warehouses of Mexico and Veracruz**	**Bank**	50
6. **National Bank of Mexico**	**Bank**	47
7. **Laguna Bank of Encouragement**	**Bank**	10
8. Santa Maria de La Paz Co	Mining	15
9. National Railways of Mexico	Railroad	50
10. Buen Tono Cigarette Factory	Manuf.	39
11. **Bank of London And Mexico**	**Bank**	26
12. **Caja de Prestamos**	**Bank**	42
13. **Banco Mercantil de Monterrey**	**Bank**	7
14. **Mexican Bank of Commerce And Industry**	**Bank**	47
15. Interoceanic Railway of Mexico	Railroad	10

Sources: The network of corporate interlocks was created by the author from lists of directors by company in *Brazilian Year Book 1909* and *Mexican Year Book 1909*. Bonacich centrality was estimated by the author using Borgatti, Everett, and Freeman, UCINET 6.0 Version 1.00.
Note:
[a] Degree represents the number of board interlocks of each company, which matters to determine centrality in the network. Yet in this table centrality is determined using the betweenness measure, which weights heavily how frequently a company is in the shortest path between any two other companies in the network.

corporations in the network of corporate interlocks in Brazil are ranked using Bonacich centrality, only three are banks. The top-ranked banks, the Societe Financiere et Commerciale Franco-Bresilienne and Banca Commerciale Italo-Brasiliano, were both identified by Warren Dean as being tied to the commercial and manufacturing enterprises of immigrants.[45]

The extent to which Brazil differs from Mexico and the United States in terms of the number of connections (degree centrality) is evident in Table 8.7. Whereas most banks in Mexico and the United States had more than 20

[45] Warren Dean, *The Industrialization of São Paulo, 1880–1945*, Austin: University of Texas Press, 1969, pp. 63–64, has speculated that many immigrants founded businesses in Brazil with funds gathered in their countries of origin. Both banks, Financiere and Banca Commerciale, might have channeled funds or served as advisors to many of the immigrant ventures.

Table 8.7. *Most central corporations in Brazil, Bonacich centrality, 1909*

Company name	Sector	Degree[a]
1. Internacional de Armazens Geraes	Coffee	13
2. Refinadora Paulista	Food	9
3. Companhia de Industria e Commercio	Food	7
4. **Societe Financiere et Commerciale Franco-Bresilienne**	**Bank**	8
5. São Paulo Match Factory	Manuf.	8
6. São Paulo and Minas Railway Company Ltd	Railroad	7
7. **Banca Commerciale Italo-Brasiliano**	**Bank**	11
8. Moinho Santista	Agric.	8
9. Fabrica de Cimento Italo Brazileira	Manuf.	5
10. Tecelagem de Seda Italo Brazileira	Textile manuf.	5
11. Aliança Fiação e Tecidos	Textile manuf.	4
12. Docas do Porto da Bahia, Cessionaria Das	Port	4
13. Brazil Great Southern Railway	Railroad	2
14. Mchardy Manufactureira e Importadora	Capital goods	2
15. **Banco do Recife**	**Bank**	11

Sources: The network of corporate interlocks was created by the author from lists of directors by company in *Brazilian Year Book 1909* and *Mexican Year Book 1909*. Bonacich centrality was estimated by the author using Borgatti, Everett, and Freeman, UCINET 6.0 Version 1.00.
Note:
[a] Degree represents the number of board interlocks of each company, which matters to determine centrality in the network. Yet in this table centrality is determined using the eigenvalue or Bonacich centrality measure. This latter measure of centrality takes into account not only the degree centrality of the company, but also the centrality of the companies to which it is linked.

connections, in Brazil two banks had 11 and one had eight interlocks. The most central corporation in Brazil, the Internacional de Armazens Gerais, a company involved in the coffee trade in Sao Paulo, had only 13 interlocks.

In Table 8.8, which ranks Brazil's top 15 companies using betweenness centrality, we find only two banks. Only one bank in the previous list, the Banco do Recife, appears again, and the top central bank, Banco de Crédito Rural e Internacional, a commercial and mortgage bank in Rio de Janeiro, has only five interlocks. The latter bank's centrality most likely derived from its connections with manufacturing companies in the southeast of Brazil that it helped to link through the network of corporate interlocks to companies in other regions of the country.

Table 8.8. *Most central corporations in Brazil, betweenness centrality, 1909*

Company name	Sector	Degree[a]
1. E. F. Victoria A Minas	Railroad	5
2. São Felix, Fiação e Tecidos	Textiles	3
3. Docas De Santos	Port	5
4. E. F. Noroeste do Brazil	Railroad	4
5. Docas do Porto Da Bahia, Cessionaria Das	Port	4
6. Empreza Ind. De Melhoramentos do Brazil	Agricultural	3
7. Melhoramentos De Pernambuco, Geral De	Construction	3
8. Banco De Crédito Rural e Internacional	**Bank**	**5**
9. Manufactora Fluminese	Textiles	9
10. Assucareira, Companhia	Food	3
11. Cia. Cantareria e Viação Fluminense	Shipping	3
12. Agrícola De Juiz De Fora	Agricultural	10
13. Banco do Recife	**Bank**	**11**
14. Aliança, Fiação e Tecidos	Textile	4
15. Mercurio Fire And Marine Insurance	Insurance	7

Sources: The network of corporate interlocks was created by the author from lists of directors by company in *Brazilian Year Book 1909* and *Mexican Year Book 1909*. Bonacich centrality was estimated by the author using Borgatti, Everett, and Freeman, UCINET 6.0 Version 1.00.
Note:
[a] Degree represents the number of board interlocks of each company, which matters to determine centrality in the network. Yet in this table centrality is determined using the betweenness measure, which weights heavily how frequently a company is in the shortest path between any two other companies in the network.

The Brazilian network of board interlocks extended over a large geographical area, and many corporations were important in terms of betweenness because of their role in bridging groups in different regions. Banco do Recife, for example, bridged companies in Pernambuco (a northeastern state) to the main network of interlocks in Sao Paulo and Rio de Janeiro. Most of its 11 interlocks were to corporations in different economic centers such as Rio de Janeiro. This bank was so central to the network might be expected given the stage of development of Brazil's financial markets circa 1909. For companies in regions far from the major financial centers banks would have been almost the only source of financing, making close relationships with them more advantageous. Only large corporations could venture into the Rio de Janeiro Stock Exchange and issue debt.

One could argue that geographic factors explain the differences between the networks of Brazil and Mexico, the considerable distances between the former's cities giving rise to a more dispersed network (with fewer interlocks) and complicating interaction between companies and banks. But the role of geography, though probably important, is mitigated by the following circumstances. First, I find that clusters with companies from the state of Minas Gerais (in the central part of Brazil) are adjacent and connected to the clusters that included firms and banks from Rio Grande do Sul (in the far south) and Rio de Janeiro (in the southeast). In a similar pattern, companies in Rio de Janeiro were connected to clusters of firms in northern states such as Pernambuco and Bahia. Second, banks were, in many instances, important bridges between the companies in these different regions. One of the top central actors, Banco de Credito Rural e Internacional in Rio de Janeiro, played an important role in linking a large group of São Paulo companies with the web of interlocks in the rest of the country. Still, many clusters in distant states such as Maranhão tended to be isolated from the rest of the country, and as the clusters are not always grouped by region, geography cannot be the only factor that influenced network structure.

Multivariate Analysis of Bank Connections in Mexico and Brazil

Company-level data were used to explore the degree to which differences in the number of connections between corporations and banks and within the banking sector are explained by country characteristics and basic differences in company characteristics across two countries. Pooling all the data on bank interlocks by company for Mexico and Brazil, the following exercise calculates the differences in the number of interlocks with banks by country, controlling for company characteristics and industry fixed effects. Perhaps the most important characteristic that needed to be controlled for is size, as it could be the case that Mexican companies' greater numbers of connections with banks simply reflected their larger size or larger boards of directors. These characteristics were controlled for using a multivariate OLS regression of the following form:

$$y_i = \beta_0 + \beta_1 \log(age) + \beta_2 \log(paid\text{-}up\ capital/size\ of\ board)_i$$
$$+ \beta_3\ (Brazil\ dummy)_i + \sum_z^z \beta_{3+z}\ industry_{iz} + e_i$$

where y_i is a variable that measures the number of bankers on the board of each company i, $log(age)$ is the natural logarithm of the number of years

Table 8.9. *Summary statistics, corporate network and bank interlocks data, Brazil and Mexico, c. 1909*

Variable	Obs	Mean	Std. dev.	Min	Max
Nonbank interlocks	197	4.3	6.2	0	38
Bank interlocks	197	1.7	3.9	0	23
Bank interlock dummy	197	0.4	0.5	0	1
Interlocks with bankers of 2 banks	197	0.8	1.7	0	11
Brazilian company	197	0.6	0.5	0	1
Board size	197	6.2	3.3	1	23
Age	191	15.7	13.0	1	101
Capital in US$	197	7,969,613	33,900,000	883	460,000,000

since the company was established, *log(paid-up)* is the natural logarithm of the social capital of the company (in some specifications I substitute this variable for the size of the board of directors in each company, *i*, and also control for a series of *z* industry dummies). Because what I want to examine are differences between Brazil and Mexico in the importance of connections with banks, I include, after controlling for company characteristics, a dummy variable for whether a company is in Brazil (=1) or Mexico (=0). Thus, we expect to find large and negative coefficients for this variable.[46]

We can see from Table 8.9, which presents the summary statistics that when the data are pooled, the average number of bank interlocks per company is 1.7. Of the 40% of companies in the sample that have an interlock with a bank, 17% are Brazilian and 23% Mexican. We can also see that 60% of the companies in the sample are Brazilian, companies which, we would expect, had less propensity to have interlocks with banks. In any case, we still need to control for company characteristics in order to determine the importance of the difference in the number of bank-company interlocks in Brazil compared to Mexico.

Table 8.10 presents the results of the multivariate analysis examining the correlates of company-bank interlocks in Brazil and Mexico (using ordinary

---

[46] I also tried controlling for the whether companies had financing options other than banks, mainly bonds, by adding a continuous variable that measures the bond to paid-up capital ratio and dummy variables for companies with bond issues. But none of these variables was significantly correlated with the number of bank interlocks or with the bank interlock dummy.

Table 8.10. Correlates of company-bank interlocks in Brazil and Mexico (OLS and Probit estimates), c. 1909

	OLS	OLS	OLS	OLS	OLS	Probit	Probit	Probit	Probit	Probit
	Interlock w/ bank (1)	Interlock w/ bank (2)	Interlock w/ bank (3)	Interlock w/ bank (4)	Interlock w/ bank (5)	Interlock w/ bank (dummy) (6)	Interlock w/ bank (dummy) (7)	Interlock w/ bank (dummy) (8)	Interlock w/ bank (dummy) (9)	Interlock w/ bank (dummy) (10)
Constant	4.292 [1.029]***	-1.199 [0.962]	-1.206 [1.038]	0.093 [2.941]	-0.341 [3.058]					
Ln(age)	-0.08 [0.277]	-0.154 [0.208]	-0.138 [0.210]	-0.204 [0.341]	-0.206 [0.353]	0.127 [0.045]***	0.136 [0.047]***	0.141 [0.047]***	0.132 [0.047]***	0.133 [0.048]***
Board size		0.727 [0.119]***	0.761 [0.120]***				0.05 [0.014]***	0.061 [0.015]***		
Ln(capital)				0.314 [0.257]	0.326 [0.270]				-0.014 [0.024]	-0.011 [0.026]
Brazil	-3.709 [0.668]***	-1.878 [0.458]***	-2.17 [0.501]***	-3.358 [0.627]***	-3.325 [0.629]***	-0.381 [0.072]***	-0.301 [0.082]***	-0.384 [0.086]***	-0.396 [0.077]***	-0.447 [0.081]***
Industry dummies	N	N	Y	N	Y	N	N	Y	N	Y

(continued)

211

Table 8.10 (continued)

	OLS	OLS	OLS	OLS	OLS	Probit	Probit	Probit	Probit	Probit
	Interlock w/bank (1)	Interlock w/bank (2)	Interlock w/bank (3)	Interlock w/bank (4)	Interlock w/bank (5)	Interlock w/bank (dummy) (6)	Interlock w/bank (dummy) (7)	Interlock w/bank (dummy) (8)	Interlock w/bank (dummy) (9)	Interlock w/bank (dummy) (10)
Observations	191	191	191	191	191	191	191	191	191	191
R^2 or Pseudo R^2	0.211	0.531	0.557	0.225	0.236	0.11	0.16	0.19	0.11	0.13
Model chi-square						27.5	41.9	49.8	27.6	31.0
Log likelihood						−112.3	−106.3	−102.2	−112.1	−110.1

Notes: The dependent variable in specifications 1 through 5 is the number of board interlocks with banks, and in specifications 6 through 10 a dummy for whether the company has a bank interlock. The first five specifications are estimated with ordinary least squares, the last five using maximum likelihood estimates of a normal probability function (Probit), both with robust standard errors (in parentheses). The hypothesis tested is that Brazilian companies should have fewer interlocks with banks or be less likely to have an interlock with a bank, on average, than their Mexican counterparts, even after controlling for company characteristics and industry dummies. Coefficients for the Probit estimation are for *marginal probabilities* of an infinitesimal change in the dependent variable or the change from 0 to 1 in dummy variables.

⁺ significant at 10%, ** significant at 5%, *** significant at 1%.

212

least squares, or OLS). It is clear that, even after controlling for important company characteristics such as age, company size, board size, and industry, Brazilian companies had, on average, fewer connections with banks. In specifications one to five, the dependent variable is the number of bank interlocks per company. We can see that Brazilian companies had, on average, between 1.8 and 3.4 fewer interlocks with banks than their Mexican counterparts, depending on what we control for. I obtain more robust results and a higher R^2 when I control for board size and include the industry dummies (R^2 of almost 0.60) in specifications two and three. But even in these specifications, we know that Brazilian companies had, on average, 1.8 fewer interlocks with banks. This is a large figure if we take into account that the average number of interlocks with banks in the sample is 1.7. Basically, once we control for company characteristics, the regression results tell us that Brazilian companies for the most part did not interlock with banks beyond what would be expected for the average company in each sector.

In specifications six through 10 I use a similar approach, but the dependent variable is a dummy for whether the company has board interlocks with a bank. The coefficients represent the marginal probability of an infinitesimal change in any variable or the change from zero to one in dummy variables. For Brazilian companies, the probability of having an interlock with a bank is 30% to 40% lower than for a Mexican company. This, too, is quite large when we take into account that we are controlling for industry, size, and age. In fact, according to the Probit estimates in specifications six through 10, age and board size are important in explaining the number of connections between companies and banks.

These connections were many in Mexico. Tables 8.1 and 8.2 show clearly that Mexican companies, in general and in all sectors, used board interlocks much more often than did their Brazilian counterparts. Recent research maintains that this is because in Mexico connections to politicians were crucial to obtain concessions and protection, and substituted for many of the third party institutions that existed in Brazil to ensure enforcement of contracts and protection of property rights among business enterprises. The comparison with Mexico thus reinforces the premise I advance that it was relatively strong institutions that facilitated the development of financial markets in Brazil between the 1880s and the 1930s.

CONCLUSION

This chapter presents evidence that discredits two claims: (1) banks were market makers in Brazil, and (2) the network of connections of banks and corporations substituted for investor protections or for court enforcement of corporate debt contracts. Interlocks with banks were established far less frequently in Brazil than in either Mexico or the United States (or Germany, for that matter) circa 1909. Nor did banks play as central a role in Brazil as they did in Mexico and the United States, where large commercial and investment banks were some of the most central actors in the respective networks of corporate board interlocks. Finally, even after controlling for company characteristics such as board size, company size, company age, and industry, Brazilian corporations relied to a much lesser degree than companies in Mexico on interlocks with banks.

All of these results point to the importance of the institutional settings that prevailed in Brazil at the turn of the twentieth century. Perhaps because they were afforded alternative financing options such as corporate bonds, which were not available in countries such as Mexico, Brazil's corporations were less dependent on connections to banks for access to credit. Perhaps mandatory disclosure of financial information and relatively strong protections for minority shareholders also reduced reliance on banks as endorsers of corporations or market makers in general, roles they did play in the United States. The evidence presented here bolsters the evidence in previous chapters that development of financial markets in Brazil between the 1880s and at least the first two decades of the twentieth century seems to have been sustained by the strength of the institutions that protected shareholders within corporations and creditors in courts. In the next chapter, we explore why, given the evidence of the strength of these institutions, Brazil's financial markets declined after World War I.

## NINE

What Went Wrong after World War I?

Evidence presented in earlier chapters suggests that activity in Brazil's financial markets first peaked between the late 1880s and 1915 in part because domestic and foreign investors actively participated in the financing of corporations. These investors trusted the financial commitments companies made when they issued securities either because the companies offered strong protections for shareholders or, in the case of bonds, because the legal system protected creditors in the event of corporate bankruptcies. So what precipitated the rapid decline in the stock and bond markets after 1915? How was it that Brazil ended the twentieth century with a high concentration of ownership in large corporations, a corporate landscape dominated by family-controlled business groups, and the government owning and controlling the largest corporations in the country? This chapter and the next one answer these questions, and outline the principal changes in corporate governance and finance after World War I. The current chapter focuses on understanding the decline in financial markets and the main legal changes of the 1930s and 1940s. The following chapter explains the rise of concentrated ownership as a consequence of these changes.

EXPLANATIONS OF THE REVERSAL IN FINANCIAL DEVELOPMENT AFTER WORLD WAR I

This chapter explores, against the evidence presented for Brazil, two broad explanations of why financial development declined worldwide following World War I. The "great reversal" explanation advanced by Raguram Rajan and Luigi Zingales emphasizes the considerable extent to which trade and capital flows influenced the incentives that led domestic industrialist groups to lobby for greater or lesser financial development. They maintain that the postwar decline in capital and trade flows motivated industrialists to lobby the government to deemphasize investor protections (creditor and shareholder rights) and focus on the survival of incumbent firms (e.g., by providing subsidized credit from government banks or drafting more lenient bankruptcy laws). Enrico Perotti and Ernst-Ludwig von Thadden, by contrast, argue that the experimentation of many countries in the 1920s with higher levels of inflation precipitated changes in voter priorities that motivated governments to alter the regulation of corporate governance and finance.[1]

Rajan and Zingales observe that declining capital and trade flows following World War I (especially in the 1930s) affected the development of financial markets and changed the incentives of domestic industrialists. In their interpretation of events, industrialists initially promoted the development of markets to finance the expansion of their operations in the face of the intense international competition that prevailed before World War I. But once they had become well established and international competition become less intense (with the decline of globalization in the 1920s and 1930s), the incentives of incumbent industrialists changed significantly. Given that developed stock and bond markets would facilitate access to capital to new competitors, incumbent industrialists preferred to backtrack the development of those markets and focused on finding bank credit or government subsidized loans.

Rajan and Zingales view the Great Depression as a key inflexion point because it generated a coordinated effort by governments worldwide to restrict capital flows and increase tariffs. In this scenario, labor and industrialists welcomed self-sufficiency. The latter lobbied for government policies that would limit financial development, preferring a growth strategy whereby the source of corporate financing shifted largely from the stock markets to government subsidized loans or bank credit.[2]

The first of the two hypotheses examined here is that declining capital flows to Brazil precipitated a decline in the stock and bond markets

---

[1] See Raghuram Rajan and Luigi Zingales, "The Great Reversals: The Politics of Financial Development in the 20th Century," *Journal of Financial Economics* 69 (2003): 5–50. Some of the ideas mentioned in this chapter were also developed in Raghuram Rajan and Luigi Zingales, *Saving Capitalism from the Capitalists: Unleashing the Power of Financial Markets to Create Wealth and Spread Opportunity*, New York: Crown Business, 2003, Chapters 9–11. Also see Enrico Perotti and Ernst-Ludwig von Thadden, "The Political Economy of Corporate Control and Labor Rents," *Journal of Political Economy* 114, 1 (2006): 145–175.

[2] In *Saving Capitalism from the Capitalists*, Rajan and Zingales further develop this argument, noting that workers' increasing demands for insurance following the Great Depression, together with incumbent corporations' need for government finance, increased the role of the government in the economy for the next four to five decades.

and significant changes in investor protections. According to Rajan and Zingales, the postwar decline in trade and capital flows prompted incumbent industrialists and labor to block financing for new entrants by lobbying governments to change investor protections and block further development of stock and bond markets by changing investor protections in a way that favored controlling shareholders over smaller investors or altering creditor rights to protect incumbent industrialists and labor over creditors. Causality, in their story, runs from waning capital flows to legal changes to declining stock markets.

Evidence presented in this chapter reveals capital flows to Brazil to have fallen rapidly after World War I, but stabilized by the 1920s at the level that had prevailed at the turn of the twentieth century. In that sense, there is no clear break in capital flows (at least not from England to Brazil) after 1920. Yet equity market capitalization and turnover fell slightly in 1915, equity market turnover to GDP declining from 1.2% to 0.6% during World War I and remaining at that level until the 1950s, and bond markets and trading declined rapidly after 1915. There is thus no clear causality from declining capital flows to financial market development. Moreover, changes in bankruptcy and company laws documented here, which in Rajan and Zingales's view should explain a significant part of the postwar decline in equity and bond markets, occurred too late to be clearly linked to the initial decline in financial market development (company law changed in the 1930s, bankruptcy law in 1945). This evidence, even if does not refute their view completely, questions the argument that there was a clear sequence of events or causality unleashed by the fall in capital (and trade) flows. For the case of Brazil, at least, that does not seem to be the best explanation.

The second hypothesis tested in this chapter relates to the model proposed by Perotti and Von Thadden, the intuition for which is that the postwar inflationary shock affected countries asymmetrically. In countries in which the median voter held equity, the postinflationary episode led voters to support governments that tightened regulation and strengthened the control rights of dispersed equity holders. In countries in which shareholders were less dominant and their financial holdings drastically reduced by the inflationary shock, voters demanded that their labor income be protected, even at the expense of protections for equity owners. This model, albeit a highly stylized picture of what happened after World War I, suggests an additional testable hypothesis: postwar inflation eroded financial wealth and generated support for changes in corporate governance and regulation that weakened investor protections in order to protect labor against macroeconomic instability. These changes should have taken the form, for example, of bankruptcy laws that favored incumbent entrepreneurs and labor over creditors and a corporate governance system that emphasized stability and, perhaps, protection of incumbent controlling shareholders.[3]

A perhaps more direct test of whether inflation eroded different constituencies' support of the development of stock markets is whether it reduced bondholders' and shareholders' real returns. If inflation eroded real returns, the consensus supporting protections for shareholders and creditors may have weakened. With low returns it is easier to understand how unions, investors, and incumbent industrialists, who may have had opposing interests before, were able to form a broad coalition that lobbied to change bankruptcy and company laws. This coalition promoted legal changes in the 1930s and 1940s that ended, de jure and de facto, the status quo and created a new model of corporate governance and finance.

This chapter documents that, in the case of Brazil, negative real returns for (and few new issues of) bonds and equity disposed incumbent industrialists, labor organizations, the government, and even stockbrokers to forsake continuation of the original system of corporate governance and finance for a new system based on bank credit with government providing the bulk of funding. This story concludes in the following chapter, which explains the long-term changes in the structure of corporate ownership and finance following World War I.

BEGINNING OF THE END: THE DECLINE OF CAPITAL FLOWS AFTER 1915

There is no doubt that World War I was disastrous for Brazilian financial markets. The existence of a literature on the benefits to industrialization of Brazil's pursuit of an import substitution strategy during the war years notwithstanding, for many of the nation's large companies sources of financing dried up as capital flows suddenly ceased and coffee exports suffered as shipping was disrupted and the international payment system froze.[4]

---

[3] Perotti and von Thadden, "The Political Economy of Corporate Control and Labor Rents," 145–175. In "The Political Origin of Pension Funding" (unpublished manuscript, Amsterdam Business School, 2006), Perotti and Armin Schwienbacher make a similar argument regarding pension systems – that the countries most affected by inflation after World War I ended up with state-sponsored universal pension systems, and those less exposed to inflation developed pension systems that relied on capital markets and individual accounts, allowing that the shift in the desire for a social safety net in countries affected by war and inflation might have been a product of ideology.

[4] The literature that argues that World War I positively influenced the development of Brazil's industry is summarized in Wilson Cano, *Raízes da Concentração Industrial em São*

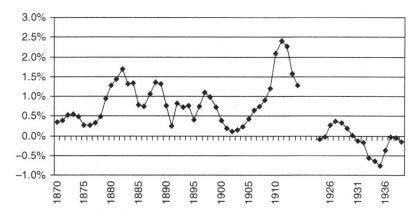

Figure 9.1. British capital exports to the private sector in Brazil, 1870–1939 (as a % of Brazil's GDP, three-year moving average, net values after 1924)

Sources: Data for 1870–1914 are from Stone, *Global Export*, pp. 102–111; data for 1915–1923 are not available. Data for 1924–1939 represent annual net flows estimated by taking the differences of the total annual stock of British investments in Brazil as reported in "British Investments in Brazil," *South American Journal*, Feb. 4, 1950. Everything is normalized using the GDP estimates from Goldsmith, *Brasil 1850–1984*, Tables 3.1 and 4.2.

I document here the rapid postwar decline in the size of the Brazilian corporate bond market and the virtual disappearance from the exchange of the trading of bonds in the 1920s and 1930s. Equity markets took a hit and capitalization had a one-time shift downward as trading was reduced to nearly half its prewar level.

The question examined here is whether the sequence of events followed the line of causality proposed by the "great reversal" hypothesis. That is, did reduced capital flows precipitate changes in investor protections and subsequent declines in stock and bond market capitalization? Figure 9.1, which plots British capital exports to Brazil (over GDP) between 1870 and 1939, clearly shows the decline of capital flows after WWI. Figure 9.2, which disaggregates the figures among railways and other private capital flows, shows the decline to be especially pronounced in the railway sector.

Even absent data for 1914 to 1924, the long-run trajectory of the series exhibits a striking similarity to the trend in Brazil's stock and bond markets. A comparison of Figure 9.1 and Figure 9.3 (which plots stock and bond market capitalization to GDP for Brazil from 1881 to 2003) – that capital flows before 1914 financed some stock and bond issues directly and indirectly

Paulo, São Paulo: T. A. Queiroz Editora, 1987, and Wilson Suzigan, *Industria Brasileira: Origem e Desenvolvimento*, São Paulo: HUCITEC, 2000.

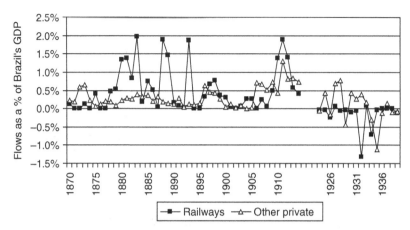

Figure 9.2. British capital exports to the private sector in Brazil, 1870–1939 (by sector, as a % of Brazil's GDP, net values after 1924)

Source: See Figure 9.1.

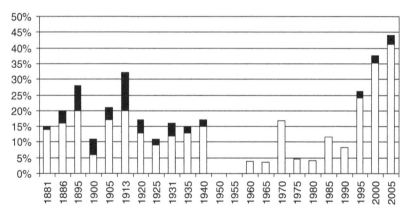

Figure 9.3. Stock and bond market capitalization to GDP, Brazil, 1881–2003

Source: See Appendix 2A.

reduced the cost of capital for companies that used the stock exchange during those years – explains why the decline in the capital flows from 3.5% of GDP to less than 0.5% is correlated with the fall in stock and bond markets from 25% in 1913 (Figure 9.1) to between 10% and 15% in the 1920s.

The decline in capital flows hit especially hard Brazilian corporate bond issues denominated in foreign currencies and cross-listed in Europe (many of the bond issues of Brazil's large railway companies, for example). The postwar disruption in British finance (e.g., the restriction of capital outflows) and instability of the Brazilian exchange rate made it difficult for Brazilian companies to reissue their bonds. For instance, Brazil was on and off the gold standard during the 1920s and abandoned it altogether in the 1930s.

The stock market crisis precipitated by World War I "was not confined to the belligerent nations in Europe but was worldwide in scope," maintains Ranald Michie, who, citing the director of the New York Stock Exchange, adds that "the crisis had developed so suddenly, and the conditions were so utterly without historical parallel, that the best informed men found themselves at a loss for guidance." In fact, the imminence of a major war in Europe had generated such panic that stock markets around the world ceased operations in July 1914.[5] By 1919, the stock markets in most countries had reopened, but they crashed again in 1920. As activity in securities markets worldwide declined in the wake of this brief recovery, government bonds became a more important proportion of total trading. The imposition of capital controls in most European countries introduced further complications.[6]

According to Alan Taylor, declining capital flows to Latin America were initially a direct consequence of the capital controls European nations imposed after the war and subsequent "inflationary war finance." The postwar disruption not only ended four decades of stability under the international gold standard, but also severely constrained Europe's capacity to export capital. "Reliant on heavy borrowing from the United States, the European core countries were no longer in any position to export capital to the developing world." In fact, Britain, which had been the main exporter of savings, "emerged from the war quite diminished, and from 1918 through the 1920s [implemented] explicit embargoes on foreign investment." But even as New York became the center of world capital markets, "the American capacity to supply funds to the rest of the world did not as rapidly fill the void left by the British."[7]

In the face of suspension of international payments and exchange rate depreciation and controls, foreign investors must have preferred to stay home rather than risk losing money in Brazil. The situation only "grew

---

[5] See Ranald C. Michie, *The Global Securities Markets: A History*, New York: Oxford University Press, 2006, quotes from pp. 156 and 157.

[6] See Michie, *The Global Securities Markets*, Chapter 6, and Lyndon Moore, "The Effect of World War One on Stock Market Integration," unpublished manuscript, Victoria University of Wellington, 2006.

[7] Alan Taylor, "Foreign Capital Flows," in Victor Bulmer-Thomas, John H. Coatsworth, and Roberto Cortés Conde (eds.), *Cambridge Economic History of Latin America*, Cambridge: Cambridge University Press, 2006, pp. 57–100, quotes from p. 81.

gloomier" in the 1930s, according to Taylor, with macroeconomic policy becoming "activist and uncooperative [with the international financial system]" and tariff and quota wars reaching full force with the passage in the United States of the Smoot-Hawley Tariff. Latin American countries responded by imposing capital controls and trying to manage multiple exchange rates.[8] Brazil, for instance, renegotiated its debt (and temporarily suspended payments) in 1930 and defaulted in 1937.[9] From 1930 on, moreover, the Brazilian government controlled all exchange rate transactions through Banco do Brasil, to which it granted a monopoly on such transactions, and required exporters to sell in advance to the bank (at an official rate) the foreign currency they would obtain for their exports. The government rationed the foreign exchange accumulated at Banco do Brasil, privileging the payment of public debt and purchase of essential imports over remittance of dividend and coupon payments from Brazilian companies to foreign investors.[10]

Capital flows to most sectors of Brazil's economy declined rapidly in the 1930s. Figure 9.1 plots the estimates of the flows of new British capital to Brazil, showing that British investors began to liquidate their positions in Brazilian companies during the Great Depression years. If capital was still flowing into Brazil in the late 1930s, the amount (in net terms) was insignificant.

Figure 9.2 separates British flows of capital to Brazil among railways and other sectors, showing that after the Great Depression the decline was more dramatic (at least in the early 1930s) in the railway sector. For other sectors net capital inflows into Brazil were basically insignificant or negative beginning in the 1920s.

In the case of stock and bond markets, there was no clear recovery of total capitalization after the war. That is, the boom experienced in the first decade of the century came to an abrupt end in 1915 and was followed by a sustained decline for at least three decades (evident in Figures 9.3 and 9.4). Figure 9.3 shows the sum of stock and bond market capitalization during

---

[8] Taylor, "Foreign Capital Flows," p. 84.
[9] Brazil selectively suspended payments on some foreign loans but continued to pay the service of the loans it got thanks to the Rotschilds in 1898 and 1914 . For details on the history of foreign debt in Brazil, see Marcelo Abreu de Paiva, "Brazil as a Debtor, 1824–1931," *Economic History Review* 59, 4 (2006): 765–787, esp. pp. 771–772.
[10] Annibal Villela and Wilson Suzigan, *Política do Governo e Crescimento da Economia Brasileira: 1889–1945,* Rio de Janeiro: IPEA/INPES, 1973, p. 333, and Marcelo de Paiva Abreu, "Crise, Crescimento e Modernização Autoritária: 1930–1945," in Marcelo de Paiva Abreu (org.), *A Ordem do Progresso: Cem Anos de Política Econômica Republicana, 1889–1989,* Rio de Janeiro: Campus Editora, 1989, p. 74.

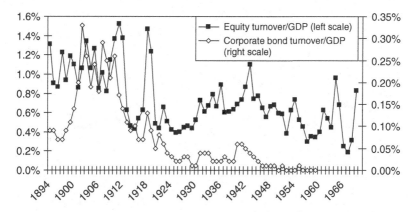

Figure 9.4. Volume of stocks and corporate bonds traded relative to GDP, 1894–1969

Sources: Bond and stock turnover rates before 1969 are from Levy, *História da Bolsa de Valores do Rio de Janeiro*, Tables 23, 26, 35, 41, 43, 44, 58, 61, and 62. Data for the years 1934, 1935, and 1939 were corrected by the author using the reports of the stockbrokers association and the *Anuário da Bolsa de Valores do Rio de Janeiro*. GDP data are from Goldsmith, *Brasil 1850–1984*, Tables 3.1, 4.2, and 6.2.

the first episode of financial development to have surpassed 25% of GDP, reaching 32% in 1913. Both aggregates began a rapid decline after that, which continued into the 1970s.

The volume of stock and bond trading in Rio de Janeiro paints a starker picture of the decline in these markets after World War I. We see in Figure 9.4, which plots the volume of stocks and corporate bonds traded in Brazil (as a percentage of GDP) between 1894 and 1969, a boom in trading between the 1890s and 1920 and then a sustained, rapid decline until the 1960s.[11]

Figure 9.5 plots together an index of capital flows (to GDP) and the turnover or volume of stocks and bonds traded in the Rio de Janeiro Stock Exchange to show how much of the decline in capital flows (in percentual terms) was mimicked by the activity in the Brazilian market. It seems that the decline of capital flows affected the bond market more heavily. The trading of stocks also fell, but almost recovered it's prewar level in the 1920s.

This implies that if the Rajan and Zingales hypothesis, of the great reversal, has some explanatory power for the case of Brazil, it is in explaining the

[11] These figures must be interpreted carefully given that in the early part of the twentieth century the trading of some stocks and most foreign-currency denominated bonds was done in London, Belgium, and Paris. In the 1990s, most trading was done domestically, and the figures for debenture trading included bonds issued by banks and other lending institutions, which had not been significant during the earlier period (e.g., I explicitly exclude all mortgage bonds issued by banks).

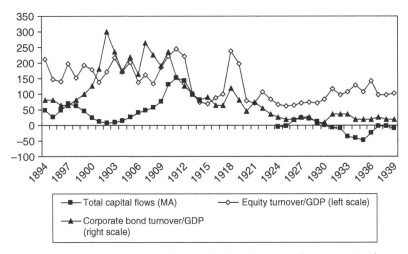

Figure 9.5. Capital flows to Brazil (from England) and stock and corporate bonds turnover (all relative to GDP, indices with 1913=100), 1894–1939

Sources: See Figures 9.1, 9.3, and 9.4.

decline in the trading of bonds in the 1920s and 1930s. This does not imply that their causal explanation is correct, since changes in investor protections came much later (and the decline in real returns for investors may also explain part of the decline in trading in the 1930s). Moreover, capital controls imposed in Brazil during the 1930s might explain why stock and bond markets did not recover their prewar levels until the last decades of the twentieth century.

The next section argues that beyond capital controls, the inflationary pressures of the postwar period ended up eroding investor interest in financial markets and facilitating the consensus around the legal changes of the 1930s and 1940s.

INFLATION, INVESTOR RETURNS, AND FINANCIAL DEVELOPMENT AFTER WORLD WAR I

An alternative explanation for the decline in stock and bond trading in Brazil could be that the deterioration of real returns on stocks and bonds consequent to higher inflation during World War I and thereafter weakened the consensus behind the status quo in corporate governance. Perotti and von Thadden's hypothesis that inflation eroded wealth and induced a change in the institutions that shape corporate governance was generated with Europe in mind, but the macroeconomic scenario of capital-receiving countries such as Brazil was quite similar to the situation in continental Europe in the 1920s and 1930s. Inflation accelerated as the Brazilian government abandoned the gold standard and elected to print money both during World War I and the early 1920s. Its attempt to reinstate the gold standard between 1926 and 1929 had to be abandoned as the Great Depression unfolded and foreign exchange reserves dried up. Following World War I, the government consolidated its control over monetary policy through the Rediscount Office at the Banco do Brasil (created in 1920) and Superintendence of Money and Credit (created in 1945).[12] But because these instances of control were, in fact, used as instruments for pursuing expansionary monetary policy, inflation accelerated in the late 1930s and even more in the 1940s.

I examined the effect of inflation on investor returns by estimating an index of average real yields of Brazilian stocks and corporate bonds (weighted by the book value of each issue). Figure 9.7 represents nominal figures for the average yields of stocks and bonds and three-year moving average of real stock and bond yields. Because there are no continuous series of stock quotations for a significant number of companies, estimated stock yields represent the dividend over the average price for the year (capital gains are not taken into account). Yields for corporate bonds are estimated as the coupon over the average price for the year and yields by company are weighted using the size of the issue relative to the sample of companies with yields for each year.

Looking at yields in Figures 9.6 and 9.7, we can see that, because nominal yields do not vary much, the disruption in financial returns during World War I and a resulting decline in yields should be attributed to inflation. The two big drops in real stock and bond yields occurred in the early 1920s and during the 1930s, both periods of rapid inflation.

One easy solution to this problem would have been for the government to allow companies to create indexed bonds (e.g., inflation indexed). Yet the legal framework did not include such provisions until the 1960s. Companies relied on foreign-currency denominated bonds in the 1890s as a way to protect buyers from macroeconomic instability, especially in the last decade of the nineteenth century. After the war, however, the Brazilian

---

[12] See Winston Fritsch, "Apogeu e Crise na Primeira República: 1900–1930," in Marcelo de Paiva Abreu (org.), *A Ordem do Progresso: Cem Anos de Política Econômica Republicana, 1889–1989*, p. 47, and Cláudio Contador, *Mercado de Ativos Financeiros no Brasil*, Rio de Janeiro: IBMEC, 1974, p. 29.

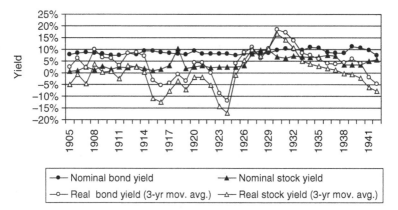

Figure 9.6. Nominal and real average yields of stocks and corporate bonds, Brazil, 1905–1942

Sources: Real average yields are estimated using annual yields (coupon or dividend payment in mil reis/average annual price of bond or stock) and subtracting annual inflation using the GDP deflator (capital gains are not included in the stock yields), then weighted by the size of each bond issue relative to the paid-up capital per company relative to the total amount of bonds or stocks included in each sample year. For bonds, yields were estimated using a sample of between 23 and 45 bond issues per year (mean = 31, median = 30), denominated in domestic currency, for multiple sectors (textiles, manufacturing in general, shipping, ports, railways, etc.). Stock yields are estimated using a sample of between 20 and 82 stocks per year (mean and median = 46). Bond and stock prices are from Bolsa de Valores do Rio de Janeiro, *Anuário da Bolsa de Valores do Rio de Janeiro*, 1932–1942.

government switched on and off the gold standard and instituted capital and exchange rate controls. Issuing bonds in foreign currencies thus would have increased too greatly the risk borne by corporations. For that reason the majority of corporations in Brazil started issuing bonds only in domestic currency. This reduced the total size of corporate bond issues and left the buyers of these bonds facing negative real returns when inflation increased.

There was only a short window in which real returns for investors were positive at the end of the 1920s. The episode of positive real yields between 1926 and 1929 illustrated in Figure 9.6 is a consequence of tight monetary policy after 1926. Prices declined rapidly in 1926 and 1927 as the Banco do Brasil raised its rediscount rates to help the federal government resume the gold standard at a stronger exchange rate than had prevailed during the earlier part of the decade. Yet, even though stock and bond yields went up again in the late 1920s and during the deflationary

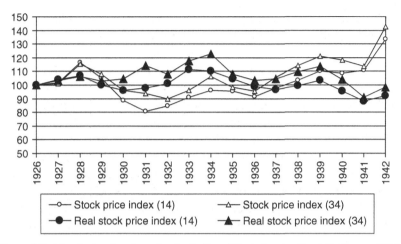

Figure 9.7. Nominal and real stock price indices, Rio de Janeiro Stock Exchange, 1926–1942 (1926=100)

Source: Estimated using two samples of stocks denominated in domestic currency. One includes 14 with complete price data, the other, 34 securities for which I have continuous stock prices save for some bad years during the Great Depression when trading declined significantly. The small sample includes three banks, two insurance companies, a manufacturing company, a port (Docas de Santos), one railway, five textile mills, and a tramway. The larger sample includes these and other companies from all industries. The stock price indices start in 1926=100, and the deflated series also uses the GDP deflator with 1926=100. Stock prices are from Bolsa de Valores do Rio de Janeiro, *Anuário da Bolsa de Valores do Rio de Janeiro*, 1932–1942.

years of the Great Depression, real yields turned negative between 1931 and 1942.[13]

These results are somewhat surprising because we would have expected investors to adjust the prices of securities (and their yields) with fluctuations in inflation. But Cláudio Contador's study of Brazilian government bond returns reveals that investors' inflationary expectations lack the sophistication to occasion adjustments to yields (by lowering prices) sufficient to keep up with inflation. His data show the yield associated with Brazilian government bonds to have been negative for most years between the 1920s and 1930s.[14]

Finding lower yields as inflation accelerated is also consistent with studies of the relationship between monetary policy and stock returns in developed countries in the post–World War II period. Michael Bordo, Michael

---

[13] For a discussion of monetary policy in the 1920s, see Fritsch, "Apogeu e Crise na Primeira República," pp. 56–58.

[14] Contador, *Mercado de Ativos Financeiros no Brasil*, p. 25.

Dueker, and David C. Wheelock, using high frequency time series to explore the relationship between stock returns and inflation in Germany, the United States, and the United Kingdom, find that stock market booms usually coincide with low inflation and their end with either tight monetary policy or higher inflation. Because monetary policy in Brazil was not tightened until the 1960s, inflation would seem to have had more of an effect on stock and bond market performance than any increase in interest rates.[15]

Evidence of the decline of stock yields in Brazil since 1929 is also corroborated by the findings of Stephen Haber's study of the nation's textile industry in the years following the Great Depression. He documents, using return on equity and similar data for dividends and stock prices for a sample of textile firms, a steady decline in rates of return on capital since the late 1920s. "[T]he Brazilian cotton textile industry," he insists, "was in serious trouble before 1929."[16]

Real stock yields in the estimates presented in Figure 9.5 declined steadily in the 1930s because dividends fell more rapidly than stock prices. We see in Figure 9.6 that stock prices did not decline more than 2% or so in real terms until the early 1940s, at which point they were 10% below their 1926 level. This suggests that most of the decline in yields is attributable to reduced dividend payments. "[A]s profits disappeared and firms were forced to the wall [in the 1930s]," Haber observes, "there was nothing, except bad news, to distribute to investors."[17]

The evidence presented here suggests that investors were unable to adapt their inflationary expectations (by adjusting securities prices) to obtain positive yields, which would have eroded investor confidence in the stock market, especially as inflation accelerated in the 1930s. With rising inflation becoming highly volatile after the 1920s and the volume of securities traded in the stock exchange so thin, it became more difficult for investors to adjust the prices of their securities sufficiently to obtain positive yields.

The equilibrium Perotti and von Thadden anticipated as a consequence of higher inflation was realized in Brazil. With investors' confidence in the market eroded by lower real returns, companies increasingly turned to bank

[15] Michael Bordo, Michael J. Dueker, and David C. Wheelock, "Monetary Policy and Stock Market Booms and Busts in the 20th Century," Federal Reserve Bank of St. Louis Working Paper 2007–020A, May 2007. This paper summarizes the literature that has looked at the relationship between inflation and stock returns.

[16] Stephen Haber, "Business Enterprise and the Great Depression in Brazil: A Study of Profits and Losses in Textile Manufacturing," *Business History Review* 66, 2 (Summer 1992): 335–362, quote from p. 351.

[17] Haber, "Business Enterprise and the Great Depression in Brazil," p. 352.

credit to fund operations and capital investment. The government also, consistent with Rajan and Zingales' hypothesis, assumed a more important role in the allocation of credit and protection of strategic sectors through subsidized loans. But whereas Rajan and Zingales expected declining capital and trade flows to precipitate, through legal changes pressed by domestic interest groups, the decline of stock and bond markets, the sequence of events was different in Brazil. In this country, the size of the stock and bond markets rapidly contracted with declining international capital flows during World War I, yet even after capital returned to Brazil, inflation eroded the performance of securities. In fact, changes to creditor and shareholder rights came decades later when interest groups formed a coalition with the government to promote significant legal changes that altered corporate governance and finance significantly.

The next section examines the political economy behind these changes in investor protections after the 1930s.

THE DECLINE OF FINANCIAL DEMOCRACY AFTER THE 1930s

The 1945 Bankruptcy Law and Decline of Creditor Rights

Following on the heels of rapidly deteriorating capital flows and low to negative real bond yields, the final blow to creditor rights and bond markets took the form of a new bankruptcy law, enacted in 1945, that eliminated most of the creditor protections contained in previous legislation. Drafted and passed by the authoritarian government of Getúlio Vargas, the law gave labor and the treasury priority over all other debts and encouraged the practice of retaining the incumbent management during the reorganization of bankrupt entities.

Upon securing the presidency of Brazil in 1930 following a brief civil war, Vargas installed a provisional government, dismissed Congress, and created a parallel judiciary system to judge political cases. After a failed counter-revolutionary movement mounted by the republican political forces of São Paulo in 1932, Vargas' provisional government tried to create a new social pact by calling a constitutional congress. A new constitution was drafted and Vargas was elected president in 1934. Although the constitution and electoral law of 1932 strengthened the secrecy of the ballot and established an electoral tribunal, the improved democratic system was not to endure. In 1937, Vargas declared a state of emergency, claiming the Communist Party was plotting a coup. Congress was subsequently dismissed and the Estado

Novo (New State), which mimicked Mussolini's corporatist model for Italy, was established.[18]

The official labor and industrialist unions created during the first years of his presidency were Vargas' main base of support. His government had since the early 1930s promoted labor legislation that introduced such basic protections for workers as a minimum wage, paid vacations, and pension funds. Most of these laws were drafted by a team of lawyers who were either former labor rights activists or known socialists. In 1943, at the zenith of his authoritarian regime, Vargas enacted the aptly named Consolidation of Labor Laws, or Consolidação das Leis do Trabalho (CLT). Alexandre Marcondes Filho, whom Vargas had appointed to run the ministries of both justice and labor, was charged with passing the legal reforms, including a new bankruptcy law, that would make the CLT work.

In 1945, Vargas enacted, as a presidential decree-law and without congressional approval, the bankruptcy reform law of 1945, which radically altered creditor rights with the aim of improving labor protections and making life easier for domestic industrialists.[19] Neither brokers nor bankers nor large bondholders (e.g., insurance companies) were permitted any input during the drafting of this law.

The new bankruptcy law was not opposed by the industrialists and unions – which included the most influential entrepreneurs of the time (e.g., Andrea Matarazzo, Roberto Simonsen, Jorge Street, and others). These industrialists worked together with Marcondes Filho to draft a new law that encouraged the continuation of going concerns over their submission to creditor control in times of insolvency.[20] Opposition might have been expected from banks

---

[18]   For a general history of the Vargas period, see Bóris Fausto, *Getúlio Vargas*, São Paulo: Companhia das Letras, 2006. Most of the history recounted in this section draws from Chapters 2 and 3.

[19]   Some of the labor protections included in the 1934 constitution were respected by the new constitution drafted by Vargas in 1937. Specific labor protections were legislated in the years that followed. A minimum wage was instituted by a 1938 law. A 1939 law transformed all unions into state and national organizations according to profession. Union contributions were made mandatory by a 1940 law. Finally, in 1941, the Justiça do Trabalho (Justice of Labor) was regulated by a law that introduced an arbitration panel to solve all labor disputes. The CLT compiled in one overarching law all previously legislated labor rights. Excluded from federal regulation, the industrialist unions remained more autonomous. On the political economy of the CLT, see John D. French, *Drowning in Laws: Labor Law and Brazilian Political Culture*, Chapel Hill: University of North Carolina Press, 2004. For the industrialist side, see Maria Antonieta P. Leopoldi, *Política e Interesses: As Associações Industriais, e Política Econômica e o Estado na Industrialização Brasileira*, São Paulo: Paz e Terra, 2000.

[20]   Information on Alexandre Marcondes Filho and his friendship with industrialists such as Roberto Simonsen is provided in Maria Antonieta P. Leopoldi, *Política e Interesses:*

and other important bondholders such as insurance companies, but the Vargas administration kept most of the relevant creditors (which comprised the opposition to the new bankruptcy law) under constant siege, preempting possible opposition from influential foreign banks and insurance companies by forcing them into nationalization and keeping national banks under close scrutiny by means of the 1933 Usury Law.[21]

The main objective of the 1945 Bankruptcy Law was to promote the survival of the going concern. As explained in Chapter 7, under this law debtors could avoid liquidation by filing for a composition scheme called *concordata preventiva*, which gave them two years to reorganize and pay all debts. In theory, the restructuring and rescheduling of debts applied only to unsecured creditors because secured creditors could collect collateral. But in practice, secured creditors rarely recovered anything as credits owed in the form of social security payments and labor injury compensation took precedence over their claims. The process whereby collateral was collected became slower over time, and after 1945, bankruptcy became an exceedingly slow judicial process, tending to last, on average, five to ten years. Adding to this problem, the post-1940s high-inflation scenario lowered the real expected recovery rate for secured creditors to zero, and when, after a few years, creditors were able to repossess collateral, the assets tended to be worthless.[22] Brazil's Congress did not change the state of creditor protections or bankruptcy procedures until 2005, when it passed a more procreditor law.

The Decline of Shareholder Protections

This chapter so far has presented evidence that the decline in the stock and bond markets was related to the impact on the Brazilian economy of reduced international capital flows and higher inflation rates. But the reasons widely held corporations decayed and democratic practices within corporations became less common have to do with changes in company

---

As Associações Industriais, e Política Econômica e o Estado na Industrialização Brasileira, pp. 86–87.

[21] Leopoldi, *Política e Interesses,* p. 86, and Maria Bárbara Levy, *A Indústria do Rio de Janeiro através de suas Sociedades Anônimas,* Rio de Janeiro: UFRJ Editoria, 1994, pp. 240–241.

[22] See Brazil, Decree-Law 7661, June 21, 1945 for the actual law. For the history of bankruptcy law in Brazil, see Paulo Penalva Santos, "Brevíssima notícia sobre a recuperação extrajudicial," *Revista do Advogado* 25, 83 (September 2005): 107–115. Inflation correction for assets and liabilities of bankrupt firms was forbidden by law until 1984. The changes in foreclosures are based on the experiences of lawyers interviewed for this book. From interviews with Luis Fernando de Paiva and Giuliano Colombo, bankruptcy specialists from Pinheiro Neto Advogados, and Thomas Felsberg, of Felsberg & Associados, São Paulo, Brazil, November 11, 2005.

laws in the 1930s and 1940s. The introduction, in 1932, of nonvoting shares reduced the cost of control and made it easier for large shareholders (with relatively low portions of total capital) to acquire full control of large corporations. The 1940 company law introduced strong shareholder protections that favored holders of common stock, but also eliminated some of the provisions, such as graduated voting schemes, that fostered more egalitarian distribution of votes among shareholders. Whereas maximum vote schemes were still allowed for holders of common stock, graduated voting schemes were fully eliminated.

Reducing investor protections would be costly for corporations in a world in which they obtained outside financing from small investors. But that is not how the financial system of Brazil operated after the 1940s. Corporations that had become more reliant on credit from banks, especially government-owned banks, were less concerned about obtaining capital in stock or bond markets, especially if doing so entailed providing strong protections for small shareholders or promoting the democratization of control. In most existing companies, a single investor or family would acquire enough common equity to exert complete control and, when issuing new shares, to opt for issues of nonvoting stock.

In this scenario, the set of investor protections discussed in Chapters 4, 5, and 6 became, in a sense, irrelevant because information about ownership and voting power within the corporation became less relevant as the majority of shareholders had nonvoting shares. Additionally, the statutes of large corporations, because rising inflation forced their continual readjustment, no longer included directors' salaries.

Some students of corporate governance in Brazil argue that family control was a logical consequence of the macroeconomic and institutional environment that prevailed after the 1930s. According to Mária Bárbara Levy,

"[T]he peculiarities of the industrialization process required the family-controlled enterprise. ... The advantages that could come with the introduction of a more rational system [with more dispersed ownership and control] were neutralized by the existence of an unstable market. .... The instability of financial and exchange rate policy, which could alter the cost structure of a corporation, increase the costs of machinery imports, complicate the projected expansion of a company, or change its borrowing policies, generated a situation in which it was necessary to have quick decision-making regarding inventory, capital investment, and capital structure. These decisions were more efficiently handled by individuals [or families].[23]

[23] Translated by the author from Levy, *A Indústria do Rio de Janeiro através de suas Sociedades Anônimas*, pp. 254–255.

Reflecting this logic, Brazil's corporate landscape had by the 1980s become dominated by family-controlled and owned business groups known as *grupos*. These diversified conglomerates with access to subsidized credit through affiliate banks or connections with the government, because they could buy or outperform their capital-starved competitors, ended up dominating and controlling large portions of the internal market for consumer and industrial products.

Preferred Shares and the Decline of Shareholder Rights

The introduction of preferred shares in the 1930s significantly altered the cost of controlling corporations. Preferred shares were regulated by Decree 21,526, passed on June 15, 1932, which set no explicit limit on the percentage of total equity such shares could represent. Preferred shares granted their owners first rights when dividends were distributed and priority when shares were repurchased or, in the event of bankruptcy, in the recovery of assets. Preferred shares usually did not carry voting rights, but it was up to the company to decide whether to give these shares control rights. In most instances, holders of preferred share issues exchanged voting rights for guaranteed dividends. Regulatory changes enacted in 1940 stipulated that if no dividends were paid for three years, preferred shares would become ordinary shares with full voting rights.[24]

Other protections were accorded preferred shares. Dissident investors who held preferred shares who disagreed with an assembly or managerial decision had the right, for example, to walk away and be paid for their shares at the fair share of total shareholders' equity, though it is unclear whether this right was ever enforced.

Preferred shares were not widely traded until the late 1940s, nearly a decade after their introduction. A review of the *Anuário da Bolsa do Rio de Janeiro* (the Rio de Janeiro Stock Exchange Annual) between 1932 and 1942 reveals that only a handful of companies issued preferred shares during the 1930s, and these accounted for less than 4% of total trading between 1926 and 1942. By way of comparison, the trading of corporate bonds represented, on average, 30% of total trading for the same period.[25]

---

[24] Tatiana Nenova argues that companies circumvented this ruling by paying token amounts in dividends. See Tatiana Nenova, "Control Values and Changes in Corporate Law in Brazil," *Latin American Business Review* 6, 3 (2005), p. 10.

[25] Estimates of total trading exclude government bonds and are compiled using the total amounts traded by each security published in the *Anuário da Bolsa de Valores do Rio de Janeiro*, 1932–1942.

One might argue that preferred shares protected smaller shareholders by guaranteeing a fixed cash flow, but issuing a large part of equity in nonvoting shares enabled insiders to acquire control of companies at low cost, a situation that worsened as Brazilian laws increasingly reduced the share of equity required to control a company. Whereas under the 1940 company law preferred shares were not permitted to exceed 50% of capital, the 1976 law permitted two-thirds of total equity to be denominated as preferred shares, which in many cases reduced the total equity needed to control a corporation from 26 to 17% (or one half of total voting shares).[26] For example, after 1976, if 33% of equity was in ordinary voting shares, holding 17% was sufficient to control a company, whereas in 1940, if 50% of equity was in ordinary shares, it was necessary to hold 26% to exercise control.

Reducing the cost of control in the unstable environment of the post–Great Depression period abetted a tendency to consolidate the control of large corporations in a few hands (or families). Moreover, not only was control more concentrated after the 1930s, but also, as financing increasingly came to be provided through bank credit and long-term credit by financial institutions controlled by the government, those well connected in these circles were able to better secure credit terms. Connectedness and strategic position as producers of manufactured goods for export or industrial products for domestic use afforded companies a significant advantage over competitors and possible new entrants. As a consequence, Brazil ended up with high market concentration in most industrial sectors. It was at this point, as capital became scarcer and tariff protections necessary for survival, that most of Brazil's largest companies began to create the large, diversified conglomerates known as business groups or *grupos*. The dynamics of this transition are explained in the following chapter.

CONCLUSION

This chapter narrates the decline in stock and bond markets after World War I by testing two hypotheses that try to explain the changes in corporate governance and finance. The evidence of the decline of Brazil's stock and bond markets does not fully conform to Rajan and Zingales' predictions. Capital flows neither directly changed the legal framework nor directly explain the decline in stock market activity. Even if the initial reduction in capital flows from Europe to Brazil after the war seems to be correlated with

---

[26] See Fran Martins, *Comentários à Lei das Sociedades Anônimas: Lei no. 6.404, de 15 de Dezembro de 1976*, Rio de Janeiro: Biblioteca Forense, 1977–1979, p. 101.

a decline in stock and bond market activity, we cannot attribute the entire decline in stock and bond markets to the postwar decline in capital flows. This is mostly because capital flows to Brazil continued in the 1920s and 1930s while stock market activity continued its decline.

The post–World War I scenario that played out in Brazil conforms perhaps more closely to Perotti and von Thadden's story of the long-lasting effects of the inflationary shock of the 1920s on corporate governance worldwide. In Brazil, inflation decimated investor returns in real terms, eroding confidence in the markets and making it easier to change labor and shareholder rights. Opposition from investors and the interest groups that protected investor rights (e.g., the stock broker association) was muted by the fact that all were losing money under existing arrangements.

Under a scenario of higher inflation and macroeconomic instability, the Brazilian government instituted capital controls. This macroeconomic environment generated negative real returns in stock and bond markets and thus eroded investor confidence in the Brazilian market, both abroad and at home. This explains the broad consensus in 1945 to make bankruptcy law more creditor and labor friendly and explains why companies gravitated from equity issues toward bank credit.

The next chapter explains how these changes played out until the end of the twentieth century and shows in detail how inflation altered the structure of corporate finance as well as some of the major changes in corporate governance in place by the end of that century.

TEN

The Rise of Concentrated Ownership in the
Twentieth Century

If Brazil started the twentieth century with a system of strong investor protections and relatively low ownership concentration, how is it that the corporate landscape in the second half of the century ended up being dominated by large conglomerates with concentrated ownership? This chapter explains the major changes effected in corporate governance and finance during the twentieth century.

The structure of corporate finance in Brazil changed radically after the 1930s and 1940s as banks supplanted the stock and bond markets as the main source of corporate finance. The government created a development bank that provided the bulk of long-term credit and commercial banks focused on short-term lending.

Ownership of large corporations ended up being highly concentrated because either families or the government seized full control of the voting equity (which became relatively easy to do subsequent to the introduction of nonvoting equity in 1932). Brazilian entrepreneurs ended up forming large, diversified conglomerates (*grupos*) with highly concentrated ownership for strategic reasons that have to do both with economics – they are helpful for overcoming many market failures – and politics – they are influential lobbying machines with sufficient clout to counter the powerful labor unions.

Finally, the government became the largest shareholder in the Brazilian economy, coming to control after World War I, and especially after World War II, the largest companies in the country by both bailing out existing companies (e.g., railways) and promoting the creation of state-owned enterprises (e.g., steel mills, mining companies, chemical plants, and banks). The rise of the state as a shareholder, however, ran counter to some of the corporate governance norms that had prevailed before World War I.

236

INFLATION AND THE "REVERSAL" IN CORPORATE FINANCE: GOVERNMENT BANKS VERSUS MARKETS

The scheme of corporate finance that had prevailed until 1930 was altered in significant ways over the course of the following two decades. Banks, which had largely focused on financing the export of agricultural commodities and were mostly providers of short-term capital for corporations, became the dominant players in the market for funding after the 1930s. This transition can only be understood when the effects of inflation in Brazil and government reaction to an accelerating inflation rate, are taken into account.

The decline of stocks and bonds as the main source of finance begins to make sense when we take into account the fact that it was hard for companies to issue securities indexed to inflation (or with inflation correction provisions). It is difficult, for example, to imagine any Brazilian corporation wanting to bear all the risk of the uncertain macroeconomic environment by issuing bonds denominated, or stocks that paid dividends, in foreign currencies, something relatively common before 1915. Moreover, by the 1930s, dealing with inflation had become part of the day-to-day business of Brazilian corporations and government regulation limited their options for making bonds and stocks attractive to investors.

The usury law passed by the Brazilian government in 1933 in response to higher levels of inflation, for example, de facto eliminated two possible forms of inflation correction for companies that wanted to increase investors' returns. Indexing contracts to a foreign currency, whether pounds or dollars, a strategy companies had used to isolate (especially foreign) investors from inflation and exchange rate depreciation, was eliminated by the stipulation that all contracts be denominated in domestic currency. Additionally a government-imposed limit on nominal interest rates of 12% per year impeded companies from indexing their bond coupon rates to inflation or the to exchange rate (not permitted until the 1960s) or raising the coupon rate such that bondholders could realize positive real yields. Although not binding during the deflationary years of the Great Depression (1929–1931), as inflation levels escalated from the 1920s to the 1960s, the 12% interest rate ceiling introduced significant distortions in the economy.[1]

Two side effects of the law further eroded the importance of stock markets as a source of capital for corporate financing. As investors lost their appetite for securities that paid negative real yields, banks, which in the face

---

[1] See Decree 23,501, November 1933. For a discussion of the effects of the usury law on treasury bond yields, see Cláudio Contador, *Mercado de Ativos Financeiros no Brasil*, Rio de Janeiro: IBMEC, 1974, pp. 24–25.

of the ceiling imposed on nominal rates were reluctant to provide long-term loans, afforded most companies access only to short-term credit (see Table 10.1), and loans from government-controlled banks became the most important source of long-term credit.

Table 10.1 reports short-term and long-term bank credit to the private sector relative to GDP between 1951 and 1972. The first side effect of the usury law is quite clear: short-term bank loans increasingly became the main source of credit for the private sector, representing 26% of GDP in 1951 and 40% in the 1970s.

Long-term loans to the private sector were a small proportion of the total private credit in the Brazilian economy. We can see in Table 10.1 that long-term bank loans to the private sector represented between 1% and 2% of GDP in the 1950s and into the 1960s, leading Brazilian economist Mário Henrique Simonsen to state that "long-term loans are virtually unavailable in Brazil." According to Simonsen this was mostly because of "uncertainty about the future rhythm of inflation" and the impossibility of charging high interest rates to compensate for that risk. Brazilian companies consequently obtained funds mostly by discounting their IOUs and bills of exchange with commercial and government-owned banks, occasionally issuing debentures for small amounts. All of this commercial paper provided short-term credit, and the maturity for corporate debentures was quite short (e.g., one year). As inflation increased in the 1950s and early 1960s, avoiding the restrictions of the usury law became more complicated, causing both short- and long-term bank credit to the private sector to contract.[2]

Banks nevertheless managed to remain profitable throughout the 1950s and 1960s by taking recourse to two mechanisms: first, they respected the usury law by paying low nominal rates on deposits, and second, they charged higher rates for loans (closer to the 12% ceiling) and, when inflation was higher than the cap on nominal interest rates, they compensated for the losses by charging high fees and forcing borrowers to keep large portions of their loans on deposit. The re-loaning of these time deposits to other borrowers was effectively an implicit fee that compensated the banks for their losses.[3]

The other side effect of the usury law was that as the government consolidated its control over the allocation of resources to the Brazilian economy, strategic and protected sectors were afforded long-term credit at low real

---

[2]   Mário Henrique Simonsen, "Inflation and the Money and Capital Markets of Brazil," in Howard Ellis (ed.), *The Economy of Brazil*, Berkeley and Los Angeles: University of California Press, 1969, p. 150.
[3]   Simonsen, "Inflation and the Money and Capital Markets of Brazil," p. 143.

Table 10.1. *Total bank loans for the private sector*
(as a % of GDP), 1951–1972

	Short-term	Long-term	Total
1951	26.2	1.2	27.4
1952	27.1	1.3	28.4
1953	27.2	1.5	28.7
1954	25.6	1.5	27.1
1955	24.2	1.5	25.7
1956	21.1	1.5	22.6
1957	21.0	1.8	22.8
1958	21.4	2.0	23.4
1959	19.7	2.1	21.8
1960	19.8	2.0	21.9
1961	18.3	1.7	20.1
1962	20.9	2.0	23.0
1963	17.8	1.8	19.6
1964	16.8	1.4	18.3
1965	17.2	1.5	18.7
1966	16.6	2.8	19.3
1967	20.5	4.3	24.8
1968	27.3	6.4	33.6
1969	30.1	8.4	38.5
1970	34.5	9.4	43.8
1971	37.7	10.7	48.3
1972	40.1	12.4	52.5

Source: Contador, *Mercado de Ativos Financeiros no Brasil*, p. 32.

interest rates by the monetary authorities and National Bank for Economic Development (Banco Nacional de Desenvolvimento Econômico [BNDE], created in 1952, renamed Banco Nacional de Desenvolvimento Econômico e Social [BNDES] in 1982). In fact, most of the long-term credit reported in Table 10.1 was provided by government controlled banks.

Moreover, companies that had access to credit from government-controlled banks paid low or negative real rates of interest. A World Bank report that examined credit market practices before the 1970s reported that real interest rates for these subsidized credits were near zero or negative, and in the 1970s, when more data is available, the World Bank found the real interest rate on BNDE loans averaged between −4% and 2% per year.[4]

This change in the system of corporate finance had important implications for the strategies of Brazilian corporations. Given that government banks controlled the allocation of long-term credit and that part of the credit provided by the BNDE was also used to buy equity and shares issued by corporations, establishing and maintaining good relations with the government and BNDE officials became an integral part of corporate strategy. In this context, the government viewed these companies as strategically important because of the employment they generated or goods they produced. Thus, these large conglomerates had greater leverage with the BNDE, something that gave them a better chance of surviving in the new environment.

In a nutshell, the corporate governance game stopped being about providing protections for outside investors who purchased shares or bonds in stock markets. When long-term credit was provided primarily by government banks (especially after the 1940s), the focus of corporations and their owners necessarily had to shift to how to access government finance and secure short-term credit from banks.

With shares and bonds relegated to a secondary role as sources of corporate finance, the volume of new issues was relatively small between the 1950s and 1964. Table 10.2 shows that new share issues represent about 2.5%, and new corporate bond issues about 0.5%, of GDP per year. The credit markets and issue of stocks and bonds began to grow again in 1964, after the government allowed companies and banks to issue securities and credit contracts with inflation correction while simultaneously contracting the money supply. Other fiscal incentives explain the rebound of share issues in the 1960s.[5]

THE RISE OF CONCENTRATED OWNERSHIP

By the end of the twentieth century, ownership of Brazilian corporations was highly concentrated, one shareholder or family usually controlling the majority of the votes. With the introduction of nonvoting, preferred shares

---

[4] World Bank, *Brazil: Financial Systems Review*, Washington, D.C.: The World Bank, 1984, pp. xiii–xiv and xix.
[5] For an explanation of the fiscal incentives used to promote the issue of new shares in Brazil between 1964 and 1972, see Aldo Musacchio, "Law and Finance in Historical Perspective: Politics, Bankruptcy Law, and Corporate Governance in Brazil, 1850–2002," unpublished Ph.D. dissertation, Stanford University, 2005, pp. 60–62.

Table 10.2. *New stock and bond issues (as a % of GDP),
Brazil, 1951–1972*

	New shares	Total share issues	Corporate bond issues
1951	1.8	2.9	
1952	2.3	3.6	
1953	1.9	3.2	
1954	2.7	4.1	
1955	2.4	3.8	
1956	2.5	7.6	0.03
1957	2.7	4.4	0.01
1958	2.7	3.4	0.04
1959	3.2	5.1	0.05
1960	2.9	4.5	0.05
1961	1.9	3.8	0.01
1962	3.1	5.1	0.04
1963	2.3	4.7	0.02
1964	1.8	9.8	0.06
1965	3.3	16.8	0.11
1966	3.3	11.3	0.06
1967	4.1	13.3	
1968	4.9	12.7	
1969	4.8	18.6	
1970	4.2	13.4	
1971	7.8	14.6	
1972	5.1	11.9	

Sources: Share issues are compiled from "Emissões de Capital,"
Conjuntura Econômica, 1951–1972, corporate bond issues from
Simonsen, "Inflation and the Money and Capital Markets of Brazil,"
Table 6, p. 150.
Note: New shares represent new issues sold to the public by existing or
new companies. Total share issues also includes the issue of shares to
incorporate retained earnings or when total equity was revalued.

in 1932, this control became possible without owning a large portion of
total equity.

After 1932, because preferred shares did not carry voting rights, corporations could issue new stock without necessarily having to disperse

control rights among new owners.[6] In relative terms, the introduction of preferred shares reduced the cost of control in Brazilian corporations. Before 1932, investors looking to acquire full control of corporations had to buy 51% (under one-share-one-vote provisions) or more (under graduated voting or maximum vote provisions) of shares, but after 1932 a shareholder with only 26% of voting equity could control a corporation that had issued 50% of its capital in nonvoting, preferred shares. The cost of capital was further reduced in 1976, when corporations were permitted to issue as much as two-thirds of their capital in nonvoting, preferred shares. In this context, the majority of the voting equity needed to control a corporation that had 66% of its capital in preferred shares was only 17% of total capital.

A good example of the transformation of the structure of ownership effected by preferential shares is that of Panair do Brasil, the Brazilian airline operated and controlled by Pan-American Airways (Pan Am) of the United States. Pan Am chartered Panair do Brasil in 1943, taking advantage of the fact that it did not have to give up control in order to raise capital in equity markets (its book value was $80,000 cruzeiros, equivalent to US$5.15 million of 1900). Pan Am controlled 57.7% of the ordinary shares of the Brazilian corporation with 57.7% of the votes in the shareholder assembly (each ordinary share had one vote). Most of Panair do Brasil's thousands of shareholders held preferential shares, and the 1,238 holders of ordinary shares had such low percentages of total equity (the second largest shareholder, Panair's workers union, controlled only about 2.5% of the ordinary shares[7]) that they could not challenge Pan Am's control.

FAMILY OWNERSHIP AND THE RISE OF BUSINESS GROUPS

Even in the absence of data that would enable us to track the evolution of ownership concentration over time for all the Brazilian corporations that existed at the beginning of the century, we know that the largest companies at the end of the twentieth century had a higher concentration of control rights than did the sample of companies studied in this book. Additional evidence that ownership concentration increased in the second half of the twentieth century is provided by the data we have for the largest conglomerates of corporations at the end of the 1970s.

---

[6]   Corporations could give voting rights to preferred shareholders, but in practice that did not happen.
[7]   "Panair do Brasil, S. A.," *Diario Official*, December 27, 1943.

By the 1970s, the dominant firms in most sectors in Brazil belonged to multifirm, largely diversified conglomerates, or grupos, usually under the direct control of a family or family-owned parent company. Table 10.3, which reports the percentage of equity controlled by the largest shareholder and three largest shareholders and name of the company or family that controlled the *grupo*, gives an idea of the degree of ownership concentration in these corporations by 1980. Ownership information is not precise. Because most of these groups were not publicly traded, or were owned by holding companies that were not publicly traded, the table is constructed from reports taken from *Balanço*, a magazine section of the financial newspaper *Gazeta Mercantil*. The magazine sent questionnaires directly to companies, and magazine staff estimated from the responses the shareholdings of the largest owners. The estimates reported in Table 10.3 are the best that can be derived from this information.[8]

In most *grupos*, the largest shareholder, usually a family or holding company, controlled more than 50% of shares with voting power. Only Brahma, one of Brazil's two largest breweries, and Alpargatas, a shoe and clothing manufacturer, had dispersed ownership (see Table 10.3).

Given that the cost of control was reduced, two questions remain. How did these business groups emerge, and why was ownership of the groups concentrated? There are two answers, one economic, the other political. The economic explanation for the emergence of business groups in developing countries in the twentieth century is that they were a "microeconomic response to well-known conditions of market failure in less developed countries," mostly in the markets for capital, managerial talent, and to some extent inputs.[9] Nathaniel Leff observes that business groups help to diversify the portfolios of large entrepreneurs, and "diversification has an obvious appeal in economies subject to the risks and uncertainties of instability and rapid structural change," which was clearly the case in Brazil in the 1930s and 1940s.[10]

Tarun Khanna and Krishna Palepu, arguing that groups in India or Brazil are perhaps a response to "a variety of market failures caused by

---

[8]   "*Grupos*," *Gazeta Mercantil: Balanço*, 4, 4 (September 1980).

[9]   Nathaniel Leff, "Industrial Organization and Entrepreneurship in Developing Countries: The Economic Group," *Economic Development and Cultural Change* 26 (1978): 661–675, esp. p. 666.

[10] Leff, "Industrial Organization and Entrepreneurship in Developing Countries," p. 667. For an argument that there is no conclusive evidence that diversification gives business groups any advantage, see Tarun Khanna and Yishay Yafeh, "Business Groups in Emerging Markets: Paragons or Parasites?" *Journal of Economic Literature* 45, 2 (June 2007): 331–372.

Table 10.3. *Ownership of the largest business groups in Brazil, 1980*

Grupo	Assets in million cruzeiros	Main sectors	Concentration of control rights (votes)		Who controls the company?
			Top shareholder (%)	Top 3 shareholders (%)	
Votorantim	27,663	Cement, aluminum, steel, heavy machinery, textiles	>50		Family Ermírio de Moraes
Matarazzo	24,276	Textiles, coffee, mining, sugar	57	>74	Family Matarazzo: Sulema S. A. (57%) and Irben S. A. (17%)
Bradesco	22,381	Banking, hotels	>50		Bradesco Bank
Bonfiglioli	19,500	Finance, foods, publicity, trade	100		Family Bonfiglioli
Villares	18,663	Steel, elevators, trade, agriculture	65		Family Villares
Caemi	17,138	Mining, steel, agriculture, trade	>50		ATA Parts and Investments (controlled by Augusto Trajano de Azevedo Antunes)
Bamerindus	14,510	Banking, agriculture	>50		Family Andrade Vieira
Dedini	14,384	Steel works, machinery and equipment	25.9	73	A.D.O.S.A. (25.9%); D.O.S.A. (24.9%); A.D. (22.4%); and Nidar (22.6%)
Itaú	13,479	Banking and data management	>50		Itaubanco Foundation

Group	(value)	Sector	%	%	Ownership
Camargo Corrêa	13,056	Construction, agriculture, textiles, finance	>50		Participaciones Morro Vermelho (controlled by Sebastião Ferraz de Camargo Pintado)
Brahma	11,485	Beer	5	<15	Dispersed ownership
Suzano-Feffer	10,184	Paper	>50	>50	Leon Feffer and Max Feffer
Real	9,899	Finance and tourism		>50	Aloysio de Andrade Faria; Augusto Esteves Neves; and Rubens Garcia Neves
Copersucar	9,874	Sugar, sugar-gasoline, coffee			Controlled by 71 sugar mills
Varig	9,533	Airline	>50		Rubem Berta Foundation
Sadia	8,659	Foods, supermarkets, insurance		~50	Attilio F. Fontana; Osório H. Fulan; Zoé Silveira D´Avila; Maria A. C. Fontana
Alpargatas	8,495	Shoes, clothing, sporting goods			Dispersed ownership (11,000 shareholders)
Comind	7,747	Finance and data management		>50	Stab S. A. and Brooklyn S. A.
Unibanco	7,722	Finance	>50		Walter Moreira Salles

Source: "Grupos," in *Gazeta Mercantil: Balanço*, 4, 4, September 1980.

information and agency problems," describe different ways in which groups can substitute for some of the markets that exist in developed countries (e.g., for managerial talent or capital).[11] But what the economic answer to the question of the emergence of business groups does not explain is why these conglomerates tend to have concentrated ownership.[12]

Following the economic logic, one could argue that business groups' concentrated ownership and close relationships between owners and managers were a strategic response to an uncertain environment. Mária Bárbara Levy argues that ownership concentration in Brazil was linked to the need for quick, consistent decision making. Business groups in Brazil were usually controlled by a single family and run by a family member, something that may have facilitated such responses.

There are also two political reasons for the emergence of large business groups with concentrated ownership. First, the accumulation of assets under the management of a single group (or family) was a response to the power of labor organizations. According to Mark J. Roe, concentrated ownership in countries such as Italy and Germany in the second half of the twentieth century was a product of political struggles between labor and management. Owners mitigated conflicts with management, he maintains, by creating large shareholding blocks that could counterbalance the power of labor. Concentrated ownership thus can be understood as a reaction to the increasing bargaining power of labor, as in Germany, for example, where labor has actively participated in the management of most companies since the 1970s, with a labor representative usually occupying a seat on the board of directors or overseeing board of most large corporations.[13]

In Brazil, the labor movement's political leverage increased in the wake of Vargas' rise to power in 1930. Labor increasingly won positions in Congress (in the early 1930s and from the 1940s until today), and labor unions were strongly supported by the Vargas government, which passed many prolabor laws between the 1930s and early 1940s. After 1941, labor disputes were

---

[11] Tarun Khanna and Krishna Palepu, "Is Group Affiliation Profitable in Emerging Markets?: An Analysis of Diversified Indian Business Groups," *Journal of Finance* 55, 2 (2000): 867–891, quote from p. 868.

[12] For a review of the literature on business groups, see Khanna and Yafeh, "Business Groups in Emerging Markets."

[13] See Mark J. Roe, *Political Determinants of Corporate Governance*, New York: Oxford University Press, 2003, esp. Chapters 1 and 4; for a discussion of the conflict between labor and owners in Germany, see Chapter 8 and Katharina Pistor, "Codetermination in Germany: A Socio-Political Model with Governance Externalities," in Margaret Blair and Mark Roe (eds.), *Employees and Corporate Governance*, Washington, D.C.: Brookings Institution Press, 1999, pp. 163–193.

required to be resolved in arbitration courts created by the government and run by government-appointed officials. If we can imagine that corporations had a hard time dealing with labor in such an environment, Roe's argument might possibly be generalizable to Brazil: to counterbalance the power of labor unions and gain more leverage with the government, corporations integrated into large, diversified holding groups with concentrated ownership (usually under the control of a single family). Concentration of ownership and control at once reduced agency costs within the corporation (by reducing friction between owners and managers) and thereby increased management's bargaining power vis-à-vis labor within the firm.

The second political reason for the rise of business groups has to do with the lobbying capacity of these holding companies. As the companies developed a diversified portfolio of businesses, most of which were large-scale ventures, the owners of these companies became more important for the government. On the one hand, these large companies employed a significant number of workers and produced strategic products (steel, cement, cars, etc.) that were part of the import substitution strategy of the government. On the other hand, many of these groups owned banks that were also crucial parts of the financing system the government used to finance its own operations. Having the ownership of these large conglomerates concentrated in a few hands helped the controlling shareholders to centralize lobbying costs in single units that became more powerful and strategically important for the government as the economic model increasingly relied on import substitution.[14]

Thanks to a large body of work that has studied business groups the world over, we now know that business groups evolved in similar ways in other common and civil law countries. Perhaps the prototypical example is that of India, where business groups evolved in a political and economic environment quite similar to that of Brazil. Business groups in Chile, Korea, and Mexico also have similar origins.[15] More research is needed, however,

[14] For a discussion of the role of business groups in Brazil and other developing economies, see Leff, "Industrial Organization and Entrepreneurship in Developing Countries," esp. pp. 669–670 regarding the specific role business groups can play in an import substitution environment.

[15] For the role and evolution of business groups in India, see Khanna and Palepu, "Is Group Affiliation Profitable in Emerging Markets?," and Tarun Khanna and Krishna Palepu, "The Evolution of Concentrated Ownership in India: Broad Patterns and a History of the Indian Software Industry," in Randall Morck (ed.), *A History of Corporate Governance around the World: Family Business Groups to Professional Managers*, Chicago and London: University of Chicago Press and NBER, 2004, pp. 283–324. For the case of Chile, see Tarun Khanna and Jan W. Rivkin, "Interorganizational Ties and Business Group Boundaries: Evidence

to establish whether political motivation was important in creating such groups and concentrating ownership, or whether such groups in other countries were responding purely to economic challenges. Interestingly, in all of these countries the government also became an important owner of large enterprises. In the final part of this chapter, we examine the evolution of the Brazilian government as an owner.

THE GOVERNMENT AS A SHAREHOLDER AND THE RISE OF STATE-OWNED ENTERPRISES

Another major change in corporate governance in Brazil in the 1930s and 1940s was the ascendance of the federal and state governments as large shareholders. By the end of the twentieth century, both directly and through holding companies or development banks, Brazil's federal and state governments were among the largest shareholders in the nation's economy. At least half of the ten largest corporations listed on the Sao Paulo Stock Exchange in the year 2005 were controlled by the government. This chapter reviews briefly how the government became the largest shareholder in Brazil and what that implied for the system of investor protections that prevailed before 1930.

Government participation in large corporations was often part of a broader agenda to place the government at the center of the development process. Consider Companhia Nacional de Alcalis, which was chartered in 1944 and specialized in the production of alkaline products that served as inputs to the production of glass and soap: the federal government owned all of the company's ordinary shares (50.5% of capital), while hundreds of shareholders owned small blocks of its preferred shares.[16]

INVESTOR PROTECTIONS AND GOVERNMENT CONTROL

The participation of the federal and state governments as shareholders in many of Brazil's large corporations does not necessarily imply the erosion of investor protections. But Brazil's federal and state governments usually owned corporations initially "created through special laws, with provisions that revoked the common law, in order to insure full control of the corporation for the government." Levy observes that the first significant "deviation

from an Emerging Economy," *Organization Science* 17, 3 (May/June 2006): 333–352. For other countries, see the survey in Khanna and Yafeh, "Business Groups in Emerging Markets?"

[16] "Companhia Nacional de Alcalis," *Diario Official*, March 7, 1944.

from common practice" in companies in which the government was the controlling shareholder was usually the nomination of the CEO. CEOs were named by the government and the rest of the directors elected by majority vote, but because the federal government usually participated in large corporations only if it controlled a majority of votes, the other directors as well were effectively chosen by the government.[17] Wherever the law impeded government control, the federal and state governments instituted exceptions. Many government-owned corporations, for example, were granted exceptions to the company law that precluded corporations from issuing more than 50% of total equity in preferred shares.[18]

The federal government began to participate actively in the ownership of large strategic corporations with the advent of economic nationalism during Vargas' first two regimes (1930–1937 and 1937–1945). Many times the reason given for government involvement and control was "national security." This was the case for Companhia Siderúrgica Nacional (National Steel Company, or CSN), a large, integrated steel mill project begun during World War II when Brazil recognized the risk reliance on imported industrial goods such as steel posed to national security. The government negotiated a loan from the U.S. Export-Import Bank to finance part of the project and enlisted the help of large numbers of domestic industrialists and financiers to fund construction. In 1941, an initial public offering was organized with the aim of raising 500 million mil reis (about 250 million dollars). When the equity offering, one of the most ambitious IPOs of the twentieth century, failed to capture the interest of Brazil's private entrepreneurs and bankers, the treasury bought most of the ordinary shares, while pension funds bought the bulk of preferred shares.[19]

The 1940 company law provided that all sales of shares including public offerings had to be conducted through officially registered stockbrokers, all of whom were members of one of the country's stockbrokers associations. The federal government's organization of its own IPO for CSN, using diverse means that included a radio campaign to attract investors, was clearly not in keeping with this law. The Rio de Janeiro Stock Brokers Association, notwithstanding its charter to protect company laws and investor interests

[17] Maria Bárbara Levy, *A Indústria do Rio de Janeiro através de suas Sociedades Anônimas*, Rio de Janeiro: UFRJ Editoria, 1994, p. 256.

[18] Levy, *A Indústria do Rio de Janeiro através de suas Sociedades Anônimas*, p. 257.

[19] For the story of entrepreneur participation in the purchase of equity of the National Steel Company, see Warren Dean, *The Industrialization of São Paulo, 1880–1945*, Austin: University of Texas Press, 1969, pp. 218–220. A complete list of ordinary and preferential shareholders can be found in "Cia. Siderúrgica Nacional," *Diario Official*, May 8, 1941.

in general, probably realizing that "its future was going to depend more on [the trading of securities issued by] government controlled corporations," not only failed to object to the government's action, but bought 500 shares of CSN.[20]

Many of the Brazilian corporations that before 1940 had dispersed ownership and many protections for minority shareholders ended up under state control in the second half of the twentieth century. Most of these interventions were the product of economic difficulties and complications arising from difficulty accessing sufficient foreign exchange (the exchange rate was controlled after 1945) to buy inputs. Railways, in particular, saw increased participation of federal and state governments in their ownership and operation. Steven Topik estimates that by 1930, railways operated by the federal government transported 30% and 53%, and the state operated rail lines 26.3% and 14%, of the nation's cargo and passengers, respectively. Brazil's federal and state governments thus controlled more than half the nation's railways after World War I. Many of these were acquired after they went bankrupt and their assets were auctioned (following the bankruptcy procedures described in Chapter 7); others simply bailed out.[21] By 1950, the federal government directly controlled most of the country's railways as well as the shipping line Lloyd and many other companies (e.g., ports, newspapers, manufacturing companies, and so forth). Moreover, the government had during World War II expropriated all German chartered companies operating in Brazil.

The state of São Paulo had over the course of the 1930s and 1940s taken over Banco do Estado de São Paulo (Banespa). Although it waited a decade to exercise its control over the company in shareholder meetings, the state government had held a majority stake since 1926, at which time it had replaced the institution's graduated voting scheme with a scheme that provided one vote for every 20 shares.[22] In the 1960s, São Paulo's E. F. Paulista and E. F. Mogyana railways were taken over by the state government, which,

[20] Levy, *A Indústria do Rio de Janeiro através de suas Sociedades Anônimas*, p. 270.
[21] Steven Topik, *The Political Economy of the Brazilian State, 1889–1930*, Austin: University of Texas Press, 1987, pp. 105–107.
[22] The explanation of the changes in governance appear in the minutes of the annual shareholder meetings between 1914 and 1926. The government of São Paulo gave a loan to Banespa that later on was converted to common equity. With this swap of debt for equity the state government ended up being the largest shareholder, in exchange the shareholders of the company agreed to change the voting provisions, eliminating maximum vote provisions. See Banco do Estado de São Paulo, *Atas da Assembléia de Acionistas do Banco do Estado de São Paulo*, Museu Banespa, São Paulo, Brazil, 1914–1926.

by 1971, had bailed out so many railway lines that it had created a holding company to manage them.

By the 1980s and early 1990s, changes in company laws and changing conditions in domestic credit markets had painted a Brazilian corporate landscape quite different from that of the 1880s and 1930s. By the 1980s, the largest private corporations in Brazil were organized as holding companies under the control of a large shareholder, often a family or the government, a consequence largely of the introduction of preferred shares, government intervention in the role of controlling shareholder, and the uncertain and at times "hostile" institutional environment in which companies operated after the Great Depression.

CONCLUSION

This chapter reviewed how the concentration of ownership increased in Brazil during the twentieth century for four primary reasons. First, ownership concentration increased as capital markets became less important as a source of finance. This happened because the government intervened in financial markets in ways that redirected companies seeking capital away from the stock markets and toward banks, especially government-owned banks. Second, changes in company laws made it easier for large shareholders to gain controlling interests in large Brazilian corporations. This was, in part, why at the end of the twentieth century most of Brazil's large corporations were owned by single families or a couple of large shareholders.

Third, the chapter examined how these controlling shareholders increased their equity stake (and thus ownership concentration in general), partly with the aim of making companies more responsive to changing circumstances when the economic environment became less stable. These controlling shareholders created business conglomerates or groups both to counter market failures and to respond to new political pressures. Families controlling large, strategically important industries concentrated power to balance that accumulated by labor organizations and as a way to increase their lobbying power in an environment in which relations with the government determined access to capital and foreign exchange as well as tariff protection against competing imports.

Finally, the chapter narrates the rise of government ownership of large corporations. Brazil's federal and state governments assumed ownership of large corporations consequent to bailouts during bad times or simply to place the state at the center of the development process. Invoking all manner of exceptions to company laws with the objective of developing powerful domestic industries, its federal and state governments emerged as important owners and controllers of some of Brazil's most important industrial corporations. The configuration of corporate finance and corporate governance that existed in Brazil at the end of the twentieth century was a consequence of economic and political circumstances and not necessarily of any colonial institutions such as legal tradition.

ELEVEN

Conclusion

This book is a detailed historical account of how Brazil's institutions of corporate governance and practices of corporate finance have changed over time. It is a study of the contingent factors that led to changes in how companies interacted with investors and how those changes, in turn, shaped the financial structure of companies (the choice of debt vs. equity). In short, it is a history of change.

This historical analysis yields three major conclusions. First, companies are not bound by the legal environment in which they operate. Companies can shape and change corporate governance practices by devising bylaws that attract outside investors to buy the equity and bonds they issue. Second, firms' financial structures respond to changes in the institutions and practices of corporate governance, driven, in some instances, by macroeconomic shocks. Third, the fact that corporate governance and finance changed so much over time implies that there has been little persistence of legal institutions in Brazil in the last two hundred years.

COMPANIES ARE NOT BOUND BY THE LEGAL
ENVIRONMENT IN WHICH THEY OPERATE

This book shows that in the absence of investor protections embodied in national laws and monitoring by specialized agencies corporations can themselves provide the needed protections, perhaps even more effectively, in their bylaws. Today there is a prevailing belief that the best way to "democratize" the control of corporations is to require at the national level that companies include one-share, one-vote provisions in their statutes. This is a requirement to be traded on Bovespa's New Market with the highest level of corporate governance standards today. But the findings of Chapters 4 and 5 suggest that maximum vote provisions and graduated voting scales can be more powerful ways to attract outside investors and democratize finance. These findings are not unique to Brazil; many companies in countries such as Japan, the United States, the United Kingdom, and Chile had these kinds of voting provisions at the end of the nineteenth century. In some cases – Japan's cotton textile industry and early corporations in New York, for example – these voting provisions also have been linked to more diffused ownership.[1]

Voting Rights Matter

This book shows, in a nutshell, that what companies do matters. In the absence of national laws that mandate investor protections, the protections companies afford in their bylaws and through their day-to-day business practices are the real drivers of investor interest in equity. Chapter 5 shows that Brazilian companies that included protections for smaller shareholders in their bylaws tended to have less concentrated ownership and control. This is because these protections not only reduced the power of large shareholders (and thereby the concentration of control rights), but also reduced the concentration of ownership in general by attracting more investors. The evidence presented in Chapter 5 suggests that investor interest in equity went beyond pure financial returns inasmuch as even investors with relatively small holdings showed up at shareholder meetings to vote and discuss the future of the companies they owned.

If companies' actions matter, then perhaps some countries fail to attract more foreign investors or some companies to attract larger numbers of smaller shareholders not because of vacuums in legislation or weak enforcement by the regulatory agencies, but rather because of company practices with respect to the potential for insider abuse. Policy recommendations for improving investor protections should not be directed exclusively to national legislators and stock market regulatory agencies, but also to corporations

---

[1] For the case of Japan see Yoshiro Miwa and J. Mark Ramseyer, "Corporate Governance in Transitional Economies: Lessons from the Prewar Japanese Cotton Textile Industry," *Journal of Legal Studies* 29, 1 (January 2000): 171–203; for the case of early corporations in New York see Eric Hilt, "When Did Ownership Separate from Control?: Corporate Governance in the Early Nineteenth Century," *Journal of Economic History* 68, 3 (September 2008): 645–685; for Chilean corporate charters see Gonzalo Islas Rojas, "Does Regulation Matter? An Analysis of Corporate Charters in a Laissez-faire Environment," unpublished manuscript, University of California Los Angeles, September 2007; for similar bylaws in England see Gareth Campbell and John D. Turner, "Protecting Outside Investors in a Laissez-faire Legal Environment: Corporate Governance in Victorian Britain," paper presented at the Business History Conference, Cleveland, June 2007.

and their insiders. A common recommendation of the World Bank and other international organizations pushing for improvements in corporate governance standards is to have national regulations that mandate that all corporations adopt a one-share, one-vote provision. One-share, one-vote is widely considered the best way to democratize the ownership and control of corporations not only because it eliminates nonvoting shares, but also because, according to some studies done in the late 1980s, it provides the right incentives to attract outside takeover offers that can discipline management.[2] The International Corporate Governance Network (a multi-country task force that issues recommendations on corporate governance), the Ethos Foundation, and other international organizations recommend one-share, one-vote as a way to reduce the disproportionate power of shareholders accorded special voting rights.[3] In contrast, graduated voting scales and maximum vote provisions have been overlooked by these organizations because they are no longer common practice in large financial markets.

Companies certified with the São Paulo Stock Exchange's highest level of corporate governance protections are required to give all shares the right to vote following the one-share, one-vote rule. Yet concentration of control remains quite high in Brazil because only some companies are adhering to the "new market" standards, and even in companies with one-share, one-vote provisions the concentration of control has not decreased. This is because, as Naomi Lamoreaux and Jean-Laurent Rosenthal found to be the case in late nineteenth-century American corporations, "the principle of one vote per share meant that shareholders who possessed enough stock to decide elections were effectively dictators."[4]

This book suggests that voting provisions that reduce the power of large shareholders are among the most effective "democratizers" of control in large corporations. Investment banks and pension funds interested in either underwriting or buying equity from companies with more democratic practices will perhaps be more attracted to these voting provisions than to one-share, one-vote schemes. Maximum vote provisions and graduated voting scales served in the past to induce smaller shareholders to buy equity and

[2] For the second part, see Sanford J. Grossman and Oliver Hart, "One Share-One Vote and the Market for Corporate Control," *Journal of Financial Economics* 20 (1988): 175–202.
[3] See International Corporate Governance Network, "ICGN Statement on Global Corporate Governance Principles," July 8, 2005, available at www.icgn.org. For voting rights, see page 4.
[4] Hilt, "When Did Ownership Separate from Control?," p. 30, and Naomi R. Lamoreaux and Jean-Laurent Rosenthal, "Corporate Governance and the Plight of Minority Shareholders in the United States before the Great Depression," in Edward Glaeser and Claudia Goldin (eds.), *Corruption and Reform*, Chicago: University of Chicago Press, 2006, pp. 127–128.

become more involved in the decision-making processes of the large corporations in which they invested. Companies truly interested in attracting smaller shareholders (perhaps because doing so lowers their cost of capital) should at least consider these voting provisions. Obviously, there are downsides. With less concentrated control, decision making can become slower, and slower decision making can put a company at risk during times of crisis or when the environment is uncertain or hostile and rapid reactions are needed to survive or succeed. But in a world in which bank credit is too expensive for corporations and it is difficult to place large corporate bond issues (perhaps because bondholders are not really protected by the courts), attracting smaller investors as well as large institutional investors preoccupied with good corporate governance practices can make a big difference. If institutional investors and underwriters are demanding more protections for smaller shareholders, voting provisions that democratize control can be a viable option.

Another downside of maximum vote provisions is that they increase the difficulty of controlling a corporation. If controlling a corporation is harder, then the market for corporate control will be deactivated. The market for corporate control is one of the ways in which capital markets keep managers focused on the maximization of shareholder value. Thus, not having this market could lead to more abuses by managers and to less incentive alignment between managers and owners. In markets in which trading is relatively thin, however, this tradeoff (of not having a market for corporate control) is in a way irrelevant. Of course one could speculate about how active markets would have been if companies had not had maximum vote provisions in Brazil, but even in companies that did not have those provisions, the market for corporate control was very small because controlling shareholders rarely sold their shares and usually monitored managers closely. The lesson is that in emerging markets with thin stock markets, companies that need outside shareholders, and for which the democratization of control is not a major obstacle, should consider adopting maximum vote provisions as a way to keep managers in check.

Disclosure Matters

In the past, most large Brazilian corporations were open books to potential investors, who could learn a great deal about them from publicly available information. Indeed, the corporate information at the disposal of the average Brazilian investor in, say, 1910 or 1920 was much greater than that available to a relatively well-informed investor today. After 1891, a corporation that wanted to sell new equity was required to publish a complete shareholder list, its corporate statutes (including voting rights), and financial statements. Financial statements had to be published at least once per year (twice for most traded companies) and statutes every time shareholders voted to change a bylaw. Today, despite improvements in financial disclosure, the information needed by investors to figure out the distribution of power within a corporation is not as complete, as companies are required to identify only the five or so largest shareholders or those with more than 10% ownership. Because ownership of most private corporations follows pyramidal schemes of cross-ownership, and it is difficult to know how proxy voting operates when full shareholder lists are not disclosed, regulators (and companies interested in attracting outside shareholders) should consider increasing transparency. Recent research by Rafael La Porta, Florencio Lopez-de-Silanes, and Andrei Shleifer finds that countries with more complete disclosure of information that can help investors evaluate and monitor the actions of corporations and their insiders tend to have significantly larger stock markets and more outside ownership (as opposed to large portions of equity in the hands of insiders).[5]

The Limits to Corporate Bylaws

The options that companies have for overcoming the institutional environment around them are limited. When macroeconomic instability is extreme or there is a big shock to the economy, companies with bylaws that offer strong protections for investors may still find it difficult to attract outside capital. That is, companies are, at the end of the day, bound by the macroeconomic environment in which they operate. When the economic situation is dire stock and bond markets lose all appeal for companies trying to access capital, simply because investors themselves drive prices down or stop trading some securities altogether.

Under extreme macroeconomic circumstances, companies need to be able to read the situation and adjust corporate governance and finance practices quickly enough to reduce their dependence on stocks or bonds to fund growth. Railways are perhaps the ultimate example of a sector that became overly dependent on the system of corporate finance that was dominant worldwide before World War I. Wedded to a financial structure that relied heavily on bond issues (and preferred equity), many railways in

---

[5] Rafael La Porta, Florencio Lopez-de-Silanes, and Andrei Shleifer, "What Works in Securities Laws?" *Journal of Finance* 61, 1 (February 2006): 1–32, see pp. 17 and 20.

Brazil and other countries sought bailouts or declared bankruptcy when financial markets dried up in the 1920s and 1930s.

DIFFERENT CORPORATE GOVERNANCE PRACTICES LEAD FIRMS TO SELECT DIFFERENT FINANCIAL STRUCTURES

This book tells the story of how different institutions around corporate governance led to different firm financial structures over time. The first part of the book describes an equilibrium in which in a somewhat stable macroeconomic environment corporate governance practices led companies to protect outside investors in a way that increased their ability to raise capital by issuing equity or bonds. Once macroeconomic shocks changed the availability of funds and the willingness of investors to buy bonds and stocks that paid low to negative real returns, companies became less interested in protecting outside investors. In this context insiders entrenched their ownership stakes and sought bank credit, especially from government development banks.

Chapters 2, 3, and 7 present evidence that stock and bond issues played a crucial role in the financing of corporations not only in São Paulo and the textile sector, but also in most economic sectors and in most of the largest states of Brazil. The corporate form afforded Brazilian entrepreneurs the possibility of selling stocks and bonds to large numbers of domestic and foreign investors and, through the financing of a railway network and banks, docks, manufacturing firms, and utility companies, accelerated the country's rate of urbanization and industrialization, even if only in the southeast and south of the country.

The shareholder protections provided by many of Brazil's largest corporations and enforcement of creditor rights by Brazilian courts might well have been stronger in the past than today, and Brazil's bond markets certainly seem to have been larger in 1913. The level of disclosure and protections for small shareholders written into company bylaws at that time also seemed to foster less concentrated ownership and control, increasing trading of Brazil's largest corporations. Indeed, the number of corporations traded on the stock exchange per million people was higher before 1920 than it has been for the past three decades.

The concluding chapters examine how a significantly different set of corporate finance practices was spawned by macroeconomic changes and reforms to the laws that regulated corporate governance in the 1930s and 1940s. Post–World War I inflation and macroeconomic instability drove stock and bond market activity down, in part because investor returns (in real terms) went negative for a good part of the 1920s and 1930s, giving rise, by the end of the 1930s, to a consensus to change the prewar institutions that had supported the development of the stock and bond markets. A broad coalition that included the government and labor as well as companies preferred a system of corporate governance and finance that promoted the continuation of the going concern over protection of investors. The new system was based on bank credit and government subsidized loans. With the explicit weakening of investor protections, corporate ownership became extremely concentrated, and the government in many cases directly financed or simply bailed out large corporations. The corporate finance system that emerged after the 1930s, by fostering the accumulation of significant market power, facilitated the rapid expansion of the surviving Brazilian firms (including state-owned enterprises).

This system of concentrated ownership, concentrated market power, and bank finance prevailed until the 1990s, when privatization and the increasing integration of Brazil into global capital markets precipitated a second renaissance (the second "great reversal") in the nation's equity and bond markets. Large corporations once again made significant changes to their financial structure, reintroducing many of the protections that had been fashionable before World War I.

NO SIGNS OF PERSISTENT EFFECTS OF BRAZIL'S LEGAL INSTITUTIONS

Variation in investor protections and financial development in Brazil calls into question the idea that effects of institutions such as a country's legal tradition persist over time. Investor protections in national laws, level of financial development, company enforcement of shareholder rights, and degree of corporate transparency seem not only to be unrelated to legal tradition, but also to have moved from one extreme to another in response either to economic shocks or to political negotiations among powerful interest groups.

Brazil seems to exemplify the sort of "great reversal" that occurred throughout most of continental Europe and the Americas after World War I. The Brazilian economy was particularly hard hit by diminishing capital flows during and after the war, which (by raising the cost of capital) made it difficult for companies to issue new bonds and stocks, destabilized the balance of payments and exchange rate, and generally complicated monetary policy. Except for brief episodes during which the government tried to reestablish the gold standard (in particular, between 1926 and 1929), monetary policy in Brazil in the wake of World War I was unpredictable at best.

Higher, more volatile inflation decimated investor returns and weakened support (especially in practice) for strong creditor and shareholder rights. Responding to changes in the political landscape, the Brazilian government in the 1930s and 1940s altered many of the legal provisions that had facilitated the development of its stock and bond markets. There was a reshuffling of power within corporations, with large shareholders consolidating control and distancing themselves from the philosophy that earlier had helped to democratize corporate control. The introduction of nonvoting shares in 1932 further abetted this transition by providing a way for companies to obtain outside capital without democratizing control.

The Brazilian government's reaction to the new macroeconomic conditions, driven by a nationalist ideology, included taking a more active role in financing existing corporations (through subsidized loans from government development banks), with the federal and state governments bailing out or taking over railways, shipping lines, utilities, and many other formerly widely held companies that had gone bankrupt as sources of new capital dried up after the war. This is what explains the Brazil of today, a country dominated by large family-controlled conglomerates and large state-owned enterprises.

The past eight years have seen significant improvements in both the legal framework and the enforcement of higher standards of corporate governance by the São Paulo Stock Exchange (Bovespa) and the main regulatory body, the Commissão de Valores Mobiliários (CVM). Both have been pressing companies to comply with the company law enacted in 2001 that strengthened, at least on paper, protections for smaller shareholders. A three-level certification mechanism devised by Bovespa to signal the relative safety of investments from insider abuse effectively functions as an incentive to improve corporate governance practices.[6] Investors' willingness

---

[6] Level-one companies must maintain a minimum free float of 25% of capital, improve quarterly disclosures, and disclose controlling shareholders' activity, among other things. To achieve level two, companies must reduce the term of office of members of the board of directors to one year, present annual financial reports following Generally Accepted Accounting Principles (GAAP), and provide nonvoting shares the right to vote on matters such as mergers, acquisitions, and contract approval when there is potential for conflict of interest. The São Paulo Stock Exchange certifies as New Market (Novo Mercado) companies that comply with all the level two provisions, give all shares the right to vote (have a one-share, one-vote provision), and assure equal treatment of all shareholders when takeover offers are tendered. Enforcement of these standards is the responsibility of an arbitration panel within Bovespa that can impose penalty fees on or delist noncompliant companies, although no cases yet have been brought before this panel. For a detailed description of the procedures and rules related to the first two levels of corporate governance, see the Bovespa Web page, available at www.bovespa.com.br.

to pay a premium for the shares of companies that improve their practices sufficiently to earn certification at the highest standard of corporate governance seem to validate the value of this mechanism.[7] Yet concentration of ownership and control in Brazil, albeit lower than ten years ago, remains quite high, and certainly higher than before 1910, which means that in practice many companies continue to embrace the system that has prevailed for the past several decades.

The realization that legal institutions are not persistent over time comes only after a deep examination of the history of corporate governance practices, in this case in Brazil. Therefore, this book is an effort to defend detailed history as necessary in order to understand how institutions and economic outcomes interact and change over time. Hence, I emphasize doing historical research explicitly rather than relying on "implicit history." Much of my main argument is based on historical evidence uncovered by doing "explicit" history. Specifically, I use archival and other historical materials to determine whether patterns of investor protections and financial development reflected persistent effects of the prevailing legal tradition. Its findings suggest that strong correlations between past variables and present economic outcomes do not always hold. That is why the book makes the case that strong correlations taken to demonstrate persistent effects over time need to be validated not only statistically but also historically.

Politics Matter

The story of change I tell in this book highlights also the fact that politics matter to the swings in the regulation of investor protections and the configuration of the market for capital in the long run. Countries reacted differently to shocks such as World War I and the Great Depression, changing the rules in terms of investor protections, sometimes in radical ways. Chapter 7 shows that changes in Brazil's bankruptcy law that favored incumbent industrialists and labor groups had a long-term impact on bond markets, such that the stock of corporate bonds (relative to GDP) has never been restored to its 1913 level.

Another one of those swings happened again at the turn of the twentieth century. In 2005, Brazil's Congress passed a major reform to the country's bankruptcy laws that made it easier for secured creditors to take possession of collateral and gave more power to creditors during company

---

[7] See, for instance, Antonio Gledson de Carvalho, "Efeitos da Migração para os Níveis de Governança da Bovespa," unpublished manuscript, Bovespa, April 2003.

reorganizations. Banks were, to a large extent, behind this push to facilitate the recovery of collateral when borrowers turn insolvent. Their argument was that such bankruptcy law would promote the deepening of the supply of mortgage and secured credit. An important question, of course, is how long these legal provisions will remain in place, whether they will endure long enough, for example, to encourage the issuing of long-term bonds and mortgage bonds. Creditor protections being notoriously dependent on politics and the interests of large, well organized coalitions (e.g., labor and banks), international shocks or sudden changes in the macroeconomic environment (heightened inflation or a major world crisis, for example) could generate consensus for a return to post-1945 bankruptcy procedures. In a country such as Brazil, in which labor unions are powerful and organized, this is a latent possibility that perhaps might only be forestalled by socializing more broadly the gains credit markets can yield when these institutions are in place. One way to socialize these benefits is to make them accessible to a large share of the population that is dependent on creditor rights by increasing access to mutual and pension funds or by increasing the securitization of debts and mortgages (under close regulation by the securities commission). If more people have to gain from a deeper mortgage market, it will be harder to see radical reversals in market operations. By contrast, a weakly monitored securitization of mortgages could lead to a financial catastrophe (as happened in the United States in 2007 and 2008) and to the discredit of securities markets.

The radical legal changes that occurred in Brazil (and European countries such as Italy and France) after the 1930s seem to have been a product of the fact that legal and constitutional safeguards in civil law countries (as opposed to common law countries such as England and the United States) were insufficient to forestall the erosion of investor protections. This may be why the law and finance literature found (on paper) such strong correlations between legal origin and investor protections in the 1990s. This correlation reflects not, however, the persistence of weak investor protections in civil law countries, but rather the fact that political institutions in these countries were less resistant to change in the wake of large macroeconomic shocks.

MIGHT A "GREAT REVERSAL" SUCH AS THAT EXPERIENCED AFTER WORLD WAR I OCCUR AGAIN?

Perhaps a final lesson to be learned from the transformation of financial markets in the twentieth century concerns the importance of the roles played by reduced capital flows and higher inflation in reshaping institutions and financial markets after World War I. After the war and the Great Depression destabilized the Brazilian export model and reduced the capital flows that had helped to finance its early industrialization, Brazil experienced high levels of inflation for several decades. It was not until the 1990s that Brazil's stock markets regained the trust of foreign and domestic investors, in part because the government brought inflation under control. Inflation is not likely to be a problem again because Brazil's central banks have learned a great deal about its dangers, but what is less certain is whether the wave of financial liberalization that has swept the world over the past two decades will be a permanent state.

Before the subprime crisis that started in the United States in 2007 and the market crash of 2008 most citizens of the globally integrated world believed that globalization was an unstoppable force. Likewise, people thought globalization was unstoppable before 1914 – yet history proved them wrong.

Between 1870 and 1914, the world enjoyed a period of globalization characterized by the almost completely free movement of labor, capital, and goods. In the richer European countries that had benefited from global integration, the common citizen "regarded this state of affairs as normal, certain, and permanent, except in the direction of further improvement, and any deviation from it as aberrant, scandalous and avoidable."[8] Writing in the late 1920s, Eugene Staley, a professor of political science at the University of Chicago, observed:

transoceanic aviation, streamlined land transport on still growing networks of steel and concrete, world-wide telephony and picture transmission, the development of scientific management techniques making possible central planning of larger and larger productive units – not to speak of such wonders as stratosphere navigation and the tapping of atomic energy that may be looming on the scientific horizon – make it a fairly safe prediction that the technological forces of the future will still be toward the economic integration of the world, implying larger fixed investments over larger areas. If that is the case, there is no doubt about the future bringing world-wide investment relationships ... *except* for the possible interference of the political factors broadly denoted by the term "nationalism." It is quite possible that a sufficiently widespread and intense political nationalism might continue to block the basic technological forces tending toward world economic integration.[9]

[8] John Maynard Keynes, *The Economic Consequences of the Peace*, New York: Dover Publications, 1994 [1920], pp. 9–10.
[9] Eugene Staley, *War and the Private Investor: A Study in the Relations of International Politics and International Private Investment*, New York: Doubleday, Doran & Company, Inc., 1935, p. 16.

Even acknowledging the forces at play against the first wave of globalization, Staley firmly believed that nationalism eventually would give way to the forces of economic integration. Today, we know that him and all the optimists before 1914 were wrong and that financial integration came to an end after World War I to a large extent because of nationalism.[10] Partly because of nationalism and partly as a reaction against the rigid adjustment mechanism under the gold standard, most countries moved away from financial integration and imposed capital controls in one form or another after the war.[11]

In Latin America, the economic shocks of the postwar period generated a backlash against integration with the world. As Jeffrey Williamson put it, "rising inequality in resource abundant Latin America, where inequality was already very extensive and where the vote was limited to the wealthy few, served to inhibit political liberalism."[12]

As the twenty-first century dawns, it is unclear how long the current wave of globalization will persist, and whether, unless its benefits reach greater numbers of citizens, a third "great reversal" inducing a backlash against financial integration will occur.[13] If events unravel propitiously, corporations should ride the wave that is sweeping stock markets and use the lessons learned from their predecessors a century earlier to attract outside investors in large numbers. Corporations should play the disclosure and voting cards to make their investors active stockholders invested not only in corporate shares but in financial development in general. Only if the masses can be made to gain from financial development and international financial integration is a near-term backlash against financial markets and financial integration likely to be avoided.

---

[10] For a discussion of nationalism and the causes of World War II, see Niall Ferguson, *The War of The World: Twentieth Century Conflict and the Descent of the West*, New York: Penguin Press, 2006, and *The Cash Nexus: Money and Power in the Modern World, 1700–2000*, New York: Basic Books, 2001, Chapter 13.

[11] See Maurice Obstfeld and Alan Taylor, *Global Capital Markets: Integration, Crisis, and Growth*, Cambridge: Cambridge University Press, 2004, Chapter 1 and Rawi Abdelal, *Capital Rules: The Construction of Global Finance*, Cambridge, Mass.: Harvard University Press, 2007, Chapters 1 and 3.

[12] Jeffrey Williamson, *Globalization and the Poor Periphery Before 1950*, Cambridge, Mass.: MIT Press, 2006, p. 148.

[13] Rawi Abdelal argues that changes in capital market integration (e.g., when capital controls became the norm around the world in the 1930s or when liberalization occurred after the 1980s) are driven by politics. The findings of his book imply that a great reversal in international financial integration could take place again if the political opposition to financial markets were widespread around the world, or at least in developed countries. See Abdelal, *Capital Rules*.

As I write the last words of this book, however, it appears likely that things will unravel in a way that will take the United States to a new equilibrium that looks like Brazil after the 1940s. In the wake of the 2008 crash, the sentiment occasioned by poor returns might lead investors to turn their backs on the equity markets. If stocks are abandoned and government bailouts of companies and banks continue, the model of corporate finance that we have known since the 1990s might change dramatically, with commercial bank and government credit likely to play a crucial role in the new scenario and small investors to become largely irrelevant as large shareholders, including the government, take control of troubled companies. Perhaps, yet again, history will repeat itself.

Bibliography

Brazil's National Archive, Rio de Janeiro

Arquivo Nacional, Juizo de Orfãos, Caetano Pinto de Miranda Montenegro, Inventário, caixa 1385, No. 149.

Arquivo Nacional, Juizo de Orfãos, Michaella de Paula Costa Montenegro, Inventário, caixa 4256, No. 2466.

Bolsa de Valores do Rio de Janeiro (BVRJ), Sociedades Anônimas, Banco Mercantil do Rio de Janeiro, various caixas.

Bolsa de Valores do Rio de Janeiro (BVRJ), Sociedades Anônimas, Transportes, Caixa 406.

Banco da Republica do Brasil, *Relação dos Accionistas do Banco da Republica do Brazil e Suas Agencias em 1905*. Rio de Janeiro: Typografia do Jornal do Commercio, 1905.

Banco de Credito Universal, Sentence of Liquidation, in Corte de Apelação, no. 200, maço 243, Réu: Companhia Geral de Estradas de Ferro no Brasil /Autor: Banco de Crédito Universal, Liquidação Forçada, 1894, pp. 217–242.

Banco do Estado de São Paulo, *Atas da Assembléia de Acionistas do Banco do Estado de São Paulo,* Museu Banespa, São Paulo, Brazil, 1889–1950.

Banco Dos Funcionarios Públicos, *Relatorio Apresentado Pelo Presidente do Banco dos Funcionarios Publicos. Anno 1904.* Rio de Janeiro, Typographia Leuzinger, 1904.

Banco Mercantil do Rio de Janeiro, *Lista dos Accionistas do Banco Mercantil do Rio de Janeiro em 31 de Julho de 1911*, Rio de Janeiro, Typografia Leuzinger, 1911.

Bolsa de Valores do Rio de Janeiro (BVRJ), Sociedades Anônimas, Transportes, caixa 406 and 2166.

Companhia Petropolitana, *Relatorio da Directoria da Companhia Petropolitana Apresentado à Assembléa Geral Ordinaria dos Snrs. Accionistas,* Rio de Janeiro: Typografia Do jornal do Commércio, 1928 and 1929.

Corte de Apelação, Juízo Comercial do Tribunal Civil e Comercial, No. 3892 maço 3133, Réu: Companhia Anônima União Industrial dos Estados Unidos do Brasil / Autor: Francisco de Paula Valladares, Liquidação Forçada, 1896.

Corte de Apelação, Juízo Câmara Comercial do Tribunal Civil e Criminal, No 708 maço 268, Réu: Companhia Estrada de Ferro Leopoldina / Autor: Edward Herdman, Liquidação Forçada, 1897.

Corte de Apelação, Juízo Comercial do Tribunal Civil e Comercial, No. 581 maço 262, Réu: Companhia Viação Férrea Sapucahy / Autor: Syndicos da Liquidação Forçada da Companhia Viação Férrea Sapucahy, Prestação de Contas, 1899.

Corte de Apelação, Juízo Comercial do Tribunal Civil e Comercial, No. 3892 maço 3133, Réu: Cervejaria Bavaria / Autor: Banco de Depositos e Descontos, Liquidação Forçada, 1900.

Corte de Apelação, Juízo da 1a Vara Comercial, No. 1823 maço 3105, Réu: Estrada de Ferro do Espírito Santo e Minas (Chemins de Fer Espírito Santo et Minas) / Autor: Pinto de Souza Castro e outros, Liquidação Forçada, 1907.

Corte de Apelação, Juízo de Direito da Primeira Vara Comercial, No. 113 maço 3046, Réu: Companhia Ferro Carril Carioca / Autor: Veiga & Cia and Terra & Irmão, Liquidação Forçada, 1908.

Corte de Apelação, Juízo de Direito da Primeira Vara Comercial, No. 127 maço 3047, Réu: Companhia Ferro Carril Carioca / Autor: Companhia Edificadora, Falencia, 1910.

Corte de Apelação, Juízo Comercial do Tribunal Civil e Comercial, No. 188 maço 3051, Réu: Companhia de Tecidos e Fiação Santo Aleixo / Autor: Fernandes Moreira & Co., Liquidação Forçada, 1916.

Corte de Apelação, No. 270 maço 3056, Câmara Comercial do Tribunal Civil e Criminal, Réu: Companhia Anônima Coudelaria Cruzeiro / Autor: Emílio de Barros e Companhia, Liquidação Forçada, 1892.

Corte de Apelação, No. 200 maço 243, Réu: Companhia Geral de Estradas de Ferro do Brasil / Autor: Banco de Crédito Universal, Liquidação Forçada, 1894.

Corte de Apelação, No. 2411 maço 356, Vara Comercial do Tribunal Civil e Comercial, Réu: Lloyd Brazileiro / Autor: Banco intermediário do Rio de Janeiro, 1901.

Corte de Apelação, No. 3090 maço 3115, Réu Companhia de Fiação e Tecidos Santa Maria, Liquidação Forçada, 1909.

Corte de Apelação, No. 1548 maço 3033, 3ª Vara Cível, Réu: Companhia de Construções Prediais "O Prédio" / Autor: Luis Alves Casas, Liquidação Forçada, 1915.

Corte de Apelação, No. 101 maço 3045, Galeria A, 4ª Vara Cível, Réu: Companhia Nacional Mineira / Autor: Costa Garcia e Companhia, Petição de Contas, 1916.

Corte de Apelação, No. 1827 maço 3038, 3ª Vara Cível, Réu: Companhia Vidraria "Carmita," Falência, 1916.

Firmas, Juízo da 2ª Vara do Comércio, No. 5 maço 1774, Galeria A, Firma: A. A. Figueira e Companhia / Autor: Alexandro Wagner, Justificação de Falência, 1879.

Firmas, Juízo da 1ª Vara do Comércio, No. 1869 maço 1695, Galeria A, Firma: A. Coruja e Companhia / Autor: Antonio Coruja, Falência, 1880.

Firmas, Juízo da 1ª Vara do Comércio, No. 3651 maço 3128, Galeria A, Firma: A. Coruja e Companhia / Autor: Antonio Coruja, 1888.

Paulista de Estradas de Ferro, Cia. *Estatutos da Companhia Paulista de Estradas de Ferro Reformados em Assembléa Geral Extraordinária Celebrada a 25 de Junho de 1926.* Sao Paulo, 1926.

Paulista de Estradas de Ferro, Cia. *Presença de Acionistas em Assembléia Geral Extraordinária de 25 de Junho de 1935.* Sao Paulo, 1935.

Processos Comerciais, 1ª Vara do Comércio, No. 1655 Caixa 1314, Firma: João Monteiro Ornellas, Falência, 1863.

Processos Comerciais, 2ª Vara do Comércio, No. 20 maço 196, Galeria A, Firma: Alberto da Fonseca & Cia. E outro / Autor: José Carlos de Mello Barreto, Falência, 1859.

Processos Comerciais, 2ª Vara do Comércio, No. 5 maço 1751, Galeria A, Firma: Aguiar & Cunha / Autor: Antônio Pinto Gomes & Cia, Falência, 1861.

Processos Comerciais, 2ª Vara do Comércio, No. 20 maço 1765, Galeria A, Firma: Azevedo Lima & Cia / Autor: Júlio Cárdia de Azevedo Lima, Falência, 1874.

Processos Comerciais, 2ª Vara do Comércio, No. 3982 caixa 1896, Firma: A. Guimarães & Cia, Liquidação, 1881.

Processos Comerciais, 2ª Vara do Comércio, No. 6 maço 176, Galeria A, Firma: A. J. da Cunha & Cia / Autor: Félix Antonio Gonçalves Vianna, Justificação de Falência, 1882.

Processos Comerciais, 2ª Vara do Comércio, No. 2 maço 11, Firma: Camacho & Cia / Autor: S. Brito & Cia, Justificação de Falência, 1887.

Processos Comerciais, 2ª Vara do Comércio, No. 10437 maço 720, Firma: A. Gomes & Cia / Autor: Ferreira & Carneiro, Justificação de Falência, 1888.

Viação Férrea Sapucahy, Proposta de Concordata aos Debenturistas e mais credores da Companhia Viação Férrea Sapucahy, April 14, 1899 in BVRJ, Sociedades Anônimas, Transportes, Notação 6498 a 6527, caixa 406.

Viação Férrea Sapucahy, Various documents including the agreements between shareholders and debenture holders of the Companhia Viação Férrea Sapucahy 1899–1900, in BVRJ, Sociedades Anônimas, Transportes, Notação 6498 a 6527, caixa 406.

"Companhia Fiação e Tecelagem Alegria," in *Diário Oficial,* 12/06/1919.

"Companhia Luz e Força de Santa Cruz," in *Diário Oficial,* 10/23/1909.

"Companhia Petropolis Industrial," in *Diário Oficial,* 30/11/1912.

"Companhia Renascença Industrial," in *Diário Oficial do Estado de Minas Gerais,* 3/19/1937.

"Estatutos da Sociedade Anônyma Lanificios Minerva," in *Diário Oficial,* 1/6/1922.

"Estrada de Ferro do Dourado," Bolsa de Valores do Rio de Janeiro, Sociedades Anônimas, Transportes, caixa 2166.

"Fiação e Tecelagem Divinopolis S.A., Extraordinária," in *Diário Oficial do Estado de Minas Gerais,* 22/03/1942.

"Lanari Engenharia, Industria e Comercio,"in *Diário Oficial do Estado de São Paulo,* 08/12/1951.

"Santa Luzia Industrial S.A.," in *Diário Oficial do Estado de Minas Gerais,* 2/23/1926.

"Sociedade Anonyma Companhia Chimica Braziliera," in 8/20/1912.

"Tecidos Cometa," in *Diário Oficial,* 5/12/1903.

"Usinas Nacionais," in *Diário Oficial,* 6/3/1911.

Company Documents Available at the São Paulo State Archive, São Paulo

Antarctica, Cia. *Atas da Assambléia de Acionistas da...*, São Paulo, 1891–1927.

Estatutos da Companhia Antarctica Paulista, 1891–1913, published in Decree 217, May 2, 1891; Decree 3348, July 17 1899; Decree 10,036, February 6, 1913.

Estatutos da Companhia Industrial de São Paulo, São Paulo: Typographia a Vapor de Jorge Seckler & Comp., 1891.

Estatutos da Companhia Industrial Rodovalho, São Paulo: Companhia Impressora Paulista, 1891.

270   *Bibliography*

Estatutos da Companhia São Paulo Fabril, São Paulo: Companhia Impressora Paulista, 1890.

Estrada de Ferro São Paulo e Rio, *Relatório da diretoria, 1876*, São Paulo, 1877

Estrada de Ferro Sorocabana, *Relatório Apresentado Pela Superintendência aos Syndicos da Liquidação Forçada. Anno de 1903*. São Paulo: Typografia A Vap. Rosehan & Meyer, 1904.

Estrada de Ferro Sorocabana, *Relatório. Anno de 1904*. São Paulo: Typografia A Vap. Rosehan & Meyer, 1905.

Fiação e Tecidos Santa Rosa, Cia. *Estatutos*, 07/09/1913.

Paulista de Estradas de Ferro, Cia. *Estatutos da Companhia Paulista de Estradas de Ferro Reformados em Assembléa Geral Extraordinária Celebrada a 25 de Junho de 1926.* Sao Paulo, 1926.

Paulista de Estradas de Ferro, Cia. *Presença de Acionistas em Assembléia Geral Extraordinária de 25 de Junho de 1935.* Sao Paulo, 1935.

Paulista de Estradas de Ferro, Cia. *Presença de Acionistas em Assembléia ...* São Paulo, 1869–1957.

Mogyana (Mojiana) de Estradas de Ferro, *Cia. Relatório da Diretoria em Assembléia Geral ...* 1878–1922.

"Estatutos da Companhia Fabricadora de Papel (Klabin)," in *Diário Oficial do Estado de São Paulo*, 6/15/1909, and "Cia. Fabricadora de Papel (Klabin)," in *Diário Oficial do Estado de São Paulo*, 5/8/1937.

"Cia. Matarazzo," in *Diario Oficial do Estado de São Paulo*, 6/2/1891.

"Cia. Matarazzo, Decreto n. 17544 – de 10 de Novembro de 1926," in *Diario Oficial do Estado de São Paulo,*1/4/1927.

"Cia. Matarazzo, Decreto N. 2 – de 25 de Julho de 1934," in *Diário Oficial do Estado de São Paulo*, 8/15/1934.

"Companhia Paulista de Força e Luz," in *Diário Oficial do Estado de São Paulo*, 11/16/1912.

"Companhia Puglise," in *Diário Oficial do Estado de São Paulo*, 10/17/1907.

"Companhia Puglise," in *Diário Oficial do Estado de São Paulo*, 8/9/1923.

"Companhia Puglise," in *Diário Oficial do Estado de São Paulo*, 9/23/1923.

"Companhia S. Bernardo Fabril," in *Diário Oficial do Estado de São Paulo*, 2/7/1908.

"Companhia S. Bernardo Fabril," in *Diário Oficial do Estado de São Paulo*, 2/7/1915.

"Companhia Telephonica do Estado de São Paulo," in *Diário Oficial do Estado de São Paulo*, 1/30/1913.

"Cotonificio Rodolpho Crespi," in *Diário Oficial do Estado de São Paulo*, 4/1/1909.

"Estatutos da Companhia S. Paulo Industrial," in *Diário Oficial do Estado de São Paulo*, 10/21/1891.

"Estatutos da Sociedade Anônyma Tecelagem Italo-Brazileira," in *Diário Oficial do Estado de São Paulo*, 4/25/1907.

"Indústrias Reunidas Fábricas Matarazzo," in *Diario Oficial do Estado de São Paulo*, 12/14/1911.

"Publica Forma. Primero Traslado de Escriptura de Constituição de Sociedade Anônyma (Comp. Brasileira de Ar Liquido)," in *Diário Oficial do Estado de São Paulo*, 9/3/1912.

"Sociedade Anônima Indústrias Reunidas Fábrica Matarazzo," in *Diario Oficial do Estado de São Paulo*, 7/12/1916.

Other Primary Documents and Data Sources

"Panair do Brasil, S. A.," in *Diário Oficial*, 12/27/1943.

"Sociedade Anonyma Fabrica de Tecidos Esperança," in *Diario Official*, 6/16/1919.

"A novísima lei de fallencias," *São Paulo Judiciário*, October, 2003, p. 157.

Annuaire du Brésil Économique 1913, Rio de Janeiro, Le Brésil Économique, 1914.

Boletin Financiero y Minero, Mexico City, 1905–1910.

Bolsa de Valores do Rio de Janeiro. *Anuário da Bolsa de Valores do Rio de Janeiro*, Rio de Janeiro: Typografia Do Jornal do Commércio, 1932–1942.

Bolsa Oficial de Valores de São Paulo. *Anuário da Bolsa Oficial de Valores de São Paulo*, São Paulo, 1939.

Brazil Company Handbook. Rio de Janeiro, 1987–2002.

Brazil. *Anuário Estatístico do Brasil (1908–1912)*. Rio de Janeiro: Typografia da Estatística, 1917.

Brazil. *Anuário Estatístico do Brasil*. Rio de Janeiro: Instituto Brasileiro de Geografia e Estatística, Ano 5, 1939/1940.

Brazil. *Colecção das Leis e Decretos do Império*. Rio de Janeiro: Imprensa Nacional, 1808–1888.

Brazil. *Colecção das Leis e Decretos*. Rio de Janeiro: Imprensa Nacional, 1888–1930.

Brazil. *Diario Oficial da União*. Rio de Janeiro, 1890–1950.

Brazil. Instituto Brasileiro de Geografia e Estatística (IBGE). *Estatísticas Históricas do Brasil*, Rio de Janeiro: IBGE, 1992.

Brazil. Ministério da Justiça. *Relatório do Ministério da Justiça*. Rio de Janeiro: Typografia Universal de Laemmert, 1866.

Brazil. Ministério de Agricultura, Indústria e Comércio. *Recenseamento do Brasil Realizado em 1 de Setembro de 1920*. Rio de Janeiro: Typografia da Estatística, 1929.

Brazil. *Relatório do Ministro da Fazenda em Janeiro de 1880*. Rio de Janeiro: Imprensa Nacional, 1880.

Brazil. *Relatório do Ministro da Fazenda em Janeiro de 1891*. Rio de Janeiro: Imprensa Nacional, 1891.

Brazil. *Retrospecto Comercial do Journal do Commercio*. Rio de Janeiro, 1906–1919.

Brazil. *Sociedades Mercantis Autorizadas a Funcionar no Brasil* (1808–1946). Rio de Janeiro, Departamento Nacional de Indústria e Comércio, 1947.

Brazilian Year Book 1909. London: McCorquodale & Co, 1910.

Câmara Sindical de Corretores de Fundos Públicos da Bolsa de Valores do Rio de Janeiro. *Relatorio da Câmara Sindical de Corretores de Fundos Públicos da Bolsa de Valores do Rio de Janeiro*. Rio de Janeiro: Imprensa Nacional, 1890–1947.

El Economista Mexicano. Mexico City, 1905–1910.

English Statutes: The Bankrutpcy Act, 1969 (32 & 33 Vict., c. 71, 1869) and The Companies (Consolidation) Act 1908 (8 Edw. 7, c. 69, 1908).

Gazeta Mercantil: Balanço. 4, 4 (September 1980).

Investor's Monthly Manual. London, 1871–1930.

Jornal do Commércio. Rio de Janeiro, 1827–1930.

McKinsey & Company. *Investor Opinion Survey (2000)*. McKinsey and Company, 2000.

Mexican Year Book. A Statistical, Financial, and Economic Annual, Compiled from Official and Other Returns, 1909–1910. London: McCorquodale & Co, 1910.

O Estado de São Paulo. São Paulo, Brazil, 2001–2002.
Retrospecto Commercial do Jornal do Commércio. Rio de Janeiro, 1870–1930.
Revista de Jurisprudencia, 1897.
The Economist. Weekly, 2004–2007.
The stock exchange official intelligence for … London: Spottiswoode, Ballantyne, 1899–1930.
United Kingdom. *Companies (Consolidation) Act 1908*, 8 Edw. 7, c. 69.

Resources on the Internet

Bovespa, www.bovespa.com.br (last accessed 05/05/09).
Brazil. Senado Federal. *Portal de Legislação Federal*. 1931–present, www.senado.gov.br (last accessed 05/05/09).
Fundação Getúlio Vargas, CPDOC. "A Era Vargas – 1º tempo – dos anos 20 a 1945," www.cpdoc.fgv.br (last accessed 05/05/09).
Centro de Pesquisa e Documentação de História Contemporânea do Brasil, CPDOC, www.cpdoc.fgv.br (last accessed 05/05/09).
Comissão de Valores Mobiliários, www.cvm.com.br (last accessed 05/05/09).
Global Financial Data, www.globalfinancialdata.com (last accessed 05/05/09).
Instituto de Pesquisa Econômica Aplicada, Ipeadata, www.ipeadata.gov.br (last accessed 05/05/09).
NBER, *Macroeconomic History* Data, www.nber.org/databases/macrohistory/contents (last accessed 05/05/09).
Oxford Latin American Economic History Database, oxlad.qeh.ox.ac.uk (last accessed 05/05/09).
Serviço Nacional de Debêntures, www.debenture.com.br (last accessed 05/05/09).
Supremo Tribunal Federal, www.stf.jus.br (last accessed 05/05/09).

Interviews

Luis Fernando de Paiva and Giuliano Colombo, interview with the author, Pinheiro Neto Advogados, São Paulo, Brazil, November, 2005.
Thomas Felsberg, Felsberg & Associados, interview with the author, São Paulo, Brazil, November, 2005.

Secondary Sources

Abdelal, Rawi. *Capital Rules: The Construction of Global Finance*. Cambridge, Mass.: Harvard University Press, 2007.
Abreu, Marcelo de Paiva (org.) *A Ordem do Progresso: Cem Anos de Política Econômica Republicana, 1889–1989*. Rio de Janeiro: Campus Editora, 1989.
Abreu, Marcelo de Paiva. "Crise, Crescimento e Modernização Autoritária: 1930–1945." In Marcelo de Paiva Abreu (org., ed.), *A Ordem do Progresso: Cem Anos de Política Econômica Republicana, 1889–1989*. Rio de Janeiro: Campus Editora, 1989, pp. 73–104.
Abreu, Marcelo de Paiva. "Os Funding Loans Brasileiros." *Pesquisa e Planejamento Econômico* 32, 3 (2002): 515–540.

Abreu, Marcelo de Paiva. "Brazil as a Debtor, 1824-1931." *Economic History Review* 59, 4 (2006): 765-787.

Acemoglu, Daron. "The Form of Property Rights: Oligarchic vs. Democratic Societies." unpublished manuscript, Massachusetts Institute of Technology, 2003.

Acemoglu, Daron, Simon Johnson, and James Robinson. "The Colonial Origins of Comparative Development: An Empirical Investigation." *American Economic Review* 91 (2001): 1369-1401.

Adelman, M. A. "Comment on the 'H' Concentration Measure as a Numbers-Equivalent." *Review of Economics and Statistics* 51, 1 (February 1969): 99-101.

Adler, John (ed.) *Capital Movements and Economic Development.* London: McMillan, 1967.

Aganin, Alexander and Paolo Volpin. "The History of Corporate Ownership in Italy." In Randall Morck (ed.), *A History of Corporate Governance Around the World: Family Business Groups to Professional Managers.* Chicago and London: University of Chicago Press and NBER, 2006, pp. 325-361.

Aoki, Masahiko. "Toward an Economic Model of the Japanese Firm." *Journal of Economic Literature* 28, 1 (March 1990): 1-27.

Aoki, Masahiko. *Toward a Comparative Institutional Analysis.* Cambridge, Mass.: MIT Press, 2001.

Barata, Carlos Eduardo de Almeida,and Antonio Henrique da Cunha Bueno (org.). *Dicionário das Famílias Brasileiras, vol. 2.* São Paulo: Ibero América, 2000.

Bates, Robert. *Open Economy Politics.* Princeton: Princeton University Press, 1997.

Bayer, Christian and Carsten Burhop. "Corporate Governance and Incentive Contracts: Historical Evidence from a Legal Reform." Unpublished manuscript, Universität Dortmund and Max Planck Institut für Gemeinschaftsgüter, September 2007.

Beck, Thorsten, Asli Demirgüç-Kunt and Ross Levine. "A New Database on Financial Development and Structure," *World Bank Economic Review* 14 (2000): 597-605.

Beck, Thorsten, Asli Demirguç-Kunt and Ross Levine. "Law and Finance: Why Does Legal Origin Matter?" *Journal of Comparative Economics* 31 (2003a): 653-675.

Beck, Thorsten, Asli Demirguç-Kunt and Ross Levine. "Law, Endowments, and Finance." *Journal of Financial Economics* 70, 2 (2003b): 137-181.

Beck, Thorsten and Ross Levine. "Legal Institutions and Financial Development." In Claude Menard and Mary Shirley (eds.), *The Handbook of New Institutional Economics.* Dordrecht, The Netherlands: Springer, 2005, pp. 251-279.

Berglöf, Erik and H. Rosenthal. "The Political Economy of American Bankruptcy: Evidence from Roll Call Voting, 1800-1978." Unpublished manuscript, Princeton University, 2000.

Berkowitz, Daniel, Katharina Pistor and Jean-Francois Richard. "Economic Development, Legality, and the Transplant Effect." *European Economic Review* 47 (2003): 165-195.

Berle, Adolf A. and Gardiner C. Means. *The Modern Corporation and Private Property,* rev. ed. New York: Hartcourt, Brace & World, Inc., 1967 [1932].

Bevilaqua, Achilles. *Falência Dec.-lei n. 7661, de 21 de Junho de 1945.* São Paulo: Revista Forense, 1958.

Binder, John. 1985. "Measuring the Effects of Regulation with Stock Price Data." *Rand Journal of Economics* 16, 2 (1985): 167-183.

Blair, Margareth and Mark Roe (eds.) *Employees and Corporate Governance*. Washington, D.C.: Brookings Institution Press, 1999.

Bloch, Marc. *The Historian's Craft: Reflections on the Nature and Uses of History and the Techniques and Methods of Those Who Write it*. New York: Vintage Books, 1953, p. 30.

Bordo, Michael, Michael J. Dueker and David C. Wheelock. "Monetary Policy and Stock Market Booms and Busts in the 20th Century." Federal Reserve Bank of St. Louis Working Paper 2007-020A, May 2007.

Bordo, Michael and Hugh Rockoff. "The Gold Standard as a 'Good Housekeeping Seal of Approval'." *Journal of Economic History* 56, 2 (1996): 389–428.

Borgatti, S. P., M. G. Everett and L. C. Freeman. UCINET 6.0 Version 1.00. Natick: Analytic Technologies, 1999.

Boyle, A. J. *Minority Shareholders' Remedies*. Cambridge: Cambridge University Press, 2002.

Brecht, Marco and Bradford DeLong. "Why Has There Been So Little Block Holding in America?" In Randall Morck (ed.), *A History of Corporate Governance Around the World: Family Business Groups to Professional Managers*. Chicago and London, University of Chicago Press and NBER, 2006, pp. 613–666.

Briones, Ignacio. "Capital Market development and economic Performance: A General Overview Over the Chilean experience 1870–1995." Paper presented at the European Historical Economics Society, Summer School, Trinity College, Ireland, 2001.

Brown, Richard. "Comparative Legislation in Bankruptcy." *Journal of the Society of Comparative Legislation* 2 (1900): 251–270.

Byrd, Daniel and Mark S. Mizruchi. "Bankers on the Board and the Debt Ratio of Firms." *Journal of Corporate Finance* 11 (September 2005): 129–173.

Campbell, Gareth and John D. Turner. "Protecting Outside Investors in a Laissez-faire Legal Environment: Corporate Governance in Victorian Britain." Paper presented at the Business History Conference, Cleveland, June 2007.

Cano, Wilson. *Raízes da Concentração Industrial em São Paulo*. São Paulo: T. A. Queiroz Editora, 1987.

Cardozo, Fernando Henrique and Enzo Faletto. *Dependency and Development in Latin America*. Berkeley: University of California Press, 1979.

Carlos, Anne and Frank D. Lewis. "International Financing of Canadian Railroads: The Role of Information." In Michael Bordo and Richard Sylla (eds.), *Anglo-American Finance: Financial Institutions and Markets in the Twentieth Century*. New York and Burr Ridge, Illinois: New York University Press and Irwin Press, 1995, pp. 383–414.

Carosso, Vincent P. *Investment Banking in America: A History*. Cambridge, Mass: Harvard University Press, 1970.

Catão, Luis A. V. "A New Wholesale Price Index for Brazil during the Period 1870–1913." *Revista Brasileira De Economia* 46, 4 (1992): 519–533.

Cerutti, Mario. *Burguesía y Capitalismo en Monterrey*. México: Claves Latinoamericanas, 1983.

Cerutti, Mario. *Burgesía, Capitales e Industria en el Norte de México*. Mexico: Alianza and Universidad Autonoma de Nuevo Leon, 1992.

Chang, Sea Jin and Unghwan Choi. "Strategy, Structure and Performance of Korean Business Groups: A Transactions Cost Approach." *Journal of Industrial Economics* 37, 2 (1988): 141–158.

Chirino, Jorge. "Pozos, de Coyotes, Crac, y Optimismo: Origen y Clausura de la Bolsa de México, 1895–1896." B.A. thesis, Instituto Tecnológico Autónomo de México, 1999.

Claessens, Stijn and Leora F. Klapper. "Bankruptcy around the World: Explanations of Its Relative Use." *American Law and Economics Review* 7 (2005): 253–283.

Coatsworth, John and Alan Taylor (eds.) *Latin America and the World Economy Since 1800.* Cambridge, Mass.: DRCLAS/Harvard University Press, 1998.

Coffee, John C. "Convergence and Its Critics: What Are the Preconditions to the Separation of Ownership and Control?" Columbia Center for Law and Economics Working Paper No. 179, Columbia University, 2000.

Cohen, Jim. "Divergent Paths: How Capital Market Development Affected Differentiation in Transportation Structures, U.S. and France, 1840–1940." Paper presented at Financer le Entreprises face aux Mutations Économiques do XX Siècle, Institut de la Gestion Publique et du Dévelopment Économique, Paris, France, March 2007.

Contador, Cláudio. *Mercado de Ativos Financeiros no Brasil.* Rio de Janeiro: IBMEC, 1974.

Contador, Cláudio and Claudio Haddad. "Produto Real, Moeda e Preços: A Experiência Brasileira no Período 1861–1970." *Revista Brasileira de Estatística* 36, 143 (1975): 407–440.

Davis, Gerald and Mark S. Mizruchi. "The Money Center Cannot Hold: Commercial Banks in the U.S. System of Corporate Governance." *Administrative Science Quarterly* 44, 2 (1999): 215–239.

de Carvalho, Antonio Gledson. "Efeitos da Migração para os Níveis de Governança da Bovespa." Mimeo, Bovespa, April 2003.

De Long, Bradford. "Did J. P. Morgan's Men Add Value?: An Economist's Perspective on Financial Capitalism." In Peter Temin (ed.), *Inside the Business Enterprise: Historical Perspectives on the Use of Information.* Chicago: University of Chicago Press, 1991, pp. 205–250.

de Sá, Chrockatt. *Brazilian Railways: Their History, Legislation and Development.* Rio de Janeiro: Typografia de C. Leuzinger & filhos, 1893.

Dean, Warren. *The Industrialization of São Paulo, 1880–1945.* Austin: University of Texas Press, 1969.

Del Angel, Gustavo. "Paradoxes of Financial Development: The Construction of the Mexican Banking System, 1941–1982." Unpublished Ph.D. dissertation, Stanford University, 2002.

Del Angel, Gustavo. "Networks, Discipline, and Idiosyncratic Risks in Mexican Banks, 1950–1980." Paper presented at the Business History Conference Annual Meeting, Le Creusot, France, June 17–19, 2004.

Dewing, Arthur Stone. *The Financial Policy of Corporations,* 2 vols. New York: The Roland Press Co., 1941.

Di Martino, Paolo. "Bankruptcy Law and Banking Crises in Italy (c. 1890–1938)." *Revista di Storia Economica* 20, 1 (April 2004): 65–85.

Di Martino, Paolo. "Approaching Disaster: Personal Bankruptcy Legislation in Italy and England, c. 1880–1939." *Business History* 47, 1 (January 2005): 22–43.

Diamond, Douglas W. "Financial Intermediation and Delegated Monitoring." *Review of Economic Studies* 51, 3 (July 1984): 393–414.

Dimson, Elroy, Paul Marsh and Mike Staunton. *The Triumph of the Optimists: 101 Years of Global Investment Returns.* Princeton: Princeton University Press, 2002.

Djankov, Simeon, Rafael La Porta, Florencio Lopez de Silanes and Andrei Shleifer. "The Regulation of Entry." *Quarterly Journal of Economics* 117, 1 (February 2002): 1–37.

Djankov, Simeon, Rafael La Porta, Florencio Lopez de Silanes and Andrei Shleifer. "Courts: The Lex Mundi Project." *Quarterly Journal of Economics* 118, 2 (May 2003): 453–517.

Dunlavy, Colleen. "Corporate Governance in Late 19th-Century Europe and the U.S.: The Case of Shareholder Voting Rights." In Klaus J. Hopt, H. Kanda, Mark J. Roe, E. Wymeersch and S. Prigge (eds.), *Corporate Governance: The State of the Art of Emerging Research*. Oxford: Clarendon Press, 1998, pp. 5–39.

Dunlavy, Colleen. "From Citizens to Plutocrats: 19th-Century Shareholder Voting Rights and Theories of the Corporation." In Kenneth Lipartito and David B. Sicilia (eds.), *Constructing Corporate America: History, Politics, Culture*. Oxford: Oxford University Press, 2004, pp. 66–93.

Engerman, Stanley and Kenneth Sokoloff. "Factor Endowments, Institutions, and Differential Paths of Growth." In Stephen Haber (ed.), *Why Latin America Fell Behind*. Stanford: Stanford University Press, 1997, pp. 260–304.

Faria, Antônio Bento de. *Das Fallencias (Lei n. 859 de 16 de agosto de 1902): Annotada de Accordo com a Doutrina, a Legislação e a Jurisprudencia e Seguida de um Formulário por Antonio Bento de Faria, Bacharel em Sciencias Jurídicas e Sociais*. Rio de Janeiro: Jacintho Ribeiro dos Santos, 1902.

Fausto, Boris. *História do Brasil*. São Paulo: Edusp, 1994.

Fausto, Boris. *Getúlio Vargas*. São Paulo: Companhia das Letras, 2006.

Fear, Jeffrey and Christopher Kobrak. "Diverging Paths: Accounting for Corporate Governance in America and Germany." *Business History Review* 80-1 (2006): 1–48.

Fear, Jeffrey and Christopher Kobrak. "Banks on Board: Banks in German and American Corporate Governance, 1870–1914." Unpublished manuscript, Harvard Business School, May 2007.

Ferguson, Niall. *The Cash Nexus: Money and Power in the Modern World, 1700–2000*. New York: Basic Books, 2001.

Ferguson, Niall. *The War of the World: Twentieth Century Conflict and the Descent of the West*. New York: The Penguin Press, 2006.

Flandreau, Marc and Frédréric Zumer. *The Making of Global Finance, 1880–1913*. Paris: OECD, 2004.

Fohlin, Caroline. "The History of Corporate Ownership and Control in Germany." In Randall Morck (ed.) *A History of Corporate Governance Around the World: Family Business Groups to Professional Managers*. Chicago: University of Chicago Press and NBER, 2006, pp. 223–283.

Fohlin, Caroline. "Does Civil Law Tradition and Universal Banking Crowd Out Securities Markets?: Pre-World War I Germany as a Counter-Example." *Enterprise & Society* 8-3 (September 2007): 602–641.

Franco, Gustavo. "A Primeira Década Republicana." In Marcelo de Paiva Abreu (org., ed.) *A Ordem do Progresso: Cem Anos de Política Econômica Republicana, 1889–1989*. Rio de Janeiro: Campus Editora, 1989, pp. 11–30.

Frank, Zephyr. *Dutra's World. Wealth and Family in Nineteenth-Century Rio de Janeiro*. Albuquerque: University of New Mexico Press, 2004.

Franks, Julian, Colin Mayer and Stefano Rossi. "Ownership: Evolution and Regulation." Institute of Finance and Accounting Working Paper FIN 401, London Business School, 2004.

Franks, Julian, Colin Mayer and Stefano Rossi. "Spending Less Time with the Family: The Decline of Family Ownership in the UK." In Randall Morck (ed.) *A History of Corporate Governance Around the World: Family Business Groups to Professional Managers.* Chicago and London: University of Chicago Press and NBER, 2004, pp. 581–607.

Franks, Julian, Colin Mayer and Hannes F. Wagner. "The Origins of the German Corporation: Finance, Ownership and Control." *Review of Finance* 10, 4 (2006): 537–585.

French, John D. *Drowning in Laws: Labor Law and Brazilian Political Culture.* Chapel Hill: University of North Carolina Press, 2004.

Fritsch, Winston. "Apogeu e Crise na Primeira República: 1900–1930." In Marcelo de Paiva Abreu (org., ed.) *A Ordem do Progresso: Cem Anos de Política Econômica Republicana, 1889–1989.* Rio de Janeiro: Campus Editora, 1989, pp. 31–72.

Furtado, Celso. *Formação Econômica do Brasil.* Mexico: Fondo de Cultura Económica, 1959.

Glaeser, Edward and Andrei Shleifer. "Legal Origins." *Quarterly Journal of Economics* 117, 4 (November, 2002): 1193–1230.

Goldsmith, Raymond W. *Comparative National Balance Sheets: A Study of Twenty Countries, 1688–1978.* Chicago: University of Chicago Press, 1985.

Goldsmith, Raymond. *Brasil 1850–1984: Desenvolvimento Financeiro sob um Século de Inflação.* Rio de Janeiro: Banco Bamerindus and Editora Harper & Row do Brasil, 1986.

Gómez-Galvarriato, Aurora. "The Impact of the Revolution: Business and Labor in the Mexican Textile Industry, Orizaba, Veracruz, 1900–1930." Ph.D. dissertation, Harvard University, 1999.

Gómez-Galvarriato, Aurora. "The Political Economy of Protectionism: The Evolution of Labor Productivity, International Competitiveness, and Tariffs in the Mexican Textile Industry, 1900–1950." NBER Inter-American Seminar in Economics 2004, New Perspectives on Economic History, El Colegio de México, Mexico City, December 2–4, 2004.

Gómez-Galvarriato, Aurora and Aldo Musacchio. "Un Nuevo índice de Precios para Mexico, 1886–1929." *El Trimestre Económico* 67, 265 (2000): 47–93.

Gómez-Galvarriato, Aurora and Aldo Musacchio. "Organizational Choice in a French Civil Law Underdeveloped Economy: Partnerships, Corporations and the Chartering of Business in Mexico, 1886–1910." Unpublished manuscript, Centro de Investigacion y Docencia Economicas (CIDE), Mexico, 2004.

Gompers, Paul, Joy Ishii and Andrew Metrick, "Corporate Governance and Equity Prices." *Quarterly Journal of Economics* 118, 1 (February 2003): 107–155.

Gourevitch, Peter A. and James Shinn. *Political Power and Corporate Control: The New Global Politics of Corporate Governance.* Princeton: Princeton University Press, 2005.

Graham, Richard. *Britain and the Onset of Modernization in Brazil, 1850–1914.* London: Cambridge University Press, 1968.

Granovetter, Mark. "Economic Action, Social Structure, and Embeddedness." *American Journal of Sociology* 91, 3 (1985): 481–510.

Granovetter, Mark. "Business Groups." In N. Smelser and R. Swedberg (eds.), *Handbook of Economic Sociology*. Princeton: Princeton University Press, 1994, pp. 453–475.

Greif, Avner. "Cultural Beliefs and the Organization of Society: A Historical and Theoretical Reflection on Collectivist and Individualist Societies." *Journal of Political Economy* 102, 5 (1994): 912–950.

Greif, Avner. "Commitment, Coercion and Markets: The Nature and Dynamics of Institutions Supporting Exchange." In Claude Menard and Mary Shirley (eds.), *The Handbook of New Institutional Economics*. Dordrecht, The Netherlands: Springer, 2005, pp. 727–785.

Greif, Avner. *Institutions and the Path to the Modern Economy: Lessons from Medieval Trade*. Cambridge: Cambridge University Press, 2006.

Haber, Stephen. *Industry and Underdevelopment*. Stanford: Stanford University Press, 1989.

Haber, Stephen. "Industrial Concentration and the Capital Markets: A Comparative Study of Brazil, Mexico and the United States, 1830–1930." *Journal of Economic History* 51 (September 1991): 559–580.

Haber, Stephen. "Business Enterprise and the Great Depression in Brazil: A Study of Profits and Losses in Textile Manufacturing." *Business History Review* 66, 2 (Summer 1992): 335–362.

Haber, Stephen (ed.) *How Latin America Fell Behind: Essays on the Economic Histories of Brazil and Mexico, 1800–1914*. Stanford: Stanford University Press, 1997.

Haber, Stephen. "The Efficiency Consequences of Institutional Change: Financial Market Regulation and Industrial Productivity Growth in Brazil, 1866–1934." In John Coatsworth and Alan Taylor (eds.), *Latin America and the World Economy Since 1800*. Cambridge, Mass.: DRCLAS and Harvard University Press, 1998, pp. 275–322.

Haber, Stephen and Herbert S. Klein. "The Economic Consequences of Brazilian Independence." In Stephen Haber (ed.), *How Latin America Fell Behind: Essays on the Economic Histories of Brazil and Mexico, 1800–1914*. Stanford: Stanford University Press, 1997, pp. 243–259.

Haber, Stephen, Armando Razo and Noel Maurer. *The Politics of Property Rights: Political Instability, Credible Commitments, and Economic Growth in Mexico, 1876–1929*. Cambridge: Cambridge University Press, 2003.

Haber, Stephen, Douglass C. North, and Barry Weingast (eds.), *The Politics of Financial Development*, Stanford: Stanford University Press, 2007.

Haddad, Cláudio. *Growth of Brazilian Real Output, 1900–1947*. Chicago: University of Chicago Press, 1974.

Haddad, Cláudio. "Crescimento Econômico do Brasil, 1900–1976." In Paulo Neuhaus (coord.), *Economia Brasileira: Uma Visão Histórica*. Rio de Janeiro: Editora Campus, 1980.

Hanley, Anne. "Capital Markets in the Coffee Economy: Financial Institutions and Economic Change in São Paulo, Brazil, 1850–1905." Ph.D. dissertation, Stanford University, 1995.

Hanley, Anne. "Business Finance and the São Paulo Bolsa, 1886–1917." In John Coatsworth and Alan Taylor (eds.), *Latin America and the World Economy Since 1800*. Cambridge, Mass.: DRCLAS and Harvard University Press, 1998, pp. 115–138.

Hanley, Anne. "Is It Who You Know? Entrepreneurs and Bankers in São Paulo, Brazil at the Turn of the Twentieth Century." *Enterprise and Society* 5, 2 (2004): 187–225.

Hanley, Anne. *Native Capital: Financial Institutions and Economic Development in São Paulo, Brazil, 1850–1920.* Stanford: Stanford University Press, 2005.

Hannah, Leslie. "Comment on 'The Global Securities Market in the 20th Century: Trends, Events, Governments and Institutions' by Ranald Michie." Paper presented at the Workshop on Global Stock Market History in the Twentieth Century, University of Tokyo, July 25, 2006

Hannah, Leslie. "The Divorce of Ownership From Control from 1900: Re-calibrating Imagined Global Historical Trends." *Business History* 49, 4 (July 2007): 404–438.

Hannah, Leslie. "Pioneering Modern Corporate Governance: A View from London in 1900." *Enterprise and Society* 8 (September 2007): 642–686.

Hart, Oliver. *Firms, Contracts, and Financial Structure.* Oxford: Clarendon Press; New York: Oxford University Press, 1995.

Hart, Oliver. "Different Approaches to Bankruptcy." Unpublished manuscript, Harvard University, 1999.

Hart, Oliver and John Moore. "Property Rights and the Nature of the Firm." *Journal of Political Economy* 98, 6 (December 1990): 1119–1158.

Hautcoeur, Pierre-Cyrille. "Le Marché Boursier et le Financement des Enterprises Françaises (1890–1939)." Unpublished Ph.D. dissertation, Université de Paris I Panthéon-Sorbonne, 1994.

Hautcoeur, Pierre-Cyrille and Nadine Levratto. "Bankruptcy Law and Practice in 19th-Century France." Unpublished manuscript, Paris-Jourdan Sciences Économiques, 2006.

Hawkins, David F. "The Development of Modern Financial Reporting Practices among American Manufacturing Corporations." *Business History Review* 37 (1963): 135–168.

Healy, Paul and Krishna Palepu. "Information asymmetry, corporate disclosure, and the capital markets: A review of the empirical disclosure literature." *Journal of Accounting and Economics* 31 (2001): 405–440.

Hilt, Eric. "When Did Ownership Separate from Control?: Corporate Governance in the Early Nineteenth Century." In *The Journal of Economic History* 68, 3 (September 2008): 645–685.

Hirschman, Albert O. "The Paternity of an Index." *American Economic Review* 54, 5 (September 1964): 761.

Hoshi, Takeo and Anil Kashyap. *Corporate Financing and Governance in Japan: The Road to the Future.* Cambrid

Hoshi, Takeo, Anil Kashyap and David Scharfstein. "The Role of Banks in Reducing the Costs of Financial Distress in Japan." NBER Working Paper 3435, 1990.

Howard, Margaret and Peter A. Alces. *Cases and Materials on Bankruptcy.* St. Paul, Minn.: West Group, 2001.

Huebner, Salomon. "The Distribution of Stockholdings in American Railways." *Annals of the American Academy of Political and Social Science* 22 (November 1903): 63–78.

International Corporate Governance Network. "ICGN Statement on Global Corporate Governance Principles." July 8, 2005, www.icgn.org (last accessed 05/05/09).

Islas Rojas, Gonzalo. "Does Regulation Matter?: An Analysis of Corporate Charters in a Laissez-faire environment." Unpublished manuscript, University of California Los Angeles, September 2007.

Jensen, Michael C. and William H. Meckling. "Theory of the Firm: Managerial Behavior, Agency Costs and Ownership Structure." *Journal of Financial Economics* 3, 4 (October 1976): 305–360.

Johnson, Simon, Rafael La Porta, Florencio Lopes-de-Silanes and Andrei Shleifer. "Tunneling." *American Economic Review Papers and Proceedings* 90 (2000): 22–27.

Jones, Matthew T. and Maurice Obstfeld. "Saving, Investment, and Gold: A Reassessment of Historical Current Account Data." In Guillermo A. Calvo, Rudi Dornbusch and Maurice Obstfeld (eds.), *Money, Capital Mobility, and Trade: Essays in Honor of Robert Mundell*, Cambridge, Mass.: MIT Press, 2001, pp. 303–364.

Keynes, John Maynard. *The Economic Consequences of the Peace*. New York: Dover Publications, 1994 [1920].

Khanna, Tarun and Krishna Palepu. "Is Group Affiliation Profitable in Emerging Markets?: An Analysis of Diversified Indian Business Groups." *Journal of Finance* 55, 2 (2000): 867–891.

Khanna, Tarun and Krishna Palepu. "The Evolution of Concentrated Ownership in India: Broad Patterns and a History of the Indian Software Industry." In Randall Morck (ed.), *A History of Corporate Governance around the World: Family Business Groups to Professional Managers*. Chicago, and London: University of Chicago Press and NBER, 2004, pp. 283–324.

Khanna, Tarun and Jan W. Rivkin. "Interorganizational Ties and Business Group Boundaries: Evidence from an Emerging Economy." *Organization Science* 17, 3 (May/June 2006): 333–352.

Khanna, Tarun and Yishay Yafeh. "Business Groups in Emerging Markets: Paragons or Parasites?" *Journal of Economic Literature* 45, 2 (June 2007): 331–372.

King, Robert G. and Ross Levine. "Finance and Growth: Schumpeter Might Be Right." *Quarterly Journal of Economics* 108, 3 (1993): 717–737.

Kroszner, Randall S. and Philip E. Strahan. "Bankers on Boards: Monitoring, Conflicts of Interest, and Lender Liability." *Journal of Financial Economics* 62, 3 (December 2001): 415–452.

La Porta, Rafael and Florencio Lopez-de-Silanes. "Creditor Protection and Bankruptcy Law Reform." In Stijin Claessens, Simeon Djankov and Ashoka Mody (eds.), *Resolution of Financial Distress: An International Perspective on the Design of Bankruptcy Laws*. Washington, D.C.: The World Bank, 2001, pp. 65–90.

La Porta, Rafael, Florencio Lopez-de-Silanes and Andrei Shleifer. "Corporate Ownership around the World." *Journal of Finance* 54, 2 (1999): 471–517.

La Porta, Rafael, Florencio Lopez-de-Silanes and Andrei Shleifer. "What Works in Securities Laws?" *Journal of Finance* 61, 1 (February 2006): 1–32.

La Porta, Rafael, Florencio Lopez-de-Silanes and Andrei Shleifer. "The Economic Consequences of Legal Origins." *Journal of Economic Literature* 46, 2 (2008): 285–332.

La Porta, Rafael, Florencio Lopez-de-Silanes, Andrei Shleifer and Robert Vishny. "Legal Determinants of External Finance." *Journal of Finance* 52, 3 (1997): 1131–1150.

La Porta, Rafael, Florencio Lopez-de-Silanes, Andrei Shleifer and Robert Vishny. "Law and Finance." *Journal of Political Economy* 106, 6 (1998): 1113–1155.

La Porta, Rafael, Florencio Lopez-de-Silanes, Andrei Shleifer and Robert Vishny. "Investor Protection and Corporate Governance." *Journal of Financial Economics* 58, 1 (2000): 1–25.

Lamoreaux, Naomi. "Information Problems and Banks' Specialization in Short-Term Commercial Lending: New England in the Nineteenth Century." In Peter Temin (ed.), *Inside the Business Enterprise: Historical Perspectives on the Use of Information.* Chicago and London: NBER, 1991, pp. 161–204.

Lamoreaux, Naomi. *Insider Lending: Banks, Personal Connections, and Economic Development in Industrial New England.* Cambridge: Cambridge University Press, 1994.

Lamoreaux, Naomi and Jean-Laurent Rosenthal. "Corporate Governance and the Plight of Minority Shareholders in the United States before the Great Depression." In Edward Glaeser and Claudia Goldin (eds.), *Corruption and Reform.* Chicago: University of Chicago Press, 2006, pp. 125–152.

Leal, Ricardo P. C. and André Carvalhal da Silva. "Corporate Governance and Value in Brazil (and in Chile)." In Alberto Chong and Florencio López-de-Silanes (eds.), *Investor Protection and Corporate Governance: Firm Level Evidence Across Latin America.* Stanford: Stanford University Press and Inter-American Development Bank, 2007, pp. 213–287.

Leff, Nathaniel. "Industrial Organization and Entrepreneurship in Developing Countries: The Economic Group." *Economic Development and Cultural Change* 26 (1978): 661–675.

Leff, Nathaniel. *Underdevelopment and Development in Brazil, 2 vols.* London: George Allen & Unwin, 1982.

Leopoldi, Maria Antonieta P. *Política e Interesses: As Associações Industriais, e Política Econômica e o Estado na Industrialização Brasileira.* São Paulo: Paz e Terra, 2000, pp. 86–87.

Levine, Ross, Norman Loayza and Thorsten Beck. "Financial Intermediation and Growth: Causality and Causes." *Journal of Monetary Economics* 46 (2000): 31–77.

Levine, Ross and Sara Zervos. "Stock Markets, Banks, and Economic Growth." *American Economic Review* 88 (June, 1998): 537–558.

Levy, Maria Bárbara. *Historia da Bolsa de Valores do Rio de Janeiro.* Rio de Janeiro: IBMEC, 1977.

Levy, Maria Bárbara. *A Indústria do Rio de Janeiro através de suas Sociedades Anônimas.* Rio de Janeiro: UFRJ Editora, 1994.

Lima, Adamastor. *Nova lei das Fallencias: Decreto n. 5.746 de 9 de Dezembro de 1929, Comparada com a lei n. 2.024 de 1908.* Rio de Janeiro: Coelho Branco, 1929.

Lipartito, Kenneth and Yumiko Morii. "Rethinking the Separation of Ownership from Management in American History." Unpublished manuscript, Johns Hopkins University, 2007.

Lobo, Mária Eulália Lahmeyer. "O Encilhamento." *Revista Brasileira De Mercado De Capitais* 2, 5 (1976): 261–301.

Lobo, Mária Eulália Lahmeyer. *História do Rio de Janeiro: Do Capital Comercial ao Capital Industrial e Financeiro.* Rio de Janeiro: IBMEC, 1978.

Love, Joseph LeRoy. "Political Participation in Brazil, 1881–1969." *Luso-Brazilian Review* 7, 2 (1970): 3–24.

Ludlow, Leonor and Carlos Marichal. *Banca y Poder en México, 1800–1925.* Historia: Colección Enlace. México: Grijalbo, 1986.

Ludlow, Leonor and Alicia Salmerón. *La Emisión de Papel Moneda en México: Una Larga Negociación Político-Financiera.* México: SHCP/Talleres de Impresión de Estampillas y Valores, 1997.

Marichal, Carlos and Mario Cerutti. *Historia de las Grande Empresas en México, 1850–1930.* Obras De Economía Latinoamericana: Economía Latinoamericana (Mexico City, Mexico). Nuevo León, México: Universidad Autónoma de Nuevo León, Fondo de Cultura Económica, 1997.

Markham, Lester V. *Victorian Insolvency: Bankruptcy, Imprisonment for Debt, and Company Winding-Up in Nineteenth Century England.* Oxford: Clarendon Press; New York: Oxford University Press, 1995.

Marques, Maria Teresa De Novaes. "Capital, Cerveja e Consumo de Massa: Trajetória da Brahma, 1888/1933." Unpublished Ph.D. dissertation, Universidade de Brasília, Brasilia, 2003.

Marques, Maria Teresa De Novaes. "Bancos e Desenvolvimento Industrial: Uma Revisão das Teses de Gerschenkron à Luz da História da Cervejaria Brahma, 1888/1917." *História e Economia* 1, 1 (September 2005): 87–119.

Martins, Fran. *Comentários à Lei das Sociedades Anônimas: Lei no. 6.404, de 15 de Dezembro de 1976.* Rio de Janeiro: Biblioteca Forense, 1977–1979.

Maurer, Noel. "Finance and Oligarchy: Banks, Politics, and Economic Growth in Mexico, 1876–1928." Unpublished Ph.D. dissertation, Stanford University, 1997.

Maurer, Noel. *The Power and the Money: Credible Commitments and the Financial System in Mexico, 1876–1934.* Stanford: Stanford University Press, 2003.

Maurer, Noel and Stephen Haber. "Institutional Change and Economic Growth: Banks, Financial Markets, and Mexican Industrialization." In Jeffrey L. Bortz and Stephen H. Haber (eds.), *The Mexican Economy, 1870–1930: Essays on the Economic History of Institutions, Revolution, and Growth.* Stanford: Stanford University Press, 2002.

Maurer, Noel and Tridib Sharma. "Enforcing Property Rights Through Reputation: Mexico's Early Industrialization, 1878–1913." *Journal of Economic History* 61, 4 (2001).

Merryman, John Henry. *The Civil Law Tradition.* Stanford: Stanford University Press, 1985.

Merryman, John Henry. "The French Deviation." *American Journal of Comparative Law* 44 (1996): 109–119.

Michie, Ranald C. *The Global Securities Markets: A History.* New York: Oxford University Press, 2006.

Mitchell, B. R. *International Historical Statistics, 1750–2000.* New York: Palgrave Macmillan, 2003.

Mitchie, R. C. *The London and New York Stock Exchanges, 1850–1914.* London: Allen & Unwin, 1987.

Miwa, Yoshiro and J. Mark Ramseyer. "Corporate Governance in Transitional Economies: Lessons from the Prewar Japanese Cotton Textile Industry." *Journal of Legal Studies* 29, 1 (January 2000): 171–203.

Miyajima, Hideaki, Julian Franks and Colin Mayer. "Evolution of Ownership: The Curious Case of Japan." Unpublished manuscript, Waseda University, 2007.

Mizruchi, Mark S. *The American Corporate Network: 1904–1974.* Beverly Hills, Calif.: Sage, 1982.

Mizruchi, Mark S. and Linda Brewster Stearns. "A Longitudinal Study of the Formation of Interlocking Directorates." *Administrative Science Quarterly* 33 (1988): 194–210.

Moore, Lyndon. "The Effect of World War One on Stock Market Integration." Unpublished manuscript, Victoria University of Wellington, 2006.

Moss, David. *When All Else Fails: Government as the Ultimate Risk Manager.* Cambridge, Mass. and London, England: Harvard University Press, 2002.

Murphy, Antoine. "Corporate Ownership in France: The Importance of History." In Randall Morck (ed.) *A History of Corporate Governance Around the World: Family Business Groups to Professional Managers.* Chicago and London: University of Chicago Press and NBER, 2006, pp. 185–223.

Murphy, Mary E. "Revision of British Company Law." *American Economic Review* 36, 4 (September 1946): 659–660.

Musacchio, Aldo. "Ordem (na corte) e Progresso: O Poder Judiciário e o Mercado Financeiro na Transformação Econômica Republicana." *Acervo: Revista do Arquivo Nacional*, Rio de Janeiro (November 2002).

Musacchio, Aldo. "Law and Finance in Historical Perspective: Politics, Bankruptcy Law, and Corporate Governance in Brazil, 1850–2002." Unpublished Ph.D. dissertation, Stanford University, 2005.

Musacchio, Aldo and Ian Read. "Bankers, Industrialists and their Cliques: Elite Networks in Mexico and Brazil During Early Industrialization." *Enterprise and Society* 8, 4 (December 2007): 842–880.

Nakamura, Leonard and Carlos Zarazaga. "Economic Growth in Argentina in the Period 1900–1930: Some Evidence from Stock Returns." In John Coatsworth and Alan Taylor (eds.), *Latin America and the World Economy Since 1800.* Cambridge. Mass.: DRCLAS and Harvard University Press, 1998, pp. 247–269.

Nenova, Tatiana. "Control Values and Changes in Corporate Law in Brazil." *Latin American Business Review* 6, 3 (2005): 1–37.

Nenova, Tatiana. "The Value of Corporate Voting Rights and Control: A Cross-Country Analysis." *Governance: An International Perspective* 2 (2005): pp. 352–378.

Neuhaus, Paulo. *História Monetária do Brasil, 1900–1945.* Rio de Janeiro: Instituto Brasileiro de Mercado de Capitais, 1975.

Neymarck, Alfred. "Les Chemineaux De L'épargne." *Journal de la Société de Statistique de Paris* 52, 4 (1911Ç): 122–166.

Nicolau, Jairo. *História do Voto no Brasil.* Rio de Janeiro: Jorge Zahar, 2002.

North, Douglass C. *Institutions, Institutional Change, and Economic Performance.* Cambridge: Cambridge University Press, 1990.

North, Douglass C. "Economic Performance Through Time." Nobel Prize Lecture, Stockholm, December 9, 1993.

North, Douglass and Barry Weingast. "Constitutions and Commitment: The Evolution of Institutions Governing Public Choice in Seventeenth Century England." *Journal of Economic History* 49 (1989): 803–832.

O'Sullivan, Mary. *Contests for Corporate Control: Corporate Governance and Economic Performance in the United States and Germany.* Oxford: Oxford University Press, 2000.

O'Sullivan, Mary. "The Expansion of the U.S. Stock Market, 1885–1930: Historical Facts and Theoretical Fashions." *Enterprise and Society* 8, 3 (September 2007): 489–542.

Obstfeld, Maurice and Alan Taylor. *Global Capital Markets: Integration, Crisis, and Growth*. Cambridge: Cambridge University Press, 2004.

Packenham, Robert. *The Dependency Movement: Scholarship and Politics in Development Studies*. Cambridge, Mass.: Harvard University Press, 1992.

Pagano, Marco and Paolo Volpin. "The Political Economy of Corporate Governance." *American Economic Review* 95, 4 (September 2005): 1005–1030.

Peláez, Carlos Manuel. "Análise Econômico do Programa Brasileiro de Sustentação do Café – 1906–1945: Teoria, Política e Medição." *Revista Brasileira De Economia* 24, 4 (1971): 5–211.

Peláez, Carlos Manuel and Wilson Suzigan. *História Monetária do Brasil*. Brasilia: Universidade de Brasília, 1976.

Perotti, Enrico and Ernst-Ludwig von Thadden. "The Political Economy of Corporate Control and Labor Rents." *Journal of Political Economy* 114, 1 (2006): 145–175.

Perotti, Enrico and Armin Schwienbacher. "The Political Origin of Pension Funding." Unpublished manuscript, Amsterdam Business School, 2006.

Petersen, Mitchell A. and Raghuram G. Rajan. "The Benefits of Lending Relationships: Evidence from Small Business Data." *Journal of Finance* 49, 1 (March 1994): 3–37.

Pinheiro, Armando Castelar. "Judiciário, Reforma e Economia: A Visão dos Magistrados." In Armando Castelar Pinheiro (ed.), *Reforma do Judiciário: Problemas, Desafios, Perspectivas*. Rio de Janeiro: IDESP and BookLink, 2003, pp. 138–206.

Pistor, Katharina. "Codetermination in Germany: A Socio-Political Model with Governance Externalities." In Margareth Blair and Mark Roe (eds.), *Employees and Corporate Governance*. Washington, D.C.: Brookings Institution Press, 1999, pp. 163–193.

Pistor, Katharina, Yoram Keinan, Jan Kleinheisterkamp and Mark West. "Innovation in Corporate Law." *Journal of Comparative Economics* 31, 4 (2003): 676–694.

Rajan, Raghuram G. and Luigi Zingales. "Financial Dependence and Growth." *American Economic Review* 88 (June 1998): 559–586.

Rajan, Raghuram G. and Luigi Zingales. "Financial Systems, Industrial Structure, and Growth." *Oxford Review of Economic Policy* 17, 4 (2001): 467–482.

Rajan, Raghuram and Luigi Zingales. "Sources of Data for 'The Great Reversals': The Politics of Financial Development in the 20th Century." Unpublished manuscript, University of Chicago, June 2001.

Rajan, Raghuram and Luigi Zingales. "The Great Reversals: The Politics of Financial Development in the 20th Century." *Journal of Financial Economics* 69 (2003): 5–50.

Rajan, Raghuram and Luigi Zingales. *Saving Capitalism from the Capitalists: Unleashing the Power of Financial Markets to Create Wealth and Spread Opportunity*. New York: Crown Business, 2003.

Ramirez, Carlos D. "Did J. P. Morgan's Men Add Liquidity?: Corporate Investment, Cash Flow, and Financial Structure at the Turn of the Twentieth Century." *Journal of Finance* 50, 2 (1995): 661–678.

Razo, Armando. "Social Networks and Credible Commitments in Dictatorships: Political Organization and Economic Growth in Porfirian Mexico (1876–1911)." Unpublished Ph.D. dissertation, Stanford University, 2003.

Riberiro de Andrada, Carlos. *Bancos de Emissão no Brasil*. Rio de Janeiro: Leite de Ribeiro, 1923.

Rix, M.S. "Company Law: 1844 and Today." *Economic Journal* 55, 218/219 (June–September 1945): 242–260.

Roe, Mark J. "Political Preconditions to Separating Ownership from Corporate Control." *Stanford Law Review* 53 (2000): 539–606.

Roe, Mark J. *Political Determinants of Corporate Governance*. New York: Oxford University Press, 2003.

Roe, Mark J. "Legal Origins and Modern Stock Markets." Unpublished manuscript, Harvard Law School, November 2006.

Roe, Mark J. and Jeffrey Gordon (eds.). *Convergence and Persistence in Corporate Governance Systems*. Cambridge: Cambridge University Press, 2004.

Roe, Mark J. and Jordan Siegel. "Political Instability and Financial Development." Unpublished manuscript, Harvard Law School and Harvard Business School, February 2007.

Rousseau, Peter L. and Richard Sylla. "Emerging Financial Markets and Early US Growth." *Explorations in Economic History* 42, 1 (2005): 1–26.

Rousseau, Peter L. and Richard Sylla. "Financial Revolutions and Economic Growth: Introducing this EEH Symposium." *Explorations in Economic History* 43, 1 (2006): 1–12.

Saes, Flávio A. M. *As Ferrovias de São Paulo, 1870–1940*. São Paulo: HUCITEC, 1981.

Saes, Flávio A. M. *A Grande Empresa de Serviços Públicos na Economia Cafeeira*. São Paulo, HUCITEC, 1986.

Saes, Flávio A. M. *Crédito e Bancos no Desenvolvimento da Economia Paulista, 1850–1930*. São Paulo: Instituto de Pesquisas Econômicas, 1986.

Saes, Flávio A.M. and Tamás Szmrecsányi. "El Papel de los Bancos Extranjeros en la Industrialización Inicial de São Paulo." In Carlos Marichal (ed.), *Las Inversiones Extranjeras en América Latina, 1850–1930: Nuevos Debates y Problemas en Historia Económica Comparada*. México: Fondo de Cultura Económica, 1995, pp. 230–243.

Santos, Everett. "Liquidez de Mercado Secundário para Debêntures." Unpublished manuscript, Ibmec, Rio de Janeiro, 1973.

Santos, Paulo Penalva. "Brevíssima Notícia Sobre a Recuperação Extrajudicial." *Revista do Advogado* 25, 83 (September 2005): 107–115.

Schumpeter, Joseph. *History of Economic Analysis*. New York: Oxford University Press, 1954.

Scott, John. *Social Network Analysis: A Handbook*. London: Sage, 1991.

Sgard, Jérôme. "Do Legal Origins Matter?: Bankruptcy Laws in Europe (1808–1914)." *European Review of Economic History* 10, 3 (December 2006): 389–419.

Shleifer, Andrei, Rafael La Porta and Florencio Lopes-de-Silanes. "Ownership Around the World." *Journal of Finance* 54, 2 (1999): 471–517.

Siegel, Jordan. "Can Foreign Firms Bond Themselves Effectively by Renting U.S. Securities Laws?" *Journal of Financial Economics* 75, 2 (February 2005): 319–359.

Simonsen, Mário Henrique. "Inflation and the Money and Capital Markets of Brazil." In Howard Ellis (ed.), *The Economy of Brazil*. Berkeley and Los Angeles: University of California Press, 1969.

Staley, Eugene. *War and the Private Investor: A Study in the Relations of International Politics and International Private Investment*. New York: Doubleday, Doran & Company, Inc., 1935.

Stallings, Barbara. *Banker to the Third World: U.S. Portfolio Investment in Latin America, 1900–1986*. Studies in International Political Economy. Berkeley and Los Angeles: University of California Press, 1987.

Stearns, Linda Brewster and Mark S. Mizruchi. "Board Composition and Corporate Financing: The Impact of Financial Institution Representation on Borrowing." *Academy of Management Journal* 36, 3 (1993): 603–618.

Stein, Stanley. *The Brazilian Cotton Manufacture: Textile Enterprise in an Underdeveloped Area, 1850–1950*. Cambridge, Mass.: Harvard University Press, 1957.

Stiglitz, Joseph. "Bankruptcy Laws: Basic Economic Principles." In Stijin Claessens, Simeon Djankov and Ashoka Mody (eds.), *Resolution of Financial Distress: An International Perspective on the Design of Bankruptcy Laws*. Washington, D.C.: The World Bank, 2001, pp. 1–24.

Stone, Irving. *The Global Export of Capital From Great Britain, 1865–1914: A Statistical Survey*. New York, Palgrave Macmillan, 1999.

Summerhill, William R. III. *Order Against Progress: Government, Foreign Investment, and Railroads in Brazil, 1854–1913*. Stanford: Stanford University Press, 2003.

Summerhill, William R. III. "Political Economy of the Domestic Debt in Nineteenth-Century Brazil." Paper presented at the conference Economics, Political Institutions, and Financial Markets II: Institutional Theory and Evidence from Europe, the United States, and Latin America. Social Science History Institute, Stanford University, February 4–5, 2005.

Summerhill, William R. III. "Sovereign Credibility with Financial Underdevelopment: The Case of Nineteenth-Century Brazil." Unpublished manuscript, University of California, Los Angeles, May 2007.

Suzigan, Wilson. *Industria Brasileira: Origem e Desenvolvimento*. São Paulo: HUCITEC, 2000.

Sylla, Richard. "Financial Systems and Economic Modernization." *Journal of Economic History* 62, 2 (2002): 277–292.

Sylla, Richard. "Schumpeter Redux: A Review of Raghuram G. Rajan and Luigi Zingales's *Saving Capitalism from the Capitalists.*" *Journal of Economic Literature* 44 (June 2006): 391–404.

Taussig, F. W. and W. S. Barker. "American Corporations and Their Executives: A Statistical Inquiry." *The Quarterly Journal of Economics* 40, 1 (November 1925): 1–51.

Taylor, Alan. "Foreign Capital Flows." In Victor Bulmer-Thomas, John H. Coatsworth and Roberto Cortés Conde (eds.), *Cambridge Economic History of Latin America*. Cambridge: Cambridge University Press, 2006, pp. 57–100.

Topik, Steven. *The Political Economy of the Brazilian State, 1889–1930*. Austin: University of Texas Press, 1987.

Triner, Gail. "Banks and Brazilian Economic Development: 1906–1930." Unpublished Ph.D. dissertation, Columbia University, 1994.

Triner, Gail. *Banking and Economic Development: Brazil, 1889–1930*. New York: Palgrave, 2000.

Union of South Africa. Union Office of Census and Statistics. *Official Year Book of the Union of South Africa*, no. 2 (1918): 729.

Villela, Annibal and Wilson Suzigan. *Política do Governo e Crescimento da Economia Brasileira: 1889–1945*. Rio de Janeiro: IPEA/INPES, 1973.

Wasserman, Mark. "La Inversión Extranjera en México, 1876–1910: Un Estudio de Caso del Papel de las *élites* Regionales." In Enrique Cárdenas (comp.), *Historia Económica de México*, vol. 3. México: Fondo de Cultura Económica, 1992, pp. 267–289.

Wasserman, Stanley. *Social Network Analysis: Methods and Applications*. Cambridge: Cambridge University Press, 1997.

Weinstein, David E. and Yishay Yafeh. "On the Costs of Bank-Centered Financial System: Evidence from the Changing Main Bank Relations in Japan." *Journal of Finance* 53, 2 (April 1998): 635–672.

Wellhoff, S. *Sociétés par Actions*. Alexandria: Société de Publications Égyptiennes, 1917.

Williamson, Jeffrey. *Globalization and History: The Evolution of a Nineteenth-Century Atlantic Economy*. Cambridge, Mass.: MIT Press, 1999.

Williamson, Jeffrey. *Globalization and the Poor Periphery Before 1950*. Cambridge, Mass.: MIT Press, 2006.

Windolf, Paul. "The Emergence of Corporate Networks in the United States and Germany 1896–1938." Presented at the annual meeting of the American Sociological Association, Philadelphia, Penn., August 2005.

Wood, E.R. *Review of the Bond Market in Canada*. Montreal: Dominion Securities Corporation, 1911–1914.

World Bank. *Brazil: Financial Systems Review*. Washington, D.C.: The World Bank, 1984.

World Bank. *Doing Business Report, 2006*, www.doingbusiness.org (last accessed 05/05/09).

Zingales, Luigi. "Corporate Governance." In Peter Newman (ed.), *The New Palgrave Dictionary of Economics and Law*. New York: Palgrave, McMillan, 2004.

Zingales, Luigi and Alexander Dyck. "Private Benefits of Control: An International Comparison." *Journal of Finance* 49 (April 2004): 537–600.

Index

minority shareholder protections,
84–86
ownership concentration in, 9
property rights protection, 14–15
public vs. private enforcement of
investor rights, 12–13
"Law of Impediments"
(*"Lei dos entraves"*), 34–36
Leff, Nathaniel, 243
legal families
features of, 10–11
types of, 4
legal institutions
effects of, 259–261
variance across countries, xv
legal systems
hybrid forms of, 11
transplant countries, 12
legal traditions
and investor protections, xvi, 9
types of, 4
Lei da Boa Razão, 166
"Lei dos entraves" ("Law of
Impediments"), 34–36
Leopoldina Railway Company, 175–176,
176–177
lessons learned
on corporate by-laws, 253–254,
257–258
on disclosure, 256–257
on financial structure selection,
258–259
on inflation effects, 262–263
on legal institutions, 259–261
on political impacts, 261–262
on reduced capital flows, 262–263
on voting rights/provisions, 254–256
Levine, Ross, 67
Levy, Maria Bárbara, 36, 246, 232–233,
248–249
liability, limited, 38, 90
liquidação amigável (bankruptcy
arrangement), 172–173. *See also*
bankruptcy laws
liquidação forçada (forced liquidation),
171. *See also* bankruptcy laws
loans, long-term, 238

lobbying activities, of business groups, 247
Lopez-de-Silanes, Florencio, 4, 12–13,
93–94, 257
Luttuga, Vicente, 180

macroeconomic conditions, and financial
market development, 50–53
Marcondes Filho, Alexandre, 168–169,
230
market capitalization, equity, 40
market makers, bankers as. *See also*
corporate-bank interlocks
centrality of banks, 202–209
corporate network connections,
197–202
hypothesis for, 186–188, 213–214
in Mexico, 193–194
in the United States, 190–192
Marques, Teresa Cristina de Novaes, 62
Matarazzo, Francisco de, 62–63, 123–124,
146, 154
Mauá, Viscount of, 167
Maurer, Noel, 193, 200
Mayer, Colin, 84–85, 94, 120
Means, Gardiner C., 7
Meckling, William H., 7
Merryman, John H., 10
Mexico
bank-corporate interlocks, 193–194,
202–209, 209–213
comparisons with Brazil, 51–52, 195
corporate network connections,
197–200
Michie, Ranald, 221
Miwa, Yoshiro, 121–122
Mizruchi, Mark S., 192, 202–203
monarchy, Brazil as constitutional, 31
monetary policy
and inflation, 227–228
in stock market growth, 41–42
Montenegro, Caetano Pinto de Miranda,
181–182
Morgan, J. P., 156, 191

Napoleonic code
and colonization, 10
and commerce, xvii, 4, 166–167

Printed in the United States
By Bookmasters